Introduction:

Agony in the Key of AX

What astonishes me about learning how to program is not that it's so hard, but that it's so *easy*. Am I nuts? Hardly. It's just that my curse is the curse of a perfect memory, and I remember *piano lessons*.

My poor mother paid $600 in 1962 for a beautiful cherrywood spinet, and every week for two years I trucked off to Wilkins School of Music for a five dollar lesson. It wasn't that I was a reluctant student; I love music and I genuinely wanted to master the damned thing. But after two years, the best I could do was play "Camelot" well enough to keep the dog from howling. I can honestly say that nothing I ever tried and failed to achieve after that (including engineering school and sailboarding) was anything close to that difficult.

That's why I say: if you can play the piano, you can learn to program in assembly language. Even if you can't play the piano, I hold that you can learn to program in assembly language, if:

- You've ever done your own long-form taxes
- You've earned a degree in medicine, law, or engineering
- You've ever put together your kid's swing set
- You've ever cooked a five-course dinner for eight and gotten everything to the table, hot, at all the right times

Still, playing the piano is the acid test. There are a lot more similarities than there are differences. To wit:

In both cases, you sit down in front of a big expensive machine with a keyboard. You try to memorize a system of notation that seems to have originated on Mars. You press the keys according to incomprehensible instructions in stacks of books. Ultimately, you sit there and grit your teeth while making so many mistakes your self-confidence dribbles out of your pores and disappears into the carpet padding. In many cases, it gets so bad that you hurl the books against the wall and stomp off to play Yahtzee with your little brother.

The differences are fewer: mistakes committed while learning assembly language won't make the dog howl. And, more crucially, what takes *years* of agony in front of a piano can be done in a couple of months in front of your average PC.

Furthermore, I'll do my best to help.

That's what this book is for: to get you started as an assembly-language programmer from a dead stop. I'll assume that you know how to run your machine. That is, I won't go through all that nonsense about flipping the big red switch and inserting a disk in a drive and holding down the Ctrl key while pressing the C key. Van Wolverton can teach you all that stuff.

On the other hand, I won't assume that you know *anything* about programming, nor very much about what happens inside the box itself. That means the first few sections will be the kind of necessary groundwork that will start you nodding off if you've been through it already. There's no helping that. Skip to Section 3 or so if you get bored.

I also have to come clean here and admit that this book is not intended to be a complete tutorial on assembly language, or even close to it. What I want to do is get you familiar enough with the jargon and the assumptions of assembly language so that you can pick up your typical "introduction" to assembly language and not get lost by page 6. I specifically recommend Tom Swan's excellent book, *Mastering Turbo Assembler*, which will take you the rest of the way if you use Borland's assembler. A comparable book devoted to Microsoft's MASM has not yet been written, but even if you use MASM, Tom's book will still be valuable and you'll learn a lot from it. *Mastering Turbo Assembler* can occasionally be found in bookstores, or you can order it by mail through *PC TECHNIQUES* Bookstream.

Assembly language is almost certainly the most difficult kind of computer programming, but keep in mind that we're speaking in relative terms here. Five pushups are harder to do than five jumping jacks—but compared to running the Marathon, both amount to almost nothing. Assembly language is more difficult to learn than Pascal, but compared to raising your average American child from birth to five years, it's a cakewalk.

So don't let the mystique get you. Assembly-language programmers feel pretty smug about what they've learned to do, but in our workaday lives we are forced to learn and do things that put even assembly language to shame. If you're willing to set aside a couple months' worth of loose moments, you can pick it up too. Give it a shot. Your neighbors will thank you.

And so will the dog.

—Jeff Duntemann
    Scottsdale, AZ
    March 1992

Assembly Language:
Step-by-Step

Assembly Language: Step-by-Step

Jeff Duntemann

John Wiley & Sons, Inc.
New York • Chichester • Brisbane • Toronto • Singapore

Recognizing the importance of preserving what has been written, it is a policy of John Wiley & Sons, Inc. to have books of enduring value published in the United States printed on acid-free paper, and we exert our best efforts to that end.

Library of Congress Cataloging-in-Publication Data

Duntemann, Jeff.   1952 –
    Assembly language : step-by-step / Jeff Duntemann.
      p.   cm.
    Includes index.
    ISBN 0-471-57814-2 (paper : alk. paper)
    1. Assembler language (Computer program language)   I. Title.
QA76.73.A8D87   1992
005.265--dc20   92-16665
                                           CIP

Printed in the United States of America

92 93 10 9 8 7 6 5 4 3 2 1

For Kathleen M. Duntemann, Godmother…

*…who gave me books
when all I could do was put teeth marks in them.*

It was a good investment.

Acknowledgments

To the host of people who sent me feedback on the first edition, especially Michael Covington, John Sprung, and A. Wesley Jones.

Also, to Michael Abrash, who coached me on the dusty corners of the CPU and the traps waiting there for the unwary.

And, of course, to Carol, who watched patiently as it happened, and urged me through the walls as I hit them.

(Yes, Mr. Byte. You too. Sit down. Here's a Milk Bone. We did it.)

A Note to People Who Have Never Programmed Before

More than anyone else, this book was written for you. Starting with assembly language would not be most people's first choice in a computer language, but it's been done; it *can* be done, and it can be done with less agony than you might think. Still, it's a novel aim for a computer book, and I'd like you to do a little quality control for me and tell me how I'm doing.

While you're going through this book, ask yourself once in a while: is it working? And if not, why not?

If I lose you somewhere in the discussion, jot a note in the margin. Tell me where I lost you. If possible, tell me why. (And saying, "I just don't get it" is perfectly acceptable, as long as you tell me where in the book you were when you started *not* to get it.)

As with all my books, I hope to keep this one in print well into the 21st century, revising it as need be to hone my technique and follow the technology. Telling me how the book works or doesn't work will, in time, help me make a better book.

Write to me at:

Jeff Duntemann
PC TECHNIQUES Magazine
7721 E. Gray Road #204
Scottsdale, AZ 85260

I can't reply individually to all letters, (not if I ever intend to get another book written!) but you'll have my eternal gratitude nonetheless.

How to Get the Most from this Book

By design, this is a serial-access book. I wrote it to be read like one of those bad/wonderful novels, starting at page one and moving right along to the end. Virtually all of the chapters depend on the chapters that came before them, and if you read a chapter here and a chapter there, there's some danger that the whole thing won't gel.

If you're already familiar with programming, you could conceivably skip Chapters 0,1, and 2. But why not assume there's a hole or two in parts of your experience and a little rust on the rest? Skill is not simply knowledge, but the resonance that comes of seeing how different facets of knowledge reinforce one another.

Do it all. Get the big picture. (Keep in mind that I've hidden some funny stories in there as bait!)

Contents

Another Pleasant Valley Saturday

Understanding What Computers Really Do

0.1 It's All in the Plan

Quick, get the kids up, it's past 7. Nicky's got Little League at 9 and Dione's got ballet at 10. Mike, give Max his heartworm pill! (We're out of them, ma, remember?) Your father picked a great weekend to go fishing...here, let me give you ten bucks and go get more pills at the vet's...my God, that's right, Hank needed gas money and left me broke. There's a teller machine over by K-Mart, and I if I go there I can take that stupid toilet seat back and get the right one.

I guess I'd better make a list.

It's another Pleasant Valley Saturday, and thirty-odd million suburban home-makers sit down with a pencil and pad at the kitchen table to try and make sense of a morning that would kill and pickle any lesser being. In her mind, she thinks of the dependencies and traces the route:

Drop Nicky at Rand Park, go back to Dempster and it's about ten minutes to Golf Mill Mall. Do I have gas? I'd better check first—if not, stop at Del's Shell or I won't make it to Milwaukee Avenue. Bleed the teller machine at Golf Mill, then cross the parking lot to K-Mart to return the toilet seat that Hank bought last weekend without checking what shape it was. Gotta remember to throw the toilet seat in back of the van—write that at the top of the list.

By then it'll be half past, maybe later. Ballet is all the way down Greenwood in Park Ridge. No left turn from Milwaukee—but there's the sneak path around behind the Mall. I have to remember not to turn right onto Milwaukee like I always do—jot that down. While I'm in Park Ridge I can check and see if Hank's new glasses are in—should call but they won't even be open until 9:30. Oh, and groceries—can do that while Dione dances. On the way back I can cut over to Oakton and get the dog's pills.

In about ninety seconds flat the list is complete:

- Throw toilet seat in van
- Check gas—if empty, stop at Del's Shell
- Drop Nicky at Rand Park
- Stop at Golf Mill teller machine
- Return toilet seat at K-Mart
- Drop Dione at ballet (remember back path to Greenwood)
- See if Hank's glasses are at Pearle Vision—if they are, make double sure they remembered the extra scratch coating
- Get groceries at Jewel
- Pick up Dione
- Stop at vet's for heartworm pills
- Drop off groceries at home

- If it's time, pick up Nicky. If not, collapse for a few minutes, then pick up Nicky.
- Collapse!

In what we often call a "laundry list" (whether it involves laundry or not) is the perfect metaphor for a computer program. Without realizing it, our intrepid homemaker has written herself a computer program, and then set out (acting as the computer) to execute it completely before noon.

Computer programming is nothing more than this: You the programmer write a list of steps and tests. The computer then performs each step and test in sequence. When the list of steps has been executed, the computer stops.

A computer program is a list of steps and tests, nothing more.

Steps and Tests

Think for a moment about what I call a "test" in the laundry list shown above. A test is the sort of either/or decision we make dozens or hundreds of times on even the most placid of days, sometimes nearly without thinking about it.

Our homemaker performed a test when she jumped into the van to get started on her adventure. She looked at the gas gauge. The gas gauge would tell her one of two things: 1) She has enough gas, or 2) no, she doesn't. If she has enough gas, she takes a right and heads for Rand Park. If she doesn't have enough gas, she takes a left down to the corner and fills the tank at Del's Shell. (Del takes credit cards.) Then, with a full tank, she continues the program by taking a U-turn and heading for Rand Park.

In the abstract, a test consists of those two parts:

- First you take a look at something that can go one of two ways.
- Then you do one of two things, depending on what you saw when you took a look.

Toward the end of the program, our homemaker got home, took the groceries out of the van, and took a look at the clock. If it wasn't time to get Nicky back from Little League, she has a moment to collapse on the couch in a nearly empty house. If it *is* time to get Nicky, there's no rest for the ragged: She sprints for the van and heads back to Rand Park. (Any guesses as to whether she really gets to collapse when the program is complete?)

More than Two Ways?

You might object that many or most tests involve more than two alternatives. Ha-hah, sorry, you're dead wrong—in every case. Furthermore, you're wrong whether you think you are or not.

Except for totally impulsive behavior, every human decision comes down to the choice of one of two alternatives.

What you have to do is look a little more closely at what goes through your mind when you make decisions. The next time you buzz down to Moo Foo Goo for fast Chinese, observe yourself while you're poring over the menu. The choice might seem, at first, to be of one item out of 26 Cantonese main courses. Not so—the choice, in fact, is between choosing one item and *not* choosing that one item. Your eyes rest on Cashew Chicken. Naw, too bland. *That was a test.* You slide down to the next item. Chicken with Black Mushroom. Hmmm, no, had that last week. *That was another test.* Next item: Kung Pao Chicken. Yeah, that's it! *That was a third test.*

The choice was not among Cashew Chicken, Chicken with Black Mushrooms, or Kung Pao Chicken. Each dish had its moment, poised before the critical eye of your mind, and you turned thumbs up or thumbs down on it, individually. Eventually, one dish won, but it won in that same game of "To eat or Not to eat."

Many of life's most complicated decisions come about because 99% of us are not nudists. You've been there: You're standing in the clothes closet in your underwear, flipping through your rack of pants. The tests come thick and fast. This one? No. This one? No. This one? No. This one? Yeah. You pick a pair of blue pants, say. (It's a Monday, after all, and blue would seem an appropriate color.) Then you stumble over to your sock drawer and take a look. Whoops, no blue socks. *That was a test.* So you stumble back to the clothes closet, hang your blue pants back on the pants rack, and start over. This one? No. This one? No. This one? Yeah. This time it's brown pants, and you toss them over your arm and head back to the sock drawer to take another look. Nertz, out of brown socks, too. So it's back to the clothes closet....

What you might consider a single decision, or perhaps two decisions inextricably tangled (like picking pants and socks of the same color, given stock on hand) is actually a series of small decisions, always binary in nature: Pick 'em or don't pick'em. Find 'em or don't find 'em. The Monday morning episode in the clothes closet is a good analog of a programming structure called a *loop*: You keep doing a series of things until you get it right, and then you stop. (Assuming you're not the kind of guy who wears blue socks with brown pants.) But whether you get everything right always comes down to a sequence of simple, either/or decisions.

Computers Think Like Us

I can almost hear what you're thinking: "Sure, it's a computer book, and he's trying to get me to think like a computer." Not at all. Computers think like *us.*

We designed them; how else could they think? No, what I'm trying to do is get you to take a long hard look at how *you* think. We run on automatic for so much of our lives that we literally do most of our thinking without really thinking about it.

The very best model for the logic of a computer program is the very same logic we use to plan and manage our daily affairs. No matter what we do, it comes down to a matter of confronting two alternatives and picking one. What we might think of as a single large and complicated decision is nothing more than a messy tangle of many smaller decisions. The skill of looking at a complex decision and seeing all the little decisions in its tummy will serve you well in learning how to program. Observe yourself the next time you have to decide something. Count up the little decisions that make up the big one. You'll be surprised.

And, surprise! You'll be a programmer.

0.2 Had This Been the Real Thing...

Do not be alarmed. What you have just experienced was a metaphor. It was not the real thing. (The real thing comes later.)

I'll be using metaphors a lot in this book. A metaphor is a loose comparison drawn between something familiar (like a Saturday morning laundry list) and something unfamiliar (like a computer program.) The idea is to anchor the unfamiliar in the terms of the familiar, so that when I begin tossing facts at you you'll have someplace comfortable to lay them down. The facts don't start until Chapter 1. (That's why I call this Chapter 0: Metaphors only, please.)

The most important thing for you to do right now is keep an open mind. If you know a little bit about computers or programming, don't pick nits. Yes, there are important differences between a homemaker following a scribbled laundry list and a computer executing a program. I'll mention those differences all in good time.

For now, it's still Chapter 0. Take these initial metaphors on their own terms. Later on, they'll help a lot.

0.3 Do Not Pass GO

"There's a reason *bored* and *board* are homonyms," said my best friend Art one evening, as we sat (two super-sophisticated twelve-year-olds) playing some game in his basement. (He may have been unhappy because he was losing.) Was it Mille Bornes? Or Stratego? Or Monopoly? Or something else entirely? I confess I don't remember. I simply recall hopping some little piece of plastic shaped like a pregnant bowling pin up and down a series of colored squares that told me to do dumb things like go back two spaces or put $100 in the pot or nuke Outer Mongolia.

Outer Mongolia notwithstanding, there are strong parallels to be drawn between that peculiar American obsession, the board game, and assembly-language programming. First of all, everything we said before still holds: Board games, by and large, consist of a progression of steps and tests. In some games, like Trivial Pursuit, *every* step on the board is a test: To see if you can answer, or not answer, a question on a card. In other board games, each little square on the board contains some sort of instruction: Lose One Turn; Go Back Two Squares; Take a Card from Community Chest; and, of course, Go to Jail.

Certain board games made for some lively arguments between Art and me (it was that or be bored, as it were) concerning what it meant to Go Forward or Backward Five Steps. It seemed to me that you should count the square you were already on. Art, traditionalist always, thought you should start counting with the first step in the direction you had to go. This made a difference in the game, of course. (I conveniently forgot to press my point when doing so would land me on something like Park Place with fifteen of Art's hotels on it...)

The Game of Big Bux

To avoid getting in serious trouble, I have invented my own board game to continue with this particular metaphor. In the sense that art mirrors life, the Game of Big Bux mirrors life in Silicon Valley, where money seems to be spontaneously created (generally in somebody else's pocket) and the three big Money Black Holes are fast cars, California real estate, and messy divorces.

A portion of the Big Bux game board is shown on the following page. The line of rectangles on the left side of the page continues all the way around the board. In the middle of the board are cubbyholes to store your play money and game pieces; stacks of cards to be read occasionally; and short "detours" with names like Messy Divorce and Start a Business, which are brief sequences of the same sort of action rectangles as those forming the path around the edge of the board.

Unlike many board games, you don't throw dice to determine how many steps around the board you take. Big Bux requires that you move *one* step forward on each turn, *unless* the square you land on instructs you to move forward or backward or go somewhere else, like through a detour. This makes for a considerably less random game. In fact, Big Bux is a pretty deterministic game, meaning that whether you win or lose is far less important than just going through the ringer and coming out the other side. (Again, this mirrors Silicon Valley, where you come out either bankrupt or ready to flee to Peoria and open a hardware store. That *other* kind of hardware.)

There is some math involved. You start out with one house, a cheap car, and $50,000 in cash. You can buy CDs at a given interest rate, payable each time you make it once around the board. You can invest in stocks and other securities whose value is determined by a changeable index in economic indicators, which fluctuates based on cards chosen from the stack called The

Figure 0.1. The Game of Big Bux

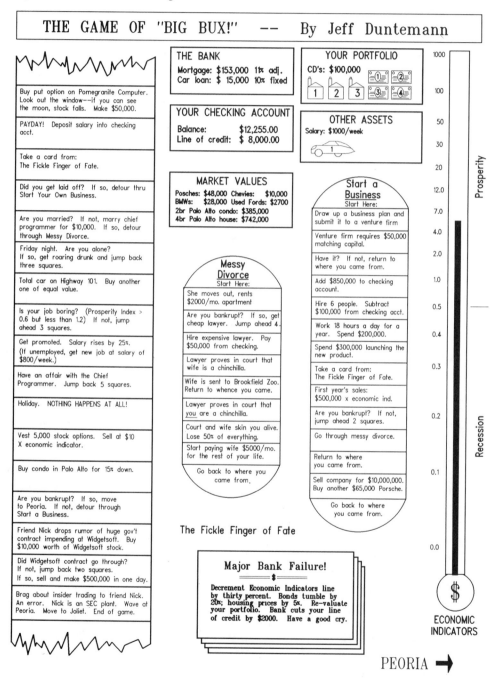

Fickle Finger of Fate. You can sell cars on a secondary market, buy and sell houses, and wheel and deal with the other players. Each time you make it once around the board you have to recalculate your net worth. All of this involves some addition, subtraction, multiplication, and division, but there's no math more complex than compound interest. Most of Big Bux involves nothing more than taking a step and following the instructions at each step.

Is this starting to sound familiar?

Playing Big Bux

At one corner of the Big Bux board is the legend Move In, since that's how people start life in California—no one is actually *born* there. Once you're moved in, you begin working your way around the board, square by square, following the instructions in the squares.

Some of the squares simply tell you to do something, like *Buy condo in Palo Alto for 5% down.* Many of the squares involve a test of some kind. For example, one square reads: *Is your job boring? (Prosperity Index 0.3 but less than 4.0) If not, jump ahead 3 squares.* The test is actually to see if the Prosperity Index has a value between 0.3 and 4.0. Any value outside those bounds (i.e., runaway prosperity or Four Horsemen class recession) are defined as Interesting Times, and cause a jump ahead by three squares.

You always move one step forward at each turn, unless the square you land on directs you to do something else, like jump forward three squares or jump back five squares.

The notion of taking a detour is an interesting one. Two detours are shown in the portion of the board I've provided. Taking a detour means leaving the main run around the edge of the game board and stepping through a series of squares elsewhere on the board. The detours involve some specific process; i.e., starting a business or getting divorced.

You can work through a detour, step by step, until you hit the bottom. At that point you simply pick up your journey around the board right where you left it. You may also find that one of the squares in the detour instructs you to go back to where you came from. Depending on the logic of the game (and your luck and finances) you may completely run through a detour, or get thrown out somewhere in the middle.

Also note that you can take a detour from within a detour. If you detour through Start a Business and your business goes bankrupt, you leave Start a Business temporarily and detour through Messy Divorce. Once you leave Messy Divorce you return to where you left Start a Business. Ultimately, you also leave Start a Business and return to wherever it was you were when you took the detour.

The same detour (for example, Start a Business) can be taken from any of several different places along the game board.

Assembly Language Programming as a Board Game

Now that you're thinking in terms of board games, take a look at Figure 0.2. What I've drawn is actually a fair approximation of assembly language as it was used on some of our simpler microprocessors about ten or twelve years ago. The PROGRAM INSTRUCTIONS column is the main path around the edge of the board, of which only a portion can be shown here. This is the assembly language computer program, the actual series of steps and tests that, when executed, causes the computer to do something useful. Setting up this series of program instructions is what programming in assembly language actually is.

Everything else is odds and ends in the middle of the board that serve the game in progress. You're probably noticing (perhaps with sagging spirits) that there are a *lot* of numbers involved. (They're weird numbers, too—what, for example, does "004B" mean? I'll deal with that issue in *Chapter 2: Alien Bases.*) I'm sorry, but that's simply the way the game is played. Assembly language, at the innermost level, is nothing *but* numbers, and if you hate numbers the way most people hate anchovies, you're going to have a rough time of it.

I should caution you that the Game of Assembly Language represents no real computer processor like the 8088. Also, I've made the names of instructions more clearly understandable than the names of the instructions in 86 assembly language. In the real world, instruction names are typically things like **STOSB**, **DAA**, **INC**, **SBB**, and other crypticisms that cannot be understood without considerable explanation. We're easing into this stuff sidewise, and in this chapter I have to sugar-coat certain things a little to draw the metaphors clearly.

Code and Data

Like most board games (including Big Bux), the assembly language board game consists of two broad categories of elements: Game steps and places to store things. The "game steps" are the steps and tests I've been speaking of all along. The places to store things are just that: The cubbyholes into which you can place numbers, with the confidence that those numbers will remain where you put them until you take them out or change them somehow.

In programming terms, the game steps are called *code*, and the numbers in their cubbyholes (as distinct from the cubbyholes themselves) are called *data*. The cubbyholes themselves are usually called *storage*.

The Game of Big Bux works the same way. Look back to Figure 0.1 and note that in the **Start a Business** detour, there is an instruction that reads **Add $850,000 to checking account.** The checking account is one of several different kinds of storage in this game, and money values are a type of data. It's no different conceptually from an instruction in the Game of Assembly Language that reads **ADD 5 to Register A**. An **ADD** instruction in the code alters a data value stored in a cubbyhole named Register A.

Figure 0.2 The Game of Assembly Language

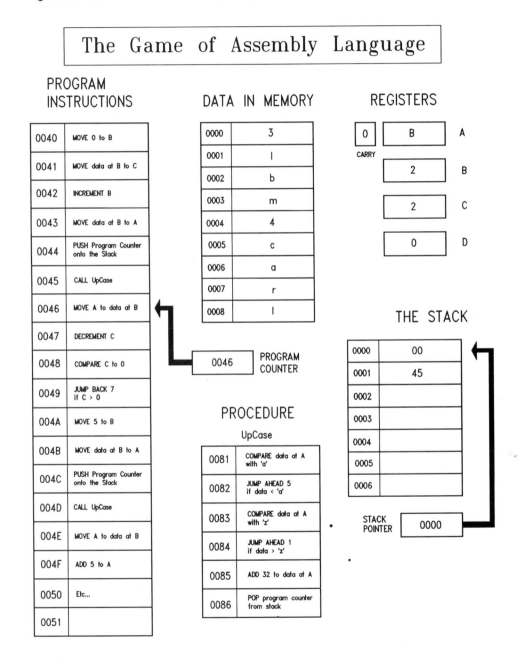

Code and data are two very different kinds of critters, but they interact in ways that make the game interesting. The code includes steps that place data into storage (**MOVE** instructions) and steps that alter data that is already in storage (**INCREMENT** and **DECREMENT** instructions.) Most of the time you'll think of code as being the master of data, in that the code writes data values into storage. Data does influence code as well, however. Among the tests that the code makes are tests that examine data in storage (**COMPARE** instructions). If a given data value exists in storage, the code may do one thing; if that value does not exist in storage, the code will do something else, as in the **JUMP BACK** and **JUMP AHEAD** instructions.

The short block of instructions marked **PROCEDURE** is a detour off the main stream of instructions. At any point in the program you can duck out into the procedure, perform its steps and tests, and then return to the very place from which you left. This allows a sequence of steps and tests that is generally useful and used frequently to exist in only one place rather than exist as a separate copy everywhere it is needed.

Addresses

Another critical concept lies in the funny numbers at the left side of the program step locations and data locations. Each number is unique, in that a location tagged with that number appears only once inside the computer. This location is called an *address*. Data is stored and retrieved by specifying the data's address in the machine. Procedures are called by specifying the address at which they begin.

The little box (which is also a storage location) marked **PROGRAM COUNTER** keeps the address of the next instruction to be performed. The number inside the program counter is increased by one (we say, "incremented") each time an instruction is performed *unless the instruction tells the program counter to do something else*.

Notice the **JUMP BACK 7** instruction at address 0049. When this instruction is performed, the program counter will back up by seven counts. This is analogous to the "go back three spaces" concept in most board games.

Metaphor Check!

That's about as much explanation of the Game of Assembly Language as I'm going to offer for now. This is still Chapter 0, and we're still in metaphor territory. People who have had some exposure to computers will recognize and understand more of what Figure 0.2 is doing. (There's a real, traceable program going on in there—I dare you to figure out what it does—and how!) People with no exposure to computer innards at all shouldn't feel left behind for being utterly lost. I created the Game of Assembly Language solely to put across the following points:

- *The individual steps are very simple.* One single instruction rarely does more than move a single byte from one storage cubbyhole to another, or compare the value contained in one storage cubbyhole to a value contained in another. This is good news, because it allows you to concentrate on the simple task accomplished by a single instruction without being overwhelmed by complexity. The bad news, however, is that...

- *It takes a lot of steps to do anything useful.* You can often write a useful program in Pascal or BASIC in five or six lines. A useful assembly language program cannot be implemented in fewer than about fifty lines, and anything challenging takes hundreds or thousands of lines. The skill of assembly language programming lies in structuring these hundreds or thousands of instructions so that the program can be read and understood. And finally,

- *The key to assembly language is understanding memory addresses.* In languages like Pascal and BASIC, the compiler takes care of *where* something is located—you simply have to give that something a name, and call it by that name when you want it. In assembly language, you must *always* be cognizant of where things are in your computer's memory. So in working through this book, pay special attention to the concept of *addressing*, which is nothing more than the art of specifying where something is. The Game of Assembly Language is peppered with addresses and instructions that work with addresses. (Such as **MOVE data at B to C**, which means move the data stored at the address specified by register B to the address specified by register C.) Addressing is by far the trickiest part of assembly language, but master it and you've got the whole thing in your hip pocket.

Everything I've said so far has been orientation. I've tried to give you a taste of the big picture of assembly language and how its fundamental principles relate to the life you've been living all along. Life is a sequence of steps and tests, and so are board games—and so is assembly language. Keep those metaphors in mind as we proceed to "get real" by confronting the nature of computer numbers.

Alien Bases

Getting Your Arms around Binary and Hexadecimal

1.1 The Return of the New Math Monster

1966. Perhaps you were there. New Math burst upon the grade school curricula of the nation, and homework became a turmoil of number lines, sets, and alternate bases. Middle-class fathers scratched their heads with their children over questions like, "What is 17 in base 5?" and "Which sets does the Null Set belong to?" In very short order (I recall a period of about two months) the whole thing was tossed in the trash as quickly as it had been concocted by addle-brained educrats with too little to do.

This was a pity, actually. What nobody seemed to realize at the time was that, granted, we were learning New Math—except that *Old* Math had never been taught at the grade school level either. We kept wondering of what possible use it was to know what the intersection of the set of squirrels and the set of mammals was. The truth, of course, was that it was no use at all. Mathematics in America has always been taught as *applied* mathematics—arithmetic—heavy on the word problems. If it won't help you balance your checkbook or proportion a recipe, it ain't real math, man. Little or nothing of the logic of mathematics has *ever* made it into the elementary classroom, in part because elementary school in America has historically been a sort of trade school for everyday life. Getting the little beasts fundamentally literate is difficult enough. Trying to get them to appreciate the beauty of alternate number systems simply went over the line for practical middle-class America.

I was one of the few who enjoyed fussing with math in the New Age style back in 1966, but I gladly laid it aside when the whole thing blew over. I didn't have to pick it up again until 1976, when, after working like a maniac with a wire-wrap gun for several weeks, I fed power to my COSMAC ELF computer, and was greeted by an LED display of a pair of numbers in *base 16!*

Mon dieu, New Math *redux...*

This chapter exists because at the assembly-language level, your computer does not understand numbers in our familiar base 10. Computers, in a slightly schizoid fashion, work in base 2 and base 16—all at the same time. If you're willing to confine yourself to BASIC or Pascal, you can ignore these alien bases altogether, or perhaps treat them as an advanced topic once you get the rest of the language down pat. Not here. *Everything* in assembly language depends on your thorough understanding of these two number bases. So before we do anything else, we're going to learn how to count all over again—in Martian.

1.2 Counting in Martian

There is intelligent life on Mars.

That is, the Martians are intelligent enough to know from watching our TV programs these past forty years that a thriving tourist industry would not be to their advantage. So they've remained in hiding, emerging only briefly to carve big rocks into the shape of Elvis's face to help the *National Enquirer* ensure that no one will ever take Mars seriously again. The Martians do occasionally communicate with us science fiction writers, knowing full well that nobody has ever taken *us* seriously. Hence the information in this section, which involves the way Martians count.

Martians have three fingers on one hand, and only one finger on the other. Male Martians have their three fingers on the left hand, while females have their three fingers on the right hand. This makes waltzing and certain other things easier.

Like human beings and any other intelligent race, Martians started counting by using their fingers. Just as we used our ten fingers to set things off in groups and powers of ten, the Martians used their four fingers to set things off in groups and powers of four. Over time, our civilization standardized on a set of ten digits to serve our number system. The Martians, similarly, standardized on a set of four digits for their number system. The four digits follow, along with the names of the digits as the Martians pronounce them: θ (Xip), ʃ (Foo), ∩ (Bar), ≡ (Bas).

Like our zero, xip is a placeholder representing no items, and while Martians sometimes count from xip, they usually start with foo, representing a single item. So they start counting: *Foo, bar, bas…*

Now what? What comes after bas? Table 1.1 demonstrates how the Martians count to what we would call twenty-five.

Table 1.1. Counting in Martian, base fooby

Martian Numerals	Martian Pronunciation	Earth Equivalent
θ	Xip	0
ʃ	Foo	1
∩	Bar	2
≡	Bas	3
ʃθ	Fooby	4
ʃʃ	Fooby-foo	5
ʃ∩	Fooby-bar	6
ʃ≡	Fooby-bas	7
∩θ	Barby	8
∩ʃ	Barby-foo	9
∩∩	Barby-bar	10
∩≡	Barby-bas	11
≡θ	Basby	12
≡ʃ	Basby-foo	13
≡∩	Basby-bar	14
≡≡	Basby-bas	15

continued

Table 1.1. Counting in Martian, base fooby (*continued*)

Martian Numerals	Martian Pronunciation	Earth Equivalent
⌠ΘΘ	Foobity	16
⌠Θ⌠	Foobity-foo	17
⌠Θ∩	Foobity-bar	18
⌠Θ≡	Foobity-bas	19
⌠⌠Θ	Foobity-fooby	20
⌠⌠⌠	Foobity-fooby-foo	21
⌠⌠∩	Foobity-fooby-bar	22
⌠⌠≡	Foobity-fooby-bas	23
⌠∩Θ	Foobity-barby	24
⌠∩⌠	Foobity-barby-foo	25

With only four digits (including the one representing zero) the Martians can only count to bas without running out of digits. The number after bas has a new name, *fooby*. Fooby is the base of the Martian number system, and probably the most important number on Mars. Fooby is the number of fingers a Martian has. We would call it *four*.

The most significant thing about fooby is the way the Martians write it out in numerals: ⌠Θ. Instead of a single column, fooby is expressed in two columns. Just as with our decimal system, each column has a value that is a power of fooby. This only means that as you move from the rightmost column toward the left, each column represents a value fooby multiplied by the column to its right.

The rightmost column represents units, in counts of foo. The next column over represents fooby multiplied by foo, or (given that arithmetic works the same way on Mars as here, New Math notwithstanding) simply fooby. The next column to the left of fooby represents fooby multiplied by fooby, or foobity, and so on. This relationship should become clearer through Table 1.2.

Table 1.2. Powers of fooby

⌠	Foo	× Fooby =
⌠Θ	Fooby	× Fooby =
⌠ΘΘ	Foobity	× Fooby =
⌠ΘΘΘ	Foobidity	× Fooby =
⌠ΘΘΘΘ	Foobididity	× Fooby =
⌠ΘΘΘΘΘ	Foobidididity	and so on...

Dissecting a Martian Number

Any given column may contain a digit from xip to bas, indicating how many instances of that column's value are contained in the number as a whole. Let's work through an example. Look at Figure 1.1, which is a dissection of the Martian number ⌒≡ʃΘ, pronounced "Barbididity-basbidity-foobity-bas." (A visiting and heavily-disguised Martian precipitated the doo-wop craze while standing at a Philadelphia bus stop in 1954, counting his change.)

The rightmost column tells how many units are contained in the number. The digit there is bas, indicating that the number contains bas units. The second column from the right carries a value of fooby multiplied by foo (essentially fooby times one) or fooby. A xip in the fooby column indicates that there are no foobies in the number. The xip digit in ⌒≡ʃΘ≡ is a placeholder, just as zero is in our numbering system. Notice also that in the columnar sum shown to the right of the digit matrix, the foobies line is represented by a double xip. Not only is there a xip to tell us that there are no foobies, but also a xip holding the foos place as well. This pattern continues in the columnar sum as we move toward the more significant columns to the left.

Figure 1.1. The anatomy of ⌒≡ʃΘ≡

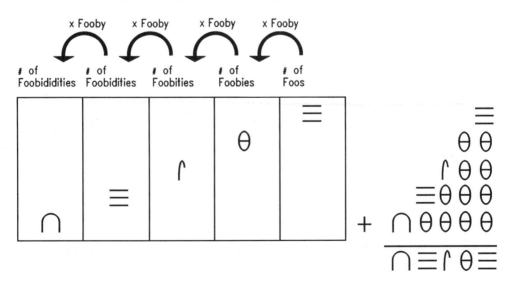

Consider the Martian Number ⌒≡ʃΘ≡

Each column carries a value fooby multiplied by the column on its right.

Fooby multiplied by fooby is foobity, and the ⌠ digit tells us that there is foo foobity (a single foobity) in the number. The next column, in keeping with the pattern, is foobity multiplied by fooby, or foobidity. In the columnar notation, foobidity is written as ⌠ΘΘΘ. The ≡ digit tells us that there are bas foobidities in the number. Bas foobidities is a number with its own name, basbidity, which may be written as ≡ΘΘΘ. Note the presence of basbidity in the columnar sum.

The next column to the left has a value of fooby multiplied by foobidity, or foobididity. The ∩ digit tells us that there are bar foobididities in the number. Bar foobididities (written ∩ΘΘΘ) is also a number with its own name, barbidity. Note also the presence of barbidity in the columnar sum, and the four xip digits that hold places for the empty columns.

The columnar sum expresses the sense of the way a number is assembled: The number contains barbidity, basbidity, foobity, and bas. Roll all that together by simple addition and you get ∩≡⌠Θ≡. The name is pronounced simply by hyphenating the component values: Barbidity-basbidity-foobity-bas. Note that there is no part in the name representing the empty fooby column. We don't, for example, pronounce the number 401 as "four hundred, zero tens, one." We simply say, "four hundred one." In the same manner, rather than say "xip foobies" the Martians just leave it out.

As an exercise, given what I've told you so far about Martian numbers, figure out the Earthly value equivalent to ∩≡⌠Θ≡.

The Essence of a Number Base

Since tourist trips to Mars are unlikely to begin any time soon, of what Earthly use is knowing the Martian numbering system? Just this: it's an excellent way to see the sense in a number base without getting distracted by familiar digits and our universal base 10.

In a columnar system of numeric notation like both ours and the Martians', the *base* of the number system is the magnitude by which each column of a number exceeds the magnitude of the column to its right. In our base 10 system, each column represents a value ten multiplied by the column to its right. In a base fooby system, each column represents a value fooby multiplied by that of the column to its right. (In case you haven't already caught on, the Martians are actually using base 4—but I wanted you to see it from the Martians' own perspective.) Each has a set of digit symbols, the number of which is equal to the base. In our base 10, we have ten symbols, from 0 through 9. In base 4, there are four digits from 0 through 3. *In any given number base, the base itself can never be expressed in a single digit!*

1.3 Octal: How the Grinch Stole 8 and 9

Farewell to Mars. Aside from lots of iron oxide and some terrific *a capella* groups, they haven't much to offer us ten-fingered folk. There are some similarly odd number bases in use here, and I'd like to take a quick detour through one that occupies a separate world right here on Earth: The world of Digital Equipment Corporation, better known as DEC.

Back in the '60s, DEC invented the minicomputer as a challenger to the massive mainframes pioneered by IBM. To ensure that no software could possibly be moved from an IBM mainframe to a DEC minicomputer, DEC designed its machines to understand only numbers expressed in base *8*.

Let's think about that for a moment, given our experience with the Martians. In base 8, there must be eight digits. DEC was considerate enough not to invent their own digits, so what they used were the traditional digits from 0 through 7. *There is no digit 8 in base 8!* That always takes a little getting used to, but it's part of the definition of a number base. DEC gave a name to its base 8 system: *octal*.

A columnar number in octal follows the rule we encountered in thinking about the Martian system: Each column has a value 8 multiplied by that of the column to its right.

Who Stole 8 and 9?

Counting in octal starts out in a very familiar fashion: One, two, three, four, five, six, seven…*ten*.

This is where the trouble starts. In octal, ten comes after seven. What happened to eight and nine? Did the Grinch steal them? (Or the Martians?) Hardly. They're still there—but they have different names. In octal, when you say "ten" you mean "eight." Worse, when you say "eleven" you mean "nine."

Unfortunately, what DEC did *not* do was invent clever names for the column values. The first column is, of course, the units column. The next column to the left of the units column is the tens column, just as it is in our own decimal system. But here's the rub, and the reason I dragged Mars into this: *Octal's "tens" column actually has a value of 8.*

A counting table will help. Table 1.3 counts up to thirty octal, which has a value of 24 decimal. I dislike the use of the terms eleven, twelve, and so on in bases other than ten, but the convention in octal has always been to pronounce the numbers as we would in decimal, only with the word "octal" after them.

Remember, each column in a given number base has a value base multiplied by the column to its right, so the tens column in octal is actually the eights column. (They call it the tens column because it is written 10, and pronounced "ten.") Similarly, the column to the left of the tens column is the hundreds

---

Table 1.3. Counting in octal, base 8

Octal Numerals	Pronunciation	Decimal Equivalent
0	Zero	0
1	One	1
2	Two	2
3	Three	3
4	Four	4
5	Five	5
6	Six	6
7	Seven	7
10	Ten	8
11	Eleven	9
12	Twelve	10
13	Thirteen	11
14	Fourteen	12
15	Fifteen	13
16	Sixteen	14
17	Seventeen	15
20	Twenty	16
21	Twenty-one	17
22	Twenty-two	18
23	Twenty-three	19
24	Twenty-four	20
25	Twenty-five	21
26	Twenty-six	22
27	Twenty-seven	23
30	Thirty	24

---

column (because it is written 100) but the hundreds column actually has a value of 8 multiplied by 8, or 64. The next column over has a value of 64 multiplied by 8, or 512, and the column left of that has a value of 512 multiplied by 8, or 4096.

This is why if someone talks about a value of "ten octal" they mean 8; "one hundred octal" they mean 64, and so on. Table 1.4 summarizes the octal column values and their decimal equivalents.

A digit in the first column (the units, or 1's column) tells how many units are contained in the octal number. A digit in the next column to the left, the tens column, tells how many 8's are contained in the octal number. A digit in the third column, the hundreds column, tells how many 64's are in the number, and so on. For example, 400 octal means that the number contains 4 64's; that is, 256 in decimal.

Table 1.4. Octal columns as powers of 8

Octal		Power of 8		Decimal	
1	=	8^0	=	1	× 8 =
10	=	8^1	=	8	× 8 =
100	=	8^2	=	64	× 8 =
1000	=	8^3	=	512	× 8 =
10000	=	8^4	=	4096	× 8 =
100000	=	8^5	=	32768	× 8 =
1000000	=	8^6	=	262144	× 8 =

It is confusing. The best way to make it all gel is to dissect a middling octal number, just as we did with a middling Martian number. This is what's happening in Figure 1.2: The octal number 76225 is pulled apart into columns and added up again.

Figure 1.2. The anatomy of 76225 octal

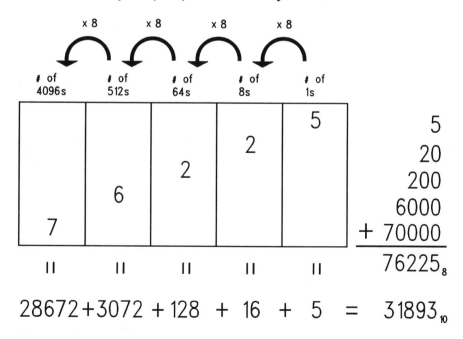

Consider the Octal Number 76225

Each column carries a value
eight multiplied by the column on its right.

The sum of each column's decimal equivalent
is the value of the octal number in decimal.

It works the same way it does in Martian, or decimal, or any other number base. In general: Each column has a value consisting of the number base raised to the power represented by the ordinal position of the column minus one. That is, the value of the first column is the number base raised to the 1–1, or 0, power. Since any number raised to the zero power is one, the first column in *any* number base always has the value of one and is called the *units column*. The second column has the value of the number based raised to the 2–1, or 1st power, which is the value of the number base itself. In octal this is 8; in decimal, 10; in Martian base fooby, fooby. The third column has a value consisting of the number base raised to the 3–1, or 2nd power, and so on.

Within each column, the digit holding that column tells how many instances of that column's value is contained in the number as a whole. Here, the 6 in 76225 octal tells us that there are six instances of its column's value in the total value 76225 octal. The six occupies the fourth column, which has a value of 8^{4-1}, which is 8^3, or 512. This tells us that six 512 values are in the number as a whole.

You can convert the value of a number in any base to decimal (our base 10) by determining the value of each column in the alien base, then multiplying the value of each column by the digit contained in that column, (to create the decimal equivalent of each digit) and then finally taking the sum of the decimal equivalent of each column. This is done in Figure 1.2, and the octal number and its decimal equivalent are both shown.

Now that we've looked at columnar notation from both a Martian and an octal perspective, make sure you understand how columnar notation works in any arbitrary base before we go on.

Log in Please

You may use an octal number every day. You may, in fact, have it memorized. This number is your ID number on the CompuServe timesharing system. CompuServe runs on a (large) bank of DEC computers, and their user IDs are all in octal. Notice, if you use CompuServe, that *nowhere* in *any* of the ID numbers attached to the messages you read will you find either the digit 8 or the digit 9.

1.4 Hexadecimal: Solving the Digit Shortage

Octal is unlikely to be of use to you unless you choose to become a minicomputer programmer, which is about as exciting as blowing packing peanuts into boxes on somebody else's shipping dock. As I mentioned earlier, the *real* numbering system to reckon with in the microcomputer world is base 16, which we call *hexadecimal,* or (more affectionately) simply *hex.*

Hexadecimal shares the essential characteristics of any number base, including both Martian and octal: It is <u>a columnar notation, in which each column has a value *sixteen* times the value of the column to its right.</u> It has sixteen digits, running from 0 to...what?

We have a shortage of digits here. From zero through nine we're in fine shape. Ten, eleven, twelve, thirteen, fourteen, and fifteen, however, need to be expressed in single digits. Without any additional numeric digits, the people who developed hexadecimal notation in the early 1950s borrowed the first six letters of the alphabet to act as the needed digits.

Counting in hexadecimal, then, goes like this: 0, 1, 2, 3, 4, 5, 6, 7, 8, 9, A, B, C, D, E, F, 10, 11, 12, 13, 14, 15, 16, 17, 18, 19, 1A, 1B, 1C and so on. Table 1.5 restates this in a more organized fashion, with the decimal equivalents up to 32.

Table 1.5. Counting in hexadecimal, base 16

Hexadecimal Numerals	Pronunciation (follow with "hex")	Decimal Equivalent
0	Zero	0
1	One	1
2	Two	2
3	Three	3
4	Four	4
5	Five	5
6	Six	6
7	Seven	7
8	Eight	8
9	Nine	9
A	A	10
B	B	11
C	C	12
D	D	13
E	E	14
F	F	15
10	Ten (or, One-oh)	16
11	One-one	17
12	One-two	18
13	One-three	19
14	One-four	20
15	One-five	21
16	One-six	22
17	One-seven	23
18	One-eight	24

continued

Table 1.5. Counting in hexadecimal, base 16 (*continued*)

Hexadecimal Numerals	Pronunciation (follow with "hex")	Decimal Equivalent
19	One-nine	25
1A	One-A	26
1B	One-B	27
1C	One-C	28
1D	One-D	29
1E	One-E	30
1F	One-F	31
20	Twenty (or, Two-oh)	32

One of the conventions in hexadecimal that I favor is the dropping of words like "eleven" and "twelve" that are too tied to our decimal system and only promote gross confusion. Confronted by the number 11 in hexadecimal (usually written 11H to let us know what base we're speaking) we would say, "one-one hex." Don't forget to say "hex" after a hexadecimal number, again to avoid gross confusion. This is unnecessary with the digits 0 through 9, which represent the exact same values in both decimal and hexadecimal.

Some people still say things like "twelve hex", which is valid, and means 18 decimal. But I don't care for it, and advise against it. This business of alien bases is confusing enough without giving the aliens Charlie Chaplin masks.

Each column in the hexadecimal system has a value 16 multiplied by that of the column to its right. (The rightmost column, as in *any* number base, is the units column and has a value of 1.) As you might imagine, the values of the individual columns goes up frighteningly fast as move from right to left. Table 1.6 shows the values of the first seven columns in hexadecimal. For comparison's sake, note that the seventh column in decimal notation has a value of 1,000,000, while the seventh column in hexadecimal has a value of 16,777,216.

Table 1.6. Hexadecimal columns as powers of 16

Decimal		Power of 16		Hexadecimal	
1H	=	16^0	=	1	× 16 =
10H	=	16^1	=	16	× 16 =
100H	=	16^2	=	256	× 16 =
1000H	=	16^3	=	4096	× 16 =
10000H	=	16^4	=	65536	× 16 =
100000H	=	16^5	=	1048576	× 16 =
1000000H	=	16^6	=	16777216	etc...

Figure 1.3. The anatomy of 3C0A9 hex

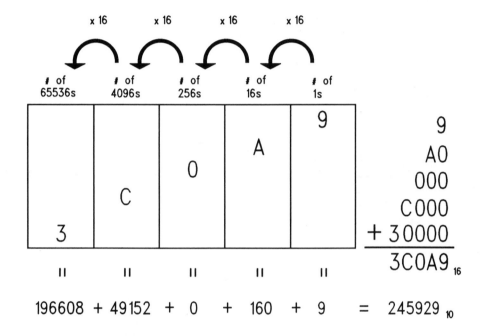

Consider the Hexadecimal Number 3C0A9

Each column carries a value sixteen times
that of the column on its right.

x 16   x 16   x 16   x 16

of   # of   # of   # of   # of
65536s   4096s   256s   16s   1s

			9
		0	A
	C		
3			

```
        9
       A0
      000
     C000
  + 30000
  ---------
    3C0A9 ₁₆
```

196608 + 49152 + 0 + 160 + 9 = 245929 ₁₀

The sum of each column's decimal equivalent
is the value of the hex number in decimal.

To help you understand how hexadecimal numbers are constructed, I've dissected a typical hex number in Figure 1.3, in the same fashion that I dissected numbers earlier in both Martian base fooby, and in octal. Just as in octal, zero holds a place in a column without adding any value to the number as a whole. Note in Figure 1.3 that no 256 values are present in the number 3C0A9H.

As in Figure 1.2, the decimal values of each column are shown beneath the column, and the sum of all columns is shown in both decimal and hex.

1.5 From Hex to Decimal and From Decimal to Hex

Most of the manipulation of hex numbers you'll be performing will be simple conversions between hex and decimal, in both directions. The easiest way to perform such conversions is by way of a hex calculator, either a "real" calculator like the venerable TI Programmer (which I still have, wretched battery-eater that it is) or a TSR software calculator like Sidekick. This demands nothing of your grey matter, of course, and won't help you understand the hexadecimal number system any better. So while you're a green student, lay off anything that understands hex, hardware, software, or human associates.

In fact, the best tool is a simple four-function memory calculator. The conversion methods I'll describe here all make use of such a calculator, since what I'm trying to teach you is number base conversion, not decimal addition or long division.

From Hex to Decimal

As you'll come to understand, converting hex numbers to decimal is a good deal easier than going the other way. The general method is to do what we've been doing all along in the dissection figures: Derive the value represented by each individual column in the hex number, and then add up the total of all the column values in decimal.

Let's try an easy one. The hex number is 7A2. Start at the right column. This is the units column in any number system. You have 2 units, so enter 2 into your calculator. Now store that 2 into memory. (Or press the SUM button, if you have one.)

So much for units. Keep in mind that you're keeping a running tally of the values of the columns in the hex number. Move to the next column to the left. Remember that each column represents a value 16 times the value of the column to its right. So the second column from the right is the 16s column. (Refer to Table 1.6 if you lose track of the column values.) The 16s column has an A in it. A in hex is decimal 10. The total value of that column, therefore, is 16 × 10, or 160. Perform that multiplication on your calculator, and add the product to the 2 that you stored in memory. (Again, the SUM button is a handy way to do this if your calculator has one.)

Remember what you're doing: Evaluating each column in decimal and keeping a running total. Now, move to the third column from the right. This one contains a 7. The value of the third column is 16 × 16, or 256. Multiply 256 by 7 on your calculator, and add the product to your running total.

You're done. Retrieve the running total from your calculator memory. The total should be 1954, which is the decimal equivalent of 7A2 hex.

Let's try it again, with a little less natter and a much larger number: C6F0DB.

Evaluate the units column. B × 1 = 11 × 1 = 11. Start your running total.

Evaluate the 16s column. D × 16 = 13 × 16 = 208. Add 208 to your running total.

Evaluate the 256s column. 0 × 256 = 0. Move on.

Evaluate the 4096s column. F × 4096 = 15 × 2096 = 61,440. Add it to your running total.

Evaluate the 65536s column. 6 × 65536 = 393,216. Add it to the running total.

Evaluate the 1048576s column. C S 1048576 = 12 S 1048576 = 12,582,912. Add it to your total.

The running total should be 13037787.

Finally, do it yourself, using the hex number 1A55BE.

From Decimal to Hex

The lights should be coming on about now. This is good, because going in the other direction, from our decimal base 10 to hex, is *much* harder, and involves more math. What we have to do is find the hex column values within a decimal number—and that involves some considerable use of that fifth-grade boogeyman, long division.

But let's get to it; again, starting with a fairly easy number: 449. The calculator will be handy, in spades. Tap in the number 449 and store it in the calculator's memory.

What we need to do first is find the *largest* hex column value that is contained in 449 at least *once*. Remember grade-school "gazintas"? (12 gazinta 855 how many times?) It's something like that. Looking back at Table 1.6, we can see that 256 is the largest power of 16, and hence the largest hex column value, that is present in 449 at least once. (The next largest power of 16, 512, is obviously too large to be present in 449.)

So we start with 256, and determine how many times 256 gazinta 449. 449 ÷ 256 = 1.7539. At least once, but not quite twice. So 449 contains only one 256. Write down a 1 on paper. *Don't enter it into your calculator.* We're not keeping a running total here; if anything, we could say we're keeping a running remainder. The 1 is the leftmost hex digit of the hex value equivalent to decimal 449.

We know that there is only one 256 contained in 449. What we must do now is subtract that 256 from the original number, now that we've counted it by writing a 1 down on paper. Subtract 256 from 449. Store the difference, 193, into memory.

The 256 column has been removed from the number we're converting. Now we move to the next column to the right, the 16s. How many 16s are contained in 193? 193 ÷ 16 = 12.0625. This means the 16s column in the hex equivalent of 449 contains a…12? Hmmmm…remember the digit shortage, and the fact that in hex, the value we call 12 is represented by the letter C. From a hex perspective, we have found that the original number contains C in the 16s column. Write a C down to the right of your 1: 1C. So far so good.

We've got the 16s column, so just as with the 256s, we have to remove the 16s from what's left of the original number. The total value of the 16s column is C × 16 = 12 × 16 = 192. Bring the 193 value out of your calculator's memory, and subtract 192 from it. A lonely little 1 is all that's left.

So we're down to the units column. There is one unit in one, obviously. Write that 1 down to the right of the C in our hexadecimal number: 1C1. Decimal 449 is equivalent to hex 1C1.

Now perhaps you'll begin to understand why Sidekick is so popular.

Let's glance back at the big picture of the decimal-to-hex conversion. We're looking for the hexadecimal columns "hidden" in the decimal value. We find the largest column contained in the decimal number, find that column's value, and subtract that value from the decimal number. Then we look for the next smallest hex column, and the next smallest, and so on, removing the value of each column from the decimal number as we go. In a sense, we're dividing the number by consecutively smaller powers of 16, and keeping a running remainder by removing each column as we tally it.

Let's try it again. The secret number is 988,664.

The largest column contained in 988,664 from Table 1.6 is 65536. Divide 988,664 by 65536 = 15 and change. Ignore the change. 15 = F in hex. Write down the F.

Subtract the sum of F × 65536 from 988,664. Store the remainder (5624).

Move to the next smallest column. 5624 ÷ 4096 = 1 and change. Write down the 1.

Remove 1 × 4096 from the remainder: 5624 − 4096 = 1528. Store the new remainder: 1528.

Move to the next smallest column. 1528 ÷ 256 = 5 and change. Write down the 5.

Remove 5 × 256 from the stored remainder, 1528. Store 248 as the new remainder.

Move to the next smallest column. 248 ÷ 16 = 15 and change. 15 = F in hex. Write down the F.

Remove F × 16 from stored remainder, 248. The remainder, 8, is the number of units in the final column. Write down the 8.

There you have it. 988,664 decimal = F15F8H.

Again, note the presence of the H at the end of the hex number. From now on, every hex number in the text of this book will have that H affixed to its hindparts. It's important, because not *every* hex number contains letter digits. There is a 157H as surely as a 157 decimal, and the two are *not* the same number. Don't forget to include the H when writing your assembler programs, as I'll be reminding you later on.

Practice. Practice! PRACTICE!

The best (actually, the only) way to get a gut feel for hex notation is to use it lots. Convert *each* of the following hex numbers to decimal. Lay each number out on the dissection table and identify how many 1s, how many 16s, how many 256s, how many 4096s, and so on, are present in the number, and then add them up in decimal.

```
CCH
157H
D8H
BB29H
7AH
8177H
A011H
99H
2B36H
FACEH
8DB3H
9H
```

That done, now turn it inside out, and convert each of the following decimal numbers to hex. Remember the general method: From Table 1.6, choose the largest power of 16 that is *less* than the decimal number to be converted. Find out how many times that power of 16 is present in the decimal number, and write it down as the leftmost converted hex digit. Then subtract the total value represented by that hex digit from the decimal number. Then repeat the process, using the next smallest power of 16 until you've subtracted the decimal number down to nothing.

decimal to hex

```
39
413
22
67,349
6,992
41
1,117
44,919
12,331
124,217
91,198
307
112,374,777
```

(Extra credit for that last one...) If you need more practice, choose some decimal numbers and convert them to hex, and then convert them back.

1.6 Arithmetic in Hex

As you become more skilled in assembly language, you'll be doing more arithmetic in base 16. You may even (good grief) come to do it in your head. (I tend to do most of mine on my memory resident hex calculator.) Still, it takes some practice.

Addition and subtraction are no different than what we know in decimal, with a few extra digits tossed in for flavor. The trick is nothing more than knowing your addition tables to 0FH. This is best done not by thinking to yourself, "Now, if C is 12 and F is fifteen, then C + F is twelve plus fifteen, which is 27 decimal but 1BH." Instead, you should simply say inside your head, "C + F are 1BH."

Yes, that's asking a lot. But I ask you now, as I will ask you again on this journey, Do you wanna hack DOS...or do you just wanna fool around? It takes practice to learn the piano, and it takes practice to get really greased up on the foundation concepts of assembly language programming.

So let me sound like an old schoolmarm and tell you to memorize the following. Make flash cards if you must:

```
  9        8        7        6        5
+ 1      + 2      + 3      + 4      + 5
 0AH      0AH      0AH      0AH      0AH

  A        9        8        7        6
+ 1      + 2      + 3      + 4      + 5
 0BH      0BH      0BH      0BH      0BH

  B        A        9        8        7        6
+ 1      + 2      + 3      + 4      + 5      + 6
 0CH      0CH      0CH      0CH      0CH      0CH

  C        B        A        9        8        7
+ 1      + 2      + 3      + 4      + 5      + 6
 0DH      0DH      0DH      0DH      0DH      0DH

  D        C        B        A        9        8        7
+ 1      + 2      + 3      + 4      + 5      + 6      + 7
 0EH      0EH      0EH      0EH      0EH      0EH      0EH

  E        D        C        B        A        9        8
+ 1      + 2      + 3      + 4      + 5      + 6      + 7
 0FH      0FH      0FH      0FH      0FH      0FH      0FH

  F        E        D        C        B        A        9        8
+ 1      + 2      + 3      + 4      + 5      + 6      + 7      + 8
 10H      10H      10H      10H      10H      10H      10H      10H

  F        E        D        C        B        A        9
+ 2      + 3      + 4      + 5      + 6      + 7      + 8
 11H      11H      11H      11H      11H      11H      11H

  F        E        D        C        B        A        9
+ 3      + 4      + 5      + 6      + 7      + 8      + 9
 12H      12H      12H      12H      12H      12H      12H

  F        E        D        C        B        A
+ 4      + 5      + 6      + 7      + 8      + 9
 13H      13H      13H      13H      13H      13H

  F        E        D        C        B        A
+ 5      + 6      + 7      + 8      + 9      + A
 14H      14H      14H      14H      14H      14H

  F        E        D        C        B
+ 6      + 7      + 8      + 9      + A
 15H      15H      15H      15H      15H

  F        E        D        C        B
+ 7      + 8      + 9      + A      + B
 16H      16H      16H      16H      16H
```

```
    F            E            D            C
  + 8          + 9          + A          + B
   17H          17H          17H          17H

    F            E            D            C
  + 9          + A          + B          + C
   18H          18H          18H          18H

    F            E            D
  + A          + B          + C
   19H          19H          19H

    F            E            D
  + B          + C          + D
   1AH          1AH          1AH

    F            E
  + C          + D
   1BH          1BH

    F            E
  + D          + E
   1CH          1CH

    F
  + E
   1DH

    F
  + F
   1EH
```

If nothing else, this exercise should make you glad computers don't work in base 64.

Columns and Carries

With all of the single-column additions committed (more or less) to memory, you can tackle multicolumn addition. It works pretty much the same way it does with decimal. Add each column starting from the right, and carry into next column anytime a single column's sum exceeds 0FH.

For example:

```
 1           1
   2 F 3 1 A DH
 + 9 6 B A 0 7H
   C 5 E B B 4H
```

Work this one through, column by column. The sum of the first column (the rightmost) is 14H, which cannot fit in a single column, so we must carry the one into the next column to the left. Even with the additional 1, however, the sum of the second column is 0BH, which fits in a single column and no carry is required.

Keep on adding moving left. The second-to-last column will again overflow, and you will need to carry the one into the last column. As long as you have your single-digit sums memorized, it's a snap.

Well, more or less.

Now, here's something you should take note of:

> The most you can ever carry out of a single-column addition of two numbers is *1.*

It doesn't matter what base: 16, 10, fooby, or 2. You will either carry a 1 out of a column, or carry nothing at all. This is important when you add numbers on paper or within the silicon of your CPU, as we'll learn a few chapters on.

Subtraction and Borrows

If you have your single-column sums memorized, you can usually grim your way through subtraction with a shift into a sort of mental reverse: if E + 6 equals 14H, then 14H – E must equal 6. The alternative is memorizing an even larger number of tables, and since I haven't memorized them, I won't ask you to.

But over time, that's what tends to happen. In hex subtraction, you should be able to dope out any given single-column subtraction by turning a familiar hexadecimal sum inside-out. And just as with base 10, multicolumn subtractions are done one column at a time:

```
  F76CH
- A05BH
  5711H
```

During your inspection of each column, you should be asking yourself, "What number added to the bottom number yields the top number?" Here, you should know from your tables that B + 1 = C, so the difference between B and C is 1. The leftmost column is actually more challenging: what number added to A gives you F? Chin up; even I have to think about it on an off day.

The problems show up, of course, when the top number in a column is smaller than its corresponding bottom number. Then (like the federal government on a bomber binge) you have no recourse but to borrow.

Borrowing is one of those grade-school rote-learned processes that very few people really understand. (To understand it is tacit admittance that something of New Math actually stuck. Horrors!) From a height, what happens in a borrow is that one count is taken from a column and applied to the column on its right. I say "applied" rather than "added to" because in moving from one column to the column on its right, that single count is multiplied by 10, where "ten" represents the number base. (Remember that "ten" in octal has a value of 8, while "ten" in hexadecimal has a value of 16.)

It sounds worse than it is. Let's look at a borrow in action, and you'll get the idea.

```
  9 2H
- 4 FH
```

Here, the subtraction in the rightmost column can't happen as-is, because F is larger than 2. So we borrow from the next column to the left.

Nearly thirty years out of the past, I can still hear old Sister Marie Bernard toughing it out on the blackboard, albeit in base 10: "Cross out the 9; make it an 8. Make the 2 a 12. And 12 minus F is what, class?" 3, Sister. And that's how borrowing works. (I hope the poor dear will forgive me for putting hex bytes in her mouth...)

Think about what happened there, functionally. *We subtracted 1 from the 9 and added 10H to the 2.* One obvious mistake is to subtract 1 from the 9 and add 1 to the 2, which (need I say) won't work. Think of it this way: We're moving part of one column's surplus value over to its right, where some extra value is needed. The overall value of the upper number doesn't change (which is why we call it "borrowing" and not "stealing") but the recipient of the loan is increased by *10*, not *1*.

After the borrow, what we have looks something like this:

```
  8 12H
- 4 FH
```

And of course, once we're here the columnar subtractions all work out, and we discover that the difference is 43H.

People sometimes ask if you ever have to borrow more than 1. The answer, plainly, is no. If you borrow 2, for example, you would add 20 to the recipient column, and *20 minus any single digit remains a 2-digit number.* That is, the difference won't fit into a single column. Subtraction contains an important symmetry with addition:

> The most you ever need to borrow in any single-column subtraction of two numbers is *1*.

Borrowing Across Multiple Columns

Understanding that much about borrowing gets you most of the way there. But, as life is wont, you will *frequently* come across a subtraction similar to this:

```
  F 0 0 0H
- 3 B 6 CH
```

Column 1 needs to borrow, but neither column 2 nor column 3 have anything at all to lend. Back in grade school, Sister Marie Bernard would have rattled out with machine-gun efficiency: "Cross out the F, make it an E. Make the 0 a 10. Then cross it out, make it an F. Make the next 0 a 10; cross it out, make it an F. Then make the last 0 a 10." Got that?

What happens is that the middle two 0s act as loan brokers between the F and the rightmost 0, keeping a commission in the form of enough value to allow for subtraction in their own columns. Each column to the right of the last column borrows 10 from its neighbor to the left, and loans 1 to the neighbor on its right. After all the borrows trickle through the upper number, what we have looks like this (minus all those cross-outs):

```
  E F F ¹0H
- 3 B 6 CH
```

At this point, each columnar subtraction can take place, and the difference is B494H.

In remembering your grade-school machinations, don't fall into the old rut of thinking, "cross out the 10, make it a 9." In the world of hexadecimal, 10H − 1 = F. Cross out the 10, make it an *F*.

What's the Point?

Even if you have a hex calculator or a hex-capable screen calculator to do your figuring for you, the point I'm getting at is *practice*. Hexadecimal is the *lingua franca* of assemblers, to multiply-mangle a metaphor. The more you burn a gut-level understanding of hex into your reflexes, the easier assembly language will be. Furthermore, understanding the internal structure of the machine itself will be much easier if you have that intuitive grasp of hex values. We're laying important groundwork here. Take it seriously now and you'll lose less hair later on.

1.7 Binary

Hexadecimal is excellent practice for taking on the strangest number base of all: Binary. Binary is base 2. Given what we've learned about number bases so far, we can surmise the following about base 2.

- Each column has a value two times the column to its right.
- There are only two digits (0 and 1) in the base.

Counting is a little strange in binary, as you might imagine. It goes like this: 0,1,10,11,100,101,110,111,1000... Because it sounds absurd to say, "Zero, one, ten, eleven, one hundred...," in binary, you simply enunciate the digits, followed by the word "binary." For example, most people say "one zero one one one zero one binary" instead of "one million, eleven thousand, one hundred one binary" when pronouncing the number 1011101—which sounds enormous until you consider that its value in decimal is only 93.

Odd as it may seem, binary follows all of the same rules regarding number bases that we've discussed in this chapter. Converting between binary and decimal is done using the same methods described for hexadecimal in Section 1.5.

Because counting in binary is as much a matter of counting columns as counting digits (since there are only two digits) it makes sense to take a long, close look at Table 1.7, which shows the values of the binary number columns out to 32 places.

One look at that imposing pyramid implies that it's even hopeless to think of pronouncing the larger columns as strings of digits: "One zero zero zero zero zero zero zero…" and so on. There's a crying need for a shorthand notation here, so I'll provide you with one in a little while (and its identity will surprise you).

Table 1.7. Binary columns as powers of 2

Binary		Power of 2		Decimal
1	=	2^0	=	$1 \times 2 =$
10	=	2^1	=	$2 \times 2 =$
100	=	2^2	=	$4 \times 2 =$
1000	=	2^3	=	$8 \times 2 =$
10000	=	2^4	=	$16 \times 2 =$
100000	=	2^5	=	$32 \times 2 =$
1000000	=	2^6	=	$64 \times 2 =$
10000000	=	2^7	=	$128 \times 2 =$
100000000	=	2^8	=	$256 \times 2 =$
1000000000	=	2^9	=	$512 \times 2 =$
10000000000	=	2^{10}	=	$1024 \times 2 =$
100000000000	=	2^{11}	=	$2048 \times 2 =$
1000000000000	=	2^{12}	=	$4096 \times 2 =$
10000000000000	=	2^{13}	=	$8192 \times 2 =$
100000000000000	=	2^{14}	=	$16384 \times 2 =$
1000000000000000	=	2^{15}	=	$32768 \times 2 =$
10000000000000000	=	2^{16}	=	$65536 \times 2 =$
100000000000000000	=	2^{17}	=	$131072 \times 2 =$
1000000000000000000	=	2^{18}	=	$262144 \times 2 =$
10000000000000000000	=	2^{19}	=	$524288 \times 2 =$
100000000000000000000	=	2^{20}	=	$1048576 \times 2 =$
1000000000000000000000	=	2^{21}	=	$2097152 \times 2 =$
10000000000000000000000	=	2^{22}	=	$4194304 \times 2 =$
100000000000000000000000	=	2^{23}	=	$8388608 \times 2 =$
1000000000000000000000000	=	2^{24}	=	$16777216 \times 2 =$
10000000000000000000000000	=	2^{25}	=	$33554432 \times 2 =$
100000000000000000000000000	=	2^{26}	=	$67108864 \times 2 =$
1000000000000000000000000000	=	2^{27}	=	$134217728 \times 2 =$
10000000000000000000000000000	=	2^{28}	=	$268435456 \times 2 =$
100000000000000000000000000000	=	2^{29}	=	$536870912 \times 2 =$
1000000000000000000000000000000	=	2^{30}	=	$1073741824 \times 2 =$
10000000000000000000000000000000	=	2^{31}	=	$2147483648 \times 2 =$
100000000000000000000000000000000	=	2^{32}	=	4294967296 etc…

You might think that such large numbers as the bottommost in the table aren't likely to be encountered in ordinary programming. Sorry, but a 32-bit microprocessor like the 80386 can swallow numbers like that in one electrical gulp, and eat billions of them for lunch. You *must* become accustomed to thinking in terms of numbers like 2^{32}, which, after all, is only a trifling four billion in decimal. You can't even run NASA on numbers like that, and it's the poor orphan at the Federal trough.

Just as with hexadecimal, there can be identity problems when using binary. The number 101 in binary is not the same as 101 in hex, or 101 in decimal. For this reason, always append the letter B to your binary values to make sure people reading your programs (including you, six weeks after the fact) know what base you're working from.

Values in Binary

Converting a value in binary to a value in decimal is done the same way it's done in hex—more simply in fact. You no longer have to count how many times a value is present in its corresponding column. That is, in hex, you have to see how many 16s are present in the 16s column, and so on. In binary, a column's value is either present (1 time) or not present (0 times.)

Running through a simple example should make this clear. The binary number 11011010B is a relatively typical binary value in small-time computer work. (On the small side, actually—many common binary numbers are twice this size.) Converting 11011010B to decimal comes down to scanning it from right to left with the help of Table 1.7, and keeping a tally of each column's value when that column contains a 1. Ignore any column containing a 0.

Clear your calculator and let's get started:

Column 0 contains a 0; skip it.

Column 1 contains a 1. That means its value, 2, is present in the value of the number. So we punch 2 into the calculator.

Column 2 contains a 0; skip it.

Column 3 contains a 1. This column's value is 2^3, or 8; add 8 to the tally.

Column 4 also contains a 1. This columns value is 2^4 or 16; Add 16 to the tally.

Column 5 contains a 0; skip it.

Column 6 contains a 1. This column's value is 64; add 64 to the tally.

Column 7 contains a 1. This column's value is 2^7, or 128; add 128 to the tally. What do we have? 218. It's as easy as that.

Converting from decimal to binary, while more difficult, is done *exactly* the same way as converting from decimal to hex. Go back and read that section again, searching for the *general method* used. (You can also see section 1.8 for more information.) In other words, see what was done and separate the essential principles from any references to a specific base like hex.

I'll bet by now you can figure it out without much trouble.

As a brief aside, perhaps you noticed that I started counting columns from 0 rather than 1. A peculiarity of the computer field is that we always begin counting things from 0. Actually, that's unfair; the computer's method is the reasonable one, because 0 is a perfectly good number and should not be discriminated against. The rift occurred because in our world, counting things tells us *how many* things are there, while in the computer world counting things is more generally done to *name* them. That is, we need to deal with bit 0, and then bit 1, and so on, far more than we need to know how many bits there are.

This is not a quibble, by the way. The issue will come up again and again in connection with memory addresses, which as I have said and will say again, are the key to understanding assembly language.

> In programming circles, *always* begin counting from 0!

This is a good point to get some practice in converting numbers from binary to decimal and back. Sharpen your teeth on these:

```
110
10001
11111
11
101
110001011101010010
11000
1011
```

When that's done, convert these decimal values to binary:

```
77
42
106
255
18
6309
121
58
18,446
```

Why Binary?

If it takes eight whole digits (11011010) to represent an ordinary three-digit number like 218, binary as a number base would seem to be a bad intellectual investment. Certainly for us it would be a waste of mental bandwidth, and even aliens with only two fingers would probably have come up with a better system.

The problem is, lights are either on or they're off.

This is just another way of saying (as I'll discuss in detail in the next chapter) that at the bottom of it, *computers are electrical devices*. In an electrical device, voltage is either present or it isn't; current either flows or it doesn't. Very early in the game, computer scientists decided that the presence of a voltage in a computer circuit would indicate a 1 digit, while lack of a voltage at that same point in the circuit would indicate a 0 digit This is the only reason we use binary, but it's a pretty compelling one, and we're stuck with it. However, you will not necessarily drown in 1s and 0s, because I've already taught you a form of shorthand.

1.8 Hexadecimal as Shorthand for Binary

The number 218 expressed in binary is 11011010B. Expressed in hex, however, the same value is quite compact: DAH. The two hex digits comprising DAH merit a closer look.

AH (or 0AH as your assembler will require it for reasons I'll explain later) represents 10 decimal. Converting any number to binary simply involves detecting the powers of 2 within it. The largest power of 2 within 10 decimal is 8. Jot down 1 and subtract 8 from 10. What's left is 2. Even though 4 is a power of two, no 4's are hiding within 2. Write a 0 to the right of the 1. The next smallest power of 2 is 2, and there is a 2 in 2. Jot down another 1 to the right of the 0. Subtract 2 from 2 and you get 0, so there are no 1s left in the number. Jot down a final 0 to the right of the rest of the numbers to represent the 1s column. What you have is this:

```
1 0 1 0
```

Look back at the binary equivalent of 218: 11011010. The last four digits are 1010. 1010 is the binary equivalent of 0AH.

The same will work for the upper half of DAH. 0DH, if you work out the binary equivalence as we just did (and it would be good mental exercise), is 1101. Look at the binary equivalent of 218 this way:

```
   218    decimal
1101 1010 binary
  D    A  hex
```

It should be dawning on you that you can convert long strings of binary 1s and 0s into more compact hex format by converting every four binary digits (starting from the right, *not* from the left) into a single hex digit.

As an example, here is a 32-bit binary number that is not the least bit remarkable:

```
11110000000000001111101001101110
```

This is a pretty obnoxious collection of bits to remember or manipulate, so let's split it up into groups of four from the right:

```
1111 0000 0000 0000 1111 1010 0110 1110
```

Each of these groups of four binary digits can be represented by a single hexadecimal digit. Do the conversion now. What you should get is the following:

```
1111 0000 0000 0000 1111 1010 0110 1110
  F    0    0    0    F    A    6    E
```

In other words, the hex equivalent of that mouthful is

```
F000FA6E
```

In use, of course, you would append an H on the end, and also put a 0 at the beginning, so the number would actually be written 0F000FA6EH.

This is still a good-sized number, but such 32-bit addresses are the largest quantities you will typically encounter in journeyman-level, assembly language-programming. Most hexadecimal numbers you will encounter are either four or two hex digits long instead. Furthermore, the PC's CPU likes to deal with 32-bit addresses 16 bits at a time, so most of the time you will look upon enormous hex numbers like 0F00FA6EH as the pair 0F00H and 0FA6EH.

Suddenly, this business starts looking a little more graspable.

Hexadecimal is the programmer's shorthand for the computer's binary numbers.

This is why I said earlier that computers use base 2 (binary) and base 16 (hexadecimal) both at the same time in a rather schizoid fashion. What I didn't say is that the computer isn't really the schizoid one; *you* are. At their very heart (as I'll explain in the next chapter) computers use *only* binary. Hex is a means by which you and I make dealing with the computer easier. Fortunately, every four binary digits may be represented by a hex digit, so the correspondence is clean and comprehensible.

Prepare to Compute

Everything up to this point has been necessary groundwork. I've explained conceptually what computers *do* and given you the tools to understand the slightly alien numbers they use. But I've said nothing so far about what computers actually *are*, and it's well past time. We'll return to hexadecimal numbers again and again in this book; I've said nothing about hex multiplication or bit-banging. The reason is plain: Before you can bang a bit, you must know where the bits live. So let's lift the hood and see if we can catch a few in action.

Lifting The Hood

Discovering What Computers Actually *Are*

2.1 RAXie, We Hardly Knew Ye...

In 1970, I was a senior in high school, and the Chicago Public Schools had installed a computer somewhere. A truckful of these fancy typewriter gimcracks was delivered to Lane Tech, and a bewildered math teacher was drafted into teaching computer science (they had the nerve to call it) to a high school full of rowdy males.

I figured it out fairly quickly. You pounded out a deck of these goofy computer cards on the card punch, dropped them into the hopper of one of the typewriter gimcracks, and watched in awe as the typewriter danced its little golfball over the greenbar paper, printing out your inevitable list of error messages. It was fun. I got straight As. I even kept the first program I ever wrote that did something useful: a little deck of cards that generated a table of parabolic correction factors for hand-figuring telescope mirrors.

The question that kept gnawing at me was exactly what sort of beast RAX (the computer's wonderfully appropriate name) actually was. What we had were ram-charged typewriters that RAX controlled over phone lines. But what was RAX?

I asked the instructor. In brief, the conversation went something like this:

ME: "Umm, sir, what exactly *is* RAX?"

HE: "Eh? Um, a computer. An electronic computer."

ME: "That's what it says on the course notes. But I want to know what RAX is made of and how it works."

HE: "Well, I'm sure RAX is all solid-state."

ME: "You mean, there's no levers and gears inside."

HE: "Oh, there may be a few. But no radio tubes."

ME: "I wasn't worried about tubes. I suppose it has a calculator in it somewhere. But what makes it remember that A comes before B? How does it know what FORMAT means? How does it tell time? What does it have to do to dial the phone?"

HE: "Now, come on, that's why computers are so great! They put it all together so that we don't have to worry about that sort of thing! Who cares what RAX is? RAX knows FORTRAN, and will execute any correct FORTRAN program. That's what matters, isn't it?"

He was starting to sweat. So was I. End of conversation.

That June, I graduated with three inches of debugged and working FOR-TRAN punch cards in my bookbag, and still had absolutely no clue as to what RAX was.

It has bothered me to this day.

Gus to the Rescue

I was thinking about RAX six years later, while on the Devon Avenue bus heading for work, with the latest copy of *Popular Electronics* in my lap. The lead story involved a little thing called the COSMAC ELF, which consisted of a piece of perfboard full of integrated circuit chips, all wired together, plus some toggle switches and a pair of LED numeric displays.

It was a computer. (Said so right on the label.) The article told us how to put it together, and that was about all. What did those chips do? What did the whole thing do? It was driving me nuts.

As usual, my friend Gus Flassig got on the bus at Ashland Avenue and sat down beside me. I asked him what the damned thing did. He was the first human being to make the concept hang together for me:

> "These are memory chips. You load numbers into the memory chips by flipping these switches in different code patterns. Each number means something to the CPU chip. One number makes it add; another number makes it subtract; another makes it write different numbers into memory, and lots of other things. A program consists of a bunch of these instruction numbers in a row in memory. The computer reads the first number, does what the number instructs it to do, and then reads the second one, does what *that* number says to do, and so on until it runs out of numbers."

If *you* don't find that utterly clear; don't worry. I had the advantage of being an electronics hobbyist (so I knew what some of the chips did) and had already written some programs in RAX's FORTRAN. But for me, my God, everything suddenly hit critical mass and exploded in my head until the steam started pouring out of my ears.

No matter what RAX was, I knew that he had to be something like the COSMAC ELF on a larger scale. I built an ELF. It was quite an education, and allowed me to understand the nature of computers at a very deep level. I don't recommend that anybody but total crazies wirewrap their own machines out of loose chips anymore, although it was a common enough thing to do in the mid- to late Seventies. In this chapter, I'll try and provide you with some of the insights that I obtained while assembling my own machine the hard way. (You wonder where the "hard" in "hardware" comes from? Not from the sound it makes when you bang it on the table, promise…)

2.2 Switches, Transistors, and Memory

Switches remember.

Think about it. You flip the switch by the door, and the light in the middle of the ceiling comes on. It stays on. When you leave the room, you flip the switch down again, and the light goes out. It stays out. Poltergeists notwith-standing, the switch will remain in the position you last left it until you (or someone else) come back and flip it to its other position.

In a sense, it remembers what its last command was until you change it, and "overwrite" that command with a new one. In this sense, a light switch represents a sort of rudimentary memory element.

Light switches are more mechanical than electrical, which does not prevent them from acting as memory; in fact, the very first computer (Babbage's 19th-century difference engine) was entirely mechanical. In fact, the far larger version he designed but never finished was to have been *steam powered.* Babbage's machine had lots of little cams that could be flipped by other cams from one position to another. Numbers were encoded and remembered as patterns of cam positions.

One if by Land

Whether a switch is mechanical, electrical, hydraulic, or something else is irrelevant. What counts is that a switch contains a pattern: On or off; up or down, flow or no flow. To that pattern can be assigned a meaning. Paul Revere told his buddy to set up a code in the Old North Church: "One if by land, two if by sea." Once lit, the lamps in the steeple remained lit (and thus remembered that very important code) long enough for Paul to call out the militia and whup the British.

In general then, what we call "memory" is an aggregate of switches that will retain a pattern long enough for that pattern to be read and understood by a person or a mechanism. For our purposes, those switches will be electrical, but keep in mind that both mechanical and hydraulic computers have been proposed and built with varying degrees of success.

Memory consists of containers for alterable patterns that retain an entered pattern until someone or something alters the pattern.

Transistor Switches

One problem with building a computer memory system of light switches is that light switches are pretty specialized: they require fingers to set them, and their "output" is a current path for electricity. Ideally, a computer memory switch should be operated by the same force it controls to allow the patterns in memory locations to be passed on to other memory locations. In the gross electromechanical world, such a switch is called a "relay."

A relay is a switch that is operated by electricity, and also controls electric-ity. You "flip" a relay by feeding it a pulse of electricity, which powers a little hammer that whaps a lever to one side or another. This lever then opens or closes a set of electrical contacts, just as your garden-variety light switch does. Computers have been made out of relays, although as you might imagine (with a typical relay being about the size of an ice cube) they weren't especially powerful computers.

Fully electronic computers are made out of transistor switches. Transistors are tiny crystals of silicon that use the peculiar electrical properties of silicon to act as switches. I won't try to explain what those peculiar properties are, since that explanation would take an entire (fat) book unto itself. Let's consider a transistor switch a sort of electrical "black box" and describe it in terms of inputs and outputs.

Figure 2.1 shows a transistor switch. When an electrical current is fed through pin 1, current flows between pins 2 and 3. When the current ceases flowing through pin 1, current ceases to flow between pins 2 and 3.

Figure 2.1. Transistor switches and memory cells

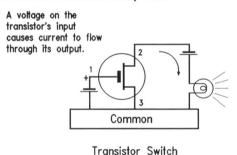

A voltage on the transistor's input causes current to flow through its output.

Transistor Switch

Memory Cell

In real life, a tiny handful of other components (typically diodes and capacitors) are necessary to make things work smoothly in a computer memory context. These components are not necessarily little gizmos connected by wires to the outside of the transistor (although in early transistorized computers they were), but are now cut from the same silicon crystal the transistor itself is cut from, and occupy almost no space at all. Taken together, the transistor switch and its support components are called a *memory cell*. I've hidden the electrical complexity of the memory cell within an appropriate black-box symbol in Figure 2.1.

A memory cell keeps current flow through it to a minimum, because electrical current flow produces heat, and heat is the enemy of electrical components. The memory cell's circuit is arranged so that if you put a tiny voltage on its input pin and a similar voltage on its *select* pin, a voltage will appear *and remain* on its output pin. That output voltage will remain in its set state until you take away the voltage from the cell as a whole, or remove the voltage from the input pin while putting a voltage on the select pin.

The "on" voltage being applied to all of these pins is kept at a consistent level. (Except, of course, when it is removed entirely.) In other words, you don't put 12 volts on the input pin and then change that to 6 volts or 17 volts. The computer designers pick a voltage and stick with it. (Most memory cells operate at a constant 5 volts, although many operate at 12 volts.) The pattern is binary in nature: you either put a voltage on the input pin or you take away the voltage entirely. Likewise, the output pin either holds a fixed voltage or no voltage at all.

We apply a code to that state of affairs: *the presence of voltage indicates a binary 1, and the lack of voltage indicates a binary 0.* This code is arbitrary. We could as well have said that the *lack* of voltage indicates a binary 1 and vise versa (and computers have been built this way for obscure reasons) but the choice is up to us. Having the *presence* of something indicate a binary 1 is more natural, and that is the way things have evolved in the computing mainstream.

A single computer memory cell, such as the transistor-based one we're speaking of here, holds one binary digit, either a 1 or a 0. This is called a *bit*. A bit is the indivisible atom of information. There is no half-a-bit, and no bit-and-a-half. (This has been tried. It works badly. But that didn't stop it from being tried.)

> A bit is a single binary digit, either 1 or 0.

The Incredible Shrinking Bit

One bit doesn't tell us much. To be useful, we need to bring a lot of memory cells together. Transistors started out small (the originals from the Fifties looked a lot like stove-pipe hats for tin soldiers) and went down from there. The first transistors were created from little chips of silicon crystal about an eighth of an inch square. The size of the crystal chip hasn't changed outrageously since then, but the *transistors* have shrunk incredibly.

In the beginning, one chip held one transistor. In time, the designers crisscrossed the chip into four equal areas, making each area an independent transistor. From there it was an easy jump to adding the other minuscule components needed to turn a transistor into a computer memory cell.

The silicon chip was a tiny and fragile thing, and was encased in an oblong molded plastic housing, like a stick of Dentyne gum with metal legs for the electrical connections.

What we had now was a sort of electrical egg carton: four little cubbyholes, each of which could contain a single binary bit. Then the shrinking process began: first 8 bits, then 16 bits, then multiples of 8 and 16, all on the same tiny silicon chip. By the late Sixties, 256 memory cells could be made on one chip of silicon, usually in an array of 8 cells by 32. In 1976, my COSMAC ELF computer contained two memory chips. On each chip was an array of memory cells 4 wide and 256 long. (Picture a *real* long egg carton.) Each chip could thus hold 1024 bits.

This was a pretty typical memory chip capacity at that time. We called them *1K RAM chips*, because they held roughly 1000 bits of *random access memory* (RAM). The "K" comes from "kilobit," that is, one thousand bits. We'll get back to the notion of what "random access" means shortly.

Toward the mid-seventies, the great memory shrinking act was kicking into high gear. 1K chips were further divided into 4K chips containing 4096 bits of memory. The 4K chips were almost immediately divided into 16K chips (16,384 bits of memory). These 16K chips were the standard when the IBM PC appeared in 1981. By 1982 the chips had been divided once again, and 16K became 64K, with 65,536 bits inside that same little gumstick. Keep in mind that we're talking more than 65,000 transistors (plus other odd components) formed on a square of silicon about a quarter-inch on a side.

Come 1985 and the 64K chip had been pushed aside by its drawn-and-quartered child, the 256K chip (262,144 bits). Chips always increase in capacity by a factor of 4 simply because the current-generation chip is divided into four equal areas, onto each of which is then placed the same number of transistors that the previous generation of chip had held over the whole silicon chip.

Today, in late 1992, that 256K chip is history. It was subdivided into four areas in the mid- to late Eighties, (producing a chip containing 1,048,576 bits) and again in 1990. Now, for our mainstream memory container we have the 4M chip. The "M" stands for "mega," which is Greek for million, and the critter has a grand total of 4,194,304 bits in its tummy, still no larger than that stick of Dentyne gum.

Will it stop here? Ha. The Japanese, patrons of all things small, have begun making quantities of chips containing 16,777,216 bits. Some physicists think that even the Japanese will have trouble dividing that little wafer one more time, since the transistors are now so small that it gets hard pushing more than one electron at a time through them. At that point some truly ugly limitations of life called quantum mechanics begin to get in the way. More than likely, the next generation of chips will be stacked vertically for greater capacity. Many people are off in the labs looking for other tricks, and don't make the oft-made mistake of assuming that they won't find any.

Random Access

These chips are called RAM chips, because they contain random access memory. Newcomers sometimes find this a perplexing and disturbing word, because random often connotes chaos or unpredictability. What the word really means is at random, meaning you can reach into a megabit memory chip and pick out any of those million-plus bits without disturbing any of the others, just as you might select one book at random from a library's many shelves of thousands of books without sifting through them in order.

Memory didn't always work this way. Before memory was placed on silicon chips, it was stored on magnetic gadgets of some kind, usually rotating drums or disks distantly related to the hard drives we use today. Rotating memory sends a circular collection of bits beneath a magnetic sensor. The bits pass beneath the sensor one at a time, and if you miss the one you want, like a Chicago bus in January, you simply have to wait for it to come by again. These are *serial access devices.* They present their bits to you, in a fixed order, one at a time, and you have to wait for the one you want to come up in its order.

No need remembering that; we've long since abandoned serial-access devices for main computer memory. We still use such systems for *mass storage*, as I'll describe a few pages down the road.

Random access works like this: Inside the chip, each bit is stored in its own memory cell, identical to the memory cell diagrammed in Figure 2.1. Each of the however-many memory cells has a unique number. This number is a cell's (and hence a bit's) *address*. It's like the addresses on a street: The bit on the corner is #0 Silicon Alley, and the bit next door is #1, and so on. You don't have to knock on the door of Bit #0 and ask which bit it is, then go to the next door and ask there too, until you find the bit you want. If you have the address, you can zip right down the street and park square in front of the bit you intend to visit.

Each chip has a number of pins coming out of it. (This is the computer room's equivalent of the Killer Rake: don't step on one in the dark!) The bulk of these pins are called *address pins*. One pin is called a *data pin*. (See Figure 2.2.) The address pins are electrical leads that carry a binary address code. Your address is a binary number, expressed in 1s and 0s only. You apply this address to the address pins by encoding a binary 1 as five volts and a binary 0 as zero volts. Special circuits inside the RAM chip decode this address to one of the select inputs of the numerous memory cells inside the chip. For any given address applied to the address pins, only *one* select input will be raised to five volts, thereby selecting that cell.

Depending on whether you intend to read a bit or write a bit, the data pin is switched between the memory cells' input or output, as shown in Figure 2.2.

But that's all done internally to the chip. As far as you on the outside are concerned, once you've applied the address to the address pins, *voila!* The data pin will contain a voltage representing the value of the bit you requested. If that bit contained a binary 1, the data pin will contain a 5 volt signal; otherwise, the binary 0 bit will be represented by 0 volts.

Memory Access Time

Chips are graded by how long it takes for the data to appear on the data pin after you've applied the address to the address pins. Obviously, the faster the better, but some chips (for electrical reasons that again are difficult to explain) are faster than others.

Figure 2.2. A RAM chip

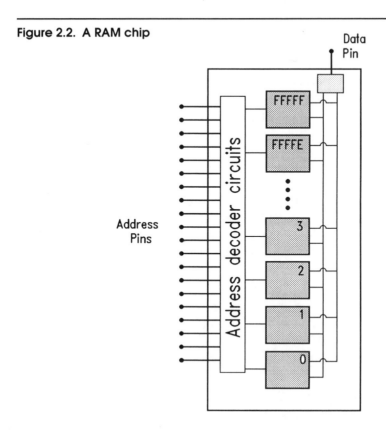

The times seem so small as to be insignificant: 100 nanoseconds is a typical memory chip access time. A nanosecond is a *billionth* of a second, so 100 nanoseconds is one ten-millionth of a second. Great stuff—but to accomplish anything useful, a computer needs to access memory hundreds of thousands or millions of times. It adds up. If you become an expert assembly language programmer, you will jump through hoops to shave the number of memory accesses your program needs to perform, because memory access is the ultimate limiting factor in a computer's performance. Michael Abrash, in fact, has published a whole book on doing exactly that: *Zen of Assembly Language*, which can be (badly) summarized in just these few words: *Stay out of memory whenever you can!* (You'll discover just how difficult this is soon enough.)

Bytes, Words, and Double Words

The days are long gone when a serious computer can exist on only one memory chip. My poor 1976 COSMAC ELF even needed at least two chips. Today's computers need dozens, or even hundreds of chips, regardless of the fact that today's chips hold megabits rather than the ELF's paltry 2,048 bits. Understanding how a computer gathers its memory chips together into a coherent *memory system* is critical when you wish to write efficient assembly-language programs. Whereas an infinity of ways exist to hook memory chips together, the system I'll describe here is that of the IBM PC type of computer, which includes the PC, XT, AT, PS/2, and a veritable plethora of clones.

Our memory system must store our information. How we organize a memory system out of a hatful of memory chips will be dictated largely by how we organize our information.

The answer begins with this thing called a *byte*. The fact that the grandaddy of all computer magazines took this word for its title indicates its importance in the computer scheme of things. From a functional perspective, memory is measured in bytes. A byte is eight bits. Two bytes side-by-side are called a *word*, and two words side-by-side are called a *double word*. There are other terms like *nybble* and *quad word*, but you can do quite well with bits, bytes, words, and double words.

> A bit is a single binary digit, 0 or 1.
> A byte is eight bits side-by-side.
> A word is two bytes side-by-side.
> A double word is two words side-by-side.

Computers were designed to store and manipulate human information. The basic elements of human discourse are built from a set of symbols consisting of letters of the alphabet (two of each for upper- and lowercase), numbers, and symbols like commas, colons, periods, and exclamation marks. Add to these the various international variations on letters like ä and ò plus the more arcane mathematical symbols, and you'll find that human information requires a symbol set of well over 200 symbols. (The symbol set used in all PC-style computers is given in Appendix A.)

Bytes are central to the scheme because one symbol out of that symbol set can be neatly expressed in one byte. A byte is eight bits, and 2^8 is 256. This means that a binary number eight bits in size can be one of 256 different values, numbered from 0 to 255. Because we use these symbols, most of what we do in computer programs is done in byte-sized chunks. In fact, except for the very odd and specialized kind of computers we are now building into intelligent food processors, *no* computer processes information in chunks smaller than one byte. Most computers today, in fact, process information either a word or a double word at a time.

Pretty Chips All in a Row

One of the more perplexing things for beginners to understand is that today's standard 1 megabit RAM chip does not even contain *one* byte…just 1,048,576 bits. Remember that today's RAM chips have only *one* data pin. To store a byte you would have to store eight bits in sequence at eight consecutive addresses, and to retrieve that byte you would have to retrieve eight bits in sequence. Since it takes 80 nanoseconds at very least to store a bit in one of those chips, storing a byte would take at least 640 nanoseconds, and in practical terms, close to a microsecond, which (believe it!) is far, far too slow to be useful.

What is actually done is to distribute a single stored byte across eight separate RAM chips, with one bit from the stored byte in each chip, at the same address across all chips. This way, when a single address is applied to the address pins of all eight chips, all eight bits appear simultaneously on the eight output pins, and we can retrieve a full byte in 80 nanoseconds instead of 640 nanoseconds. See Figure 2.3.

We call this row of eight chips a *bank* of memory, and how much memory is contained in a bank depends on the type of chips incorporated in the bank. A row of eight 64K chips contains 64K *bytes*—8 × 64K or 512K *bits*. (Remember, computers deal with information a minimum of 8 bits at a time.) A row of eight 256K chips contains 256K bytes, and so on.

This is the system used in the IBM PC, the XT, and their clones. The IBM AT and its clones process information a word at a time, so their memory systems use a row of 16 memory chips to store and retrieve a full 16-bit word at once. Furthermore, the newest generation of IBM-compatible machines using the 80386 and 80486 processors handles memory a double word at a time, so those machines access a row of 32 memory chips at a time. (A double word consists of 4 bytes, or 32 bits.)

Figure 2.3. A megabyte memory bank

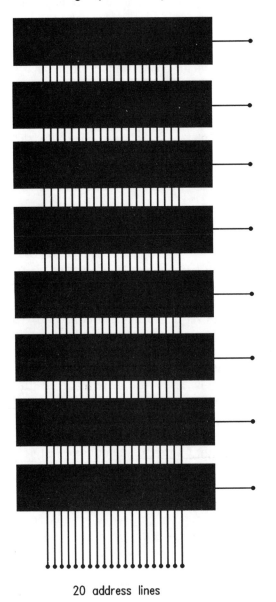

Each black box is
a chip like that shown
in Figure 2.2.

Each of eight chips
contains 1,048,576 bits.
The eight chips taken
together contain
1,048,576 bytes, with
each chip contributing
one bit to every byte.
Bytes of data may be
written to and read
from the eight data
lines shown here.

20 address lines

Actual computers combine various combinations of memory banks in various ways to produce different amounts of memory. I'll take up the subject again when we begin talking specifically about the PC in Chapter 6.

2.3 The Shop Foreman and the Assembly Line

The gist of the previous section was only this: electrically, your computer's memory consists of one or more rows of memory chips, each chip containing a *large* number of memory cells consisting of transistors and other minuscule electrical components. Most of the time, it's just as useful to forget about the transistors and even the rows of chips to avoid confusion. (My high school computer science teacher was not *entirely* wrong...but he was right for the wrong reasons.)

It's better in most cases to envision a very long row of byte-sized containers, each with its own address. Don't assume that, in computers that process information a word at a time, only *words* have addresses; it is a convention with the PC architecture that *every* byte has its own address regardless of how many bytes are pulled from memory at one time.

Every byte of memory in the computer has its own unique address, even in computers that process two bytes, or even four bytes, of information at a time.

If this seems counterintuitive, yet another metaphor will help. When you go to the library to take out the three volumes of Tolkien's massive fantasy *The Lord of the Rings*, you'll find that each of the three volumes has its own card catalog number (essentially that volume's address in the library) but that you take all three down at once and process them as a single entity. If you really *want* to, you can take only one of the books out at a time, but to do so will require yet another trip to the library to get the next volume, which is wasteful of your time and effort.

So it is with 16-bit or 32-bit computers. Every byte has its own address, but when a 16-bit computer accesses a byte, it actually reads *two* bytes starting at the address of the requested byte. You can use the second byte or ignore it if you don't need it—but if you later decide you do need the second byte you'll have to access memory again to get it. Best to save time and get it all at one swoop.

(There is an additional complication here involving whether addresses are odd or even or divisible by 4 or 16...but we'll cover that in detail later on.)

The Honcho Chip

All of this talk about reading things from memory and writing things to memory has thus far carefully skirted the question of *who* is doing the reading and writing. The who is almost always a single chip, and a remarkable chip it is, too: the *central processing unit,* or CPU. If you are the president and CEO of your personal computer, the CPU is your shop foreman. The foreman sees that your orders are carried out down in the chips where the work gets done.

Some would say that the CPU is what actually does the work, but that's an oversimplification. Plenty of real work is done in the memory system, and especially in what are called *peripherals*, like video display boards, serial and parallel ports, and modems. So while the CPU does do a good deal of the work, it parcels out quite a bit to other components within the computer. I think its role of foreman outweighs its role as assembly-line grunt.

The CPU chips used in IBM-compatible computers all come from a company called Intel, which pretty much invented the single-chip CPU back in the early seventies. Intel's first bang-up success was the 8080 chip, which helped trigger the personal computer revolution after it was chosen for the seminal MITS Altair 8800 computer introduced in *Popular Electronics*, in December of 1974. The 8080 was an eight-bit computer because it accessed memory eight bits (one byte) at a time. The 8080 is now pretty well extinct, but it gave birth to a pair of next-generation CPU chips called the 8086 and the 8088. These two chips are nearly identical except that the 8088 is an 8-bit CPU, while the 8086 is a 16-bit CPU, and accesses memory a word (two bytes) at a time. IBM chose the 8088 for its original 1981 IBM PC and later the XT, but the 8086 never made it into a true IBM computer until the somewhat forgettable PS/2 models 25 and 30 appeared in 1987.

Intel produced yet another generation of CPU chip in 1983, and by 1984 the 80286 became the beating heart of the enormously successful PC/AT. The 80286 is a more powerful 16-bit CPU, capable of everything the 8086 can do, plus numerous additional things. Early 1986 brought Intel's 80386 CPU chip to market. The 80386 upped the ante by being a 32-bit machine, which can read and write memory a double word (four bytes) at a time. The 80386 is enormously more powerful than the 80286, and a great deal faster. The newest Intel chip, the 80486, is more powerful and faster still. (I'll tell the story of the CPU wars in more detail in Chapter 11, once we've covered some more essential background.)

Many experts think that 32 bits is an ideal format for CPU memory access, and that increasing memory access beyond 32 bits at a time would begin to slow things down.

And in this business, you do *not* want to slow things down.

Talking to Memory

All the assorted Intel CPUs operate at varying speeds with various features, but they are conceptually identical, and this discussion will apply to all of them.

The CPU chip's most important job is to communicate with the computer's memory system. Like a memory chip, a CPU chip is a small square of silicon onto which a great many transistors have been placed. The fragile silicon chip is encased in a plastic or ceramic housing with a large number of pins protruding from it. Like the pins of memory chips, the CPU's pins transfer information encoded as voltage levels. Five volts indicate a binary 1, and zero volts indicate a binary 0.

Like the memory chips, the CPU chip has a number of pins devoted to memory addresses, and these pins are connected directly to the computer's banks of memory chips. When the CPU desires to read a byte (or a word or double word) from memory, it places the memory address of the byte to be read on its address pins, encoded as a binary number. About 100 nanoseconds later, the byte appears (also as a binary number) on the data pins of the memory chips. The CPU chip also has data pins, and it slurps up the byte presented by the memory chips through its own data pins. See Figure 2.4.

Figure 2.4. The CPU and memory

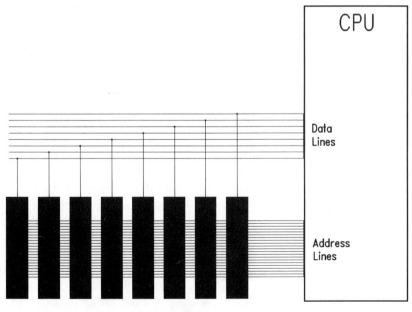

Eight megabit RAM chips, providing
1,048,576 bytes of memory total.

The process, of course, also works in reverse: to write a byte into memory, the CPU first places the memory address where it wants to write onto its address pins. Nanoseconds later, it places the byte it wishes to write into memory on its data pins. The memory chips obediently store the byte inside themselves at the requested address.

Riding the Bus

This give-and-take between the CPU and the memory system represents the bulk of what happens inside your computer. Information flows from memory into the CPU and back again. Information flows in other paths as well. Your computer contains additional devices called *peripherals* that are either sources or destinations (or both) for information.

Video display boards, disk drives, printer ports, and modems are the most common peripherals in PC-type computers. Like the CPU and memory, they are all ultimately electrical devices. Most modern peripherals consist of one or two large chips and several smaller chips that support the larger chips. Like both the CPU and memory chips, these peripheral devices have both address pins and data pins. Some, video boards in particular, have their own memory chips.

Peripherals "talk" to the CPU (i.e., pass the CPU data or take data from the CPU) and sometimes to one another. These conversations take place across the electrical connections, linking the address pins and data pins that all devices in the computer have in common. These electrical lines are called a *data bus,* and form a sort of party line linking the CPU with all other parts of the computer. There is an elaborate system of electrical arbitration that determines when and in what order the different devices can use this party line to talk with one another. But it happens the same way: an address is placed on the bus, followed by a byte (or word or double word) of data. Special signals go out on the bus with the address to indicate whether the address is of a location in memory, or of one of the peripherals attached to the data bus. The address of a peripheral is called an *I/O address* to differentiate between it and a *memory address* such as we've been discussing all along.

The data bus is the major element in the *expansion slots* present in most PC-type computers, and most peripherals are boards that plug into these slots. The peripherals talk to the CPU and to memory through the data bus connections brought out as electrical pins in the expansion slots.

The Foreman's Pockets

Every CPU contains very few data storage cubbyholes called *registers.* These registers are at once the foreman's pockets and the foreman's workbench. When the CPU needs a place to tuck something away for awhile, an empty register is just the place. The CPU could always store the data out in memory, but that takes a lot of time. Because the registers are actually inside the CPU, placing data in a register or reading it back again is *fast*.

But more important, registers are the foreman's workbench. When the CPU needs to add two numbers, the easiest and fastest way is to place the numbers in two registers and add the two registers together. The sum (in usual CPU practice) replaces one of the two original numbers that were added, but after that, the sum could then be placed in yet another register, or added to another number in another register, or stored out in memory, or any of a multitude of other operations.

> The CPU's immediate work-in-progress is held in temporary storage containers called *registers*.

Work involving registers is always fast, because the registers are within the CPU and very little movement of data is necessary.

Like memory cells and, indeed, like the entire CPU, registers are made out of transistors. But rather than having numeric addresses, registers have names like AX or DI. To make matters even more complicated, while all CPU registers have certain common properties, most registers have unique special powers not shared by other registers. Understanding the ways and the limitations of CPU registers is something like following the Watergate hearings: there are partnerships, alliances, and a bewildering array of secret agendas that each register follows. I'll be devoting most of a chapter to registers later in this book.

Most peripherals also have registers, and peripheral registers are even more limited in scope than CPU registers. Their agendas are quite explicit and in no way secret. This does not prevent them from being confusing, as anyone who has tried programming the EGA video board at a register level will attest.

The Assembly Line

If the CPU is the shop foreman, then the peripherals are the assembly line workers, and the data bus is the assembly line itself. (Unlike most assembly lines, however, the foreman works the line as hard or harder than the rest of his crew!)

As an example: information enters the computer through a modem peripheral, which assembles bits received from the telephone line into bytes of data representing characters and numbers. The modem then places the assembled byte onto the bus, from which the CPU picks it up, tallies it, and then places it back on the data bus. The video board then retrieves the byte from the bus and writes it into video memory so that you can see it on your screen.

Obviously, lots is going on inside the box. Continuous, furious communication along the data bus between CPU, memory, and peripherals is what accomplishes the work that the computer does. The question then arises: who tells the foreman and crew what to do? You do. How do you do that? You write a program. Where is the program? It's in memory, along with all the rest of the data stored in memory. In fact, the program *is* data, and that is the heart of the whole idea of programming as we know it.

2.4 The Box that Follows a Plan

Finally we come to the essence of computing: the nature of programs and how they direct the CPU to control the computer.

We've seen how memory can be used to store bytes of information. These bytes are all binary codes, patterns of 1s and 0s stored as minute electrical voltage levels and making up binary numbers. We've also spoken of symbols, and how certain binary codes may be interpreted as meaning something to us human beings, things like letters, digits, punctuation, and so on.

Just as the table in Appendix A contains a set of codes and symbols that mean something to us, there is a set of codes that mean something to the CPU. These codes are called *machine instructions, and their name is evocative of what they actually are, instructions to the CPU.*

Let's take an example or two from the venerable 8088 CPU. The binary code 01000000 (40H) means something to the 8088 chip. It is an order: *add one to register AX.* That's about as simple as they get. Most machine instructions occupy more than a single byte. The binary codes 11010110 01110011 (0B6H 73H) comprise another order: *load the value 73H into register DH.* On the other end of the spectrum, the binary codes 11110011 10100100 (0F3H 0A4H) direct the CPU to do the following (take a deep breath): *Begin moving the number of bytes specified in register CX from the 32-bit address stored in registers DS and SI to the 32-bit address stored in registers ES and DI, updating the address in both SI and DI after moving each byte, and also decreasing CX by one each time, stopping when CX becomes 0.*

The rest of the several hundred instructions understood by the Intel CPUs fall in and among those three in terms of complication and power. There are instructions that perform arithmetic operations (addition, subtraction, multiplication, and division) and logical operations (AND, OR, etc.), and instructions that move information around memory or exchange information with peripherals.

Fetch and Execute

A computer program is nothing more than a table of these machine instructions stored in memory. There's nothing special about the table nor where it is positioned in memory; it could be anywhere, and the bytes in the table are nothing more than binary numbers.

The binary numbers comprising a computer program are special only in the way that the CPU treats them. When the CPU is started running, it *fetches* a byte from an agreed-upon address in memory. This byte is read from memory and loaded into the CPU. The CPU examines the byte, and then begins performing the task that the fetched machine instruction directs it to do. In many cases, this means fetching another byte (or another two or three) from memory to complete the machine instruction before the real work begins.

For example, if it fetches the binary code 40H (as mentioned above), it immediately adds one to the value stored in register AX. But if it fetches the binary code 0B6H, it knows it must go back out to memory and fetch an additional byte to complete the instruction. When both bytes are in the CPU, *then* the CPU takes the required action, which is to load the second byte into register DH.

As soon as it finishes executing an instruction, the CPU goes out to memory and fetches the next byte in sequence. Inside the CPU is a register called the *instruction pointer* that quite literally contains the address of the next instruction to be executed. Each time an instruction is completed, the instruction pointer is updated to point to the next instruction in memory.

So the process goes: fetch and execute; fetch and execute. The CPU works its way through memory, with the instruction pointer register leading the way. As it goes it works, moving data around in memory, moving values around in registers, passing data to peripherals, and "crunching" data in arithmetic or logical operations.

> Computer programs are lists of binary machine instructions stored in memory. They are no different from any other list of data bytes stored in memory *except* in how they are treated when fetched by the CPU.

The Foreman's Innards

I made the point earlier that machine instructions are *binary* codes. This is something we often gloss over, yet to understand the true nature of the CPU, we have to step away from the persistent image of machine instructions as *numbers*. They are *not* numbers. They are binary patterns designed to throw electrical switches.

Inside the CPU are a *very* large number of transistors. Some small number of those transistors go into making the foreman's pockets—machine registers for holding information. The vast bulk of those transistors (which now number over a million in CPUs like the 80386) are switches connected to other switches, which are connected to still more switches in a mind-numbing complex network.

The machine instruction 01000000 (40H) directs the CPU to add 1 to the value stored in register AX. It's very instructive of the true nature of computers to think about the execution of machine instruction 01000000 in this way: the CPU fetches a byte containing the code 01000000 from memory. Once the byte is fully within the CPU, the CPU in essence lets the machine instruction byte push eight transistor switches. The lone 1 digit pushes its switch "up" electrically; the rest of the digits, all 0s, push their switches "down."

In a chain reaction, those eight switches flip the states of first dozens, then hundreds, then thousands, and finally tens of thousands of tiny transistor switches within the CPU. It isn't random—this furious moment of electrical activity within the CPU operates utterly according to patterns etched into the silicon of the CPU by Intel's teams of engineers. Ultimately—perhaps after hundreds of thousands of individual switch throws—the value contained in register AX is suddenly one greater than it was before.

How this happens is difficult to explain, but you must remember that *any* number within the CPU can also be looked at as a binary code, including numbers stored in registers. Also, most switches within the CPU contain more than one "handle." These switches are called *gates* and work according to the rules of logic. Perhaps two, or three, or even more "up" switch throws have to simultaneously arrive at a particular gate in order for one "down" switch throw to pass through that gate.

These gates are used to build complex internal machinery within the CPU. Collections of gates can add two numbers in a device called an *adder*, which again is nothing more than a crew of dozens of little switches working together first as gates and then as gates working together to form an adder.

As part of the cavalcade of switch throws kicked off by the binary code 01000000, the value in register AX was dumped trap-door style into an adder, while at the same time the number 1 was fed into the other end of the adder. Finally, rising on a wave of switch throws, the new sum emerges from the adder and ascends back into register AX—and the job is done.

The foreman of your computer, then, is made of switches—just like all the other parts of the computer. The chap contains a mind-boggling number of such switches, interconnected in even more mind-boggling ways. But the important thing is that whether you are boggled or (like me on off days) merely jaded by it all, the CPU, and ultimately the computer, *does what we tell it to*. We set up a list of machine instructions as a table in memory, and then, by God, that mute iron brick comes alive and starts earning its keep.

Changing Course

The first piece of genuine magic in the nature of computers is that a string of binary codes in memory tells the computer what to do, step by step. The second piece of that magic is really the jewel in the crown. *There are machine instructions that change the order in which machine instructions are fetched and executed.*

In other words, once the CPU has executed a machine instruction that does something useful, the next machine instruction may tell the CPU to go back and play it again—and again, and again, as many times as necessary. The CPU can keep count of the number of times that it has executed that particular instruction or list of instructions, and keep repeating them until a prearranged count has been met.

Or the CPU can arrange to skip certain sequences of machine instructions entirely if they don't need to be executed at all.

What this means is that the list of machine instructions in memory does not necessarily begin at the top and run without deviation to the bottom. The CPU can execute the first fifty or a hundred or a thousand instructions, then jump to the end of the program—or jump back to the start and begin again. It can skip and bounce up and down the list like a stone tossed over a calm pond. It can execute a few instructions up here, then zip down somewhere else and execute a few more instructions, then zip back and pick up where it left off, all without missing a beat or even wasting too much time.

How is this done? Recall that the CPU contains a register that always contains the address of the next instruction to be executed. This register, the instruction pointer, is not essentially different from any of the other registers in the CPU. Just as a machine instruction can add one to register AX, another machine instruction can add (or subtract) some number from the address stored in the instruction pointer. Add one hundred to the instruction pointer, and the CPU will *instantly* skip one hundred bytes down the list of machine instructions before it continues. Subtract one hundred from the address stored in the instruction pointer, and the CPU will *instantly* jump *back* one hundred bytes up the machine instruction list.

And finally, the third whammy: *the CPU can change its course of execution based on the work it has been doing.* The CPU can "decide" whether or not to execute a given instruction or group of instructions, based on values stored in memory, or based on the state of special one-bit CPU registers called *flags.* The CPU can count up how many times it needs to do something, and then do that something that number of times.

So not only can you tell the CPU what to do, you can tell it where to go. Better, you can sometimes let the CPU, like a faithful bloodhound, sniff out the best course forward in the interest of getting the work done the quickest possible way.

Back in Chapter 0, I spoke of a computer program being a sequence of steps and tests. Most of the machine instructions understood by the CPU are steps, but others are tests. The tests are always two-way tests, and in fact, the choice of what to do is always the same: jump or don't jump. *That's all.* You can test for any of numerous different conditions, but the choice is always one of jumping to another place in the program, or just keep truckin' along.

The Plan

I can sum it all up by borrowing one of the most potent metaphors for computing ever uttered: *the computer is a box that follows a plan.* These are the words of Ted Nelson, author of the uncanny book *ComputerLib/Dream Machines,* and one of those very rare people who have the infuriating habit of being right most of the time.

You write the plan. The computer follows it by passing the instructions, byte by byte, to the CPU. At the bottom of it, the process is a hellishly involved electrical chain reaction involving tens of thousands of switches composed of hundreds of thousands or even millions of transistors.

This plan, this list of machine instructions in memory, is your assembly-language program. The whole point of this book is to teach you to correctly arrange machine instructions in memory for the use of the CPU.

With any luck at all, by now you'll have a reasonable conceptual understanding of both what computers do and what they are. It's time to start looking more closely at the nature of the operations that machine instructions force the CPU to do.

3

The Right To Assemble

The Process of Making Assembly-Language Programs

3.1 Nude with Bruises and Other Perplexities

Years ago (back in the Sixties; had to be!), I recall reading about a comely female artist who produced her oil paintings by the intriguing process of rolling naked on a tarp splattered with multicolored oil paint, and then throwing herself against a canvas taped to the studio wall. (I can see the headline now: '*NUDE WITH BRUISES*' DRAWS RECORD PRICE AT NY AUCTION...)

I've seen people write programs this way. The BASIC language makes it easy: you roll in an intoxicating collection of wild and powerful program statements, and then smear them around on the screen until something works. And something invariably *does* work, no matter how little thought goes into the program's design. BASIC is like that. It's "moron-friendly," and will stoop to whatever level of carelessness goes into a program's preparation.

The programs that result, while workable in that they don't crash the machine, can take seven seconds to paint a screen, or an hour and a half to sort a database with 150 check records in it.

You can't paint *Nude with Bruises* in assembly language. Trust me.

The Sears Catalog Fallacy

But there are other perfectly proper programming paradigms that won't work with assembly language, either. One of these models is commonly used with my own beloved Turbo Pascal: decide what you want to do, sketch out a design based on a reasonable amount of forethought, and then go hunting through a veritable Sears catalog of toolbox products looking for stock procedures like:

```
SearchDataFileForFirstRecordBeginningWithStringAndDisplayInRed
```

Basically, this method glues together other people's canned procedures into programs that aren't exactly canned, but are more or less polybagged. Which is OK—I do it all the time. I also eat at Burger King a couple of times a week, because it's quick and cheap—and because I get hungry no matter how hard I try not to. When I need a software tool in a bad way and just can't get around not having it, I look for the quickest possible way of producing it.

(As an interesting side note, I once produced a necessary utility—my JRead utility—by starting with Borland's FirstEd example editor from their Editor Toolbox, and *cutting things out of it* until the program did what I needed. I ended up writing only about 20 lines of new code, all tolled. It was programming in reverse—you can't do it all the time, but this time it allowed me to make a solid, useful tool in about an hour and a half. Keep your eyes open for opportunities like that.)

There is an occasional toolbox of assembly language routines, but hardly enough to avoid having to think too much about the task at hand—which is what many people think by way of the Sears catalog fallacy.

I started this chapter this way as a warning: you can't write assembly-language programs by trial and error, nor can you do it by letting other people do your thinking for you. It is a complicated and tricky process compared to either BASIC or we-do-it-all-for-you languages like Turbo Pascal. You have to pay close attention. You have to read the sheet music. And, most of all, you have to practice.

3.2 DOS and DOS Files

In the previous chapter, I defined what a computer program is, *from the computer's perspective.* It is, metaphorically, a long journey in very small steps. A *long* list of binary codes direct the CPU to do what it must to accomplish the job at hand. These codes are, even in their hexadecimal shorthand form, gobbledegook to us here in the land of the living. Here is a perfect example:

```
FE FF A2 37 4C 0A 29 00 91 CB 60 61 E8 E3 20 00 A8 00 B8 29 1F FF 69 55 7B
F4 F8 5B 31
```

Is this a real program or isn't it? You'd probably have to ask the CPU, unless you were a machine-code maniac of the kind that hasn't been seen since 1977. (It isn't.)

But the CPU has no trouble with programs presented in this form. In fact, the CPU can't handle programs any other way. The CPU simply isn't equipped to understand a string of characters like

```
LET X = 42
```

or even something we out here would call assembly language:

```
MOV AX,42
```

To the CPU, it's binary only, and hold the text, please, ma'am.

So while it is possible to write computer programs in pure binary (I have done it, but not since 1977) it's unpleasant work, and will take you until the next Ice Age to accomplish anything useful.

The process of developing assembly-language programs is a path that runs from what we call *source code* that you can read, to something called *machine code* that the CPU can execute. In the middle is a resting-point called *object code* that we'll take up a little later.

The process of creating true machine-code programs is one of *translation.* You must start with something that you and the rest of us can read and understand, and then somehow convert that to something the CPU can understand and execute. Before examining either end of that road, however, we need to understand a little more about the land on which the road is built.

The God Above; the Troll Below

Most of all, we need to understand DOS. Some people look upon DOS as a god; others as a kind of troll. In fact, DOS is a little of both. Mostly what you must put behind you is the common notion that DOS is a part of the machine itself and somehow resides in the same sort of silicon as the CPU. Not so! DOS is a computer program of an only slightly special nature, called an *operating system.*

In part, an operating system is a collection of routines that do nothing but serve the components of the computer itself. By components I mean things like disk drives, printers, and so on. DOS acts something like a troll living under the bridge to your disk drive. You tell the troll what you want to do with the disk drive, and the troll does it, *his* way, and at some cost (in machine cycles) to you.

You could write a program to handle every little aspect of disk operation itself (many game programs do exactly that) but it would be more trouble than it's worth, because *every* program that runs on a computer needs to access the disk drives. And regardless of how grumpy the troll is, he *does* get the job done, and (assuming your disk drives aren't falling-down damaged) does it right every time. Can *you* guarantee that you know all there is to know about running a disk drive? Forgive me if I have my doubts. That is, in my opinion, what trolls are for.

The other (and more interesting thing) that operating systems do is run programs. It is here that DOS seems more godlike than troll-like. When you want to run a program on your computer, you type its name at the DOS command line. DOS goes out and searches one or more disk drives for the named program, loads it into memory at a convenient spot, sets the instruction pointer to the start of the program, and boots the CPU in the rear to get it going.

DOS then patiently waits for the program to run its course and stop. When the program stops, it hands the CPU obediently back to DOS, which again tilts a hand to its ear and listens for your next command from the command line.

So as programmers, we use DOS two ways: one is as a sort of toolkit; an army of trolls, each of which can perform some service for your program, saving your program that effort. The other is as a means of loading a program into memory and getting it going, and then catching the machine gracefully on the rebound when your program is through.

I'll be mentioning DOS again and again in this book. Everywhere you look in assembly language, you're going to see the old troll's face. Get used to it.

DOS Files: Magnetic Memory

Very simply, DOS files are memory banks stored on a magnetic coating rather than inside silicon chips. A DOS file contains some number of bytes, stored in a specific order. One difference from RAM memory is that DOS files stored on disk are sequential-access memory banks.

A disk (floppy or hard) is a circular platform coated with magnetic plastic of some sort. In a floppy disk drive, the platform is a flexible disk of tough plastic; in a hard disk the platform is a rigid platter of aluminum metal. Data is stored as little magnetic disturbances on the plastic coating in a fashion similar to that used in audio cassettes and VCRs. A sensor called a *read/write head* sits very close beside the rotating platform, and waits for the data to pass by.

A simplified illustration of a rotating disk device is shown in Figure 3.1. The area of the disk is divided into concentric circles called *tracks*. The tracks are further divided radially into *sectors*. A sector (typically containing 512 bytes) is the smallest unit of storage that can be read from or written to at one time. A DOS disk file consists of one or more sectors containing the file's data.

The read/write head is mounted on a sliding shaft that is controlled by a solenoid mechanism. The solenoid can move the head horizontally to position the head over a specific track. (In Figure 3.1, the head is positioned over track 2—counting from 0, remember!) However, once the head is over a particular track, it has to count sectors until the sector it needs passes beneath it. The *tracks* can be accessed at random, just like bytes in the computer's memory banks, but the sectors within a track must be accessed sequentially.

Perhaps the single most valuable service DOS provides is handling the headaches of distributing data onto empty sectors on a disk. Programs can hand

Figure 3.1. Rotating disk storage

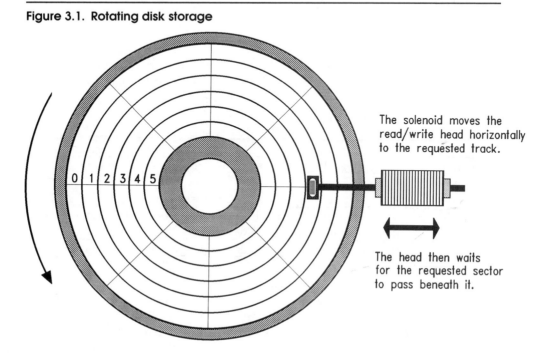

The solenoid moves the read/write head horizontally to the requested track.

The head then waits for the requested sector to pass beneath it.

sectors of data to DOS, one at a time, and let DOS worry about where on the disk they can be placed. Each sector has a number, and DOS keeps track of what sectors belong together as a file. The first sector in a file might be stored on track 3, sector 9; the second sector might be stored on track 0, sector 4, and so on. You don't have to worry about that. When you ask for sector 0 of your file, DOS looks up its location in its private tables, goes directly to track 3, sector 9 and brings the sector's data back to you.

Binary Files

The data that is stored in a file is just binary bytes and can be anything at all. Files like this, where there are *no* restrictions on the contents of a file, are called *binary files,* because they can legally contain any binary code. Like all files, a binary file consists of some whole number of sectors, with each sector (typically) containing 512 bytes. The least space any file can occupy on your disk is 512 bytes; when you see the DOS DIR command tell you that a file has 17 bytes it in, that's the count of how many bytes are *stored* in that file. But like a walk-in closet with only one pair of shoes in it, the rest of the sector is still there, empty but occupying space on the disk.

A binary file has no structure, but is simply a long series of binary codes divided into numbered groups of 512 and stored out on disk in a scheme that is best left to DOS to understand.

Text Files

If you've ever tried to use the TYPE command to display a binary file (like an .EXE or .COM file) to the screen, you've seen some odd things indeed. There's no reason for such files to be intelligible on the screen; they're intended for other "eyes," typically the CPU's.

There is a separate class of files that is specifically restricted to containing human-readable information. These files are called *text files* because they contain the letters, digits, and symbols of which printed human information (text) is composed.

Unlike binary files, text files have a certain structure to them. The characters in text files are divided into *lines.* A line in a text file is defined not so much by what it contains as by how it ends. Two invisible characters called an *end-of-line (or EOL)* marker (or EOL) tag the end of a line. The EOL marker is not one character but two: the carriage return character (called CR by those who know and love it) followed by the linefeed character (similarly called LF). You don't see these characters on the screen as separate symbols, but you see what they do: they end the line. Anywhere a line ends in an ordinary DOS text file, you'll find a mostly invisible partnership of one CR character and one LF character hanging out. The first line in a text file runs from the first byte in the file to the first EOL marker; the second line starts immediately after the first EOL marker and runs to the second EOL marker, and so on. <u>The text characters falling between two sequential EOL markers is considered a single line.</u>

Why two characters to end a line? Long ago, there was (and still is at hamfests, lordy) an incredible mechanical nightmare called a teletype machine. These were invented during World War II as robot typewriters that could send written messages over long distances through electrical signals that could pass over wires. Returning the typing carriage to the left margin of the paper (carriage return) and feeding the paper up one line to expose the next clean line of paper to the typing carriage (line feed) are separate mechanical operations. A separate electrical signal was required to do each of these operations. Although I don't know why separate signals were necessary, it has carried over into the solid-state autumn of the 20th century in the form of those two characters, CR and LF. Not only is this a case of the tail wagging the dog; it is a case of the tail walking around twenty years after the poor dog rolled over and died.

Figure 3.2 shows how CR and LF divide what might otherwise be a single meaningless string of characters into a structured sequence of lines. It's impor-

---

Figure 3.2. The structure of a text file

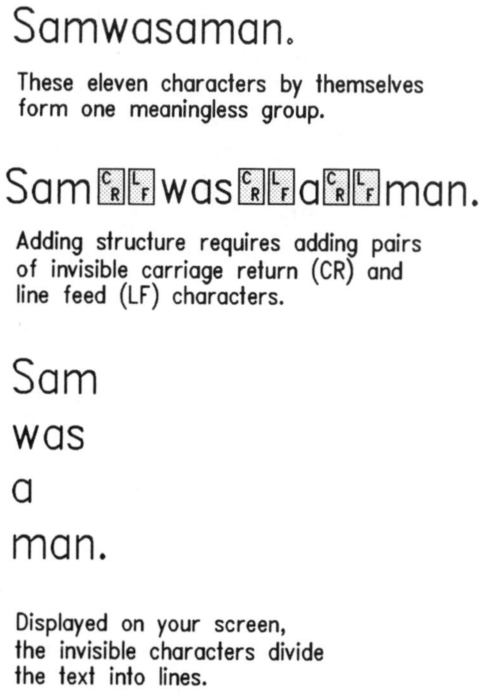

Samwasaman.

These eleven characters by themselves
form one meaningless group.

Sam⬚⬚was⬚⬚a⬚⬚man.

Adding structure requires adding pairs
of invisible carriage return (CR) and
line feed (LF) characters.

Sam

was

a

man.

Displayed on your screen,
the invisible characters divide
the text into lines.

---

tant to understand the structure of a text file because that structure dictates how some important software tools operate, as I'll explain a little later.

The CR character is actually character 13 in the ASCII character set summarized in Appendix A. The LF character is character 10. They are two of a set of several invisible characters called *whitespace*, indicating their role in positioning text characters within the white space of a text page. The other whitespace characters include the space character (character 32) the tab character (character 9) and the form feed character (character 12), which can further divide a text file into *pages.*

Another character, the *bell character* (BEL) falls in between binary and text characters. When either displayed or printed, it signals that a tone should be sounded. Back in the old teletype days, the BEL character caused the teletype machine to ring its bell. BEL characters are allowed in text files, but are generally considered sloppy practice.

One more invisible character plays an important role in the structure of a text file: The end-of-file (EOF) marker character. Unlike EOL, EOF is a single character, ASCII character 26, sometimes written as Ctrl+Z because you generate the EOF character by holding down the Ctrl key then pressing the Z key.

By convention, the EOF marker is considered the last significant character in a text file, and DOS will ignore any characters following it, *even if the file goes on for thousands of additional bytes.* Those additional bytes will be ignored by the assembler and by most text editors.

An EOF marker can be mistakenly placed in the middle of a text file by some utilities. The most frequent source of false EOF markers comes from saving a text file to disk in a word processor program's "native" mode, which may write EOF characters and many other unprintable characters into a text file. Such native mode document files are not actually text files, but are binary files intended to be read *only* by that particular word processor.

Text Editors

Manipulating a text file is done with a program called a *text editor.* A text editor is a word processor for program source code files. In its simplest form, a text editor works like this: you type characters at the keyboard and they appear on the screen. When you press the Enter key, an EOL marker is placed at the end of a line, and the cursor moves down to the next line.

A text editor also allows you to move the cursor into existing text to change, or edit, it. You can delete words and whole lines and, if necessary, replace them with new text.

Ultimately, when you are finished, you press a key like F2 or a key combination like Ctrl+KD, and the text editor saves the text you entered from the keyboard as a text file. This text file is the source code file you'll later present to the assembler for processing. Later on, you can load that same text file back into the editor to make repairs on faulty lines that cause errors during assembly or bugs during execution.

A great many people still use their word processors as program text editors. WordStar, WordPerfect, and most of the others make acceptable text editors, as long as you remember to write your text file to disk in "non-document mode" or "ASCII text mode". Most true word processors embed countless strange little codes in their text files, to control things like margin settings, font selections, headers and footers, and soft page and line breaks. These codes are not recognized ASCII characters but binary values, and actually change the document file from a text file to a binary file. The codes will give the assembler fits. *If you write a program source code file to disk as a document file, it will not assemble.* See the word processor documentation for details on how to export a document file as a pure ASCII text file.

There are numerous text editor products on the market specifically for use by assembly-language programmers. Two of the best are called Brief and Epsilon. A very good editor, Point, is often sold as an accessory with the Logitech Mouse. The Sidekick notepad editor makes a perfectly reasonable text editor for assembly-language work, as do the editors built into Microsoft's Quick language compilers and Borland's Turbo language compilers.

If you have no other editor, I have put one together and given it to various user groups around the country. If you can't find my JED editor anywhere, you can order it directly from me through the address on the flyleaf. JED works very much like the editor in the Turbo language products, because I produced it with the Turbo Pascal Editor Toolbox and Turbo Pascal 5.0.

Because there are so many different text editors in use among programmers, I'll be using JED as the example editor in this book. When you see a command line incorporating the name JED, keep in mind that you will have to substitute the name and command suite for whatever editor you may be using if you're not using JED.

Chapter 4 describes JED in detail. JED has the advantage (over editors like Brief and Epsilon) of being simple. I designed it for beginning assembly-language programmers, and if you've ever used any of the Turbo language products, JED will feel just like home.

3.3 Compilers and Assemblers

With that understanding of DOS files under your belt, you can come to understand the nature of two important kinds of programs: *compilers* and *assemblers*. Both fall into a category of programs we call *translators.*

A translator is a program that accepts human-readable source code files and generates some kind of binary file. The binary file could be an executable program file that the CPU can understand, or it could be a font file, or a compressed binary data file, or any of a hundred other types of binary file.

Program translators are translators that generate machine instructions that the CPU can understand. A program translator reads a source code file line by line, and writes a binary file of machine instructions to accomplish the actions that the source code file describes. This binary file is called an *object code file.*

A compiler is a program translator that reads in source code files written in higher-level languages like C and Pascal and outputs object code files.

An assembler is a special type of compiler. It, too, is a program translator that reads source code files and outputs object code files for the CPU. However, an assembler is a translator designed specifically to translate what we call *assembly language* into object code. In the same sense that a language compiler for Pascal or C compiles a source code file to an object code file, we say that an assembler *assembles* an assembly language source code file to an object code file. The process, one of translation, is similar in both cases. An assembler, however, has an overwhelmingly important characteristic that sets it apart from other compilers: *total control over the object code.*

Assembly Language

Some people define assembly language as a language in which one line of source code generates one machine instruction. This has never been literally true, since some lines in an assembly-language source code file are instructions to the translator program and do not generate machine instructions.

My own definition follows:

Assembly language is a language that allows total control over *every individual machine instruction* generated by the translator program.

Pascal or C compilers, on the other hand, make a multitude of invisible and inalterable decisions about how a given language statement will be translated into machine instructions. For example, the following single Pascal instruction assigns a value of 42 to a numeric variable called **I**:

```
I := 42;
```

When a Pascal compiler reads this line, it outputs a series of four or five machine instructions that take the value 42 and store it in memory at a location encoded by the name **I**. Normally, you the programmer have *no idea* what these four or five instructions actually are, and you have utterly no way of changing them, even if you know a sequence of machine instructions that is faster and more efficient than the sequence the compiler uses. The Pascal compiler has its own way of generating machine instructions, and you have no choice but to accept what it writes to disk to accomplish the Pascal statements in the source code file.

An assembler, however, has at least one line in the source code file for every machine instruction it generates. It has more lines than that to handle numerous other things, but *every* machine instruction in the final object code file is controlled by a corresponding line in the source code file.

Each of the CPU's many machine instructions has a corresponding *mnemonic* in assembly language. As the word suggests, these mnemonics began as devices to help programmers remember a particular machine instruction. For example, the mnemonic for machine instruction 9CH, which pushes the flags register onto the stack, is **PUSHF**—which is a country mile easier to remember than 9CH.

When you write your source code file in assembly language, you will arrange series of mnemonics, typically one mnemonic to a source code file text line. A portion of a source code file might look like this:

```
MOV    AH,12H      ; 12H is Motor Information Service
MOV    AL,03H      ; 03H is Return Current Speed function
XOR    BH,BH       ; Zero BH for safety's sake
INT    71H         ; Call Motor Services Interrupt
```

Here, the words **MOV**, **XOR**, and **INT** are the mnemonics. The numbers and other items to the immediate right of each mnemonic are that mnemonics's *operands.* There are various kinds of operands for various machine instructions, and some instructions (like **PUSHF** mentioned above) have no operands at all. We'll thoroughly describe each instruction's operands when we cover that specific instruction.

Taken together, a mnemonic and its operands are called an *instruction.* This is the word we'll be using most of the time in this book to indicate the human-readable proxy of one of the CPU's pure binary machine code instructions. To talk about the binary code specifically, we'll always refer to a *machine instruction.*

The assembler's most important job is to read lines from the source code file and write machine instructions to an object code file. See Figure 3.3.

Comments

To the right of each instruction is some information starting with a semicolon. This information is called a *comment,* and its purpose should be plain: to cast some light on what the associated assembly language instruction is *for.* The instruction **MOV AH,12H** places the value 12H in register AH—but *why?* The comment provides the why.

Far more than in any other programming language, comments are critical to the success of your assembly language programs. My own recommendation is that *every* instruction in your source code files have a comment to its right.

Structurally, a comment starts with the first semicolon on a line, and continues to the EOL marker at the end of that line. This is one instance where

Figure 3.3. What the assembler does

Mnemonic Operands   Comment

```
MOV AX,BX          ; Put byte count into AX
```

The assembler reads a line like this one from the source code file
and writes the equivalent machine instruction to the object code file:

```
8BH 0C3H
```

understanding how a text file is structured is very important—because in assembly language, comments end at the ends of lines. In most other languages, comments are placed *between* pairs of comment delimiters like **(*** and ***)**, and EOL markers at line ends are ignored.

Comments begin at semicolons, and end at an EOL marker.

Beware "Write-Only" Source Code!

This is as good a time as any to point out a serious problem with assembly language. The instructions themselves are almost vanishingly brief, and while each instructions states what it does, there is *nothing* to indicate the context in which that instruction operates. With some skill and discipline, you can build that context into your Pascal or BASIC code but in assembly language you can add context only through comments.

Without context, assembly language starts to turn into what we call "write-only" code. It can happen like this: on November 1, in the heat of creation, you crank out about 300 instructions in a short utility program that does something important. You go back on January 1 to add a feature to the program and discover that *you no longer remember how it works*. The individual instructions are all correct, but knowledge of how it all came together and how it works from a height have vanished under Christmas memories and eight weeks of doing other things. In other words, you *wrote* it, but you can no longer *read* it, or change it. Voila! Write-only code.

Comment like crazy. Each individual line should have a comment, and every so often in a sizable source code file, take a few lines out and make entire lines into comments, explaining what the code is up to at this point in its execution.

While comments do take room in your source code disk files, they are *not* copied into your object code files, and a program with loads of comments runs *exactly* as fast as the same program with no comments at all.

You will be investing a considerable amount of time and energy into writing your assembly-language programs. It's more difficult than just about any other way of writing programs, and if you don't comment you may end up having to simply toss out hundreds of lines of inexplicable code and write it again, *from scratch*.

Work smart. Comment till you drop.

Object Code and Linkers

There's no reason at all why an assembler could not read a source-code file and write out a finished, executable program file as its object-code file. Most assemblers don't work this way, however. Object-code files produced by the major assemblers are a sort of intermediate step between source code and executable program. This intermediate step is a type of binary file called a *relocatable object module,* or (more simply) an .OBJ file, which is the file extension used by the assembler when it creates the file. For example, a source-code file called FOO.ASM would be assembled into an object file called FOO.OBJ. (The "relocatable" portion of the concept is crucial, but a little advanced for this chapter. More on it later.)

Because .OBJ files cannot be run as programs, an additional step, called *linking,* is necessary to turn these files into executable program files.

The reason for using .OBJ files as intermediate steps is that a single, large source-code file may be divided, (using your text editor) into numerous smaller source-code files to keep them manageable in size and complexity. The assembler assembles the various component fragments separately, and the several resulting .OBJ files are woven together into a single, executable program file. This process is shown in Figure 3.4.

When you're first starting out, it's unlikely that you will be writing large programs spread out across several source-code files. Even if you only have a small source-code file that produces a single .OBJ file, you must still use the linker to change the single .OBJ file into an executable program file, as I'll explain a little later.

Figure 3.4. The assembler and linker

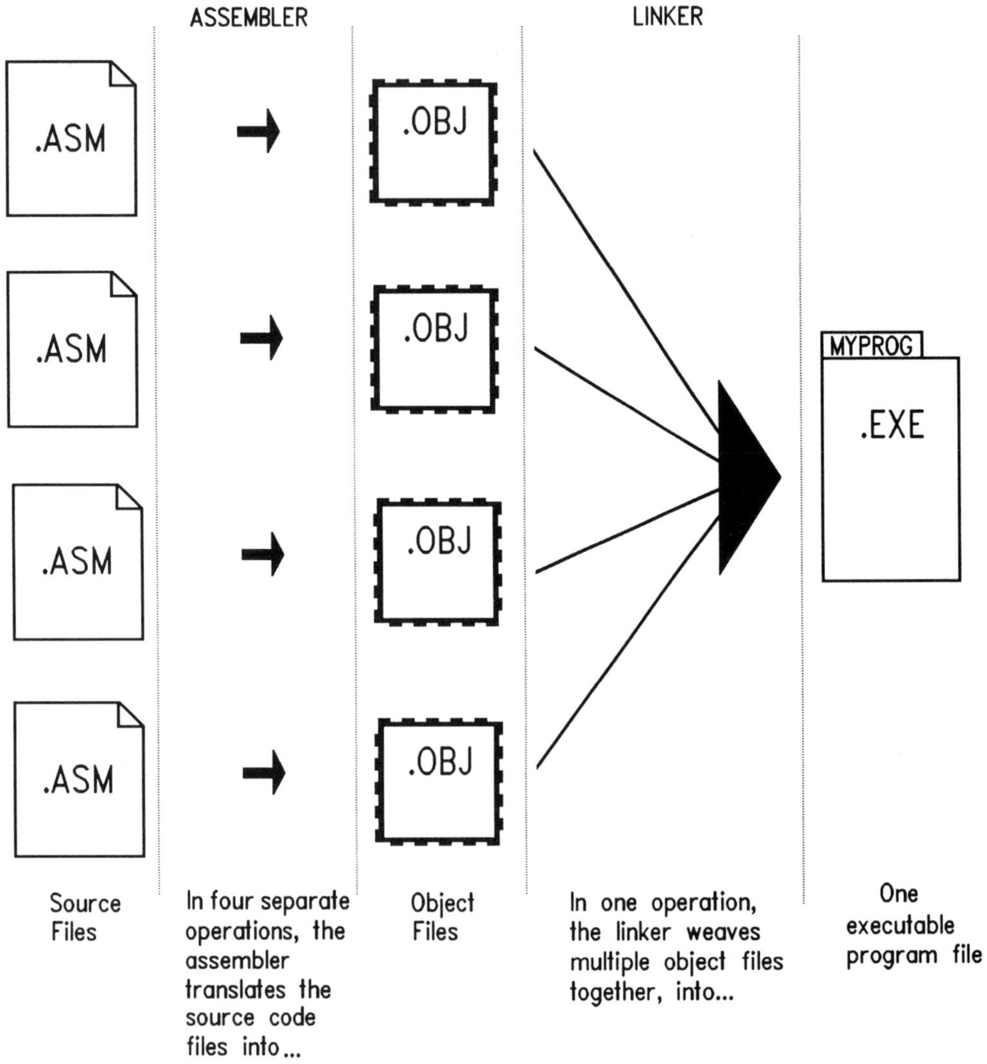

ASSEMBLER   LINKER

.ASM → .OBJ

.ASM → .OBJ   MYPROG

.EXE

.ASM → .OBJ

.ASM → .OBJ

| Source Files | In four separate operations, the assembler translates the source code files into... | Object Files | In one operation, the linker weaves multiple object files together, into... | One executable program file |

The larger your programs become, however, the more time can be saved by cutting them up into components. There are two reasons for this:

1. You can move tested, proven routines into separate libraries and link them into any program you write that might need them. This way, you can reuse code over and over again and not build the same old wheels every time you begin a new programming project in assembly language.

2. Once portions of a program are tested and found to be correct, there's no need to waste time assembling them over and over again along with newer, untested portions of a program. Once a major program gets into the tens of thousands of lines of code (and you'll get there sooner than you might think), you can save an *enormous* amount of time by only assembling the portion of a program that you are currently working on, and linking the finished portions into the final program without reassembling the whole thing every time.

Executable Program Files

The linker program may be seen as a kind of translator program, but its major role is in combining multiple object code files into a single executable program file. This executable file is sometimes called an .EXE file from the file extension that the linker appends to the file's name. For example, a source code file named FOO.ASM would be assembled to an object code file named FOO.OBJ, which would then be processed by the linker to an executable program file called FOO.EXE.

The executable file can be run by typing its name (without the .EXE extension) at the DOS prompt (for example, C:\>FOO) and then pressing Enter.

Real Assembler Products: MASM and TASM

For quite a few years there was only one assembler product in general use for the PC: Microsoft's Macro Assembler, better known as MASM. MASM is still an enormously popular program, and has established a standard for assembler operation on the PC. The source code in this book is all designed to be assembled by MASM.

MASM is by no means perfect, however, and in 1988 Borland International released their answer to MASM in the form of Turbo Assembler, which was quickly christened TASM by syllable-conserving programmers. TASM is a great deal faster than MASM, and has numerous advanced features that I won't be able to utilize in this book. However, at the level we're describing in this book, MASM and TASM are totally compatible in that they will assemble identical source code files identically. MASM and TASM are the two most popular assemblers for Intel's 86-family of CPUs, and the information in this book can be applied to either assembler.

I won't, however, attempt to describe the two assemblers' operation in detail. There are many differences in the ways the two assemblers function, and you'll have to delve into the manuals to get the full story. Very fortunately, when you're first starting out, there isn't a whole lot to using either TASM or MASM, and I'll describe the simple commands for invoking each assembler where appropriate.

The most recent releases of MASM now come with their own text editor, but for years MASM was "editor less" and you had to supply your own editor. Currently, TASM does not come with a text editor, so if you're a TASM user, you'll have to come up with a text editor on your own. I recommend using something simple, like my JED editor described in Chapter 4.

Both MASM and TASM come with their own special debugging tools, called *debuggers*. MASM's debugger is called CodeView, and TASM's debugger is called Turbo Debugger. Both are enormously sophisticated programs, and I won't be discussing either in this book, due in part to their complexity but mostly because there is a debugger shipped with every copy of PC DOS. This debugger, simply named DEBUG, is more than enough debugger to cut your teeth on, and will get you familiar enough with debugger theory to move up to CodeView or Turbo Debugger later on.

I'll be describing DEBUG much more fully in Section 3.5.

Setting Up a Working Subdirectory

The process of creating and perfecting assembly-language programs involves a lot of different kinds of DOS files and numerous separate software tools. Unlike the tidy, fully-integrated environments offered by the Turbo and Quick languages, assembly language development comes in a great many pieces with some assembly required.

I recommend setting up a development subdirectory on your hard disk and putting all of the various pieces in that subdirectory. Create, then change to a subdirectory called ASM by using these DOS commands:

```
MD ASM
CD ASM
```

Then, from within the ASM subdirectory, copy the following files or groups of files into the subdirectory:

- **Your text editor**. If you're using JED (see Chapter 4), you need only copy the file JED.EXE. If you're using a memory-resident editor like Sidekick's notepad, you may not need to copy any editor program into your development subdirectory, because it will be memory resident when you boot. For other editors like Brief, you'll need to consult the documentation.

- **Your assembler**. Again, consult the documentation to see what files are necessary to assembler a source code file. Usually, there is a single executable file like MASM.EXE or TASM.EXE and perhaps some help files or configuration files. The older versions of MASM stood alone as MASM.EXE and needed nothing else in the subdirectory to operate. Similarly, the first release of TASM allows the file TASM.EXE to work alone.

- **Your linker**. Both MASM and TASM include their own linkers. MASM's linker program is LINK.EXE. TASM's linker is TLINK.EXE. Copy the appropriate file. Both linkers stand alone and do not require any support files.

- **DEBUG**. On your DOS distribution disk (or in your DOS subdirectory, if you have a DOS subdirectory) there should be a file called DEBUG.COM. Files with a .COM extension are, like .EXE files, executable programs. .COM programs are slightly old-fashioned and not much used anymore since Turbo Pascal 3.0 was supplanted by version 4.0 in 1987. Copy DEBUG.COM into your development subdirectory.

- **Odds and ends**. A source code listing program, while not essential, can be very helpful—such programs print out neatly formatted listings on your printer. (I have written a useful one called JLIST10 that I have placed on the listings diskette for this book—but it only operates with the LaserJet laser printers.) Add anything else that may be helpful, keeping in mind that a *lot* of files are generated during assembly language development, and you should strive to keep unnecessary clutter to a minimum.

3.4 The Assembly-Language Development Process

As you can see, there are a lot of different file types and a fair number of programs involved in the cycle of writing, assembling, and testing an assembly-language program. The cycle itself sounds more complex than it is. I've drawn you a map to help you keep your bearings during the discussions in this chapter. Figure 3.5 shows the assembly-language development process in a "view from a height." At first glance it may look like a map of the L.A. freeway system, but in reality the flow is fairly straightforward. Follow along on a quick tour.

Assembling the Source-Code File

You use the text editor to first create a new text file and then to edit that same text file, as you perfect your assembly language program. As a convention, most assembly language source code files are given a file extension of .ASM. In other words, for the program named FOO, the assembly language source code file would be named FOO.ASM.

It is possible to use file extensions other than .ASM, but I feel that using the .ASM extension can eliminate some confusion by allowing you to tell at a glance what a file is for—just by looking at its name. All tolled, about nine different kinds of files can be involved during assembly language development. (We're only going to speak of four or five in this book.) Each type of file will have its own standard file extension. Anything that will help you keep all that complexity in line will be worth the (admittedly) rigid confines of a standard naming convention.

Figure 3.5. The assembly-language development process

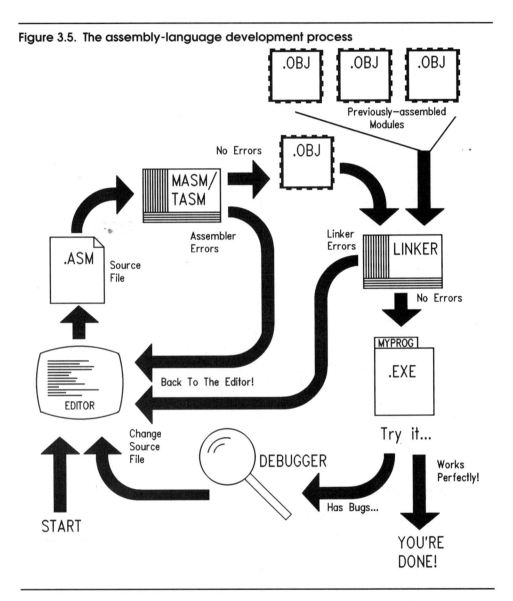

As you can see from the flow in Figure 3.5, the editor produces a source code text file, which we show as having the .ASM extension. This file is then passed to the assembler program itself, for translation to a relocatable object module file with an extension of .OBJ.

Invoking the assembler is very simple. For small standalone assembly-language programs in Turbo Assembler, it's nothing more than the name of the assembler followed by the name of the program to be assembled (for example,

C:\ASM>TASM FOO). For Microsoft's MASM, you need to put a semicolon on the end of the command. This tells MASM that no further prompts are necessary (for example C:\ASM>MASM FOO). If you omit the semicolon, nothing bad will happen, but MASM will ask you for the names of several other files, and you will have to press Enter several times to select the defaults.

DOS will load the assembler from disk and run it. The assembler will open the source code file you named after the name of the assembler, and begin processing the file. Almost immediately afterward, it will create an object file with the same name as the source file, but with the .OBJ extension.

As the assembler reads lines from the source code file, it will examine them, construct the binary machine instructions the source code lines represent, and then write those machine instructions to the object code file.

When the assembler detects the EOF marker signaling the end of the source code file, it will close both source code file and object code file and return control to DOS.

Assembler Errors

The previous three paragraphs describe what happens if the .ASM file is *correct*. By correct, I mean the file is completely comprehensible to the assembler, and can be translated into machine instructions without the assembler getting confused. If the assembler encounters something it doesn't understand when it reads a line from the source code file, we call the misunderstood text an *error*, and the assembler displays an *error message*.

For example, the following line of assembly language will confuse the assembler and summon an error message:

```
MOV AX,VX
```

The reason is simple: there's no such thing as a "VX." What came out as "VX" was actually intended to be "BX," which is the name of a register. (The V key is right next to the B key and can be struck by mistake without your fingers necessarily knowing that they done wrong.)

Typos are by far the easiest kind of error to spot. Others that take some study to find usually involve transgressions of the assembler's rules. Take for example the line:

```
MOV ES,0FF00H
```

This looks like it should be correct, since ES is a real register and 0FF00H is a real, 16-bit quantity that will fit into ES. However, among the multitude of rules in the fine print of the 86-family of assemblers is that you cannot directly move an immediate value (any number like 0FF00H) directly into a segment register like ES, DS, SS, or CS. It simply isn't part of the CPU's machinery to do that.

Instead, you must first move the immediate value into a register like AX, and *then* move AX into ES.

You don't have to remember the details here; we'll go into the rules later on. For now, simply understand that some things that look reasonable are simply "against the rules" and are considered an error.

There are much, *much* more difficult errors that involve inconsistencies between two otherwise legitimate lines of source code. I won't offer any examples here, but I wanted to point out that errors can be truly ugly, hidden things that can take a lot of study and torn hair to find. Toto, we are definitely *not* in BASIC anymore…

The error messages vary from assembler to assembler, but they may not always be as helpful as you might hope. The error TASM displays upon encountering the VX typo follows:

```
Turbo Assembler Version 1.0  Copyright (c) 1988 by Borland International

Assembling file:   FOO.ASM
**Error** FOO.ASM(74) Undefined symbol: VX
Error messages:    1
Warning messages:  None
Remaining memory:  395k
```

This is pretty plain, assuming you know what a "symbol" is. The error message TASM will present when you try to load an immediate value into ES is less helpful:

```
Turbo Assembler Version 1.0  Copyright (c) 1988 by Borland International

Assembling file:   IBYTECPY.ASM
**Error** IBYTECPY.ASM(74) Illegal use of segment register
Error messages:    1
Warning messages:  None
Remaining memory:  395k
```

It'll let you know you're guilty of performing illegal acts with a segment register, but that's it. *You* have to know what's legal and what's illegal to really understand what you did wrong. As in running a stop sign, ignorance of the law is no excuse.

> Assembler error messages do not absolve you from understanding the CPU's or the assembler's rules.

I hope I don't frighten you too terribly by warning you that for more complex errors, the error messages may be almost *no help at all.*

You may make (or *will* make; let's get real) more than one error in writing your source code files. The assembler will display more than one error message in such cases, but it may not necessarily display an error for *every* error present in the source code file. At some point, multiple errors confuse the assembler so thoroughly that it cannot necessarily tell right from wrong anymore. While it's true that the assembler reads and translates source code files line by line, there is a cumulative picture of the final assembly language program that is built up over the course of the whole assembly process. If this picture is shot too full of errors, in time the whole picture collapses.

The assembler will stop and return to DOS, having printed numerous error messages. *Start at the first one* and keep going. If the following errors don't make sense, fix the first one or two and assemble again.

Back to the Editor

The way to fix errors is to load the .ASM file back into your text editor and start hunting up the error. This "loopback" is shown in Figure 3.5.

The error message will almost always contain a line number. Move the cursor to that line number and start looking for the false and the fanciful. If you find the error immediately, fix it and start looking for the next.

Here's a little logistical snag: how do you make a list of the error messages on paper so that you don't have to memorize them or scribble them down on paper with a pencil? You may or may not be aware that you can *redirect* the assembler's error message displays to a DOS text file on disk.

It works like this: you invoke the assembler just as you normally would, but add the *redirection operator* **>** and the name of the text file to which you want the error messages sent. If you were assembling FOO.ASM with TASM and wanted your error messages written out to a disk file named ERRORS.TXT, you would invoke TASM by entering C:\ASM>TASM FOO > ERRORS.TXT.

Here, error messages will be sent to ERRORS.TXT in the current DOS directory C:\ASM. When you use redirection, the output does *not* display on the screen. The stream of text from TASM that you would ordinarily see is quite literally steered in its entirety to another place, the file ERRORS.TXT.

Once the assembly process is done, the DOS prompt will appear again. You can then print the ERRORS.TXT file on your printer and have a handy summary of all that the assembler discovered was wrong with your source code file.

Assembler Warnings

As taciturn a creature as an assembler may appear to be, it genuinely tries to help you any way it can. One way it tries to help is by displaying *warning messages* during the assembly process. These warning messages are a monumental puzzle to beginning assembly language programmers: are they errors or aren't they? Can I ignore them or should I fool with the source code until they go away?

There is no clean answer. Sorry about that.

Warnings are the assembler acting as experienced consultant, and hinting that something in your source code is a little dicey. Now, in the nature of assembly language, you may fully *intend* that the source code be dicey. In an 86-family CPU, dicey code may be the only way to do something fast enough, or just to do it at all. The critical factor is that you had better know what you're doing.

The most common generator of warning messages is doing something that goes against the assembler's default conditions and assumptions. If you're a beginner doing ordinary, 100%-by-the-book sorts of things, you should crack your assembler reference manual and figure out why the assembler is tut-tutting you. Ignoring a warning *may* cause peculiar bugs to occur later on during program testing. Or, ignoring a warning message may have no undesirable consequences at all. I feel, however, that it's always better to know what's going on. Follow this rule:

> Ignore a warning message only if you know *exactly* what it means.

In other words, until you understand why you're getting a warning message, treat it as though it were an error message. Only when you fully understand why it's there and what it means should you try to make the decision whether or not to ignore the message.

In summary, the first part of the assembly language development process (as shown in Figure 3.5) is a loop. You must edit your source code file, assemble it, and return to the editor to fix errors until the assembler spots no further errors. *You cannot continue until the assembler gives your source code file a clean bill of health.*

When no further errors are found, the assembler will write an .OBJ file to disk, and you will be ready to go on to the next step.

Linking

Theoretically, an assembler could generate an .EXE (executable) program file directly from your source code .ASM file. Some obscure assemblers have been able to do this, but it's not a common assembler feature.

What actually happens is that the assembler writes an intermediate object code file with an .OBJ extension to disk. You can't run this .OBJ file, even though it contains all the machine instructions that your assembly language source code file specified. The .OBJ file needs to be processed by another translator program, the linker.

The linker performs a number of operations on the .OBJ file, most of which would be meaningless to you at this point. The most obvious task the linker does is to weave several .OBJ files into a single .EXE program file. Creating an assembly language program from multiple .ASM files is called *modular assembly*.

Why create multiple .OBJ files when writing a single executable program? One of two major reasons is size. A middling assembly-language application might be 50,000 lines long. Cutting that single monolithic .ASM file up into multiple 8,000 line .ASM files would make the individual .ASM files smaller and much easier to understand.

The other reason is to avoid assembling completed portions of the program every time *any* part of the program is assembled. One thing you'll be doing is writing assembly language *procedures*, small detours from the main run of steps and tests that can be taken from anywhere within the assembly language program. Once you write and perfect a procedure, you can tuck it away in an .ASM file with other completed procedures, assemble it, and then simply link the resulting .OBJ file into the "working" .ASM file. The alternative is to waste time by reassembling perfected source code over and over again every time you assemble the main portion of the program.

Notice that in the upper-right corner of Figure 3.5 is a row of .OBJ files. These .OBJ files were assembled earlier from correct .ASM files, yielding binary disk files containing ready-to-go machine instructions. When the linker links the .OBJ file produced from your in-progress .ASM file, it adds in the previously assembled .OBJ files, which are called *modules*. The single .EXE file that the linker writes to disk contains the machine instructions from all of the .OBJ files handed to the linker when then linker is invoked.

Once the in-progress .ASM file is completed and made correct, its .OBJ module can be put up on the rack with the others, and added to the *next* in-progress .ASM source code file. Little by little you construct your application program out of the modules you build one at a time.

A very important bonus is that some of the procedures in an .OBJ module may be used in a future assembly language program that hasn't even been begun yet. Creating such libraries of toolkit procedures can be an extraordinarily effective way to save time by reusing code over and over again, without even passing it through the assembler again!

Something to keep in mind is that the linker must be used even when you have only *one* .OBJ file. Connecting multiple modules is only one of many essential things the linker does. To produce an .EXE file, you *must* invoke the linker, even if your program is a little thing contained in only one .ASM and hence one .OBJ file.

Invoking the linker is again done from the DOS command line. Each assembler typically has its own linker. MASM's linker is called LINK, and TASM's is called TLINK. Like the assembler, the linker understands a suite of commands and directives that I can't describe exhaustively here. Read your assembler manuals carefully.

For single-module programs, however, there's nothing complex to be done. Linking our hypothetical FOO.OBJ object file into an .EXE file using TLINK is done by entering C:\ASM>TLINK FOO at the DOS prompt.

If you're using MASM, using LINK is done much the same way. Again, as with MASM, you need to place a semicolon at the end of the command to avoid a series of questions about various linker defaults (for example, C:\ASM>LINK FOO;).

Linking multiple files involves naming each file on the command line. With TLINK, you simply name each .OBJ file on the command line after the word TLINK, with a space between each filename. You do *not* have to include the .OBJ extension—TLINK assumes that all modules to be linked end in .OBJ:

```
C:\ASM>TLINK FOO BAR BAS
```

Under MASM, you do the same thing, except that you place a plus sign (+) between each of the .OBJ filenames:

```
C:\ASM>LINK FOO+BAR+BAS
```

In both cases, the name of the .EXE file produced will be the name of the first .OBJ file named, with the .EXE extension replacing the .OBJ extension.

Linker Errors

As with the assembler, the linker may discover problems as it weaves multiple .OBJ files together into a single .EXE file. Linker errors are subtler than assembler errors and are usually harder to find. Fortunately, they are rarer and not as easy to make.

As with assembler errors, when you are presented with a linker error you have to return to the editor and figure out what the problem is. Once you've identified the problem (or *think* you have) and changed something in the source code file to fix the problem, you must reassemble and relink the program to see if the linker error went away. Until it does, you have to loop back to the editor, try something else, and assemble/link once more.

If possible, avoid doing this by trial and error. Read your assembler and linker manuals. Understand what you're doing. The more you understand about what's going on within the assembler and the linker, the easier it will be to determine who or what is giving the linker fits.

Testing the .EXE File

If you receive no linker errors, the linker will create and fill a single .EXE file with the machine instructions present in all of the .OBJ files named on the linker command line. The .EXE file is your executable program. You can run it by simply naming it on the DOS command line and pressing Enter:

```
C:\ASM>FOO
```

When you invoke your program in this way, one of two things will happen: the program will work as you intended it to, or you'll be confronted with the effects of one or more program *bugs*. A bug is anything in a program that doesn't work the way you want it to. This makes a bug somewhat more subjective than an error. One person might think red characters displayed on a blue background is a bug, while another might consider it a clever New Age feature and be quite pleased. Settling bug vs. feature conflicts like this is up to you. Consensus is called for here, with fistfights only as a last resort.

There are bugs and there are bugs. When working in assembly language, it's *quite* common for a bug to completely "blow the machine away," which is less violent than some think. A *system crash* is what you call it when the machine sits there mutely, and will not respond to the keyboard. You may have to press Ctrl+Alt+Delete to reboot the system, or (worse) have to press the reset button, or even power down and then power up again. Be ready for this—it *will* happen to you, sooner and oftener than you will care for.

Figure 3.5 announces the exit of the assembly language development process as happening when your program *works perfectly*. A very serious question is this: How do you know when it works perfectly? Simple programs assembled while learning the language may be easy enough to test in a minute or two. But any program that accomplishes anything useful will take *hours* of testing at *minimum*. A serious and ambitious application could take weeks—or months—to test thoroughly. A program that takes various kinds of input values and produces various kinds of output should be tested with as many different combinations of input values as possible, and you should examine every possible output every time.

Even so, finding every last bug is considered by some to be an impossible ideal. Perhaps—but you should strive to come as close as possible, in as efficient a fashion as you can manage. I'll have a lot more to say about bugs and debugging throughout the rest of this book.

Errors Versus Bugs

In the interest of keeping the Babel-effect at bay, I think it's important to carefully draw the distinction between errors and bugs. An *error* is something wrong with your source code file that either the assembler or the linker kick out as unacceptable. An error prevents the assembly or link process from going to completion, and will thus prevent a final .EXE file from being produced.

A *bug*, by contrast, is a problem discovered during *execution* of a program under DOS. Bugs are not detected by either the assembler or the linker. Bugs can be benign, such as a misspelled word in a screen message or a line positioned on the wrong screen row; or a bug can make your DOS session run off into the bushes and not come back.

Both errors and bugs require that you go back to the text editor and change something in your source code file. The difference here is that most errors are reported with a line number telling you where to go in your source code file to fix the problem. Bugs, on the other hand, are left as an exercise for the student. You have to hunt them down, and neither the assembler nor the linker will give you much in the line of clues.

Debuggers and Debugging

The final, and almost certainly the most painful part of the assembly language development process is *debugging*. Debugging is simply the systematic process by which bugs are located and corrected. A *debugger* is a utility program designed specifically to help you locate and identify bugs.

Debugger programs are among the most mysterious and difficult to understand of all programs. Debuggers are part X-ray machine and part magnifying glass. A debugger loads into memory *with* your program and remains in memory, side by side with your program. The debugger then puts tendrils down into both DOS and into your program, and enables some truly peculiar things to be done.

One of the problems with debugging computer programs is that they operate so quickly. Thousands of machine instructions can be executed in a single second, and if one of those instructions isn't quite right, it's long gone before you can identify which one it is by staring at the screen. A debugger allows you to execute the machine instructions in a program *one at a time*, allowing you to pause indefinitely between each one to examine the effects of the last instruction on the screen. The debugger also lets you look at the contents of any location in memory, and the values stored in any register, during that pause between instructions.

As mentioned previously, both MASM and TASM are packaged with their own advanced debuggers. MASM's CodeView and TASM's Turbo Debugger are brutally powerful (and hellishly complicated) creatures that require manuals considerably thicker than this book. For this reason, I won't try to explain how to use either CodeView or Turbo Debugger.

Very fortunately, every copy of DOS is shipped with a more limited but perfectly good debugger called DEBUG. DEBUG can do nearly anything that a beginner would want from a debugger, and in this book we'll do our debugging with DEBUG.

3.5 DEBUG and How to Use It

The assembler and the linker are rather single-minded programs. As translators, they do only one thing: translate. This involves reading data from one file and writing a translation of that data into another file.

That's all a translator needs to do. The job isn't necessarily an easy thing for the translator to do, but it's easy to describe and understand. Debuggers, by contrast, are like the electrician's little bag of tools—they do lots of different things in a great many different ways, and take plenty of explanation and considerable practice to master.

In this chapter I'll introduce you to DEBUG, a program that will allow you to *single step* your assembly language programs and examine their and the machine's innards between each and every machine instruction. This section is only an introduction—DEBUG is learned best by doing, and you'll be both using and learning DEBUG's numerous powers all through the rest of this book. By providing you with an overview of what DEBUG does here, you'll be more capable of integrating its features into your general understanding of assembly language development process as we examine it through the rest of the book.

DEBUG's Bag of Tricks

It's well worth taking a page or so simply to describe what sorts of things DEBUG can do before actually showing you how they're done. It's actually quite a list:

- **Display or change memory and files**. Your programs will both exist in and affect memory, and DEBUG can show you *any* part of memory—which implies that it can show you any part of any program or binary file as well. DEBUG displays memory as a series of hexadecimal values, with a corresponding display of any printable ASCII characters to the right of the values. We'll show you some examples a little later on. In addition to seeing the contents of memory, you can change those contents as well. And, if the contents of memory represent a file, you can write the changed file back out to disk.

- **Display or change the contents of all CPU registers**. CPU registers allow you to work *very* quickly, and you should use them as much as you can. You need to see what's going on in the registers while you use them, and with one command, DEBUG can display the contents of all machine registers and flags at one time. If you want to change the contents of a register while stepping through a program's machine instructions, you can do that as well.

- **Fill a region of memory with a single value**. If you have an area of memory that you want "blanked out," DEBUG will allow you to fill that area of memory with any character or binary value.

- **Search memory for sequences of binary values**. You can search any area of memory for a specific sequence of characters or binary value, including names stored in memory or sequences of machine instructions. You can then examine or change something that you know exists somewhere in memory but not *where*.

- **Assemble new machine instructions into memory**. DEBUG contains a simple assembler that does much of what MASM and TASM can do—one machine instruction at a time. If you want to replace a machine instruction somewhere within your program, you can type **MOV AX,BX** rather than having to look up and type 8BH 0C3H.

- **"Un-assemble" binary machine instructions into their mnemonics and operands**. The flipside of the last feature is also possible: DEBUG can take the two hexadecimal values 8BH and 0C3H and tell you that they represent the assembly language mnemonic **MOV AX,BX**. This feature is utterly essential when you need to trace a program in operation and understand what is happening when the next two bytes in memory are read into the CPU and executed. If you don't know what machine instruction those two bytes represent, you'll be totally lost.

- **Single step a program under test**. Finally, DEBUG's most valuable skill is to run a program one machine instruction at a time, pausing between each instruction. During this pause you can look at or change memory, look at or change registers, search for things in memory, "patch" the program by replacing existing machine instructions with new ones, and so on. This is what you'll do most of the time with DEBUG.

Taking DEBUG for a Spin

DEBUG can be a pretty forbidding character, terse to the point of being mute. You'll be spending a lot of time standing on DEBUG's shoulders and looking around, however, so you'd best get used to him now.

The easiest way to start is to use DEBUG to load a file into memory and examine it. On the listings disk associated with this book is a file called SAM.TXT. It's an ordinary DOS text file. (Its contents were used to demonstrate the line structuring of text files with CR and LF in Figure 3.1.) If you don't have the listings disk, you can simply load your text editor and enter the following lines:

```
Sam
was
a
man.
```

Make sure you press Enter after the period at the end of "man." Then save the file to disk as SAM.TXT.

Let's lay SAM out on DEBUG's dissection table and take a look at his innards. DEBUG will load itself and the file of your choice into memory at the same time, with only one command. Type DEBUG followed by the name of the file you want to load, as in the following example:

```
C:\ASM>DEBUG SAM.TXT
```

Make sure you use the full filename. Some programs like MASM and TASM will allow you to use only the first part of the filename and assume a file extension like .ASM, but DEBUG requires the full filename.

Like old Cal Coolidge, DEBUG doesn't say much, and never more than he has to. Unless DEBUG can't find SAM.TXT, all it will respond with is a single dash character (-) as its prompt, indicating that all is well and that DEBUG is awaiting a command.

Looking at a Hex Dump

Looking at SAM.TXT's interior is easy. Just type a D at the dash prompt. (Think dump.) DEBUG will obediently display a hex dump of the first 128 bytes of memory containing the contents of SAM.TXT read from disk. The hexadecimal numbers will probably look bewilderingly mysterious, but to their right you'll see the comforting words "Sam was a man" in a separate area of the screen. To help a little, I've taken the hex dump of SAM.TXT as you'll see it on your screen and annotated it in Figure 3.6.

This is a *hex dump*. It has three parts: the leftmost part on the screen is the address of the start of each line of the dump. Each line contains 16 bytes. An address has two parts, and you'll notice that the left part of the address does not change while the right part is 16 greater at the start of each succeeding line. The 86-family CPU's two-part addresses are a source of considerable confusion and aggravation, and I'll take them up in detail in Chapter 5. For now, ignore the unchanging part of the address and consider the part that changes to be a count of the bytes on display, starting with 100H.

The part to the right of the address is the hexadecimal representation of the 128 bytes of memory being displayed. The part to the right of the hexadecimal values are those same 128 bytes of memory displayed as ASCII characters. Now, not all binary values have corresponding printable ASCII characters. Any invisible or unprintable characters are shown as period (.) characters.

This can be confusing. The last displayable character in SAM.TXT *is* a period, and is actually the very first character on the second line of the hex dump. The ASCII side shows four identical periods in a row. To find out what's a period and what's simply a nondisplayable character, you must look back to the hexadecimal side and recognize the ASCII code for a period, which is 2EH.

Figure 3.6. Hex dump of SAM.TXT

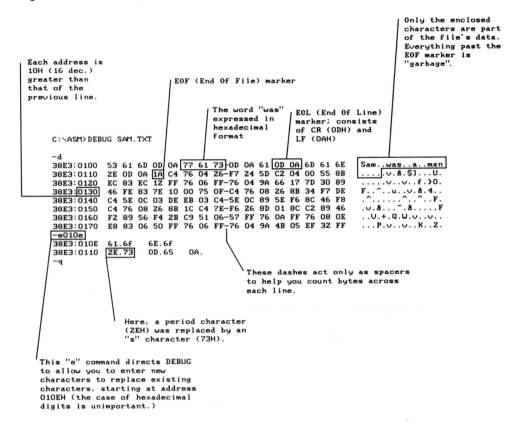

Here is a good place to point out that an ASCII table of characters and their codes is an utterly essential thing to have. Borland's Sidekick product includes a very good table, and it's always waiting in memory only a keystroke away. If you don't have Sidekick, I'd advise you to take a photocopy of the ASCII table provided in Appendix B and keep it close at hand.

Memory "Garbage"

Take a long, close look at the hexadecimal equivalents of the characters in SAM.TXT. Notice that SAM.TXT is a very short file (20 bytes), but that 128 bytes are displayed. Look for the EOF (end of file) marker on the second line.

Character 1AH is always considered the last byte of any text file. All the other bytes after the EOF marker are called "garbage," and that's pretty much what they are: random bytes that existed in memory before SAM.TXT rode in from disk. DEBUG works only from memory, and displays hex dumps of memory in 128-byte chunks by default. (You can direct DEBUG to display more bytes at a time by using some additional commands, which I won't go into here.) Only the first 20 bytes of SAM.TXT are significant information, but DEBUG obligingly shows you what's in memory well beyond the end of SAM's data.

The bytes are probably not entirely random, but instead may be part of the code or data left over from the last program to be loaded and executed in that area of memory. Because the garbage bytes fall after the EOF marker, you can safely ignore them, but should know just what they are and why they appear in your hex dump. You might occasionally see recognizable data strings from other programs in memory garbage and wonder how they got into your current program. *They didn't get into your current program.* They were just there, and now show through beyond the end of the file you last loaded under DEBUG. Knowing where legitimate information ends and where garbage begins is always important, and not usually as clear-cut as it is here.

Changing Memory with DEBUG

DEBUG can easily change bytes in memory, whether they are part of a file loaded from disk or not. The DEBUG command to change bytes is the E command. (Think enter new data.) You can use the E command to change some of the data in SAM.TXT. Part of this process is shown in Figure 3.6.

Notice the following command line:

```
-e 010e
```

To taciturn Mr. Debug, this means, "Begin accepting entered bytes at address 010EH." I show the lower case e's used in the command to put across the point that DEBUG is not case sensitive, *even for letters used as hexadecimal digits.* In other words, there is nothing sacred about using uppercase A through E for hex digits. They can be lowercase or uppercase as you choose, and you don't even have to be consistent about it.

What DEBUG does in response to the E command shown in Figure 3.6 is display the following prompt:

```
38E3:010E  61.
```

The cursor waits after the period for your input. What DEBUG has done is shown you what value is *already* at address 010EH, so that you can decide whether you want to change it. If not, just press Enter, and the dash prompt will return.

Otherwise, enter a hexadecimal value to take the place of value 61H. In Figure 3.6 I entered 6FH. Once you enter a replacement value, you have the choice of completing your change by pressing Enter and returning to the dash prompt; or changing the byte at the *next* address. If a change is your choice, press the spacebar instead of pressing Enter. DEBUG will display the byte at the next highest address and wait for your replacement value, just as it did the first time.

This is shown in Figure 3.6. In fact, Figure 3.6 shows *four* successive replacements of bytes starting at address 010EH. Notice the lonely hex byte 0A followed by a period. What happened there is that I pressed Enter *without* typing a replacement byte, ending the E command and returning to the dash prompt.

You'll also note that the next command typed at the dash prompt was "q", for Quit. Typing Q at the dash prompt will return you immediately to DOS.

The Dangers of Modifying Files

Keep in mind that what I've just demonstrated was not changing a *file*, but simply changing the contents of a file loaded into memory. A file loaded into memory through DEBUG as we did with SAM.TXT is called a *memory image* of that file. *Only the memory image of the file was changed.* SAM.TXT remains on disk, unchanged and unaware of what was happening to its doppelganger in memory.

You can save the altered memory image of SAM.TXT back to disk with a simple command: type W and then press Enter. (Think *write*.) DEBUG remembers how many bytes it read in from disk, and it writes those bytes back out again. It provides a tally as it writes:

```
Writing 0014 bytes
```

The figure is given in hex, even though DEBUG does not do us the courtesy of displaying an H after the number. 14H is 20 decimal, and there are exactly 20 bytes in SAM.TXT, counting the EOF marker. DEBUG writes out *only* the significant information in the file. It does not write out anything that it didn't load in, *unless* you explicitly command DEBUG to write out additional bytes beyond the end of what was originally read.

If you haven't already figured out what was done to poor SAM.TXT, you can dump it again and take a look. If you simply press D for another dump, however, you're in for a surprise: the new dump does not contain any trace of SAM.TXT at all. (Try it!) If you're sharp you'll notice that the address of the first line is not what it was originally, but instead is this:

```
38E3:0180
```

(The first four digits will be different on your system, but that's all right—look at the second four digits instead during this discussion.) If you know your hex, you'll see that this is the address of the *next* eight lines of dumped memory, starting immediately after where the first dump left off.

The D command works that way. Each time you press D, you get the *next* 128 bytes of memory, starting with 0100H. To see SAM.TXT again, you need to specify the starting address of the dump, which was 0100H:

```
-d 0100
```

Enter that command, and you'll see the following dump with the altered memory image of SAM.TXT:

```
38E3:0100  53 61 6D 0D 0A 77 61 73-0D 0A 61 0D 0A 6D 6F 6F   Sam..was..a..moo
38E3:0110  73 65 0A 1A C4 76 04 26-F7 24 5D C2 04 00 55 8B   se...v.&.$]...U.
38E3:0120  EC 83 EC 12 FF 76 06 FF-76 04 9A 66 17 7D 30 89   .....v..v..f.}0.
38E3:0130  46 FE 83 7E 10 00 75 0F-C4 76 08 26 8B 34 F7 DE   F..~..u..v.&.4..
38E3:0140  C4 5E 0C 03 DE EB 03 C4-5E 0C 89 5E F6 8C 46 F8   .^......^..^..F.
38E3:0150  C4 76 08 26 8B 1C C4 7E-F6 26 8D 01 8C C2 89 46   .v.&...~.&.....F
38E3:0160  F2 89 56 F4 2B C9 51 06-57 FF 76 0A FF 76 08 0E   ..V.+.Q.W.v..v..
38E3:0170  E8 83 06 50 FF 76 06 FF-76 04 9A 4B 05 EF 32 FF   ...P.v..v..K..2.
```

Sam, as you can see, is now something else again entirely.

Now, something went a little bit wrong when you changed Sam from a man to a moose. Look closely at memory starting at address 0111H. After the "e" (65H) is *half* of an EOL marker. The carriage return character (0DH) is gone, because you wrote an "e" over it. Only the line feed character (0AH) remains.

This isn't fatal, but it isn't right. A lonely line feed can cause trouble or not, depending on what you try to do with it. If you load the altered SAM.TXT into the JED editor, you'll see a ghostly "J" after the word "moose." This is how JED indicates certain invisible characters that are not EOL or EOF markers, as I'll explain in the next chapter, which describes JED in detail. The J tells you an LF character is present at that point in the file.

The lesson here is that DEBUG is a gun without a safety catch. There are no safeguards. You can change *anything* inside a file with it, whether it makes sense or not, or whether it's dangerous or not. All safety considerations are up to you. You must be aware of whether or not you're overwriting important parts of the file.

This is a theme that will occur again and again in assembly language: *safety is up to you.* Unlike BASIC, which wraps a protective cocoon around you and keeps you from banging yourself up too badly, assembly language lets you hang yourself without a whimper of protest.

Keep this in mind as we continue.

Examining and Changing Registers

If you saved SAM.TXT back out to disk in its altered state, you created a damaged file. Fixing SAM.TXT requires reconstructing the last EOL marker by inserting the CR character that you overwrote using the E command. Unfortunately, this means you'll be making SAM.TXT larger than it was when DEBUG read it into memory. To save the corrected file back out to disk, we need to somehow tell DEBUG that it needs to save more than 14H bytes out to disk. To do this we need to look at and change a value in one of the CPU registers.

Registers, if you recall, are special-purpose memory cubbyholes that exist inside the CPU chip itself, rather than in memory chips outside the CPU. DEBUG has a command that allows us to examine and change register values as easily as we examined and changed memory.

At the dash prompt, type R. (Think registers.) You'll see a display like this:

```
-r
AX=0000  BX=0000  CX=0014  DX=0000  SP=FFEE  BP=0000  SI=0000  DI=0000
DS=1980  ES=1980  SS=1980  CS=1980  IP=0100    NV UP EI PL NZ NA PO NC
1980:0100 53          PUSH  BX
```

The bulk of the display consists of register names followed by equal signs, followed by the current values of the registers. The cryptic characters NV UP EI PL NZ NA PO NC are the names of *flags*, and we'll discuss them later in the book.

The line beneath the register and flag summaries is a *disassembly* of the byte at the address contained by the *instruction pointer.* (The instruction pointer is a register which is displayed by the DEBUG R command, under the shorter name IP. Find IP's value in the register display above—it should be 0100H, which is also the address of the "S" in "Sam".) This line will be useful when you are actually examining an executable program file in memory. In the case of SAM.TXT the disassembly line is misleading, because SAM is *not* an executable program and contains nothing we intend to be used as machine instructions.

The hexadecimal value 53H, however, *is* a legal machine instruction as well as the ASCII code for uppercase "S". DEBUG doesn't know what kind of file SAM.TXT is. SAM could as well be a program file as a text file; DEBUG makes no assumptions based on the file's contents or its file extension. DEBUG examines memory at the current address and displays it as though it were a machine instruction. If memory contains data instead of machine instructions, the disassembly line should be ignored.

This is once again an example of the problems you can have in assembly language if you don't know exactly what you're doing. Code and data look the same in memory. They are only different in how you interpret them. In SAM.TXT, the hex value 53H is the letter "S"; in an executable program file 53H would be the instruction **PUSH BX**. We'll be making good use of the disassembly line later on in the book, when we get down to examining real assembly language programs. For now, just ignore it.

When DEBUG loads a file from disk, it places the number of bytes in the file in the CX register. CX is a general-purpose register, but it is often used to contain such count values, and is therefore sometimes called the *count register*.

Notice that the value of CX is 14H—just the number DEBUG reported when it wrote the altered SAM.TXT out to disk in response to the W command. If we change the value in CX, we change the number of bytes DEBUG will write to disk.

So let's fix SAM.TXT. In changing the word "man" to "moose" we wrote over two characters: the period at the end of the sentence and the CR character portion of the last line's EOL marker. We could start at address 0112H and enter a period character (2EH—use your ASCII table!) followed by a CR character (0DH). In doing so, however, we would overwrite the LF character and the EOF marker character, which is just as bad or worse.

Unlike a text editor, DEBUG will not just "shove over" the values to the right of the point where you wish to insert new values. DEBUG has no insert mode. You have to enter all four characters: the period, the CR, the LF, and the EOF.

Use the E command to enter them, and then display a dump of the file again:

```
-e 0112
1980:0112  0D.2e   0A.0d   1A.0a   0D.1a
```

CR ⇒ 0DH
LF ⇒ 0AH
EOF ⇒ 1AH

```
-d 0100
38E3:0100  53 61 6D 0D 0A 77 61 73-0D 0A 61 0D 0A 6D 6F 6F   Sam..was..a..moo
38E3:0110  73 65 2E 0D 0A 1A 04 26-F7 24 5D C2 04 00 55 8B   se.....&.$]...U.
38E3:0120  EC 83 EC 12 FF 76 06 FF-76 04 9A 66 17 7D 30 89   .....v..v..f.}0.
38E3:0130  46 FE 83 7E 10 00 75 0F-C4 76 08 26 8B 34 F7 DE   F..~..u..v.&.4..
38E3:0140  C4 5E 0C 03 DE EB 03 C4-5E 0C 89 5E F6 8C 46 F8   .^......^..^..F.
38E3:0150  C4 76 08 26 8B 1C C4 7E-F6 26 8D 01 8C C2 89 46   .v.&...~.&.....F
38E3:0160  F2 89 56 F4 2B C9 51 06-57 FF 76 0A FF 76 08 0E   ..V.+.Q.W.v..v..
38E3:0170  E8 83 06 50 FF 76 06 FF-76 04 9A 4B 05 EF 32 FF   ...P.v..v..K..2.
```

Now the file is repaired, and we can write it back to disk. Except—SAM.TXT in memory is now two bytes longer than SAM.TXT on disk. We need to tell DEBUG that it needs to write two additional bytes to disk when it writes SAM.TXT back out.

DEBUG keeps its count of SAM's length in the BX and CX registers. The count is actually a 32-bit number split between the two 16-bit registers BX and CX, with BX containing the high half of the 32-bit number. This allows us to load very large files into DEBUG, with byte counts that cannot fit into a single 16-bit register like CX. 16-bit registers can only contain values up to 65,535. If we wanted to use DEBUG on an 80,000 byte file (which is not all that big, as files go) we'd be out of luck if DEBUG only kept a 16-bit count of the file size in a single register.

But for small changes to files, or for working with small files, we only have to be aware of and work with the count in CX. Adding 2 to the byte count only changes the low half of the number, contained in CX. Changing the value of CX is done with the R command, by specifying CX after R:

```
-r cx
```

DEBUG responds by displaying the name "CX," its current value, and a colon prompt on the next line:

```
CX 0014
:
```

To add 2 to the value of CX, enter 0016 at the prompt, then press Enter. DEBUG simply returns the dash prompt—remember, it's a utility of few words.

Now, however, when you enter a W command to write SAM.TXT back to disk, DEBUG displays this message:

```
Writing 0016 bytes
```

The new, longer SAM.TXT has been written to disk in its entirety. Problem solved.

One final note on saving files back out to disk from DEBUG: if you change the values in either BX or CX to reflect something other than the true length of the file, and then execute a W command to write the file to disk, DEBUG will write as many bytes to disk as are specified in BX and CX. This could be 20,000 bytes more than the file contains, or it could be 0 bytes, leaving you with an empty file. You can destroy a file this way. Either leave BX and CX alone while you're examining and "patching" a file with DEBUG, or write the initial values in BX and CX down, and enter them back into BX and CX just before issuing the W command.

The Hacker's Best Friend

There is a *great* deal more to be said about DEBUG, but most of it involves concepts we haven't yet covered. DEBUG is the single most useful tool you have as an assembly-language programmer, and I'll be teaching you more of its features as we get deeper and deeper into the programming process itself.

The next chapter describes JED, a simple program editor and development environment I created for people who have not purchased a commercial editor product like Brief or Epsilon. If you do not intend to use JED, you can skip Chapter 4 and meet us on the other side in Chapter 5, where we begin our long trek through the 86-family instruction set.

4

Learning and Using Jed

A Programming Environment
for Assembly Language

99

4.1 A Place to Stand with Access to Tools

"Give me a lever long enough, and a place to stand, and I will move the Earth."

Archimedes was speaking literally about the power of the lever, but behind his words there is a larger truth about work in general: To get something done, you need a place to work, with access to tools. My radio bench in the garage is set up that way: A large, flat space to lay ailing transmitters down, and a shelf above where my oscilloscope, VTVM, frequency counter, signal generator, and dip meter are within easy reach.

Much of the astonishing early success of Turbo Pascal was grounded in that truth. For the first time, a compiler vendor gathered up the most important tools of software development and put them together in an intuitive fashion so that the various tasks involved in creating software flowed easily from one step to the next. From a menu that was your place to stand, you pressed one key, and your Pascal program was compiled. You pressed another one, and the program was run. It was simple, fast, and easy to learn. Turbo Pascal literally took Pascal from a backwater language favored by academics to the most popular compiled language in history, BASIC not excluded.

What Borland so boldly introduced in 1983 was adopted (reluctantly at times) by their major competitor, Microsoft. Today, Turbo Pascal, Turbo C, Turbo BASIC, Turbo Prolog, Quick C, and Quick BASIC are what we call *integrated development environments*. They provide well-designed menus to give you that place to stand, and a multitude of tools that are only one or two keystrokes away.

A little remarkably, there is no true equivalent to Turbo Pascal in the assembly-language field. Neither MASM nor Borland's own Turbo Assembler have that same comfortable place to stand. The reasons for this may seem peculiar to you, the beginner: seasoned assembly-language programmers either create their own development environments (they are, after all, the programming elite) or they simply work from the naked DOS prompt. The appeal of a Turbo Pascal-type environment is not so strong to them as it is to you. An integrated development environment for MASM and TASM may happen in time, but you must understand that both Microsoft and Borland are catering to their most important audience, the established assembly-language programmer.

That doesn't do much good for you. One glance back at Figure 3.5 can give you the screaming willies. Assembly-language development not a simple process, and grabbing all the tools from the DOS prompt is complicated and error prone; rather like standing on a ball-bearing bar stool to get the shot glasses down from the high shelf over the bar.

So, to make things a little easier for you, I've created a program called JED. JED is a beginner's development environment for either MASM or TASM. It's nowhere near as powerful as the environments provided with the Turbo or Quick languages, but it's powerful enough to get you started on the long road toward assembly-language proficiency.

Laying Hands on JED

JED.EXE is written in Turbo Pascal 5.0. You can get a copy from many of the larger user groups around the country. Perhaps your friends have a copy; ask around. I've allowed people to copy it freely in the hopes that it will be widely used. If you can't find it anywhere, you can order the listings diskette from me through the coupon on the flyleaf. Both source code and .EXE versions of JED are included on the listings diskette. You don't need Turbo Pascal to run JED.EXE. It's fully compiled and ready to run.

I must emphasize that not quite all of the source code for JED is on the listings diskette. JED contains a powerful text editor provided with Borland's Turbo Pascal Editor Toolbox. You can get JED's source code from the listings diskette, but keep in mind that it's not all there; you *must* buy the Turbo Pascal Editor Toolbox *and* own Turbo Pascal 5.0 in order to compile or modify JED.

I need to emphasize right now that you don't *need* to have JED to work with assembly language, or to use this book. JED smoothes access to your tools like TASM and TLINK, and provides a very good text editor to boot, but you can work very well from the DOS prompt using some other text editor. I'll be referencing JED as I discuss the assembly language *process* in this book; there are a multitude of ways to work with assembly language and I have to settle on something. But the information on assembly language itself is independent of the text editor and programming environment you may choose to use.

4.2 JED's Place to Stand

Like Turbo Pascal and the other integrated development environments from both Borland and Microsoft, JED's most visible part is a text editor. If you'll look back once again to Figure 3.5, you'll see that all roads seem to lead back to the text editor in good time. In general, you do most of your *thinking* while staring at the text editor screen, so it seems a logical location to put your place to stand.

Running JED is easy. The first time you want to work on a particular source code file, you type the name JED followed by the name of the source code file:

```
C:\ASM>JED EAT2.ASM
```

(Here, EAT2.ASM is the name of a source code file described a little later in this book.) DOS will load and run JED, and then JED will load the text file EAT2.ASM into its editor workspace. You'll get a view like that shown in Figure 4.1.

The Status Line

Apart from the very top line, everything on the edit screen is a display of your text file. This top line, the *status line*, contains several important items of information about the file that JED is displaying in the edit screen, which is

Figure 4.1. JED's Edit screen

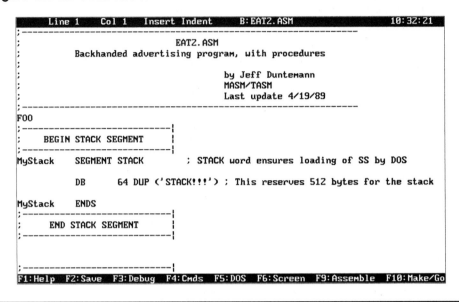

```
 Line 1    Col 1    Insert Indent     B:EAT2.ASM                 10:32:21
;----------------------------------------------------------------------
;                           EAT2.ASM
;           Backhanded advertising program, with procedures
;
;                              by Jeff Duntemann
;                              MASM/TASM
;                              Last update 4/19/89
;----------------------------------------------------------------------
FOO
;----------------------------------;
;    BEGIN STACK SEGMENT           !
;----------------------------------!
MyStack    SEGMENT STACK         ; STACK word ensures loading of SS by DOS

           DB        64 DUP ('STACK!!!') ; This reserves 512 bytes for the stack

MyStack    ENDS
;----------------------------------!
;    END STACK SEGMENT             !
;----------------------------------!


;----------------------------------!
F1:Help  F2:Save  F3:Debug  F4:Cmds  F5:DOS  F6:Screen  F9:Assemble  F10:Make/Go
```

called the *current file*. The first two items tell you the position of the cursor in terms of line number and column number. In case you're unfamiliar with such things, the line numbers run from top to bottom with line 1 at the top, and column numbers run from left to right, with column 1 at the left margin. As you move the cursor around the file using the cursor-control keys (see Section 4.4) the cursor position will be updated in the status line.

The word Insert will display in the status line if JED's editor is in insert mode. Insert mode indicates that characters typed at the keyboard will be inserted at the cursor position, pushing ahead the characters to the right of the cursor position. When the word Insert is *not* present, JED's editor is in *overwrite mode*. Overwrite mode indicates that characters typed at the cursor position will *replace* or overwrite characters that already exist on the screen, and that those underlying characters will be lost. I'll say more on this item later in this chapter.

Similarly, the word Indent indicates that the editor is in *indent mode*. In indent mode, indenting one line by spacing over from the left margin will cause subsequent lines to automatically indent to the same number of spaces from the margin. Again, more on this later in this chapter.

The name of the current file also displays in the status line. Finally, the current time according to DOS's clock, is shown in the upper-right hand corner of the screen.

The Prompt Bar

At the bottom of the screen, highlighted in blue (if you have a color monitor) is a single line bar that summarizes most of JED's important commands. This bar is called the *prompt bar.* It provides always-visible reminders as to which tools are available while you are standing at JED's Edit screen. Each tool is invoked by pressing one of the PC's ten function keys.

Eight of the ten function keys are summarized in the prompt bar. The two that are not present, F7 and F8, are actually text editing commands, and will be discussed along with all of the other editing commands in Section 4.4.

JED's Help Screen

Perhaps the single most important command to remember while you're still a beginner is the Help command, F1. Pressing F1 instantly brings up a 24-line help display of all its commands and most of the text editing commands. If you ever forget a command or are unsure of what one of the prompt bar reminders means (like F4:Cmds, which is something less than obvious) simply press F1 and read the available information. JED's Help screen is shown in Figure 4.2.

Once the Help screen is displayed, you can put it away and return to the Edit screen by pressing any *non-shift* key. (That is, any key but the Shift, Ctrl, or Alt keys.)

Figure 4.2. JED's Help screen

```
Version 1.0 -- Released 1/8/89  --  ALT-X EXITS!

(c) 1988, 1989  Jeff Duntemann -- ALL RIGHTS RESERVED

───────────────────────── COMMAND SET ─────────────────────────
F1:  Display this screen            ^KD: Quit and save file
F2:  Save current source code file  ^KQ: Quit without saving
F3:  Invoke DEBUG on current .EXE file ^KW: Write marked block to disk
F4:  Update assemble/link command lines ^KR: Read a file to cursor position
F5:  Shell out to DOS               ^KH: Hide/unhide the marked block
F6:  Show last assemble/link screen ^KY: Delete marked block
F7:  Mark beginning of block        ^KV: Move marked block
F8:  Mark end of block              ^KC: Copy marked block
F9:  Assemble only                  ^QL: Undo changes to line
F10: Assemble/link (if needed) and Go! Alt-F: Change current source code file

^QR: Move to start of file    ^Y: Delete line   ^T: Delete word  ^QY: Del. to EOL
^QC: Move to end of file      ^QF: Find  ^QA: Find/Replace  ^L: Find/repl. again
^A:  Move 1 word left         Options: N: Without asking  W: Whole words only
^F:  Move 1 word right            G: Global  U: Ignore case  B: Backwards

    <<REMEMBER!!>> If your .ASM file is not a standalone program, but a device
    driver or a library of procedures, pressing F10 may lock up your system!!
```

4.3 Using JED's Tools

The very best way to explain JED's commands and how they are used is to run through a simple JED session with a real assembly language program and explain what happens as we go. The program we'll use is EAT2.ASM, which is shown in chapter X.X. EAT2.ASM is not much of a program, but gets you started in understanding the internal mechanisms of a real, working assembly-language program. When you run EAT2.EXE from the DOS prompt, this simple message displays on your screen:

```
Eat at Joe's...
...ten million flies can't ALL be wrong!
```

After it displays those two lines, this program ends and returns control to DOS.

EAT2.ASM is the source-code file from which the executable program file EAT2.EXE is assembled and linked. EAT2.ASM is present on the disk with JED. If you have somehow obtained JED without the rest of the example files from this book, you can type EAT2.ASM into JED after running JED.

If you, as I suggested earlier, created a subdirectory on your hard disk called ASM, copy all of the files on the JED disk into subdirectory ASM. In order for JED to operate correctly, the following files must be present in the subdirectory with JED:

- **Your assembler**. This can be any command-line oriented assembler, but will typically be either MASM.EXE or TASM.EXE.

- **Your assembler's linker**. Assemblers are usually shipped with their own linker. This is certainly true of MASM and TASM. Some assemblers may not use their own linker, but will use the DOS linker, LINK.EXE, instead.

- **The DOS debugger, DEBUG.COM**. Some versions of DOS are no longer shipped with DEBUG, which is offered as part of an additional utilities disk. Prior to DOS 3.2, all versions have DEBUG.COM. If you don't have DEBUG.COM, you will find it slow going, since nearly all of the debugging skills I'll be teaching in this book center on DEBUG.COM.

Of course, other files can be present without any hindrance to your work.

Invoking JED

Make the current directory your working assembly-language subdirectory, which I have suggested you call ASM. From the DOS prompt, invoke JED and load EAT2.ASM

```
C:\ASM>JED EAT2
```

Notice that you don't have to type the .ASM extension at the end of the filename. JED has a *default file extension* of .ASM. In other words, if you don't enter a file extension, JED will append the file extension .ASM on the end of the name you enter on the command line. (You can also enter the full filename including extension.) In either case, JED will consider the name of the current file to be EAT2.ASM.

Now, either EAT2.ASM exists on your disk or it doesn't. JED won't mind if the file doesn't exist—new files have to start somewhere! If JED can't find the file you entered on the command line, it will display the words "New file" in the upper-left corner of the Edit screen and create an empty text file on your hard disk. When you type text into the Edit screen, JED will save the text into that new file.

The file may well exist on disk, and if it does, JED will load the file into the editor screen and display it for you. Assuming you entered the name EAT2, the screen should look almost identical to that shown in Figure 4.1.

You might wonder what will happen if you simply type JED at the DOS command line without specifying filename. One of two things will happen:

- JED will load the file that you last worked on from within JED. JED keeps a record of this file in a small file named JED.CFG. If it can find JED.CFG, and if the file named in JED.CFG is in current subdirectory, JED will load that file. JED updates JED.CFG automatically.

- If there is no JED.CFG on your disk, JED will create a file imaginatively named NONAME.ASM and store your text into a new file with that name. NONAME.ASM is a pretty rank name for any assembly-language program, so you might as well think of a better name and enter that when invoking JED.

JED's ability to remember the name of the last file you worked on makes it unnecessary for *you* to remember what project you were in the middle of when you pulled the plug and went to bed. Furthermore, JED also remembers the cursor position when you saved your file and exited from JED.

Moving around the Edit Screen

Your place to stand is JED's text editor, and when nothing else is going on (like assembling, linking, debugging, or running your program) you'll be in the text editor.

When you're in the text editor, any characters you type will be inserted into the current file and displayed on the Edit screen. You can move the cursor around the current file by using any of a number of cursor control keys.

The easiest to remember are the PC's keypad keys. The four arrow keys will move the cursor one character position in the direction the arrow points. The PgUp key will move the cursor one page up the size of your screen; typically 25, 43, or 50 lines, whereas PgDn will move the cursor one page down. The Home key will move the cursor immediately to the left screen margin, and the End key will move the cursor immediately to the end of the current line. (End of the line is defined as the character *after* the rightmost *non blank* character in the line.)

There are numerous other cursor control keys that you can use within JED. I'll describe them all in detail in Section 4.4.

Take a few moments scooting around inside EAT2 until you feel comfortable with it.

Making Changes to the File

The simplest way to change the file is to enter something from the keyboard. All characters you type will appear at the cursor position. The cursor will move one position to the right as you enter each character.

You can insert a new line beneath the current line by pressing Enter.

Getting rid of unwanted text is as important as adding new text. You can delete one character at a time by moving the cursor to the immediate right of the offending character, and pressing Backspace to back the cursor over it. The character will disappear.

You can delete an entire line by placing the cursor on the line and pressing Ctrl+Y. Be careful when using Ctrl+Y! You don't want to accidentally lose a line that you may or may not have in your head or written down on paper.

JED contains numerous other ways to delete text, all of which will be described in Section 4.4. For the sake of the current guided tour through JED, move the cursor to the blank line immediately beneath EAT2's comment header (line 9 in the file) and type the word "FOO". That done, press Enter and add a new line beneath it.

Saving Changes to a File

As they say in Chicago, that grand old (and cold) town where I grew up, "Vote early and often." The same philosophy applies to saving the changes you make to your current file under JED. Every so often, perhaps when you kick back in your chair to think for a bit, save your work. It's easy: one keystroke, the function key F2. JED will display the word "Saving..." in the status line at the top of the screen while it saves your file to disk. If you have a fast hard disk this will rarely take more than a second. If you're still working on diskettes, the process may take a few seconds more, especially if the current file is a good size.

Get in the habit of pressing F2 once in a while. Keep in mind that if you save your work every five minutes, you will never lose more than five minutes of work!

JED keeps an eye on things and does its level best to keep you from losing any of your work. If you try to exit JED without saving your file to disk, JED will remind you with the following prompt:

```
File modified.  Save it? (Y/N)
```

If you press "Y", JED will save your work to disk. Pressing "N" will allow you to exit JED without saving your work. All other keys but Y and N will be ignored.

JED also automatically saves your work every time you go out to use the assembler, linker, or debugger, or when you run the program you're developing, as I'll explain a little later.

Changing the Current File

If you want to change the current file while you're in JED, simply press Alt+F. (Think File.) A window will appear in the center of the screen displaing the name of the current file above a field where you can enter the name of the new file.

The name of the current file will be in the field. You can do one of two things to the name:

- **Begin typing a new name**. The old name will vanish as soon as you press a printable character key.
- **Backspace over some portion of the old name**. This allows you to change the name of the current file from EAT2.ASM to EAT3.ASM without typing the whole name.

When you press Enter, JED will attempt to load the specified file. If the file does not exist, or if you left the name field blank, JED will create a new file according to the rules summarized in the previous section.

Checking and Changing the Assemble and Link Commands

The whole point of JED is to help you do your work in assembly language, and the central task in assembly-language work is processing a correct file through an assembler. JED can execute your assembler program and assemble your current file with only one keystroke on your part. That keystroke is function key F9, as you'll see from the prompt bar at the bottom of the screen. Before you press F9 on our tour, however, we'd better make sure JED has your assembler and linker commands straight.

As programs go, JED is pretty clever, but it doesn't read minds. It can make use of any assembler that operates from the DOS command line, but you have to tell JED how to invoke the assembler you've chosen. MASM and TASM are invoked in different ways, and JED must know which assembler you're using to invoke the assembler program from disk and make use of it.

Pressing function key F4 displays a whole new screen that allows you to specify your assembler. See Figure 4.3. The screen contains two command lines, one that invokes your assembler, and another that invokes your linker. I've set JED up to assume the use of Borland's Turbo Assembler TASM, which is faster and in many ways more sophisticated than Microsoft's MASM. If you are using TASM, you needn't change JED's built-in default command lines. Figure 4.3 shows the default command lines for TASM.

To use MASM or some other assembler, however, you'll need to change both command lines. This will require some knowledge of how your assembler and linker operate. I'll provide you with some basic information about MASM and TASM; for other assemblers (or for using specialized features of MASM and TASM) you're on your own.

The line beneath the prompt "Assemble command" is the line JED will use to invoke your assembler. The default is

```
TASM ~
```

which will invoke Borland's Turbo Assembler with all default conditions in force. The tilde character ~ is used to indicate where in the line JED is to substitute the name of the current file. In other words, when JED goes out to

---

Figure 4.3. Changing JED's assembler and link commands

```
              \\JED\\  Assemble/link command edit screen



                        Assemble command:
 TASM ~.................................................................


                          Link command:
 TLINK ~


 Line editing commands:

 CR:      Accepts changes and continues
 ESC:     Abandons changes and continues
 Ctrl-X:  Clears entire field to empty string
 BS:      Destructive backspace
```

DOS to execute TASM on the file EAT2.ASM, it will substitute EAT2.ASM for the tilde, using the following line for invoking TASM:

```
TASM EAT2.ASM
```

If you're using MASM instead, you must change the Assemble command. Invoking MASM with all defaults in force (using the tilde to indicate the position of the filename) requires this command line:

```
MASM ~;
```

Again, in our example JED would automatically expand the line to read:

```
MASM EAT2.ASM;
```

The semicolon is very important, and prevents MASM from going into interactive mode. If you omit the semicolon, MASM will stop and begin asking questions from the keyboard. JED is not equipped to answer these questions, and while you yourself could answer MASM's questions from the keyboard, there's no point to it if all we want to do is use MASM's defaults. If you're using MASM, make sure you enter that semicolon!

Modifying a command line isn't difficult. You can backspace over the existing command line and replace it with a new one, or zap the whole line at once by pressing Ctrl+X, and then typing in your new command line.

When the changes are the way you want them, press Enter to retain the changes and record them in JED.CFG. If somehow you change your mind after zapping or otherwise altering the existing command line, you can abandon your changes and leave the original command line untouched by simply pressing Esc.

You'll notice that while you're editing a command line, a line of periods runs from the end of the command line to the right margin. These periods indicate how large the command line can be. You can type as far as the periods allow. If you try to type further, JED will quite literally say "uh-uh." Try it and see!

Changing the link command line is done the same way. TASM's link command line is this:

```
TLINK ~
```

MASM's link command line, on the other hand, requires a semicolon, and for the same reasons mentioned before:

```
LINK ~;
```

These are the absolute simplest command lines possible, and will suffice for simple learning programs like EAT2.ASM. For more advanced work you may need to use assembler or linker *options*, which are additional commands that provide special information to the assembler or linker about the job at hand.

For example, under MASM you can specify that the assembler write the program's segments to disk in alphabetical order (don't mind for now if you don't know what that means) by using the /A option. This requires that you enter the /A option as part of the assemble command line:

```
MASM /A ~;
```

Both TASM and MASM have numerous options of this type. You won't need any of them while working your way through this book. Later on, when you graduate to larger, more sophisticated assembly-language work, you will need to understand and use these options. If you continue to use JED at that stage, you'll have to add the desired options to the assemble and link command lines.

Assembling the Current File

If you're satisfied that the assemble and link command lines are correct, it's time to assemble EAT2. Press F9, and the following things happen:

- **JED saves the current file to disk**. Any time JED transfers control outside of itself (by executing the program under development or by executing one of the utilities) it saves the current file.

- **The screen clears, and JED invokes your assembler using the assemble command line described in the previous subsection**. The assembler displays its copyright notice and certain other information on the screen. (Precisely what information displays depends on the assembler you're using.) This information will include error messages, if your source code file contains any errors.

- **When the assembler is finished, JED saves the contents of the screen**. You can recall the information (typically error messages) back for examination later on. Saving the screen's contents happens invisibly and takes almost no time.

- A prompt reading "Press any key to return to JED" appears in the center of the bottom line of the screen. JED then waits for a keystroke, which allows you to take time to read the displayed error messages. When you're ready to resume work, press a key and the Editor screen will reappear. An example of the screen at this point is shown in Figure 4.4.

If you recall, you made a change to EAT2.ASM a little earlier, by typing the word "FOO" on line 9. This word at this location in the file means nothing, and it will generate an assembler error message. You can see this error message as

---

Figure 4.4. A TASM error message

```
Turbo Assembler  Version 2.0  Copyright (c) 1988, 1990 Borland International

Assembling file:    EAT2.ASM
**Error** EAT2.ASM(9) Illegal instruction
Error messages:    1
Warning messages:  None
Passes:            1
Remaining memory:  93k










              Press any key to return to JED...
```

TASM presents it, along with TASM's copyright notice and other information, in Figure 4.4. TASM calls the word "FOO" an illegal instruction because no **FOO** instruction exists in the 86-family instruction set. If you misspelled a genuine instruction (say, by fumble-fingering **MOV** into **MVO**) you would most likely see the same error message.

Both MASM and TASM are helpful in that they identify the line where they first noticed an error. (This line is not always where the error actually *is*, but we'll return to that matter later in the book.) This time, the error is a pretty obvious one and no assembler should have any trouble telling you that the problem exists in line 9 of the source code file. Once you press a key and return to JED's Edit screen, move to line 9 and delete the offending line. Just press Ctrl+Y and the line will vanish. Save the repaired file by pressing F2. Finally, invoke the assembler again by pressing F9. This time you *won't* see any error messages.

"Make"ing and Running an Executable File

What, exactly, does running the assembler actually accomplish? By itself, not much. Invoking the assembler alone is useful to determine if there are any errors in your source code file. If the file contains no errors, you still don't have an executable program file after the assembler has done its job. What you *do* have is a relocatable object file, with the same name as the current file but with an .OBJ file extension. In our example here, the assembler read in the current file, EAT2.ASM, and produced a new file, EAT2.OBJ.

You can't run EAT2.OBJ, and you can't read it or print it. You can't do much of anything with it, in fact, except *link* it. As I explained in the previous chapter, linking is a process by which one or more .OBJ files are translated into an executable program file with an .EXE extension. It's called linking because more than one .OBJ file can be combined into a single .EXE file through the linking process. However, even if you only have one .OBJ file (as we do here with EAT2) you must still perform the link step on that file to create an executable program file.

JED can perform the link step very easily. It does not, however, perform the link step all by itself. Running the assembler alone is useful to identify errors, but running the linker alone is pretty pointless unless you intend to run the executable program file produced by the link step. JED combines the link step with the step of actually running your new assembly language program to see what it does. Furthermore, it performs the assemble step again, so that you can do it all in one keystroke: assemble, link, and away you go!

When you press F10, JED will do basically the same things it did when you pressed F9, and then some:

- **JED saves the current file to disk**. The first time you run *any* new assembly-language program, you had better prepare to reboot your machine. It happens to the best of us now and then, and it will happen to you with dismaying frequency. Because we humans sometimes forget to save the source code file before running the .EXE file, JED *never* forgets.

- **JED executes the assembler**. If there are no errors in the file JED produces an .OBJ version of the current file. If errors are detected, no .OBJ file is generated and JED immediately takes control back from the assembler without performing the link and "go" (that is, execute) steps. JED will wait for a keystroke so that you can stare at the error messages for awhile.

- **If there were no assembler errors, JED executes the linker**. The .OBJ file is translated into a .EXE file. Again, there is the possibility that linker errors will occur, although they are much less common than assembler errors. If errors are detected, JED takes control back directly from the linker and the .EXE file will not be run. In the event of an error, JED waits for a keystroke so that you can examine the wreckage before pressing a key and going on.

- **The .EXE file is executed**. Your fledgling program runs, and when it finishes JED will once again wait for a keystroke as you examine your program's output. In our test case of EAT2, this output consists of those two lines of text shown earlier about eating at Joe's.

At this point, I have a confession to make.

What I just told you was the truth, but not the *whole* truth. The F10 command is a little more complicated than just those four steps. Suppose, for example, that you use the F10 command to create and run an .EXE file as we just did. Then suppose that you wanted to see it work again almost immediately, without making any further changes to the program. You press F10, expecting to have to wait through the assemble and link step again.

But no...

The second time you press F10, the .EXE file executes *immediately*, with neither the assembler nor the linker doing their thing.

What gives?

JED is pretty clever after all. Since you didn't make any further changes to the source code file, there was no need for JED to reassemble and relink to re-create an .EXE file no different from the one created a few seconds earlier. JED simply executed the .EXE file as it did the first time, without making you wait through a needless assemble step and link step.

Here's what happens: when you press F10, JED looks at two files on disk. The first one is the .EXE file. If no .EXE file exists on disk, obviously, JED has to create one by executing both the assembler and the linker. But if the .EXE file does exist, JED looks at the file's *time stamp* and stores a copy of the time stamp.

A time stamp is DOS's way of knowing when a file was last changed. Every file created under DOS has both a time and a date attached to it. When you execute a DIR command from the DOS command line, the files listed tell you when they were last changed by displaying their time stamps as date and time values:

```
Volume in drive C is DISK1_VOL1
Directory of  C:\TURBO\JED
JED      BAK    27659   1-08-89    4:39p
JED      PAS    27633   1-08-89    4:39p
JED      EXE    31920   1-08-89    4:39p
JED      CFG      326   1-08-89    5:25p
4 File(s)  10803200 bytes free
```

The two rightmost columns are the date and time portions of each file's time stamp.

Once it stores a copy of the .EXE file's time stamp, JED examines the current source code .ASM file, and stores a copy of its time stamp. Once JED has both time stamps, it compares them.

If the .ASM file's time stamp shows a time more recent than the .EXE file's time stamp, JED re-creates the .EXE file by invoking both the assembler and the linker. If the .ASM file's time stamp says the .ASM file is *older* than the .EXE file, JED simply runs the .EXE file without re-creating it.

Think about that for a moment until it makes perfect sense. (It's important!) If the .ASM file is older than the .EXE file, there is *no* possibility that changes made to the .ASM file have not been reflected in the .EXE file. However, if the .ASM file is newer than the .EXE file, it might mean that changes were made to the .ASM file that have not yet been reflected in the .EXE file. JED therefore updates the .EXE file so that it is guaranteed to reflect all possible changes made in the source code .ASM file.

This process is a common one among software development tools. The name of the process is "make," meaning that when necessary, JED will choose to "make" the .EXE file from the .ASM file by invoking the assembler and the linker. The make process is efficient because it only happens when it has to. If the .EXE file is found to be up-to-date, the assemble and link steps are skipped.

As I've hinted before, running a brand new assembly-language program is dangerous business, *especially* for new assembly-language programmers. High-level languages like Pascal and C protect you to a considerable extent from your own ignorance. Assembly language offers almost no such protection. Until you really *really* know what you're doing, your assembly-language programs will crash your machine hard more often than they let it live. (This is why most assembly-language programmers choose machines with hard-reset buttons on the front panel. Pushing RESET is much gentler on the machine than turning it off and on again.)

So don't get discouraged when you crash. As that old Desiderata poem on your day-glo sixties psychedelic posters takes pains to point out, "No doubt the universe is unfolding as it should." Crashing is part of the process. What *is* stupid is crashing again and again without knowing why. Figuring out why you're crashing is one of the most difficult and rewarding facets of assembly-language programming, as we'll see by and by.

Taking Another Look at Your Error Messages

The assembler won't give you a lot of clues as to where you went wrong when it detects an error, so you have to make the most of what clues you get. The assembler displays error messages during the assemble step. It would be handy to keep those error messages around and refer to them when you're back in JED's Edit screen, staring at your errant source code.

JED can do it. Before JED clears the assembler's error messages from the screen and returns you to the text editor, it saves the screen information in memory. Later on, you can redisplay the screen as it was immediately after the assemble step by pressing F6.

The only time this system fails a little bit is if you have so many errors in the source code file that they begin to scroll off the top of the screen. This means, first of all, that you have some wholesale error hunting to do. But there is a way to avoid losing the first few error messages of a multi error assemble step. As soon as the first few error messages appear, halt the assemble step by pressing Ctrl+C. It's wise to treat the first error messages first, because error messages sometimes breed other error messages, and getting rid of the first one might well purge five or fifteen others further down the file.

If you try to recall an error message screen before running the assembler, JED will clear the screen and explain the situation.

You should also keep in mind that if an assemble step occurs without errors, you will still be able to recall the assembler's copyright notice and status information by pressing F6. JED is not particular; whether errors occur or not, it saves the screen from the last time the assembler was run.

Running DEBUG

An important part of developing assembly language programs is using the DEBUG utility. JED can run DEBUG for you with a single keystroke. Once you've produced a working EAT2.EXE file, press F3. JED will invoke DEBUG.COM, using the current .EXE file as its command-line parameter. DEBUG will execute and in turn load your .EXE file into memory. The screen will clear, and you'll see DEBUG's terse little dash prompt.

Press D, and DEBUG will dump the first 128 bytes of EAT2.EXE as it was loaded into memory. Press R, and DEBUG will show you the current state of the registers. You can actually run EAT2.EXE by pressing G (for *Go*) at DEBUG's prompt. Finally, you can quit DEBUG by pressing Q. JED will take back control and wait for one final keystroke so you can grab a last look at what DEBUG has displayed.

One additional feature is that the last screenful of information displayed by DEBUG is saved in memory by JED, and can be recalled by pressing F6, just as with assembler error screens. This is handy when you need to refer back to a hex dump of a region of memory while examining a berserk source code file in the Edit screen.

"Ducking Out" to DOS

For all that it does do, JED is a modest program and doesn't try to do everything. I was tempted to build printer support into it so that you could create a printed listing of the current file by pressing a single key, but decided against it. There are a multitude of different kinds of printers out there, each with its own font sizes and setup strings and control sequences. Rather than try to cover all the printer bases, I decided to build a quick trap door into JED so that you can quickly duck out to DOS and run your own listing program, or do anything else that can be done from DOS.

To exit to DOS, press F5. JED will (to be safe) save the current file to disk, clear the screen, and take you back out to the DOS command prompt. It looks very much like JED has terminated and returned control to DOS, but not so: JED is very much alive in memory, waiting patiently for you to finish your business with DOS and come back home.

From DOS you can do things like search the directory for a lost file, make room on your disk by erasing some clutter, or even (in a pinch) run another major program like Turbo Pascal. The only caution here is that JED and your program take up a certain amount of memory, memory that is therefore not available to other programs like Turbo Pascal. Very large programs like Ventura Publisher or Paradox may not execute at all if you try to execute them from "beneath" JED, not because you've done anything wrong but only because such large programs barely run at all even in 640K of RAM, and need the memory JED is taking up.

By actual examination using the CHKDSK utility, I've found that JED and its workspace take up about 180K of RAM. That's a lot of RAM, and you have to take its loss into account when you try to do things with JED waiting in memory.

Getting back into JED is easy. Just type the command EXIT at the DOS command prompt. JED will instantly take you back with open arms, and you can continue work as though you had never taken a DOS break at all.

One interesting thing to do: create and run a .EXE file by pressing F10, then duck out to DOS by pressing F5, and delete the .EXE file. Return to JED, and press F10 again. Even though you made no additional changes to the source code file, JED will search for the .EXE file before attempting to run it. Since no .EXE file exists, JED has no choice but to remake it.

4.4 JED's Editor in Detail

As JED's beating heart, the text editor deserves a little space all to itself. JED's editor is the Borland Binary Editor, essentially the same editor as used in the Turbo languages and Sidekick. Borland disengaged the editor module from its other products and made it available in linkable form (essentially one of those .OBJ files I described a while back) and placed it in the Turbo Pascal Editor Toolbox. If you own the Turbo Pascal Editor Toolbox, you can read up on the Binary Editor's many commands in the Editor Toolbox documentation. I'll describe them all briefly in this section.

Loading Files into the Editor

When you invoke JED and it begins running, it loads either the file you named on the command line or the last file it worked on, as recorded in JED.CFG. The file is loaded into an area of memory called the *editor workspace*. The editor workspace is limited to 64K in size, and any file to be loaded must fit into memory in its entirety. If the file is too large to fit in available memory, you will see this message:

```
Insufficient text buffer size
```

JED will then have no choice but to throw up its hands and return to DOS. You'll have to cut the monster file up into smaller files (which is a good idea anyway) and invoke JED again on only a portion of the oversized file.

Also keep in mind that individual lines within an edit file are limited to 248 characters. Loading a file with longer lines will cause the editor to insert hyphens at the 248-character point.

Moving the Cursor

Apart from the keypad keys and F7 and F8 function keys (used for marking text blocks, as I'll explain below) all editor commands are control keystrokes. That is, you must hold the Ctrl key down while pressing another key or two keys. All of the keys that control cursor movement are grouped together for you in a cluster toward the left hand side of the keyboard:

W   E   R   •
A   S   D   F
Z   X   C

This arrangement of cursor control keys will be familiar to anyone who has worked with the WordStar word processor.

One Character at a Time

Moving the cursor one character at a time can be done in all four directions: pressing Ctrl+E or Up Arrow moves the cursor Up one character; pressing Ctrl+X or Down Arrow moves the cursor Down one character; pressing Ctrl+S or Left Arrow moves the cursor Left one character; and pressing Ctrl+D or Right Arrow moves the cursor Right one character.

The position of these four keys (E, X, S, and D) provide a hint as to which way they move the cursor. Look at how they are arranged on the keyboard:

E
S   D
X

Until the directions become automatic to your fingers (as they will, if you do enough editing!) thinking of the *magic diamond* will remind you which way the cursor will move for which keypress.

When you move the cursor to the bottom of the screen and press Ctrl+X one more time, the screen will *scroll.* All the lines on the screen will jump up by one, and the top line will disappear. As long as the cursor is on the bottom line of the screen and you continue to press Ctrl+X, the screen will scroll upward. If use Ctrl+E to move the cursor back in the opposite direction (upward) until it hits the top of the screen, continually pressing Ctrl+E will scroll the screen downward one line per Ctrl+E.

One Word at a Time

JED will also move the cursor left or right one word at a time: pressing Ctrl+A or Ctrl+Left Arrow moves the cursor Left one word; while pressing Ctrl+F or Ctrl+Right Arrow moves the cursor Right one word.

More hints are given here, since the A key is on the left side of the magic diamond, and the F key is on the right side of the magic diamond.

One Screen at a Time

It is also possible to move the cursor upward or downward through the file one entire screen at a time. "Upward" in this sense means toward the beginning of the file; "downward" means toward the end of the file: pressing Ctrl+R or PgUp moves the cursor Up one screen; while pressing Ctrl+C or PgDn moves the cursor down one screen.

A screen is the height of your CRT display (25, 43, or 50 lines, depending on what display adapter is installed and what font is currently loaded) minus two lines for the editor status line at the top of the screen and the prompt bar at the bottom of the screen.

Moving the Cursor by Scrolling the Screen

I have described how the screen will scroll when you use the one-character-at-a-time commands to move upward (Ctrl+E) from the top line of the screen or downward (Ctrl+X) from the bottom line of the screen. You can scroll the screen upward or downward no matter where the cursor happens to be by using the scrolling commands: pressing Ctrl+W scrolls the screen Down one line; while pressing Ctrl+Z scrolls the screen Up one line.

When you scroll the screen with these commands, the cursor "rides" with the screen as it scrolls upward or downward, *until* the cursor hits the top or bottom of the screen. Then further scrolling will make the screen slip past the cursor. The cursor will always remain visible.

These are all of the cursor control commands that can be accomplished in one Ctrl keystroke. There are a few more that are accomplished by holding the

Ctrl key down and pressing *two* keys in succession. *You must hold the Ctrl key down through both keypresses!*

Moving to the End of a Line

No matter where your cursor is on the screen, it is always within a line, even if that line happens to be empty of characters. The editor provides two commands to move the cursor either to the beginning (left end) of the line (screen column 1) or to the end of the line, (the position following the last visible character on the line): pressing Ctrl+Q/S or Home sends the cursor to the Beginning of the line; while pressing Ctrl+Q/D or End sends the cursor to the End of the line.

Moving to the End of a File

The last set of cursor control commands I'll describe takes the cursor to the beginning of the file or to the end of the file. If the file you are editing is more than a few screens long, the following commands can save you a great deal of pounding on the keyboard: pressing Ctrl+Q/R or Ctrl+PgUp sends the cursor to the Beginning of the file; while pressing Ctrl+Q/C or Ctrl+PgDn sends the cursor to the End of the file.

Because all of the current file is in memory all of the time, moving between the ends of the file can be done *very* quickly.

The Status Line

At the very top of JED's Edit screen is the status line, which provides you with some important information while you are editing.

A typical instance of the status line looks like this:

```
Line 1  Col 1   Insert Indent    C:EAT2.ASM        09:04:45
```

While you were moving the cursor around, the line and column numbers were continually changing to reflect where the cursor was in the file. The column number reflects the position of the cursor within its line; the line number indicates which line in the file contains the cursor, counting from the beginning of the file, *not* from the top of the screen. At the other end of the status line is the name of the current file.

Insert and Indent, described earlier in this chapter, are the names of two *toggles*. A toggle is a condition that exists in one of two different states. A toggle is like a switch controlling the lights in a room; the switch is either on or off.

Insert determines how newly typed characters are added to your work file. When Insert is on (that is, when the word Insert appears in the status line) characters you type are *inserted* into the file. The characters appear over the cursor and immediately push the cursor and the rest of the line to the left to make room for themselves. The line becomes one character longer for each character that you type. If you press Enter, the cursor moves down one line, carrying with it the part of the line lying to its right.

When Insert is off (i.e., if the word Insert is *not* displayed in the status line) characters you type will *overwrite* characters that already exist in the file. No new characters are added to the file unless you move the cursor to the end of the line or the end of the file and keep typing. If you press Enter, the cursor will move down to the first character of the next line down, but nothing else will change. A line will only be added to the file if you press Enter with the cursor on the last line of the file.

Turning Insert on and off is done by pressing Ctrl+V.

Indent is also a toggle, which indicates whether JED's auto-indent feature is on or off. When Indent is on, the cursor will automatically move beneath the first visible character on a new line when you press Enter. In other words (assuming that Indent is on), given this little bit of text on your screen

```
Adjust:
    MOV AX, [BP] + 6
    SUB AX, Increment_  ←Before pressing Enter

    _
   ↑ After pressing Enter
```

the cursor is at the end of the last line of text. When you press Enter, the cursor will move down one line, but it will also space over automatically until it is beneath the "S" in "SUB". This allows you to begin typing the next line of code without having to space the cursor over so that it is beneath the start of the previous line.

Like Insert, Indent can be toggled on and off; however, it takes a double control keystroke to do it: press Ctrl+Q/I to toggle Indent on and off. Indent is on when the word Indent appears in the status line.

Tab Mode

The status line also displays the current tab mode. *Tabbing* is the automatic spacing to the right when the Tab key is pressed. On the PC's keyboard, there is no key labeled "Tab"; instead, the key is imprinted with two arrows pointing in opposite directions, with a vertical bar at the head of each arrow:

```
|←
→|
```

Some clone keyboards do label the Tab key. The Tab key is usually positioned directly over the Ctrl key.

There are two kinds of tabs in JED's editor. The default tabs are not tabs as most people knew them prior to the onset of Borland's Turbo Pascal. These "smart" tabs move the cursor to the position beneath the start of the next word on the previous line. That is, using the following line as our example, if the cursor was positioned beneath this line, the caret marks show where the cursor would pause at each successive press of the Tab key:

```
Think of it as evolution in action...
      ^  ^  ^  ^           ^  ^
```

This tabbing is done by inserting spaces, *not* by inserting the ASCII Tab (Ctrl+I) character.

Smart tabs, as described above, are the default tab mode in the editor. Pressing Ctrl+O/T toggles to the opposite tab mode, which supports true, eight-character fixed tabs that insert Ctrl+I characters at each press of the Tab key. If fixed tabs are in effect, the word Tab will be shown on the status line between the word Indent and the filename:

```
Line 1  Col 1  Insert Indent Tab C:EAT2.ASM          09:45:07
```

In summary on tab mode, pressing Ctrl+O/T toggles between smart tabs and fixed tabs.

Inserts and Deletes

We've already seen how to insert characters into a text file: you make sure Insert is on, then type away. Each typed character will be inserted into the file at the cursor position.

It is also possible to insert entire blank lines. One way, of course, is to move the cursor to the beginning of a line and press Enter. (Remember, Insert must be on.) A new blank line will be inserted above the line with the cursor, and the rest of the file will be pushed downward. The cursor will ride down with the text pushed downward.

Another way to insert a line independent of the insert mode is to move the cursor to the beginning of a line and press Ctrl+N. A new line will appear, pushing the rest of the file downward, *but the cursor will not move down with the other text.* That is, pressing Ctrl+N inserts a new line at the cursor position.

There are also a number of different ways to *delete* text as well. The simplest is to use the Del (Delete) key. Pressing Ctrl+G performs exactly the same delete function: pressing Del deletes one Character to the Right of the cursor, and pressing Ctrl+G deletes one Character to the Right of the cursor.

The cursor does not move. It "swallows" the character to its right, and the rest of the line to its right moves over to fill in the position left by the deleted character.

The Backspace key is used to delete characters to the *left* of the cursor; with this method the cursor rides to the left on each deletion.

You can think of backspace as "eating" one character to the left as it moves the cursor leftward.

You can also (to save a few keystrokes) delete one *word* to the right of the cursor by pressing Ctrl+T.

When you press Ctrl+T, all characters from the cursor position rightward to the end of the current word will be deleted. If the cursor happens to be on a space (or group of spaces) between words, that space (or spaces) will be deleted up to the beginning of the next word.

You can also delete from the cursor position to the end of the current line by pressing Ctrl+Q/Y.

And finally, you can delete the entire line with a single control keystroke by pressing Ctrl+Y.

The line beneath the cursor moves up to take the place of the deleted line, pulling up the rest of the file behind it.

A warning here for those of you with thick fingers: the T and Y characters are right next to one another on the keyboard. In a late night frenzy at the keyboard you may find yourself reaching for Ctrl+T to delete a word and hit Ctrl+Y instead, losing the entire line irretrievably. I've done this often enough that I simply broke myself of the habit of using Ctrl+T at all.

Undoing Changes to a Line

JED's editor keeps a "backup" copy of each line while you're working on it, and retains that copy as long as the cursor remains within the line. Therefore, if you delete a word or some other portion of the line, or add something to a line by mistake, you can undo those changes to the line as long as you haven't yet left the line. Once you leave the line, even momentarily, the editor throws away the backup copy, and "undoing" is no longer possible. You can restore a line to its previous condition by pressing Ctrl+Q/L.

One drawback is that the undo feature will *not* restore a line deleted entirely with the Ctrl+Y command. Once a line is deleted, the cursor (by necessity) leaves the line, and so the editor does not retain the backup copy of the line. Be careful how you use Ctrl+Y!

Markers and Blocks

JED's editor supports two different kinds of markers; that is, positions in the file that have a name or number and can be moved around as needed by the programmer. These are *place markers* and *block markers*.

Place Markers

There is no such thing as a page number in an editor file. You can move the cursor to the beginning or end of the file with a single command, but to move to a specific place in the file is harder. The best way is to remember a distinctive title, procedure name, or something like that and search for it. (See below.) You might also make use of the editor's place marker feature.

The editor supports four place markers, numbered 0 through 3. These can be placed at any position in a text file with a single command: pressing Ctrl+K<n> sets marker <n> within a file, when <n> is 0,1,2, or 3.

For example, to set marker 2, you would press Ctrl+K2.

Once a place marker has been set, you can move the cursor to it with a single command: pressing Ctrl+Q<n> moves the cursor to marker <n>.

For example, to move to marker 2 you would press Ctrl+Q2. If you have two or three "construction zones" within a largish source file, you might drop one of the place markers at the start of each zone, so you can shuttle between the zones with a single command.

The markers are invisible, and if you forget where they are, about all you can do is move the cursor to them with the Ctrl+Q<n> command.

Block Markers

Block markers are used to specify the beginning and end of text blocks. There are only two of these markers, B and K, and in consequence only one block may be marked within a file at any given time.

The block markers are invisible and do not appear on your screen in any way. If both are present in a file, however, all the text between them (the currently marked block) is shown as highlighted text.

Placing each block marker is a two-character control keystroke: pressing Ctrl+K/B places the B marker; the shortcut is F7. Pressing Ctrl+K/K places the K marker; the shortcut is F8.

Note the two function key shortcuts, which are extremely convenient and fast.

A marker is placed at the cursor position and remains there until you move it elsewhere. You cannot delete or remove a marker once placed, although you can "hide" the block of text that lies between the markers, which effectively gets the markers out of the picture. (See below for more on hiding marked blocks.)

Moving the Cursor to a Block Marker

There are also commands to move the cursor to the block markers: pressing Ctrl+Q/B moves the cursor to the B marker; while pressing Ctrl+Q/K moves the cursor to the K marker.

Hiding and Unhiding Blocks of Text

The major use of markers, however, is to define a block of text. There are a number of commands available in JED's editor that manipulate the text that lies between the B and K markers.

You probably noticed while experimenting with setting markers that as soon as you positioned *both* the B and K markers in a file, the text between them became highlighted. The highlighted text is a marked text block. As we mentioned before, there is no way to remove a marker completely from a file once it has been set. You can, however, suppress the highlighting of text between the two markers. This is called *hiding* a block: pressing Ctrl+K/H will hide a block of text.

Remember that the markers are still there. Ctrl+K/H is a toggle. You invoke it once to hide a block, and you can invoke it a second time to *unhide* the block and bring out the highlighting again on the text between the two blocks.

Something else to keep in mind: the other block commands we'll be looking at below work *only* on highlighted blocks. Once a block is hidden, it is hidden from the block commands as well as from your eyes.

Marking a Word as a Block

Ordinarily, to mark a word as a block, you'd have to move the cursor to the beginning of the word, press F7, then move to the end of the word and press F8. The editor, however, includes a short form of this command sequence: move the cursor to any position within a word and press Ctrl+K/T.

Block Commands

The simplest block command to understand is *delete block*. Getting rid of big chunks of text that are no longer needed is easy: mark the text as a block using the B and K markers, then press Ctrl+K/Y.

The markers themselves are not deleted with the block of text. They close up and occupy the same single cursor position, but they are still there, and you can move the cursor to them with the Ctrl+Q/B or Ctrl+Q/K commands.

Copy block is useful when you have some standard text construction (a standard boilerplate comment header for procedures, perhaps) that you need to use several times within the same text file. Rather than retyping the block each time, you type it once, mark it as a block, and then place a copy of the original into each position where you need it. Simply position the cursor where the first character of the copied text must go, then press Ctrl+K/C.

Moving a block of text is similar to copying a block of text. The difference, of course, is that the original block of text that you marked vanishes from its original position and reappears at the cursor position. To move a block of text you must first mark the text, then position the cursor where you wish the marked text to go, and then press Ctrl+K/C.

The last two block commands allow you to write a block of text to disk, or to read (place a copy of) a text file from disk into the current file. To write a block to disk, you begin by marking the block you want saved as a separate text file, then you press Ctrl+K/W.

The editor needs to know the name of the disk file into which you want to write the marked block of text. It prompts you for the filename with a dialog box entitled "Write Block To File." You must type the name of the file, with full path if you intend the block to be written outside of the current directory, and then press Enter. The block is written to disk and remains highlighted in the editor. Note that the cursor does not move.

Reading a text file from disk into your work file is also easy. You position the cursor where the first character of the text from the file should go, and then press Ctrl+K/R.

Just as with the write block command, the editor will prompt you for the name of the file you want to read from disk with a dialog box entitled "Read Block From File."

There is one small "gotcha" that you must be aware of in connection with filenames. If you enter a filename *without* a period or file extension (that is, a filename like FOO rather than FOO.ASM) JED's editor will first look for a file named FOO. If it does not find one, it will then look for a file named FOO.ASM. If it still cannot find the file, it will issue this error message within an alarming red (if you have a color monitor) box:

```
Unable to open FOO.ASM.  Press <ESC>
```

Pressing Esc cancels the command entirely. To enter the name correctly you will need to issue the Ctrl+K/R command again.

When JED finds the text file, it will insert the file as a marked block into your work file at the cursor position. You will have to issue the hide block command to remove the highlighting. Remember also that reading a block of text from disk will effectively move your two block markers from elsewhere in your file and place them around the text that was read in.

The editor is not especially picky about the type of files you read from disk. Text files need not have been generated by JED's editor. In fact, files need not be text files at all, but remember, reading raw binary data into a text file can cause the file to appear foreshortened—the first binary 26 (Ctrl+Z) encountered in a text file is assumed to signal the end of the file. Data after that first Ctrl+Z may or may not be accessible. Furthermore, the editor will attempt to display the binary characters as is, and loading (for example) an .EXE file will fill the screen with some pretty lively garbage.

Finding and Replacing

Much of the power of electronic text editing lies in the ability to search for a particular character pattern in a text file. Furthermore, once found, it is a logical extension of the search concept to replace the found text string with a different text string. For example, if you decide to change the name of a variable to something else to avoid conflict with another identifier in a program, you might wish to have the text editor locate every instance of the old variable name in a program and replace each one with the new variable name.

JED's editor can perform both Find and Find/Replace operations with great ease. Being able to locate a given text string in a program is often better than having page numbers (which JED's editor does not) in a file. If you wish to work on the part of a program that contains a particular procedure, all you need do is search for that procedure's name by pressing Ctrl+Q/F and JED will move the cursor right to the spot you want.

When you issue the Find command, the editor prompts you with a single word:

```
Find:
```

You must then type the text string you want found, and then press Enter. The editor then prompts you for command options:

```
Options:
```

There are several command options that you can use with both the Find and Find/Replace commands. These options are single letters (or numbers) that can be grouped together in any order without spaces in between:

```
Options: BWU
```

We'll be discussing each option in detail shortly. When you press Enter after keying in the options (if any) the editor executes the command. For the Find command, the cursor will move to the first character of the found text string. If the editor cannot find any instance of the requested text string in the work file, it displays this message:

```
Search string not found. Press <ESC>
```

You must then press Esc to continue editing.

Find/Replace

The Find/Replace command goes that extra step for you. Once the search text is found, it will replace the search text with a replacement text. The options mean everything here: you can replace only the first instance of the search text; you can replace all instances of the search text; and you can have the editor ask permission before replacing, or simply go ahead and do the deed to as many instances of the search text as it finds. (This last operation is especially beloved of programmers, who call it a "search and destroy".)

As with Find, the editor prompts for the search text and options. It must also (for Find/Replace) prompt for the replacement string:

```
Replace with:
```

If you have not specified any options, the editor will locate the first instance of the search string, place the cursor beneath it, and give you the permission prompt:

```
Replace (Y/N):
```

If you type a Y here (no Enter required) the editor will perform the replacement. If you type an N, nothing will change.

Find/Replace Options

The editor's find/replace options allow you to "fine-tune" a Find or Find/Replace command to cater to specific needs. For example, without any options the Find command is case sensitive. In other words, "FOO", "foo", and "Foo" are three distinct text strings, and searching for "FOO" will not discover instances of "foo." With the U option in force, however, "FOO", "foo", and "Foo" are considered identical and searching for any of the three forms will turn up instances of any of the three that are present. There are several such options to choose from within the editor. In general they are the same Find/Replace options used by WordStar:

- **B is the Search Backwards option**. Ordinarily, a search will proceed from the cursor position toward the end of the file. If the object of the search is closer to the beginning of the file than the cursor, the search will not find it. With the B option in force, the search proceeds *backwards* through the file, toward the beginning.

- **G is the Global Search option**. As mentioned above, searches normally begin at the cursor position and proceed toward one end of the file or the other, depending on whether or not the B option is in force. With the G option in force, searches begin at the beginning of the file and proceed to the end, ignoring the cursor position. The G option overrides the B option.

- **N is the Replace Without Asking option**. Without this option, the editor (during a Find/Replace) will prompt you for a yes/no response each time it locates an instance of the search text. With N in force, it simply does the replacement. Combining the G and N options means that the editor will search the entire file and replace every instance of the search text with the replacement text, without asking. *Make sure you set it up right,* or you can cause wholesale damage to your work file. In general, *don't use G and N together without W.* (See below for details on the W option.)

- **U is the Ignore Case option**. Without this option, searches are case sensitive. "FOO" and "foo" are considered distinct and searching for one will not find the other. With the U option in force, corresponding upper- and lowercase characters are considered identical. "FOO" and "foo" will both be found on a search for either.

- **W is the Whole Words option**. Without this option, the search text will be found even when it is embedded in a larger word. For example, searching for "LOCK" will find both "BLOCK" and "CLOCK." With W in force, the search text must be bounded by spaces to be found. This option is especially important for global Find/Replace commands, when (if you omit W) replacing all instances of "LOCK" with "SECURE" will change all instances of "BLOCK" to "BSECURE" and all instances of "CLOCK" to "CSECURE."

You may also give a number as one of the options. For the Find command, this tells the editor to find the nth instance of the search text. For Find/Replace, a number tells the editor to find and replace text n times.

Find or Find/Replace Again

The editor remembers the last Find or Find/Replace command—search text, replacement text, options, and all. You can execute that last Find or Find/Replace command again simply by issuing the Find or Find/Replace again command: pressing Ctrl+L will perform the last Find or Find/Replace command again.

Ctrl+L can save you some considerable keystroking. Suppose, for example, you wanted to examine the header line of every procedure in a large (perhaps 1000 line) program with thirty or forty procedures. The way to do it is to search for the string "PROC" with the G, U, and W options in force. The first time you execute this command, the editor will find the first procedure in your program file. To find the next one, simply press Ctrl+L. You need not reenter the search text or the options. Each time you press Ctrl+L, the editor will find the next instance of the reserved word "PROC" until it runs out of file, or until you issue a new and different Find or Find/Replace command.

Saving Your Work

It is *very* important to keep in mind what is happening while you edit text files with the editor. *You are editing entirely within memory.* Nothing goes out to disk while you are actually doing the edit. You can work on a file for hours, and one power failure will throw it all away. You must develop the discipline of saving your work every so often.

The easiest way to execute a Save command from within the editor is with the Save shortcut, F2. The "longcut" to saving the file from within the editor is Ctrl+K/S, (useful if you have WordStar burned into your synapses) but F2 is easier to type and remember.

Exiting the Editor

There is more than one way to get out of JED once you're finished with the job at hand. You can get out with any of these commands:

Ctrl+K/D saves the current file and exits to DOS.

Ctrl+K/Q ends the edit *without* saving and exits to DOS.

Alt+X saves the current file *if necessary* and exits to DOS.

The differences between them are subtle. Ctrl+K/D always saves the current file and exits to DOS, whether the file has been modified or not. If the current file is very large, this can mean a delay of several seconds while the file is written out to disk (*especially* if you're working from diskettes).

Ctrl+K/Q, on the other hand, may be used to exit from JED *without* saving the current file, even if the current file has been modified since it was last saved. JED, always the one for safety, will ask you if you want to abandon the changes you've made. You can answer only Y or N; Y will indeed exit to DOS without saving the current file. N, on the other hand, indicates a change of heart on your part and JED will save the current file to disk before exiting.

Finally, Alt+X is the smart way out. If you made changes to the current file since the last time it was saved to disk, JED will save the file to disk. If no changes were made, JED will not waste your time with an unnecessary save, but will drop you out to DOS immediately.

No matter how you exit to DOS, JED considerately restores the DOS screen that existed just before you invoked it.

One important use of Ctrl+K/Q is to "undo" a disastrous search-and-destroy operation that went bad using Ctrl+Q/A. If you've changed every one of 677 instances of MOV to MUV by accident, *and haven't yet saved the damaged file to disk using F2*, your only course of action is to exit to DOS without saving the damaged file to disk. That done, you can invoke JED again and load the last, undamaged version of the current file.

So be careful, huh?

5

An Uneasy Alliance

The 8086/8088 CPU and Its Segmented Memory System

As comedian Bill Cosby once said, "I told you that story so I could tell you *this* one...." We're pretty close to half finished with this book, and I haven't even begun describing the principal element in PC assembly language: The 8086/8088 CPU. Most books on assembly language, even those targeted at beginners, assume that the CPU is as good a place as any to start their story, without considering the mass of groundwork without which most beginning programmers get totally lost and give up.

That's why I began at the *real* beginning, taking half a book to get to where the other guys start.

Keep in mind that this book was created to supply that essential groundwork. It is *not* a complete course in PC assembly language. Once you run off the end of this book, you'll have one leg up on any of the multitude of "beginner" books on assembly language from other publishers.

And it's high time we got right to the heart of things, and met the foreman of the PC himself.

5.1 Through a Glass, with Blinders

But having worked my way up to the good stuff, I find myself faced with a tricky conundrum. Programming involves two major components of the PC: the CPU and memory. Most books begin by choosing one or the other and describing it. My own opinion is that you can't really describe memory and memory addressing without describing the CPU, and you can't really describe the CPU without going into memory and memory addressing.

So let's do both at once.

The Nature of a Megabyte

The 8086 and 8088 CPUs are identical in most respects, which is why we often refer to them and their cousins as the "86 family." The 8088 is used in IBM's original PC and XT and their ubiquitous clones. The 8086 is used in two of IBM's newer machines, the PS/2 models 25 and 30. Both machines can contain and use up to a megabyte of directly addressable memory. This memory is also called *real memory* or *DOS memory*. There is another kind of memory that you may have heard of, called *expanded memory*, that follows the Lotus-Intel-Microsoft (LIM) expanded memory specification (EMS). We're not speaking of expanded memory at all in this book; I consider it an advanced topic.

As I discussed briefly in Chapter 2, a megabyte of memory is actually not 1,000,000 bytes of memory, but 1,048,576 bytes. It doesn't come out even in our base 10 because computers insist on base 2. 1,048,576 bytes expressed in base 2 is 100000000000000000000B bytes. (We don't use commas in base 2—that's yet another way to differentiate binary notation from decimal, apart from the suffixed "B".) That's 2^{20}, a fact that we'll return to shortly. The number

10000000000000000000B is so bulky that it's better to express it in the compatible (and much more compact) base 16, which we call hexadecimal. 2^{20} is equivalent to 16^5, and may be written in hexadecimal as 100000H. (If the notion of number bases still confounds you, I'd recommend another trip through Chapter 1, if you haven't been through it already. Or, perhaps, even if you have.)

Now, here's a tricky and absolutely critical question: in a memory bank containing 100000H bytes, what's the address of the very last byte in the bank? The answer is *not* 100000H. The clue is the flipside to that question: what's the address of the *first* byte in the memory bank? That answer, you might recall, is 0. *Computers always begin counting from 0.* It's a dichotomy that will occur again and again in computer programming. The last in a row of four items is item 3, because the first item in a row of four is item 0. Count: 0,1,2,3.

The address of a byte in a memory bank is just the number of that byte *starting from zero.* This means that the last, or highest address in a memory bank containing one megabyte is 100000H minus one, or 0FFFFFH. (The initial zero, while not mathematically necessary, is there for the convenience of your assembler. Get in the habit of using an initial zero on any hex number beginning with the hex digits A through F.)

The addresses in a megabyte of memory, then, run from 00000H to 0FFFFFH. In binary notation, that is equivalent to the range of 00000000000000000000B to 11111111111111111111B. That's a lot of bits—20, to be exact. If you'll look back to Figure 2.3 in Chapter 2, you'll see that a megabyte memory bank has 20 address lines. One of those 20 bits is routed to each of those 20 address lines, so that any address expressed as 20 bits will identify one and only one of the 1,048,576 bytes contained in the memory bank.

That's what a megabyte of memory is: some arrangement of memory chips within the computer, connected by an address bus of 20 lines. A 20-bit address is fed to those 20 address lines to identify one byte out of the megabyte.

16-Bit Blinders

The 8088 and 8086 can "see" a full megabyte. That is, the CPU chips have 20 address pins, and can pass a full 20-bit address to the memory system. From that perspective, it seems pretty simple and straightforward. However...the bulk of all the trouble you're ever likely to have in understanding the 86-family CPUs stems from this fact: although the CPUs can see a full megabyte of memory, they are constrained to look at that megabyte through 16-bit blinders.

You may call this peculiar. (Later on, you'll probably call it much worse.) But you *must* understand it, and understand it thoroughly.

The blinders metaphor is closer to literal than you might think. Look at Figure 5.1. The long rectangle represents the megabyte of memory that the 8088 can address. The CPU is off to the right. In the middle is a piece of metaphorical cardboard with a slot cut in it. The slot is one byte wide and

Figure 5.1. Seeing a megabyte through 16-bit (64K) blinders

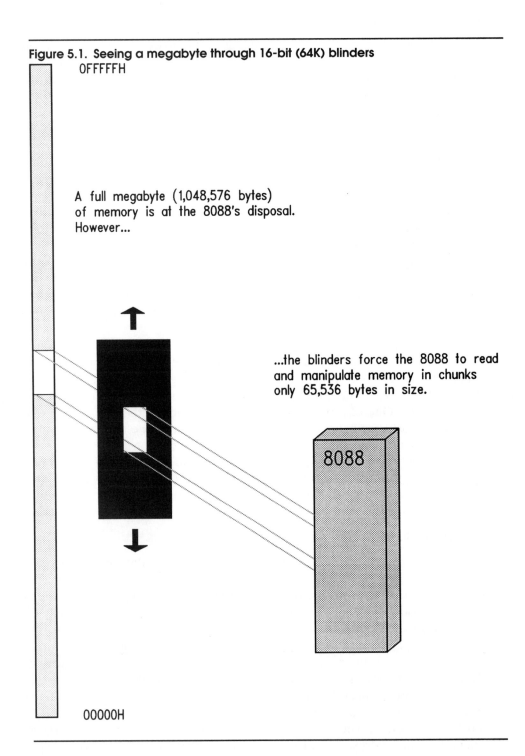

0FFFFFH

A full megabyte (1,048,576 bytes)
of memory is at the 8088's disposal.
However...

...the blinders force the 8088 to read
and manipulate memory in chunks
only 65,536 bytes in size.

8088

00000H

65,536 bytes long. The CPU can slide that piece of cardboard up and down the full length of its memory system. However, *at any one time,* it can only access 65,536 bytes.

The CPU's view of memory is peculiar. It is constrained to look at memory in chunks, where no chunk can be larger than 65,536 bytes in length.

The number 64K is important, just as 1Mb is. (We call 65,536 64K for the same reason that we call 1,048,576 "1Mb"—it's just shorthand for what is actually a binary number that "comes out even.") In fact, 64K is more important in assembly language programming than 1Mb; This is the number that circumscribes almost everything that an assembly-language programmer needs to do with the 86-family CPUs. It is, for one thing, the largest single number that the CPU can actually count and remember as an integral whole. You'll encounter it again and again and again.

Remember: 65,536 in binary is 1000000000000000B; in hex it's 10000H. The important characteristic of 64K is that the number can be expressed in 16 bits. As a multiple of one byte, 16 bits carries with it some of the magic quality of the byte as data atom in our computer universe. The 8088 and 8086 are often called 16-bit computers, because they typically and most efficiently process 16 bits at once crunch. As we begin to discuss CPU registers, you'll come to fully understand just why the magical number 65,536 is as important and all-pervasive as it is.

5.2 "They're Diggin' It up in Choonks!"

That's what Ray Walston shouted jubilantly in the marvelous film version of *Paint Your Wagon.* He was referring to gold being mined somewhere else (of course), but the metaphor to 86-family memory manipulation is apt. As we pointed out in the last section, the 8088 and its brothers *only* dig memory in chunks—that's how they're made. Furthermore, it may not be as bad an idea as most programmers think.

To cement my point, let's talk about another type of nugget: native copper. The better part of a mile under the Mesabe range in upper Michigan is an enormous nugget of native copper the size of a freight locomotive. It may even be larger; the mining company that discovered it isn't entirely sure how large it is. This super nugget was discovered before World War II and is still down there at the end of a long tunnel, basically forgotten.

Why leave a fortune in copper sitting where it was found, you ask? OK, wise guy—how do you get it out? Pure copper is a notoriously intractable metal. While not horribly hard, it is tough in ways that make cutting tools become dull and cause them to get stuck in their holes. The truth is that cutting the giant nugget up into manageable pieces would literally cost more than the copper would be worth at today's prices. Hauling out easily-crushed copper ore in fist-sized chunks is enormously easier on men and equipment—so supernugget remains in its hole, a curiosity and nothing more.

The lesson here is twofold: first of all, just as most mining companies do not encounter locomotive-sized nuggets every day (or even every century) most jobs a computer has to do not involve enormous quantities of memory *at one time*. Second, even on computers that don't have a set of 64K blinders, playing with a megabyte all at once is hard work, and costly in machine performance.

It may be that the 86-family's blinders enable it to work more quickly and efficiently within its megabyte of memory. Whether true or not, this notion of seeing memory as a number of chunks, called *segments*, is key to understanding the 86-family CPUs as well.

The Nature of Segments

In 86-parlance, a segment is a region of memory that begins on a paragraph boundary and extends for some number of bytes less than or equal to 64K (65,536). We've spoken of the number 64K before. But paragraphs?

Time out for a lesson in 86-family trivia. A *paragraph* is a measure of memory equal to 16 bytes. It is one of numerous technical terms used to describe various quantities of memory. We've spoken of some of them before, and all of them are even multiples of one byte. Bytes are data atoms, remember; loose memory bits never exist in the absence of a byte of memory to contain them. Table 5.1 lists the terms you should be aware of.

Table 5.1 lists two names for each term. One is the technical term that you and I and all the rest of the humans use in speaking. However, the assembler has its own names for these terms, which you will have to use when writing assembly-language programs. Some of these terms, like ten byte, occur very rarely, and others, like page, occur almost never. The term paragraph is almost never used, *except* in connection with the places where segments may begin.

Table 5.1. Collective terms for memory

NAME		SIZE	
Technical	**Assembler**	**Decimal**	**Hex**
Byte	BYTE	1	01H
Word	WORD	2	02H
Double word	DWORD	4	04H
Quad word	QWORD	8	08H
Ten byte	TBYTE	10	0AH
Paragraph	PARA	16	10H
Page	PAGE	256	100H
Segment	SEGMENT	65,536	10000H

Any memory address evenly divisible by 16 is called a *paragraph bound-ary*. The first paragraph boundary is address 0. The second is address 10H; the third address 20H, and so on. (Remember that 10H is equal to decimal 16.) Any paragraph boundary may be considered the start of a segment.

This *doesn't* mean that a segment actually starts every 16 bytes up and down throughout that megabyte of memory. A segment is like a shelf in one of those modern adjustable bookcases. On the back face of the bookcase are a great many little slots spaced one-half inch apart. A shelf bracket can be inserted into any of the little slots. However, there aren't hundreds of shelves, but only four or five. Most of the slots are empty. They exist so that a much smaller number of shelves may be adjusted up and down the height of the bookcase as needed.

In a very similar manner, paragraph boundaries are little slots at which a segment may start. An assembly-language program may make use of only four or five segments, but each of those segments may begin at any of the 65,536 paragraph boundaries existing in the 8088's megabyte of memory.

There's that number again: 65,536; our beloved 64K. There are 64K differ-ent paragraph boundaries where a segment may begin. Each paragraph bound-ary has a number. As always, the numbers begin from 0, and go to 64K minus one; in decimal 65,535, or in hex 0FFFFH. Because a segment may begin at any paragraph boundary, the number of the paragraph boundary at which a seg-ment begins is called the *segment address* of that particular segment. We rarely, in fact, speak of paragraphs or paragraph boundaries at all. When you see the term "segment address," keep in mind that each segment address is 16 bytes (one paragraph) farther along in memory than the segment address before it. See Figure 5.2.

In short, segments may begin at any segment address. There are 65,536 segment addresses evenly distributed across the 8088's full megabyte of memory, 16 bytes apart. A segment address is more a permission than a compulsion; for all the 64K possible segment addresses, only five or six are ever actually used to begin segments at any one time. Think of segment addresses as slots where segments may be placed.

So much for segment addresses; now, what of segments themselves? A segment may be up to 64K bytes in size, but it doesn't *have* to be. A segment may be only 1 byte long, or 256 bytes long, or 21,378 bytes long, or any length at all short of 64K bytes.

A Horizon, Not a Place

You define a segment primarily by stating where it begins. What, then, defines how *long* a segment is? Nothing, really—and we get into some really tricky semantics here. A segment is more a *horizon* than a *place*. Once you define where a segment begins, that segment can encompass any location in memory

Figure 5.2. Memory addresses vs. segment addresses

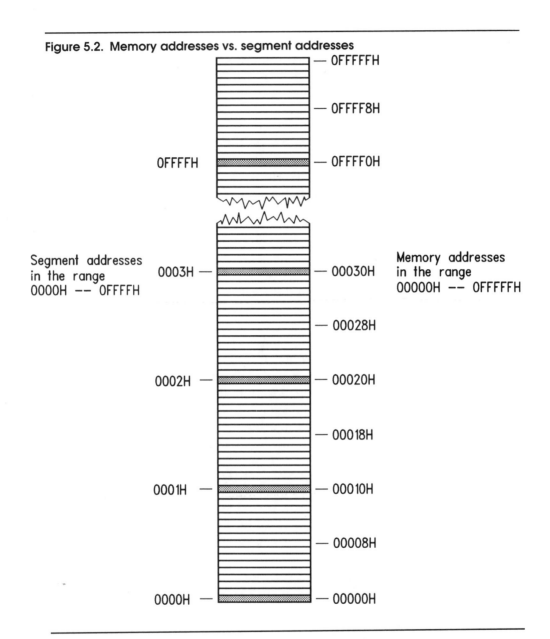

between that starting place and the horizon, which is 65,536 bytes down the line.

Nothing says, of course, that a segment must use all of that memory. In most cases, when you define a segment to exist at some segment address, you only end up considering the next few hundred bytes as part of that segment, until you get into some truly world-class programs. Most beginners read about segments and think of them as some kind of memory allocation, a protected region of memory with walls on both sides, reserved for some specific use.

This is about as far from true as you can get. Nothing is protected within a segment, and segments are not reserved for any specific register or access method. Segments can overlap. Segments don't really exist, in a very real sense, *except* as horizons beyond which a certain type of reference cannot go. It comes back to that set of 64K blinders the CPU wears, as I drew in Figure 5.1. I think of it this way: *a segment is the location in memory at which the CPU's 64K blinders are positioned*. In looking at memory through the blinders, you can see bytes starting at the segment address, and going on until the blinders cut you off, 64K bytes down the way.

The key to understanding this admittedly metaphysical definition of a segment is knowing how segments are used. And coming to understand that finally brings us to the subject of registers.

Making 20-Bit Addresses out of 16-Bit Registers

The 8088 and 8086 are often called 16-bit CPUs because their internal registers are almost all 16 bits in size. A *register*, as I've hinted before, is a memory location *inside* the CPU chip rather than outside in a memory bank. The 86 family has a fair number of registers, and they are an interesting crew indeed.

Registers do many jobs, but one of their more important jobs is holding addresses of important locations in memory. If you'll recall, the 8088 has 20 address pins, and its megabyte of memory requires addresses 20 bits in size.

How do you put a 20-bit memory address in a 16-bit register?

Easy. You don't.

You put a 20-bit address in *two* 16-bit registers.

What happens is this: all locations within the 8088's megabyte of memory have not one address but *two*. Every byte in memory is assumed to reside in a segment. A byte's complete address, then, consists of the address of its segment, along with the distance of the byte from the start of that segment. The address of the segment is (as we said before) the byte's *segment address*. The byte's distance from the start of the segment is the byte's *offset address*. Both addresses must be specified to completely describe any single byte's location within the full megabyte of memory. When written, the segment address comes first, followed by the offset address. The two are separated with a colon. Segment:offset addresses are always written in hexadecimal. Make sure the colon is there so that people know you're specifying an address and not just a couple of numbers!

I've drawn Figure 5.3 to help make this a little clearer. A byte of data we'll call "MyByte" exists in memory at the location marked. Its address is given as 0001:001D. This means that MyByte falls within segment 0001H, and is located 001DH bytes from the start of that segment. Note that when two numbers are

Figure 5.3. Segments and offsets

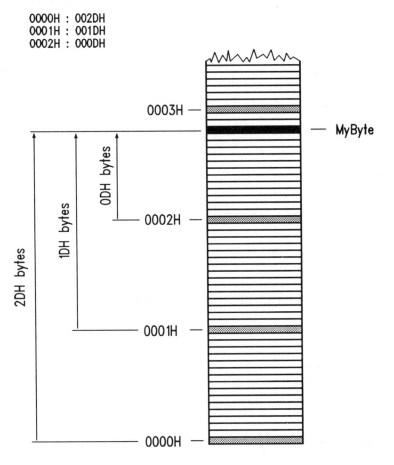

MyByte could have any of three possible addresses:

0000H : 002DH
0001H : 001DH
0002H : 000DH

used to specify an address with a colon between them, you do *not* end each of the two numbers with the hexadecimal suffix.

You can omit leading zeroes if you like; however, remember the assembly-language policy of never allowing a hex number to begin with the hex digits A through F. For example, the address 00B2:0004 could be written 0B2:4. As a good rule of thumb, however, I recommend using all four hex digits in both components of the address *except* when all four digits are zero. In other words, you can abbreviate 0000:0061 to 0:0061 or 0B00:0000 to 0B00:0.

The universe is perverse, however, and clever eyes will perceive that MyByte can have two other perfectly legal addresses: 0:002D and 0002:000D. How so? Keep in mind that a segment may start every 16 bytes throughout the full megabyte of real memory. A segment, once begun, embraces all bytes from its origin to 65,535 bytes further up in memory. There's nothing wrong with segments overlapping, and in Figure 5.3 we have three overlapping segments. MyByte is 2DH bytes into the first segment, which begins at segment address 0000H. MyByte is 1DH bytes into the second segment, which begins at segment address 0001H. It's not that MyByte is in two or three places at once. It's in only one place, but that one place may be described in any of three ways.

It's a little like Chicago's street number system. Howard Street is 76 blocks from Chicago's "origin," Madison Street. Howard Street is, however, only 4 blocks from Touhy Avenue. You can describe Howard Street's location relative to either Madison Street or Touhy Avenue, depending on what you want to do.

An arbitrary byte somewhere in the middle of the 8086's megabyte of memory may fall within literally tens of thousands of different segments. Which segment the byte is *actually* in is strictly a matter of convention.

This problem appears in real life to confront programmers of the IBM PC. The PC keeps its time and date information in a series of memory bytes that starts at address 0040:006C. There is also a series of memory bytes containing PC timer information located at 0000:046C. You guessed it—we're talking about exactly the same starting byte. Different writers speaking of that same byte may give its address in either of those two ways, and they'll all be completely correct.

The way, then, to express a 20-bit address in two 16-bit registers is to put the segment address into one 16-bit register, and the offset address into another 16-bit register. The two registers taken together identify one byte among all 1,048,576 bytes in a megabyte.

5.3 Registers and Memory Addresses

Think of the segment address as the starting position of the 8086/8088's 64K blinders. Typically, you'll move the blinders to encompass the location where you wish to work, and then leave the blinders in one place while moving around within their 64K limits.

This is exactly how registers tend to be used in 8086/8088 assembly language. The 8088, 8086, and 80286 have exactly four *segment registers* specifically designated as holders of segment addresses. (The 386 and 486 have two more—but we'll return to that in Chapter 11.) Each segment register is a 16-bit memory location existing within the CPU chip itself. No matter what the CPU is doing, if it's addressing some location in memory, the segment address of that location is present in one of the four segment registers.

The segment registers have names that reflect their general functions: CS, **DS**, **SS**, and **ES**.

- **CS stands for Code Segment**. Machine instructions exist at some offset into a code segment. The segment address of the code segment of the currently executing instruction is contained in CS.

- **DS stands for Data Segment**. Variables and other data exist at some offset into a data segment. There may be many data segments, but the CPU may only use one at a time, by placing the segment address of that segment in register DS.

- **SS stands for Stack Segment**. The *stack* is a very important component of the CPU used for temporary storage of data and addresses. I'll explain how the stack works a little later; for now simply understand that, like everything else within the 8086/8088's megabyte of memory, the stack has a segment address, which is contained in SS.

- **ES stands for Extra Segment**. The extra segment is exactly that: a spare segment that may be used for specifying a location in memory.

General-Purpose Registers

The segment registers exist only to hold segment addresses. They can be forced to do a few other things, but by and large segment registers should be considered specialists in "segment address containing." The 8086/8088 CPU has a crew of generalist registers to do the rest of the work of assembly-language computing. Among many other things, these *general-purpose registers* are used to hold the offset addresses that must be paired with segment addresses to pin down a single location in memory.

Like the segment registers, the general-purpose registers are memory locations existing inside the CPU chip itself. They all have names rather than numeric addresses: AX, BX, CX, DX, SP, BP, SI, and DI. The general-purpose registers really are generalists in that all of them share a large suite of capabilities. However, each of the general-purpose registers also has what I call its "hidden agenda": a task or set of tasks that only it can perform.

I'll explain all these hidden agendas as I go. For now, we'll concentrate on the role of the general-purpose registers in addressing memory.

Several of the general-purpose registers (BX, BP, SP, SI, and DI) may contain an offset address. This offset address may be used in combination with any of the segment registers to pinpoint any one of the 1,048,576 bytes in the mega-byte address space of the 8086/8088. All you need to do is specify which two registers are to be used together, with the segment register first and the general-purpose register second. For example:

```
SS : SP
SS : BP
ES : DI
DS : SI
CS : BX
```

Register Halves

General-purpose registers AX, BX, CX, and DX have an important property: they can be cut in half. Actually, assemblers recognize special names for the two halves of these four registers. The A, B, C, and D are retained, but instead of the X, a half is specified with an "H" for "High half" or an "L" for "Low half." Each register half is one byte (eight bits) in size, allowing the entire register to be 16 bits in size, or one word.

Thus, making up the 16-bit register AX you have byte-sized register halves AH and AL; within BX there is BH and BL, and so on. One nice thing about this arrangement is that you can read and change one half of a 16-bit number without disturbing the other half. This means that if you place the 16-bit hexadecimal value 76E9H into register AX, you can read the byte-sized value 76H from register AH, and 0E9H from register AL. Better still, if you then store the value 0AH into register AL and then read back register AX, you'll find that the original value of 76E9H has been changed to 760AH.

Being able to treat the AX, BX, CX, and DX registers as 8-bit halves can be extremely handy in situations where you're manipulating a lot of 8-bit quantities. Each register half can be considered a separate register, leaving you twice the number of places to put things while your program works. As you'll see later on, finding a place to stick a value in a pinch is one of the great challenges facing assembly-language programmers.

Keep in mind that this dual nature involves *only* general-purpose registers AX, BX, CX, and DX. The other general-purpose registers SP, BP, SI, and DI, are *not* similarly equipped. There are no SIH and SIL 8-bit registers, for example, as convenient as that would sometimes be.

The Instruction Pointer

Yet another type of register lives inside the 8086/8088 CPU. The *instruction pointer* (usually called IP) is in a class by itself. IP is far more of a specialist than are any of the segment registers. IP can do only one thing: it contains the offset address of the next machine instruction to be executed.

While executing a program, the CPU uses IP to keep track of where it is. Each time an instruction is executed, IP is *incremented* by some number of bytes. The number of bytes is the size of the instruction just executed. The net result is to bump IP further into memory, so that it points to the start of the next instruction to be executed. Instructions come in different sizes, ranging typically from one to six bytes. (Some of the more arcane forms of the more arcane instructions may be even larger.) The CPU is careful to increment IP by just the right number of bytes, so that it does in fact end up pointing to the start of the next instruction, and not merely into the middle of the last instruction.

If IP contains the offset address of the next machine instruction, where is the segment address? The segment address is kept in the code segment register CS. Together, CS and IP contain the full 20-bit address of the next machine instruction to be executed.

> The full 20-bit address of the next machine instruction to be executed is kept in CS:IP.

A *code segment* is an area of memory where machine instructions are stored. The steps and tests of which a program is made are contained in code segments. There may be many code segments in a program, but small programs like the ones in this book will most likely have only one. The *current code segment* is that code segment whose segment address is currently stored in code segment register CS. At any given time, the machine instruction currently being executed exists within the current code segment.

Typically, large programs are divided up into chunks, with each chunk considered to be part of a separate code segment. Switching from one code segment to another is done with a class of instructions called branching instructions, which I'll be covering in Chapter 9.

IP is notable in being the *only* register that can neither be read nor written to directly. It's possible to obtain the current value of IP, but the method involves some trickery that will have to wait until we discuss branching instructions in Chapter 9.

The Flags Register

There is one additional type of register inside the CPU: the Flags register. The Flags register is 16 bits in size, and most of those 16 bits are single-bit registers called *flags*. Each of these individual flags has a name, like CF, DF, OF, and so on.

When your program performs a test, what it tests is one or another of the single-bit flags in the Flags register. Since a single bit may contain one of only two values, 1 or 0, a test in assembly language is truly a two-way affair: either a flag is set to 1 or it isn't. If the flag is set to 1, the program takes one action; if the flag is set to 0, the program takes a different action.

We're concentrating on memory addressing at the moment, so for now I'll simply promise to go into flag lore in more detail at more appropriate moments later in the book.

Reading and Changing Registers with DEBUG

The DOS DEBUG utility provides a handy window into the CPU's hidden world of registers. How DEBUG does this is the blackest of all black arts and I can't begin to explain it in an introductory text. For now, just consider DEBUG a magic box.

Looking at the registers from DEBUG doesn't even require that you load a program into DEBUG. Simply run DEBUG, and at the dash prompt, type R. The display will look something very close to this:

```
-R
AX=0000  BX=0000  CX=0000  DX=0000  SP=FFEE  BP=0000  SI=0000  DI=0000
DS=1980  ES=1980  SS=1980  CS=1980  IP=0100   NV UP EI PL NZ NA PO NC
1980:0100 389A5409        CMP [BP+SI+0954],BL                  SS:0954=8A
```

I say "something very close" because details of the display will vary depending on what resident programs you have loaded in memory, which version of DOS you're using, and so on. What will vary will be the values listed as present in the various registers, and the machine instruction shown in the third line of the display (Here, **CMP [BP+SI+0954],BL**).

What will *not* vary is the fact that every CPU register has its place in the display, along with its current value shown to the right of an equal sign. The series of characters NV UP EI PL NZ NA PO NC are a summary of the current values of the flags in the flags register.

The display shown above is that of the registers when *no* program has been loaded. All of the general-purpose registers except for SP have been set to 0, and all of the segment registers have been set to the value 1980H. These are the default conditions set up by DEBUG in the CPU when no program has been loaded. (The 1980H value will probably be different for you—it represents the first available segment in memory above DOS, and where that segment falls depends on what else exists in memory both above and below DOS.)

Changing a register is done very simply, again using DEBUG's R command. To change the value of AX, type R AX

```
-R AX
AX:0000
:0A7B
-
```

DEBUG will respond by displaying the current value of AX, and then, on the following line, a colon prompt. DEBUG will then wait for you to either enter a new numeric value for AX or press Enter. If you press Enter, the current value of the register will not be changed. In the example shown above, I typed 0A7B (you needn't type the H indicating hex) and then pressed Enter.

Once you do enter a new value and then press Enter, DEBUG does nothing to verify the change. To see the change to register AX, you must display all the registers again using the R command:

```
-R
AX=0A7B  BX=0000  CX=0000  DX=0000  SP=FFEE  BP=0000  SI=0000  DI=0000
DS=1980  ES=1980  SS=1980  CS=1980  IP=0100   NV UP EI PL NZ NA PO NC
1980:0100 389A5409        CMP [BP+SI+0954],BL                 SS:0954=8A
```

Take a few minutes to practice entering new values for the general-purpose registers, then display the registers as a group to verify that the changes were made. While exploring you might find that the IP register can be changed, even though I said earlier that it can't be changed directly. The key word is *directly*; DEBUG knows all the dirty tricks.

Inspecting the Video Refresh Buffer with DEBUG

One good way to help your knowledge of memory addressing sink in is to use DEBUG to take a look at some interesting places in the PC's memory space.

One easy thing to do is look at the PC's video display adapter's refresh buffer. A *video refresh buffer* is a region of memory with a difference: any characters written to buffer memory are instantly displayed on the computer screen. This screen refresh feature is accomplished electrically through special use of the information that comes out of the memory data pins. Precisely how it is done is outside the scope of this book. For now, simply understand that writing a character to your display screen can be done by writing the ASCII code for that character into the correct address in the video refresh buffer portion of memory.

As with any memory location anywhere within the PC, the video refresh buffer has a segment address. What that segment address is depends on the kind of display installed in the PC. There are two possibilities: if your PC has a *color* screen, the segment address of the video refresh buffer is 0B800H; if your PC has a *monochrome* screen, the segment address is 0B000H.

It takes two bytes in the buffer to display a character. The first of the two (that is, first in memory) is the ASCII code of the character itself. For example, an "A" would require the ASCII code 41H; a "B" would require the ASCII code 42H, and so on. (The full ASCII code set is shown in Appendix B.) The second of the two bytes is the character's *attribute*. Think of it this way: the ASCII code says *what* character to display and the attribute says *how* to display it. The attribute dictates the color of a character and its background cell on a color screen. On a monochrome screen, the attribute specifies if a character is underlined or displayed in reverse video. (*Reverse video* is a character display mode that shows dark characters on a light background, rather than the traditional light character on a dark or black background.) Every character byte has an attribute byte and every attribute byte has its character byte; neither can exist alone.

The very first character/attribute pair in the video refresh buffer corresponds to the character you see in the upper-left corner of the screen. The next character/attribute pair in the buffer is the character at the second position on the top line of the screen, and so on. I've drawn a diagram of the relationship between characters on the screen and byte values in the video refresh buffer, in Figure 5.4.

In Figure 5.4, the three letters "ABC" are displayed in the upper-left corner of the screen. Notice that the "C" is underlined. The screen shown in Figure 5.4

Figure 5.4. The PC's video refresh buffer

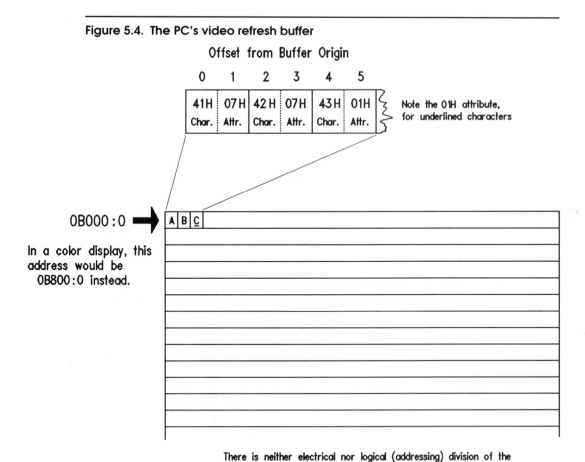

There is neither electrical nor logical (addressing) division of the buffer into lines; line structure exists only in the display.

is monochrome. The video refresh buffer therefore begins at 0B000:0. The byte located at address 0B000:0 is ASCII code 41H, corresponding to the letter "A." The byte at address 0B00:0001 is the corresponding attribute value of 07H. The value 07H as an attribute dictates normal text in both color and monochrome displays, where normal means white characters on a black background.

The byte at 0B000:0005 is also an attribute byte, but its value is 01H. On a monochrome display, 01H makes the corresponding character underlined. On a color display, 01H makes the character blue on a black background.

There is nothing about the video refresh buffer to divide it into the lines you see on the display. The first 160 characters (80 ASCII codes plus their 80 attribute bytes) are shown as the first line, and the next set of 160 characters is shown on the next line down, and so on.

You might rightfully ask what ASCII code is in the video refresh buffer for locations on the screen that show no character at all. The answer, of course, is that there *is* a character in every "empty" space: the space character, whose ASCII code is 20H.

You can inspect the memory within the video refresh buffer directly through DEBUG, by following these steps:

1. Clear the screen by entering CLS at the DOS prompt and then pressing Enter.

2. Invoke DEBUG.

3. Enter the segment address of your video refresh buffer into the ES register by using the R command. Remember: Color screens use the 0B800H segment address, while monochrome screens use the 0B000H segment address. Note that 0B800H must be entered into DEBUG as "B800," *without* the leading zero. TASM and MASM *must* have that leading zero, and DEBUG *cannot* have it. Sadly, no one ever said that all parts of this business had to make perfect sense.

4. Enter D ES:O to dump the first 128 bytes of the video refresh buffer.

5. Enter the D command (by itself) a second time to dump the next 128 bytes of the video refresh buffer.

What you'll see should look a lot like the session dump shown below:

```
C:\ASM>debug
-r es
ES 1980
:b800
-d es:0
B800:0000  20 07 20 07 20 07 20 07-20 07 20 07 20 07 20 07   . . . . . . . .
B800:0010  20 07 20 07 20 07 20 07-20 07 20 07 20 07 20 07   . . . . . . . .
B800:0020  20 07 20 07 20 07 20 07-20 07 20 07 20 07 20 07   . . . . . . . .
B800:0030  20 07 20 07 20 07 20 07-20 07 20 07 20 07 20 07   . . . . . . . .
B800:0040  20 07 20 07 20 07 20 07-20 07 20 07 20 07 20 07   . . . . . . . .
B800:0050  20 07 20 07 20 07 20 07-20 07 20 07 20 07 20 07   . . . . . . . .
```

```
B800:0060  20 07 20 07 20 07 20 07-20 07 20 07 20 07 20 07    . . . . . . . .
B800:0070  20 07 20 07 20 07 20 07-20 07 20 07 20 07 20 07    . . . . . . . .
-d
B800:0080  20 07 20 07 20 07 20 07-20 07 20 07 20 07 20 07    . . . . . . . .
B800:0090  20 07 20 07 20 07 20 07-20 07 20 07 20 07 20 07    . . . . . . . .
B800:00A0  43 07 3A 07 5C 07 41 07-53 07 4D 07 3E 07 64 07    C . : . \ . A . S . M . > . d .
B800:00B0  65 07 62 07 75 07 67 07-20 07 20 07 20 07 20 07    e . b . u . g . . . . .
B800:00C0  20 07 20 07 20 07 20 07-20 07 20 07 20 07 20 07    . . . . . . . .
B800:00D0  20 07 20 07 20 07 20 07-20 07 20 07 20 07 20 07    . . . . . . . .
B800:00E0  20 07 20 07 20 07 20 07-20 07 20 07 20 07 20 07    . . . . . . . .
B800:00F0  20 07 20 07 20 07 20 07-20 07 20 07 20 07 20 07    . . . . . . . .
```

The first 80 character/attribute pairs are the same: 20H/07H, which display as plain ordinary blank space. When you execute the CLS command on most machines, the screen is cleared, and the DOS prompt reappears on the *second* line from the top of the screen, *not* the top line. The top line is typically left blank, as is the case here.

You'll see in the second block of 128 dumped bytes the DOS prompt and the invocation of DEBUG in lowercase. Keep in mind when reading DEBUG hex dumps that any character not readily displayed as one of the standard ASCII letters, numbers, or punctuation marks is represented as a period character. This is why the 07H attribute character on the right portion of DEBUG's display is shown as a period character, since the ASCII code 07H has no displayable equivalent.

You can keep dumping further into the video refresh buffer by pressing DEBUG's D command repeatedly.

Reading the BIOS Revision Date

Another interesting item that's easy to locate in your PC is the revision date in the ROM BIOS. *Read-only memory (ROM)* chips are special memory chips that retain their contents when power to the PC is turned off. The *BIOS* (Basic Input/Output System) is a collection of assembly-language routines that perform basic services for the PC: disk handling, video handling, printer handling, etc. The BIOS is kept in ROM at the very top of the PC's megabyte of address space.

The BIOS contains a date, indicating when it was declared finished by its authors. This date is always at the same address, and can be easily displayed using DEBUG's D command. The address of the date is 0FFFF:0005. The DEBUG session is shown below. Note again that the hex number 0FFFFH must be entered without its leading zero:

```
-d ffff:0005
FFFF:0000                         30 34 2F-33 30 2F 38 37 00 FC B8      04/30/87...
FFFF:0010  00 00 00 00 00 00 00 00-00 00 00 00 00 00 00 00    . . . . . . . . . . . . . . .
FFFF:0020  00 00 00 00 00 00 00 00-00 00 00 00 00 00 00 00    . . . . . . . . . . . . . . .
FFFF:0030  00 00 00 00 00 00 00 00-00 00 00 00 00 00 00 00    . . . . . . . . . . . . . . .
```

```
FFFF:0040  00 00 00 00 00 00 00 00-00 00 00 00 00 00 00 00    ................
FFFF:0050  00 00 00 00 00 00 00 00-00 00 00 00 00 00 00 00    ................
FFFF:0060  00 00 00 00 00 00 00 00-00 00 00 00 00 00 00 00    ................
FFFF:0070  00 00 00 00 00 00 00 00-00 00 00 00 00 00 00 00    ................
FFFF:0080  00 00 00 00 00
```

One peculiarity of DEBUG illustrated here is that when you begin a hex dump of memory at an address that is *not* evenly divisible by 16, DEBUG spaces the first byte of the dump over to the right so that paragraph boundaries still fall at the left margin.

Another rather peculiar thing to keep in mind while looking at the dump shown above is that *only the first line of memory shown in the dump really exists*. The segment 0FFFFH begins only sixteen bytes before the end of the 8086/8088's megabyte of memory space. (See Figure 5.2 for a good illustration of this.) The byte at 0FFFF:000F is the *last* byte in memory. Addresses from 0FFFF:0010 to 0FFFF:0FFFF would require more than 20 address bits to express, so they simply don't exist. DEBUG won't tell you that, it'll just give you endless pages of zeroes for memory beyond the 8086/8088 megabyte pale. (Several readers have told me that certain versions of DEBUG take a different approach: DEBUG "wraps" their display around to the *bottom* of memory instead, and begins displaying bytes at 0000:0000 once it runs out of *high* memory. It's something to watch out for, and if memory "beyond" the FFFF:000F point are *not* zeroes, you're in fact seeing such a wrap to *low* memory.)

Transferring Control to Machine Instructions in ROM

So far we've looked at locations in memory as containers for data. All well and good—but memory contains machine instructions as well. A very effective illustration of a machine instruction at a particular address is also provided by the ROM BIOS—and right next door to the BIOS revision date, at that.

The machine instruction in question is located at address 0FFFF:0. Recall that, by convention, the *next* machine instruction to be executed is the one whose address is stored in CS:IP. Run DEBUG. Load the value 0FFFFH into code segment register CS, and 0 into instruction pointer IP. Then dump memory at 0FFFF:0:

```
-r cs
CS 1980
:ffff
-r ip
IP 0100
:0
-r
AX=0000  BX=0000  CX=0000  DX=0000  SP=FFEE  BP=0000  SI=0000  DI=0000
DS=1980  ES=1980  SS=1980  CS=FFFF  IP=0000   NV UP EI PL NZ NA PO NC
```

```
FFFF:0000  EA5BE000F0      JMP F000:E05B
-d cs:0
FFFF:0000  EA 5B E0 00 F0 30 34 2F-33 30 2F 38 37 00 FC B8   .[...04/30/87...
FFFF:0010  00 00 00 00 00 00 00 00-00 00 00 00 00 00 00 00   ................
FFFF:0020  00 00 00 00 00 00 00 00-00 00 00 00 00 00 00 00   ................
FFFF:0030  00 00 00 00 00 00 00 00-00 00 00 00 00 00 00 00   ................
FFFF:0040  00 00 00 00 00 00 00 00-00 00 00 00 00 00 00 00   ................
FFFF:0050  00 00 00 00 00 00 00 00-00 00 00 00 00 00 00 00   ................
FFFF:0060  00 00 00 00 00 00 00 00-00 00 00 00 00 00 00 00   ................
FFFF:0070  00 00 00 00 00 00 00 00-00 00 00 00 00 00 00 00   ................
```

Look at the third line of the register display, which we've been ignoring up until now. To the right of the address display is this series of five bytes: **EA5BE000F0**.

These five bytes make up the machine instruction we want. Notice that the first line of the memory dump begins with the same address, and, sure enough, shows us the same five bytes.

Trying to remember what machine instruction **EA5BE000F0** is would try anyone's intellect, so DEBUG is a good sport and translates the five bytes into a more readable representation of the machine instruction. We call this process of translating binary machine codes back into human-readable, assembly-language mnemonics *unassembly* or, more commonly, *disassembly.*

```
JMP F000:E05B.
```

What this instruction does, quite simply, is tell the CPU to "jump" to the address 0F000:0E05B and begin executing the machine instructions located there. If we execute the machine instruction at CS:IP, that's what will happen: the CPU will jump to the address 0F000:0E05B and begin executing whatever machine instructions it finds there.

All PC's have a **JMP** instruction at address 0FFFF:0. The address to which that **JMP** instruction jumps will be different for different makes and models of PC. This is why on your machine you won't necessarily see the exact five bytes **EA5BE000F0**, but whatever five bytes you find at 0FFFF:0, they will *always* begin with 0EAH. The 0EAH byte specifies that this instruction will be a **JMP** instruction. The remainder of the machine instruction is the address to which the CPU must jump. If that address as given in the machine instruction looks a little scrambled, well, it is...but that's the way the 86-family of CPUs do things. We'll return to the issue of funny-looking addresses a little later.

DEBUG has a command, G (for Go) that begins execution at the address stored in CS:IP. If you enter the G command and press Enter, the CPU will jump to the address built into the **JMP** instruction and begin executing machine instructions. What happens then?

Your machine will go into a *cold boot*, just as it would if you powered down and powered up again. (So make sure you're ready for a reboot before you try it!)

This may seem odd. But consider this: the CPU chip has to begin execution somewhere. When the CPU wakes up after being off all night with the power removed, it must get a first machine instruction from somewhere and start executing. Built into the silicon of the 8086/8088 CPU chips is the assumption that a legal machine instruction will exist at address 0FFFF:0. When power is applied to the CPU chip, the first thing it does is place 0FFFH in CS, and 0 in IP. Then it starts fetching instructions from the address in CS:IP and executing them, one at a time, in the manner that CPUs must.

This is why *all* PC's have a **JMP** instruction at 0FFFF:0, and why this **JMP** instruction always jumps to the routines that bring the PC up from stone cold dead to fully operational.

So go ahead: load 0FFFFH into CS and 0 into IP, and press G. Feel good? It's what we call the feeling of *power*.

Following Your Instructions

Meeting Machine Instructions Up Close and Personal

Machine instructions, those atoms of action that are the steps a program must take to get its work done, are the most visible part of any assembly-language program. The collection of instructions supported by a given CPU is that CPU's *instruction set.* The 8086 and 8088 CPUs share the same instruction set, which is why most people consider them the same CPU.

This cannot be said for the 80286 and 80386, both of which offer additional instructions not found in the 8086/8088. By and large, I'll only be introducing instructions in this book that the 8086/8088 understand. (I'll show you a few more from the more advanced CPUs in Chapter 11, but there are fewer truly useful new instructions than you might have hoped for.) Furthermore, I can't cover *all* machine instructions in this book, even limiting myself to the 8086/8088. Those that I will describe are the most common and most useful.

Nor will I abandon my discussion of memory addressing begun in Chapter 5. As I've said before, understanding how the CPU and its instructions address memory is more difficult but probably more important than understanding the instructions themselves. In and around the descriptions of the machine instructions I'll present from this point on there will be discussions and elaborations on memory addressing. Pay attention! If you don't learn the concepts of memory addressing, memorizing the entire instruction set will do you no good at all.

6.1 Assembling and Executing Machine Instructions with DEBUG

The most obvious way to experiment with machine instructions is to build a short program out of them and watch it go. This can easily be done (and we'll be doing it a lot in later chapters) but it's far from the fastest way to do things. Editing, assembling, and linking all take time, and when you only want to look at *one* machine instruction in action (rather than a crew of them working together) the full development cycle is overkill.

Once more, we turn to DEBUG.

At the close of the last chapter we got a taste of a DEBUG feature called *unassembly,* which is a peculiar way of saying what most of us call *disassembly.* This is the reverse of the assembly process we looked at in detail in Chapter 3. Disassembly is the process of taking a binary machine instruction like 42H and converting it into its more readable assembly-language equivalent, **INC DX**.

In addition to all its other tools, DEBUG also contains a simple assembler, suitable for taking assembly-language mnemonics like **INC DX** and converting them to their binary machine code form. Later on we'll use a standalone assembler like TASM or MASM to assemble complete assembly-language programs. For the time being, we can use DEBUG to do things one or two instructions at a time.

Assembling a MOV Instruction

The single most common activity in assembly-language work is getting data from here to there. There are several specialized ways to do this, but only one truly general way: the **MOV** instruction. <u>**MOV** can move a byte or word of data</u> <u>from one register to another, from a register into memory, or from memory into</u> <u>a register. What **MOV** *cannot* do is move data directly from one address in</u> <u>memory to a different address in memory.</u>

<u>The name **MOV** is a bit of a misnomer, since what is actually happening is</u> <u>that data is *copied* from a source to a destination.</u> Once copied to the destination, however, the data does not vanish from the source, but continues to exist in both places. This process conflicts a little with our intuitive notion of moving, which usually means that something disappears from a source and reappears at a destination.

Because **MOV** is so general and obvious in its action, it's a good place to start in working with DEBUG's assembler.

Invoke DEBUG and use the R command to display the current state of the registers. You should see something like this:

```
-r
AX=0000  BX=0000  CX=0000  DX=0000  SP=FFEE  BP=0000  SI=0000  DI=0000
DS=1980  ES=1980  SS=1980  CS=1980  IP=0100   NV UP EI PL NZ NA PO NC
1980:0100 701D          JO  011F
```

We ignored the third line of the register display before. Now let's think a little bit more about what it means.

<u>When DEBUG is loaded without a specific file to debug, it simply takes the</u> <u>empty region of memory where a file would have been loaded (had a file been</u> <u>loaded when DEBUG was invoked) and treats it as though a program file were</u> <u>really there. The registers all get default values, most of which are zero. **IP**,</u> <u>however, starts out with a value of 0100H, and the code segment register CS</u> <u>gets the segment address of DEBUG's workspace,</u> which is theoretically empty.

Memory is never really "empty." A byte of memory always contains some value, whether true garbage that happened to reside in memory at power-up time, or a leftover value remaining from the last time that byte of memory was used. In the above register dump, memory at **CS:IP** contains a **JO** (jump on overflow) instruction. This rather obscure instruction was not placed there deliberately, but is simply DEBUG's interpretation of the two bytes 701DH that happen to reside at **CS:IP**. Most likely, the 701D value was part of some data table belonging to the last program to use that area of memory. It could have been part of a word-processor file, a spreadsheet, or anything else. Just don't think that some program *necessarily* put a **JO** instruction in memory. Machine instructions are just numbers, after all, and what numbers do in memory depends completely on how you interpret them—and what utility program you feed them to.

DEBUG's internal assembler assembles directly into memory, and places instructions one at a time—as you enter them at the keyboard—into memory at **CS:IP.** Each time you enter an instruction, **IP** is incremented to the next free location in memory. So by continuing to enter instructions, you can actually type an assembly-language program directly into memory.

Try it. Type the A (assemble) command and press Enter. DEBUG responds by displaying the current value of **CS:IP**, and then waits for you to enter an assembly-language instruction. Type **MOV AX,1** and press Enter. DEBUG again displays **CS:IP** and waits for a second instruction. It will continue waiting for instructions until you press Enter without typing anything. Then you'll see DEBUG's dash prompt again.

Now, use the R command again to display the registers. You should see something like this:

```
-r
AX=0000  BX=0000  CX=0000  DX=0000  SP=FFEE  BP=0000  SI=0000  DI=0000
DS=1980  ES=1980  SS=1980  CS=1980  IP=0100   NV UP EI PL NZ NA PO NC
1980:0100 B80100        MOV AX,0001
```

The registers haven't changed—but now the third line shows that the **JO** instruction is gone, and that the **MOV** instruction you entered has taken its place. Notice once again that **CS** contains 1980H, and **IP** contains 0100H. The address of the **MOV** instruction is shown as **1980:0100**; in other words, at **CS:IP.**

Executing a MOV Instruction with the Trace Command

Note that you haven't *executed* anything. You've simply used DEBUG's command to write a machine instruction into a location in memory.

There are two ways to execute machine instructions from within DEBUG. One way is to execute a program in memory, starting at **CS:IP**. This means that DEBUG will simply start the CPU executing whatever sequence of instructions begins at **CS:IP**. We looked at the G command very briefly at the end of the last chapter, when we found the **JMP** instruction that reboots your PC on power up, and used G to execute that instruction. The command is quite evocative: **G**o. But don't type G just yet....

You haven't entered a program. You've entered *one* instruction, and one instruction does not a program make. The instruction *after* your **MOV** instruction could be anything at all, recalling that DEBUG is simply interpreting garbage values in memory as random machine instructions. A series of random machine instructions could easily go berserk, locking your system into an endless loop or writing zeroes over an entire segment of memory that may contain part of DOS or of DEBUG itself. We'll use DEBUG's G command a little later, once we've constructed a complete program in memory.

For now, consider the mechanism DEBUG has for executing one machine instruction at a time. It's called Trace, and you invoke it by typing T. The T command will execute the machine instruction at **CS:IP**, then give control of the machine back to DEBUG. Trace is generally used to "single-step" a machine-code program one instruction at a time, in order to watch what it's up to every step of the way. For now, it's a fine way to execute a single instruction and examine that instruction's effects.

> DEBUG's G command executes programs in memory starting at CS:IP; DEBUG's T command executes the single instruction at **CS:IP**.

So type T. DEBUG will execute the **MOV** instruction you entered at CS:IP, and then immediately display the registers before returning to the dash prompt. You'll see this:

```
-r
AX=0001  BX=0000  CX=0000  DX=0000  SP=FFEE  BP=0000  SI=0000  DI=0000
DS=1980  ES=1980  SS=1980  CS=1980  IP=0103   NV UP EI PL NZ NA PO NC
1980:0103 6E          DB 6E
```

Look at the first line. DEBUG says **AX** is now equal to 0001. It held the default value 0000 before; obviously, your **MOV** instruction worked.

And there's something else to look at here: the third line shows an instruction called **DB** at CS:IP. Not quite true—**DB** is not a machine instruction, but an assembly-language *directive* that means *define byte*. (We'll return to **DB** later on, in Chapter 7.) It's DEBUG's way of saying that the number 6EH does not correspond to *any* machine instruction. It is truly a garbage byte sitting in memory, doing nothing. Executing a 6EH byte as though it were an instruction, however, could cause your machine to do unpredictably peculiar things, up to and including locking up hard.

6.2 Machine Instructions and Their Operands

As we said earlier, **MOV** copies data from a source to a destination. **MOV** is an extremely versatile instruction, and understanding its versatility demands a little study of this notion of source and a destination.

Source and Destination Operands

Many machine instructions, **MOV** included, have one or more *operands*. In the machine instruction **MOV AX,1** there are two operands. The first is **AX**, and the second is "1."

By convention in assembly language, the first operand belonging to a machine instruction is the *destination operand*. The second operand is the *source operand.*

With the **MOV** instruction the sense of the two operands is pretty literal: The source operand is copied to the destination operand. In **MOV AX,1**, the source operand 1 is copied into the destination operand **AX**. The sense of source and destination is not nearly so literal in other instructions, but a rule of thumb is this: whenever a machine instruction causes a new value to be generated, that new value is placed in the destination operand.

There are three different flavors of data that may be used as operands: *memory data, register data,* and *immediate data.* I've blown some example **MOV** instructions up to larger-than-life size in Figure 6.1, to give you a flavor for how the different types of data are specified as operands to the **MOV** instruction.

Immediate data is the easiest to understand. We'll look at it first.

Immediate Data

The **MOV AX,1** machine instruction that you entered into DEBUG was a good example of what we call *immediate data* which is accessed through an addressing mode called *immediate addressing*. Immediate addressing gets its name from the fact that the item being addressed is immediate data built right into the machine instruction. The CPU does not have to go anywhere to find

---

Figure 6.1. MOV and its operands

Instruction	Destination Operand	Source Operand	
MOV	AX,	1	Immediate Data
MOV	BX,	CX	16—bit Register Data
MOV	DL,	BH	8—bit Register Data
MOV	[BP],	DI	Memory Data at SS:BP
MOV	DX,	[SI]	Memory Data at DS:SI
MOV	BX,	ES:[BX]	Memory Data at ES:BX

immediate data. It's not in a register, or stored in a data segment somewhere out in memory. Immediate data is always right inside the instruction being fetched and executed—in this case, the source operand, 1.

Immediate data must be of an appropriate size for the operand. In other words, you can't move a 16-bit immediate value into an 8-bit register half like **AH** or **DL**. Neither DEBUG nor the standalone assemblers will allow you to assemble an instruction like this:

```
MOV CL,67EFH
```

Because it's built right into a machine instruction, you might think immediate data would be quick to access. This is true only to a point: fetching *anything* from memory takes more time than fetching anything from a register, and instructions are, after all, stored in memory.

So, while addressing immediate data is somewhat quicker than addressing ordinary data stored in memory, neither is anywhere near as quick as simply pulling a value from a CPU register.

Also keep in mind that *only* the source operand may be immediate data. The destination operand is the place where data *goes*, not where it comes from. Since immediate data consists of literal constants (numbers like 1, 0, or 7F2BH) trying to copy something *into* immediate data rather than *from* immediate data simply has no meaning.

Register Data

Data stored inside a CPU register is known as *register data*, and is accessed directly through an addressing mode called *register addressing*. Register addressing is done by simply naming the register you want to work with. Here are some examples of register data and register addressing:

```
MOV AX,BX
MOV BP,SP
MOV BL,CH
MOV ES,DX
ADD DI,AX
AND DX,SI
```

The last two examples point up the fact that we're not speaking *only* of the **MOV** instruction here. Register addressing happens any time data in a register is acted on directly.

The assembler keeps track of certain things that don't make sense, and one such situation is having a 16-bit register and an 8-bit register half within the same instruction. Such operations are not legal—after all, what would it mean to move a two-byte source into a one-byte destination? And while moving a one-byte source into a two-byte destination might seem more reasonable, the CPU does not support it and it cannot be done.

Playing with register addressing is easy using DEBUG. Bring up debug and assemble the following series of instructions:

```
MOV AX,67FE
MOV BX,AX
MOV CL,BH
MOV CH,BL
```

Now, reset the value of **IP** to 0100 using the R command. Then execute each of the machine instructions, one by one, using the T command. The session under DEBUG should look like this:

```
-A
333F:0100 MOV AX,67FE
333F:0103 MOV BX,AX
333F:0105 MOV CL,BH
333F:0107 MOV CH,BL
333F:0109
-R IP
IP 0100
:0100
-R
AX=0000  BX=0000  CX=0000  DX=0000  SP=FFEE  BP=0000  SI=0000  DI=0000
DS=333F  ES=333F  SS=333F  CS=333F  IP=0100   NV UP EI PL NZ NA PO NC
333F:0100 B8FE67        MOV AX,67FE
-T

AX=67FE  BX=0000  CX=0000  DX=0000  SP=FFEE  BP=0000  SI=0000  DI=0000
DS=333F  ES=333F  SS=333F  CS=333F  IP=0103   NV UP EI PL NZ NA PO NC
333F:0103 89C3          MOV BX,AX
-T

AX=67FE  BX=67FE  CX=0000  DX=0000  SP=FFEE  BP=0000  SI=0000  DI=0000
DS=333F  ES=333F  SS=333F  CS=333F  IP=0105   NV UP EI PL NZ NA PO NC
333F:0105 88F9          MOV CL,BH
-T

AX=67FE  BX=67FE  CX=0067  DX=0000  SP=FFEE  BP=0000  SI=0000  DI=0000
DS=333F  ES=333F  SS=333F  CS=333F  IP=0107   NV UP EI PL NZ NA PO NC
333F:0107 88DD          MOV CH,BL
-T

AX=67FE  BX=67FE  CX=FE67  DX=0000  SP=FFEE  BP=0000  SI=0000  DI=0000
DS=333F  ES=333F  SS=333F  CS=333F  IP=0109   NV UP EI PL NZ NA PO NC
333F:0109 1401          ADC AL,01
```

Keep in mind that the T command executes the instruction displayed in the third line of the most recent R command display. The **ADC** instruction in the last register display is yet another garbage instruction, and although executing it would not cause any harm, I recommend against executing random instructions just to see what happens. Executing certain jump or interrupt instructions could wipe out sectors on your hard disk or, worse, cause internal damage to DOS that would not show up until later on.

Let's recap what these four instructions accomplished. The first instruction is an example of immediate addressing—the hexadecimal value 067FEH was moved into the **AX** register. The second instruction used register addressing to move register data from **AX** into **BX**. (Keep in mind that the way the operands are arranged is slightly contrary to the common-sense view of things. The destination operand comes *first*. Moving something from **AX** to **BX** is done by executing **MOV BX,AX**. Assembly language is just like that sometimes.)

The third instruction and fourth instruction both move data between register halves rather than full, 16-bit registers. These two instructions accomplish something interesting. Look at the last register display, and compare the value of **BX** and **CX**. By moving the value from **BX** into **CX** a byte at a time, it was possible to reverse the order of the two bytes making up **BX**. The high half of BX (what we sometimes call the *most significant byte*, or MSB, of **BX**) was moved into the low half of **CX**. Then the low half of **BX** (what we sometimes call the *least significant byte*, or LSB, of **BX**) was moved into the high half of **CX**. This is just a sample of the sorts of tricks you can play with the general-purpose registers.

Just to disabuse you of the notion that the **MOV** instruction should be used to exchange the two halves of a 16-bit register, let me suggest that you do the following: before you exit DEBUG from your previous session, assemble this instruction and execute it using the T command:

```
XCHG CL,CH
```

The **XCHG** instruction exchanges the values contained in its two operands. What was interchanged before is interchanged again, and the value in **CX** will match the values already in **AX** and **BX**. A good idea while writing your first assembly-language programs is to double check the instruction set periodically to see that what you have cobbled together with four or five instructions is not possible using a single instruction. The 8086/8088 instruction set is very good at fooling you in that regard!

Memory Data

Immediate data is built right into its own machine instruction, and register data is stored in one of the CPU's limited collection of internal registers. In contrast, *memory data* is stored somewhere in the megabyte vastness of 8086/8088 external memory. Specifying that address is much more complicated than simply reaching into a machine instruction or naming a register.

You should recall that a memory location must be specified in two parts: a *segment address,* which is one of 65,536 locations spaced every 16 bytes in memory; and an *offset address,* which is the number of bytes by which the specified byte is offset from the start of the segment. Within the CPU, the segment address is kept in one of the four segment registers, while the offset address (generally just called the offset) may be in one of a select group of general-purpose registers. To pin down a single byte within the 8086/8088's megabyte of memory, you need both the segment and offset components. We generally write them together, specified with a colon to separate them, as either literal constants or register names: **0B00:0167**, **DS:SI** or **CS:IP**.

BX's Hidden Agenda

One of the easiest mistakes to make early on is to assume that you can use *any* of the general-purpose registers to specify an offset for memory data. Not so! If you try to specify an offset in **AX,CX**, or **DX**, the assembler will flag an error. Register SP is a special case, and addresses data located on the *stack* as I'll explain in Chapter 7.)

> Only BP, BX, SI, and DI may hold an offset for memory data.

So, in fact, general-purpose registers **AX**, **CX**, and **DX** aren't quite so general after all. Why was general-purpose register **BX** singled out for special treatment? Think of it as the difference between dreams and reality for Intel. In the best of all worlds, every register could be used for all purposes. Unfortunately, when CPU designers get together and argue about what their nascent CPU is supposed to do, they are forced to face the fact that there are only so many transistors on the chip to do the job.

Each chip function is given a "budget" of transistors (sometimes numbering in the tens or even hundreds of thousands), and if the desired logic cannot be implemented using that number of transistors, the expectations of the designers have to be brought down a notch, and some CPU features shaved from the specification.

The 8086 and 8088 are full of such compromises. There were not enough transistors available at design time to allow all general-purpose registers to do everything, so in addition to the truly general-purpose ability to hold data, each 8086/8088 register has what I call a "hidden agenda." Each register has some ability that none of the others share. I'll describe each register's hidden agenda at some appropriate time in this book, and I'll call it out as such.

Register **BX** is the X register chosen to address memory data. None of the other X registers can be used in this fashion. By convention, and because there simply isn't enough horsepower in the CPU to allow *all* registers to do it, addressing memory data is one element of **BX's** hidden agenda.

Using Memory Data

With one or two important exceptions (the string instructions, which I cover to an degree—but not exhaustively—in Chapter 10), only *one* of an instruction's two operands may specify a memory location. In other words, you can move an immediate value to memory, or a memory value to a register, or some other similar combination, but you *can't* move a memory value directly to another memory value. This is just an inherent limitation of the CPU, and we have to live with it, inconvenient as it gets at times.

Specifying a memory address as one of an instruction's operands is a little complicated. The offset address must be resident in one of the general-purpose registers. To specify that we want the data at the memory location contained in the register rather than the data in the register itself, we use square brackets around the name of the register. In other words, to move the word at address **DS:BX** into register **AX**, we would use the following instruction:

```
MOV AX,[BX]
```

Similarly, to move a value residing in register **DX** into the word at address **DS:DI**, you would use this instruction:

```
MOV [DI],DX
```

Segment Register Assumptions

The only problem with these examples is: *where does it say to use DS as the segment register?*

It doesn't. To keep addressing notation simple, the 8086/8088 makes certain assumptions about certain instructions in combinations with certain registers. There is no particular system to these assumptions, and like dates in history or Spanish irregular verbs, you'll just have to memorize them, or at least know where to look them up. (The where is in Appendix C in this book.)

One of these assumptions is that the **MOV** instruction uses the segment address stored in segment register **DS** unless you explicitly tell it otherwise. In this case above, we did not tell the **MOV** instruction to use some segment register other than **DS**, so it fell back on its assumptions and used **DS**. However, had you specified the offset as residing in register **SP**, the **MOV** instruction would have assumed the use of segment register SS instead. This assumption involves a memory mechanism known as the *stack*, which we won't really address until the next chapter.

Overriding Segment Assumptions for Memory Data

But what if you *want* to use **CS** as a segment register with the **MOV** instruction? It's not difficult. The instruction set includes what are called *segment override prefixes*. These are not precisely instructions, but are more like the filters that may be snapped in front of a camera lens—the filter is not itself a lens, but it alters the way the lens operates.

There is one segment override prefix for each of the four segment registers: (**CS**, **DS**, **SS**, and **ES**). In assembly language these prefixes are written as the name of the segment register followed by a colon:

Override Prefix	Usage
CS:	Forces usage of code segment register CS
DS:	Forces usage of the data segment register DS
SS:	Forces usage of the stack segment register SS
ES:	Forces usage of the extra segment register ES

In use, the segment override prefix is placed immediate in front of the memory data reference whose segment register assumption is to be overridden. For example, to force a **MOV** instruction to copy a value from the **AX** register into a location at an offset (contained in **SI**) into the **CS** register, you would use this instruction:

```
MOV CS:[SI],AX
```

Without the "**CS:**", this instruction would move the value of **AX** into the **DS** register, at an address specified as **DS:SI**.

Prefixes in use are very reminiscent of how an address is written; in fact, understanding how prefixes work will help you keep in mind that in *every* reference to memory data within an instruction, there is a ghostly segment register assumption floating in the air. You may not see the ghostly "**DS:**" assumption in your **MOV** instruction, but if you forget that it is there the whole concept of memory data will begin to seem arbitrary and magical.

> *Every* reference to memory data includes either an assumed segment register or a segment override prefix to specify a segment register other than the assumed segment register.

At the machine-code level, a segment override prefix is a single binary byte. The prefix byte is placed *in front of* rather than within a machine instruction. In other words, if the binary bytes comprising a **MOV AX,[BX]** instruction (which we call that instruction's *opcode*) are 8BH 07H, adding the ES segment override prefix to the instruction (**MOV AX,ES:[BX]**) places a single 26H in front of the opcode bytes, giving us 26H 8BH 07H as the full binary equivalent.

Memory Data Summary

Memory data consists of a single byte or word in memory, addressed by way of a segment value and an offset value. The register containing the offset address is enclosed in square brackets to indicate that the contents of *memory*, rather than the contents of the register, are being addressed. The segment register used to address memory data is usually assumed according to a complex set of rules. Optionally, a segment override prefix may be placed in the instruction to specify some segment register other than the default segment register.

Figure 6.2 shows what happens during a **MOV AX,ES:[BX]** instruction. The segment address component of the full 20-bit memory address is contained inside the CPU in segment register **ES**. Ordinarily, the segment address would be in register **DS**, but the **MOV** instruction contains the **ES:** segment override prefix. The offset address component is specified to reside in the **BX** register.

The CPU sends out the values in **ES** and **BX** to the memory system side by side. Together, the two values pin down one memory location where **MyWord** begins. **MyWord** is actually two bytes, but that's fine—the 8086 CPU can bring both bytes into the CPU at once, while the 8088 brings both bytes in separately, one after the other. The CPU handles details like that and you needn't worry about it. Because **AX** is a 16-bit register, two 8-bit bytes can fit into it quite nicely.

The segment address may reside in any of the four segment registers: **CS**, **DS**, **SS**, or **ES**. However, the offset address may reside only in registers **BX**, **BP**, **SP**, **SI**, or **DI**. **AX**, **CX**, and **DX** may *not* be used to contain an offset address during memory addressing.

Limitations of the MOV Instruction

The **MOV** instruction can move nearly any register to any other register. For reasons probably having to do with the limited budget of transistors on the 8086 and 8088 chips, **MOV** can't quite do any move you can think of—here is a list of **MOV**'s limitations:

- **MOV cannot move memory data to memory data**. In other words, an instruction like **MOV [SI],[BX]** is illegal. Either of **MOV**'s two operands may be memory data, but *both* cannot be at once.

- **MOV cannot move one segment register into another**. Instructions like **MOV CS,SS** are illegal. This usage might have come in handy, but it simply can't be done.

Figure 6.2. Addressing memory data

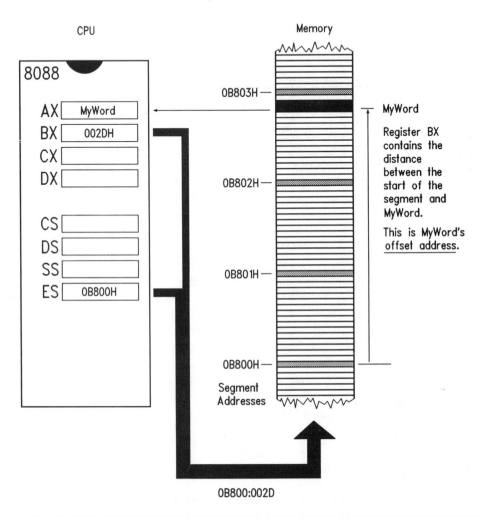

MOV AX, ES:[BX]

- **MOV cannot move immediate data into a segment register**. You can't write **MOV CS,0B800H**. Again, it would be handy but you just can't do it.

- **MOV cannot move one of the 8-bit register halves into a 16-bit register, nor vise versa**. There are easy ways around any possible difficulties here, and preventing moves between operands of different sizes can keep you out of numerous kinds of trouble.

These limitations are, of course, over and above those situations that simply don't make sense: moving a register or memory into immediate data, moving immediate data into immediate data, specifying a general-purpose register as a segment register to contain a segment, or specifying a segment register to contain an offset address. Figure 6.3 shows numerous illegal **MOV** instructions that illustrates these various limitations and nonsense situations.

6.3 Assembly-Language References

MOV is a good start. Like a medium-sized screwdriver, you'll end up using it for normal tasks and maybe some abnormal ones, just as I use screwdrivers to pry nails out of boards, club Black Widow spiders in the garage bathroom, discharge large electrolytic capacitors, and other intriguing things over and above workaday screw-turning. The 8086/8088 instruction set contains dozens of instructions, however, and over the course of the rest of this book I'll be mixing

Figure 6.3. Rogue MOV instructions

Illegal Instructions	Why they're illegal
MOV 17, 1	Only 1 operand may be immediate data
MOV 17, BX	Only the source operand may be immediate data
MOV CX, DH	Operands must be the same size
MOV [DI], [SI]	Only 1 operand may be memory data
MOV DI, DX:[BX]	DX is not a segment register
MOV ES, 0B800H	Segment registers may not be loaded from immediate data
MOV DS, CS	Only 1 operand may be a segment register
MOV [AX], BP	AX may not address memory data
MOV SI, [SS]	Segment registers may not address memory data

in descriptions of various other instructions with further discussions of memory addressing and program logic and design.

Remembering a host of tiny, tangled details involving dozens of different instructions is brutal and unnecessary. Even the "Big Guys" don't try to keep it all between their ears at all times. Most keep a *blue card* or some other sort of reference document handy to jog their memories about machine instruction details.

Blue Cards

A *blue card* is a reference summary printed on a piece of colored card stock. It folds up like a road map and fits in your pocket. The original blue card may actually have been blue, but knowing the perversity of programmers in general, it was probably bright orange. Most assemblers come with a blue card. Guard it with your life.

Blue cards aren't always cards anymore. One of the best is a full sheet of very stiff shiny plastic, sold by Micro Logic Corp. of Hackensack, NJ*. The blue card sold with Microsoft's MASM is actually published by Intel, and has grown to a pocket-sized booklet stapled on the spine.

Blue cards contain very terse summaries of what an instruction does, what operands are legal, what flags it affects, and how many machine cycles it takes to execute. This information, while helpful in the extreme, is often so brief that newcomers might not quite fathom which edge of the card is up.

6.4 An Assembly-Language Reference for Beginners

In deference to people just starting out in assembly language, I have put together a beginner's reference to the most common 8086/8088 instructions and called it Appendix A. It contains at least a page on every instruction I'll be covering in this book, plus a few additional instructions that everyone ought to know. It does *not* include descriptions on *every* instruction, but only the most common and most useful. Once you've gotten skillful enough to use the more arcane instructions, you should be able to pick up the blue card provided with your assembler and run with it.

On the next page is a sample entry from Appendix A. Refer to it during the following discussion

The instruction's mnemonic is at the top of the page, highlighted in a box to make it easy to spot while flipping quickly through the appendix. To the mnemonic's right is the name of the instruction, which is a little more descriptive than the naked mnemonic.

---

*8086/8088 Micro Chart, Micro Logic Corp. P.O. Box 174, Hackensack, NJ 07602

NEG Negate (two's complement; multiply by -1)

Flags affected:

```
O D I T S Z A P C  OF:  Overflow flag   TF: Trap flag AF: Aux carry
F F F F F F F F F  DF:  Direction flag  SF: Sign flag PF: Parity flag
*       * * * * *  IF:  Interrupt flag  ZF: Zero flag CF: Carry flag
```

Legal forms:

```
NEG r8
NEG m8
NEG r16
NEG m16
```

Examples:

```
NEG AL
NEG CX
NEG BYTE PTR [BX] ; Negates byte quantity at DS:BX
NEG WORD PTR [DI] ; Negates word quantity at DS:BX
```

Notes:

This is the assembly-language equivalent of multiplying a value by -1. Keep in mind that negation is *not* the same as simply inverting each bit in the operand. (Another instruction, NOT, does that.) The process is also known as generating the *two's complement* of a value. The two's complement of a value added to that value yields zero. -1 = $FF; -2 = $FE; -3 = $FD; etc.

If the operand is 0, CF is cleared and ZF is set; otherwise CF is set and ZF is cleared. If the operand contains the maximum negative value (-128 for 8-bit or -32768 for 16-bit) the operand does not change, but OF and CF are set. SF is set if the result is negative, or cleared if not. PF is set if the low-order 8 bits of the result contain an even number of set (1) bits; otherwise PF is cleared.

NOTE: You *must* use a type override specifier (BYTE PTR or WORD PTR) with memory data!

```
r8 = AL AH BL BH CL CH DL DH  r16 = AX BX CX DX BP SP SI DI
sr = CS DS SS ES
m8 = 8-bit memory data m16 = 16-bit memory data
i8 = 8-bit immediate data    i16 = 16-bit immediate data
d8 = 8 bit signed displacement   d16 = 16-bit signed displacement
```

Flags

Immediately beneath the mnemonic is a minichart of machine flags in the Flags register. I haven't spoken in detail of flags yet, but the Flags register is a collection of one-bit values that retain certain essential information about the state of the machine for short periods of time. Many (but by no means all) 8086/8088 instructions change the values of one or more flags. The flags may then be individually tested by one of the **JMP** instructions, which then change the course of the program depending on the state of the flags.

We'll get into this business of tests and jumps in Chapter 9. For now, simply understand that each of the flags has a name, and that for each flag is a symbol in the flags minichart. You'll come to know the flags by their 2-character symbols in time, but until then the full names of the flags are shown to the right of the minichart. Most of the flags are not used frequently in beginning assembly-language work. Most of what you'll be paying attention to, flags-wise, is the Carry flag (**CF**). It's used, as you might imagine, for keeping track of binary arithmetic when an arithmetic operation carries out of a single byte or word.

There will be an asterisk (*) beneath the symbol of any flag affected by the instruction. *How* the flag is affected depends on what the instruction does—you'll have to divine that from the Notes section of the reference sheet. When an instruction affects no flags at all, the word <none> will appear in the minichart.

In the example page, the minichart indicates that the **NEG** instruction affects the Overflow flag, the Sign flag, the Zero flag, the Auxiliary carry flag, the Parity flag, and the Carry flag. The ways that the flags are affected depend on the results of the negation operation on the operand specified. These ways are summarized in the second paragraph of the Notes section.

Legal Forms

A given mnemonic represents a single 8086/8088 instruction, but each instruction may include more than one legal form. The form of an instruction varies by the type and order of the operands passed to it.

What the individual forms actually represent are different binary number opcodes. For example, beneath the surface the **POP AX** instruction is the number 58H, whereas the **POP SI** instruction is the number 5EH.

Sometimes there will be special cases of an instruction and its operands that are shorter than the more general cases. For example, the **XCHG** instruction, which exchanges the contents of the two operands, has a special case when one of the operands is register **AX**. Any **XCHG** instruction with **AX** as one of the operands is represented by a single-byte opcode. The general forms of **XCHG** (like **XCHG r16,r16**) are always two bytes long instead. This implies that there are actually two different opcodes that will do the job for a given combination of operands (for example, **XCHG AX,DX**). True enough—and most assembler programs are "smart" enough to choose the shortest form possible in any given situation. If you are hand-assembling a sequence of raw opcode bytes, say, for use in a Turbo Pascal **INLINE** statement, you need to be aware of the special cases, and all special cases will be marked as such in the Legal forms section.

When you want to use an instruction with a certain set of operands, make sure you check the Legal forms section of the reference guide for that instruction to make sure that the combination is legal. The **MOV** instruction, for example, cannot move one segment register directly into another, nor can it move immediate data directly into a segment register. Neither combination of operands is a legal form of the **MOV** instruction.

In the example reference page on the **NEG** instruction, you'll see that a segment register cannot be an operand to **NEG**. (If it could, there would be a **NEG sr** item in the Legal forms list.) If you want to negate the value in a segment register, you'll first have to use **MOV** to move the value from the segment register into one of the general-purpose registers. Then you can use **NEG** on the general-purpose register, to move the negated value back into the segment register.

Operand Symbols

The symbols used to indicate the nature of the operands are included on every page in Appendix A. They're close to self-explanatory, but I'll take a moment to expand upon them slightly here:

- **r8**—An 8-bit register half (**AH**, **AL**, **BH**, **BL**, **CH**, **CL**, **DH**, or **DL**).
- **r16**—A 16-bit general-purpose register (**AX**, **BX**, **CX**, **DX**, **BP**, **SP**, **SI** or **DI**).
- **sr**—One of the four segment registers (**CS**, **DS**, **SS**, or **ES**).
- **m8**—An 8-bit byte of memory data.
- **m16**—A 16-bit word of memory data.
- **i8**—An 8-bit byte of immediate data.
- **i16**—A 16-bit word of immediate data.
- **d8**—An 8-bit signed displacement. We haven't covered this operand yet, but a *displacement* is a distance between the current location in the code and another place in the code to which we want to jump. It's *signed* (negative or positive) because a positive displacement jumps you higher (forward) in memory, whereas a negative displacement jumps you lower (back) in memory. We'll examine this notion in detail in Chapter 9.
- **d16**—A 16-bit signed displacement. Again, for use with jump and call instructions. See Chapter 9.

Examples

The Legal forms section shows what combinations of operands is legal for a given instruction, and the Examples section shows examples of the instruction in actual use—just as it would be coded in an assembly-language program. I've tried to put a good sampling of examples for each instruction, demonstrating the range of possibilities available with the instruction. This includes situations that require type override specifiers (which I'll cover in the next section).

Notes

The Notes section of the reference page briefly describes the instruction's action, and provides information on how it affects the flags, how it may be limited in use, and any other detail that needs to be remembered, especially things that beginners would overlook or misconstrue.

What's Not Here ...

Appendix A differs from most detailed assembly-language references in that it does not have the binary opcode encoding information or the indications of how many machine cycles are used by each form of the instruction.

The binary encoding of an instruction is the actual sequence of binary bytes that the CPU digests as the machine instruction. What we would call **POP AX** the machine sees as the binary number 58H. What we call **ADD SI,07733H** the machine sees as 81H 0C6H 33H 77H. Machine instructions are encoded into anywhere from one to four (rarely more) binary bytes depending on what instruction they are and what their operands are. Laying out the system for determining what the encoding will be for any given instruction is extremely complicated, in that its component bytes must be set up bit by bit from several large tables. I've decided that this book is not the place for that particular discussion, and have left encoding information out of Appendix A.

Finally, I've included nothing anywhere in this book that indicates how many machine cycles are expended by any given machine instruction. A *machine cycle* is one pulse of the master clock that makes the PC perform its magic. Each instruction uses some number of those cycles to do its work, and the number varies all over the map depending on criteria that I won't be explaining in this book.

Furthermore, as Michael Abrash explains in his book, *Zen of Assembly Language*, knowing the cycle requirements for individual instructions is rarely sufficient to allow even an expert assembly-language programmer to calculate how much time a given series of instructions will take. He and I both agree that it is no fit subject for beginners, and I will let him take it up in his far more advanced volume.

6.5 Rally 'Round the Flags, Boys!

We haven't studied the Flags register as a whole. The Flags register is a veritable junkdrawer of disjointed bits of information, and it's tough (and perhaps misleading) to just sit down and describe all of them in detail at once. What I'll do is describe the flags as we encounter them in discussing the various instructions in this and future chapters.

The Flags register as a whole is a single 16-bit register buried inside the CPU. Of those 16 bits, 9 are actually used as flags on the 8088/8086. The remaining seven bits are undefined and ignored. You can neither set them nor read them. Some of those seven bits become defined and useful in the more advanced processors like the 286, 386, and 486, but their uses are fairly arcane and I won't be covering them in this book, even in Chapter 11, which discusses the more advanced processors.

A flag is a single bit of information whose meaning is independent from any other bit. A bit can be *set* to 1 or *cleared* to 0 by the CPU as its needs require. The idea is to tell you, the programmer, the state of certain conditions inside the CPU, so that your program can test for and act on the states of those conditions.

I often imagine a row of country mailboxes, each with its own little red flag on the side. Each flag can be up or down, and if the Smith's flag is up, it tells the mailman that the Smiths have placed mail in their box to be picked up. The mailman looks to see if the Smith's flag is raised (a test) and if so, opens the Smith's mailbox and picks up the waiting mail.

Each of the Flags register's nine flags has a two-letter symbol by which most programmers know them. I'll use those symbols most of the time, and you should become familiar with them. The flags, their symbols, and brief descriptions of what they stand for follows:

- **OF**—The Overflow flag is set when the result of an operation becomes too large to fit in the operand it originally occupied.

- **DF**—The Direction flag is an oddball among the flags in that it tells the *CPU* something that you want it to know, rather than the other way around. It dictates the direction that activity moves (up in memory or down in memory) during the execution of string instructions. When **DF** is set, string instructions proceed from high memory toward low memory. When **DF** is cleared, string instructions proceed from low memory toward high memory. See Chapter 10.

- **IF**—The Interrupt enable flag is a two-way flag. The CPU sets it under certain conditions, and you can set it yourself using the **STI** and **CLI** instructions. When **IF** is set, interrupts (see Chapter 9) are enabled and may occur when requested. When **IF** is cleared, interrupts are ignored by the CPU.

- **TF**—When set, the Trap flag allows DEBUG's command to execute only a single instruction before the CPU calls an interrupt routine. This is not an especially useful flag for ordinary programming and I won't have anything more to say about it.

- **SF**—The Sign flag is set when the result of an operation forces the operand to become negative. By "negative," I mean that the highest order bit in the operand (the *sign bit*) becomes a 1 during a signed arithmetic operation. Any operation that leaves the sign positive will clear **SF**.

- **ZF**—The Zero flag is set when the result of an operation is zero. If the operand is some non-zero value, **ZF** is cleared.

- **AF**—The Auxiliary carry flag is used only for Binary Coded Decimal (BCD) arithmetic. BCD arithmetic treats each operand byte as a pair of 4-bit *nybbles*, and allows something approximating decimal (base 10) arithmetic to be done directly in the CPU hardware by using one of the BCD arithmetic instructions. I'll discuss BCD arithmetic briefly in Chapter 10.

- **PF**—The Parity flag will seem instantly familiar to anyone who understands serial data communications, and utterly bizarre to anyone who doesn't. **PF** indicates whether the number of set bits in the low-order byte of a result is even or odd. For example, if the result is 0F2H **PF** will be cleared, because 0F2H (11110010) contains an odd number of 1 bits. Similarly, if the result is 3AH (00111100) **PF** will be set because there is an even number (4) of 1 bits in the result. This flag is a carryover from the days when all computer communications were done through a serial port, for which a system of error detection called "parity checking" depends on knowing whether a count of set bits in a character byte is even or odd. **PF** has no other use and I won't be describing it further.

- **CF**—The Carry flag is by far the most useful flag in the Flags register, and the one you will have to pay attention to most. If the result of an arithmetic or shift operation "carries out" a bit from the operand, **CF** becomes set. Otherwise, if nothing is carried out, **CF** is cleared.

Check That Reference Page!

What I call "flag etiquette" is the way a given instruction affects the flags in the Flags register. You *must* remember that the descriptions of the flags on the previous pages are generalizations *only*, and are subject to specific restrictions and special cases imposed by individual instructions. Flag etiquette for individual flags varies widely from instruction to instruction, even though the *sense* of the flag's use may be the same in every case.

For example, some instructions that cause a 0 to appear in an operand set **ZF**, while others do not. Sadly, there's no system to it and no easy way to keep it straight in your head. When you intend to use the flags in testing by way of conditional jump instructions (See Chapter 9), you have to check each individual instruction to see how the various flags are affected.

> Flag etiquette is a highly individual matter. Check the reference for each instruction to see it affects the flags. *Assume nothing!*

A simple lesson in flag etiquette involves two new instructions, **INC** and **DEC**, and yet another interesting ability of DEBUG.

Adding and Subtracting 1 with INC and DEC

Several instructions come in pairs. Simplest among those are **INC** and **DEC**, which increment and decrement an operand by 1, respectively.

Adding 1 to something or subtracting 1 from something happens a lot in computer programming. If you're counting the number of times a program is executing a loop, or counting bytes in a table, or doing something that advances or retreats one count at a time, **INC** or **DEC** can be a very quick way to make the actual addition or subtraction happen.

Both **INC** and **DEC** take only one operand. An error will be flagged by DEBUG or your assembler if you try to use either **INC** or **DEC** with two operands, or without any.

Try both by using the Assemble command and the Trace command under DEBUG. Assemble this short program, display the registers after entering it, and then trace through it:

```
MOV AX,FFFF
MOV BX,002F
DEC BX
INC AX
```

The session should look very much like this:

```
-A
1980:0100 MOV AX,FFFF
1980:0103 MOV BX,002D
1980:0106 INC AX
1980:0107 DEC BX
1980:0108
-R
AX=0000  BX=0000  CX=0000  DX=0000  SP=FFEE  BP=0000  SI=0000  DI=0000
DS=1980  ES=1980  SS=1980  CS=1980  IP=0100   NV UP EI PL NZ NA PO NC
1980:0100 B8FFFF        MOV AX,FFFF
-T

AX=FFFF  BX=0000  CX=0000  DX=0000  SP=FFEE  BP=0000  SI=0000  DI=0000
DS=1980  ES=1980  SS=1980  CS=1980  IP=0103   NV UP EI PL NZ NA PO NC
1980:0103 BB2D00        MOV BX,002D
-T
```

```
AX=FFFF  BX=002D  CX=0000  DX=0000  SP=FFEE  BP=0000  SI=0000  DI=0000
DS=1980  ES=1980  SS=1980  CS=1980  IP=0106   NV UP EI PL NZ NA PO NC
1980:0106 40             INC AX
-T

AX=0000  BX=002D  CX=0000  DX=0000  SP=FFEE  BP=0000  SI=0000  DI=0000
DS=1980  ES=1980  SS=1980  CS=1980  IP=0107   NV UP EI PL ZR AC PE NC
1980:0107 4B             DEC BX
-T

AX=0000  BX=002C  CX=0000  DX=0000  SP=FFEE  BP=0000  SI=0000  DI=0000
DS=1980  ES=1980  SS=1980  CS=1980  IP=0108   NV UP EI PL NZ NA PO NC
1980:0108 0F             POP CS
```

Watch what happens to the registers. Decrementing **BX** predictably turns the value 2DH into value 2CH. Incrementing 0FFFFH, on the other hand, "rolls over" the register to 0. 0FFFFH is the largest unsigned value that can be expressed in a 16-bit register. Adding one to it rolls it over to 0, just as adding 1 to 99 rolls the rightmost two digits to 0 in creating the number 100. The difference with **INC** is that *there is no carry.* The Carry flag is not affected by **INC**, so don't try to use it to perform multi-digit arithmetic.

Using DEBUG to Watch the Flags

When **INC** rolled **AX** over to 0, the Carry flag was not affected, but the Zero flag (**ZF**) became set (equal to 1). The Zero flag works that way: when the result of an operation becomes 0, **ZF** is almost always set.

DEC sets the flags in the same way. If you were to execute a **DEC DX** instruction when **DX** contained 1, **DX** would become 0 and **ZF** would be set.

Apart from looking at a reference guide, how can you tell what flags are affected by a given instruction? DEBUG allows you to see the flags as they change, just as it lets you dump memory and examine the values in the general-purpose and segment registers. The second line of DEBUG's three-line register display contains eight cryptic symbols at its right margin. You've been seeing them, I'm sure, without having a clue as to their meaning.

Eight of the nine 8086/8088 flags are represented here by a two-character symbol. (The odd flag out is the Trap flag, **TF**, which is reserved for exclusive use by DEBUG itself, and cannot be examined while DEBUG has control of the machine.) Unfortunately, the symbols DEBUG uses are not the same as the standard flag symbols that programmers call the flags by. The difference is that DEBUG's flag symbols do not represent the flags' *names* but rather the flags' *values.* Each flag can be set or cleared, and DEBUG displays the state of each flag by having a unique symbol for each state of each flag, for a total of sixteen distinct symbols in all. The symbols' meanings are summarized in Table 6.1.

Table 6.1. DEBUG's flag state symbols

Flag	Set Symbol	Clear Symbol
OF—Overflow flag	OV	NV
DF—Direction flag	DN	UP
IE—Interrupt enable flag	EI	DI
SF—Sign flag	NG	PL
ZF—Zero flag	ZR	NZ
AF—Auxiliary carry flag	AC	NA
PF—Parity flag	PE	PO
CF—Carry flag	CY	NC

The best I can say for this symbol set is that it's not obviously obscene. It is, however, nearly impossible to memorize. You'd best keep a reduced copy of this table (perhaps taped to the back of a business card) near your keyboard if you intend to watch the waving of the 8086/8088's flags.

When you first run DEBUG, the flags are set to their default values NV, UP, EI, PL, NZ, NA, PO, and NC.

You'll note that all these symbols are clear symbols except for **EI**, which must be set to allow interrupts to happen. Whether you are aware of it or not, interrupts are happening constantly within your PC. Each keystroke you type on the keyboard triggers an interrupt. Every 55 milliseconds, the system clock triggers an interrupt to allow the BIOS software to update the time and date values kept in memory as long as the PC has power. If you disabled interrupts for any period of time, your real-time clock would stop and your keyboard would freeze up. Needless to say, IE must be kept set nearly all the time.

Each time you execute an instruction with the T command, the flags display will be updated. If the instruction that was executed affected any of the flags, the appropriate symbol will be displayed over the previous symbol.

With Table 6.1 in hand, go back and examine the flags display for the four-instruction DEBUG trace shown a few pages back. The first display shows the default values for all the flags, since no instructions have been executed yet. No change appears for the second and third flags displays, because the **MOV** instruction affects none of the flags.

But look closely at the flags display after the **INC AX** instruction has been executed. Three of the flags have changed state: **ZF** has gone from NZ (clear) to ZR (set), indicating that the operand of **INC** went to 0 as a result of the increment operation; **AF** has gone from NA to AC. (Let's just skip past that one; explaining what that means would be more confusing than helpful.) The Parity flag **PF** has gone from PO to PE, meaning that as a result of the increment operation, the number of bits present in the low byte of **BX** went from odd to even.

Finally, look at the last flags display after the **DEC BX** instruction has been executed. Again, **ZF**, **AF**, and **PF** changed: **ZF** went to NZ, indicating that the **DEC** instruction left a nonzero value in its operand; and **PF** went from PE to PO, indicating that the number of bits in the low byte of BX was odd after the **DEC BX** instruction.

One thing to keep in mind is that even when a flag doesn't change state from display to display, it was still *affected* by the previously executed instruction. Five out of nine flags are affected by *every* **INC** and **DEC** instruction that the CPU executes. Not every **DEC** instruction decrements its operand down to 0, but every **DEC** instruction causes some value to be asserted in **ZF**. The same holds true for the other four affected flags: even if the state of an affected flag doesn't *change* as a result of an instruction, the state is *asserted*, even if only reasserted to its existing value.

Thorough understanding of the flags comes with practice and dogged persistence. It's one of the more chaotic aspects of assembly-language programming, but as we'll see when we get to conditional branches, flags are what make the CPU truly come alive to do our work for us.

6.6 Using Type Overrides

Back on the sample reference appendix page, notice the following example uses of the **NEG** instruction:

```
NEG BYTE PTR [BX]  ; Negates byte quantity at DS:BX
NEG WORD PTR [DI]  ; Negates word quantity at DS:BX
```

What indeed is a **BYTE PTR**? Or a **WORD PTR**? Both are what we call *type overrides*, and you literally can't use **NEG** (or numerous other instructions) on memory data without one of these type overrides.

The problem is this: the **NEG** instruction negates its operand. The operand can be either a byte or a word; **NEG** works equally well on both. But...how does **NEG** know whether to negate a byte or a word? The memory data operand **[BX]** only specifies an address in memory, using **DS** as the assumed segment register. The address DS:BX points to a byte—but it also points to a word, which is nothing more than two bytes in a row somewhere in memory. So, does **NEG** negate the byte located at address **DS:BX**? Or, does it negate the *two* bytes (a word) that start at address **DS:BX**?

Unless you tell it somehow, **NEG** has no way to know.

Telling an instruction the size of its operand is what **BYTE PTR** and **WORD PTR** do. Calling them type overrides can be a little misleading sometimes, because **NEG** has no default type to override. Several other instructions that work on single operands only (like **INC**, **DEC**, and **NOT**) have the same problem.

Types in Assembly Language

So, do type overrides ever override anything? They can, sometimes.

The notion of *type* in assembly language is almost wholly a question of *size*. A word is a type, as is a byte, a double word, a quad word, and so on. The assembler is not concerned with what an assembly-language variable *means*. (Keeping track of such things is totally up to you.) The assembler only worries about how big the variable is. The assembler does not want to have to try to fit ten pounds of kitty litter in a five pound bag, which is impossible, nor five pounds of kitty litter in a ten pound bag, which can be confusing.

Register data always has a fixed and obvious type, since a register's size cannot be changed. **BL** is 1 byte and **BX** is 2 bytes. Register types cannot be overridden.

The type of immediate data depends on the magnitude of the immediate value. If the immediate value is too large to fit in a single byte, that immediate value becomes word data and you can't load it into an 8-bit register half. An immediate value that can fit in a single byte may be loaded into either a byte-sized register half or a word-sized register; its type is thus taken from the context of the instruction in which it exists, and matches that of the register data operand into which it is to be loaded.

Memory data is something else again. We've spoken of memory data so far in terms of registers holding offsets, without considering the use of named memory data. I'll be discussing named memory data in the next chapter, but in brief terms, you can define named variables in your assembly-language programs using *directives* like **DB** and **DW**. It looks like this:

```
Counter DB
MixTag  DW
```

Here, **Counter** is a variable allocated as a single byte in memory by the Define Byte (**DB**) directive. Similarly, **MixTag** is a variable allocated as a word in memory by the Define Word (**DW**) directive.

By using **DB**, you give variable **Counter** a type and a size. You must match this type when you use the variable name **Counter** in an instruction to indicate memory data. This, for example, will be accepted by the assembler:

```
MOV BL,Counter
```

This instruction will take the current value located in memory at the address represented by the variable name **Counter**, and will load that variable into register-half **BL**.

What the assembler will refuse to do is load the variable **MixTag** (which is word-sized) into a register-half, like this:

```
MOV BL,MixTag      ; Won't assemble!
```

By using a type override specifier, however, you can force the assembler to do your bidding and put *half* of **MixTag** into register **BL**:

```
MOV BL,BYTE PTR MixTag
```

The type override specifier **BYTE PTR** forces the assembler to look upon **MixTag** as being 1 byte in size. **MixTag** is *not* byte-sized, however, so what actually happens is that the least significant byte, the lowbyte, of **MixTag** will be loaded into **BL**, with the most significant byte left high and dry.

Is this useful? It can be. Is it dangerous? You bet. It is up to you to decide if overriding the type of memory data makes sense, and completely your responsibility to ensure that doing so doesn't sprinkle your code with bugs.

The best use of the type override specifiers is to clear up ambiguous instructions like **INC [DI]**, which could specify either a byte or a word as memory data pointed to by a segment register and **DI**. The other occasions will be rarer and riskier. Use your head—and know what you're doing. That's more important in assembly language than anywhere else in computer programming.

7

Our Object All Sublime

Creating Programs That Work

They don't call it "assembly" for nothing. Facing the task of writing an assembly-language program brings to mind images of Christmas morning: you've spilled 1,567 small metal parts out of a large box marked *Land Shark HyperBike* (Some Assembly Required), and now you have to somehow put them all together with nothing left over. (In the meantime, the kids seem more than happy playing in the box ….)

I've actually explained just about all you absolutely *must* understand to create your first assembly-language program. Still, there is a non-trivial leap from here to there; you are faced with many small parts with sharp edges that can fit together in an infinity of different ways, most wrong, some workable, but only a few that are ideal.

So here's the plan: on the next page I will present you with the completed and operable Land Shark HyperBike—which I will then tear apart before your eyes. This is the best way to learn to assemble: by pulling apart programs written by those who know what they're doing. Over the rest of this book we'll pull a few more programs apart, in the hope that by the time it's over you'll be able to move in the other direction all by yourself.

7.1 The Bones of an Assembly-Language Program

The listing below is perhaps the simplest correct program that will do anything visible, and still be comprehensible and expandable. This issue of comprehensibility is utterly central to quality assembly-language programming. With *no* other computer language (not even APL or that old devil FORTH) is there anything even close to the risk of writing code that looks so much like something scraped off the wall of King Tut's tomb.

The program EAT.ASM displays one (short) line of text:

```
Eat at Joe's!
```

For that you have to feed 72 lines of text file to the assembler and linker. Many of those 72 lines are unnecessary in the strict sense, but serve instead as commentary to allow you to understand what the program is doing (or more important, *how* it's doing it) six months or a year from now.

One of the aims of assembly-language coding is to use as few instructions as possible in getting the job done. This does *not* mean creating as short a source-code file as possible. The more comments you put in your file, the better you'll remember how things work inside the program the next time you pick it up. I think you'll find it amazing how quickly the logic of a complicated assembly-language file goes cold in your head. After no more than 48 hours of working on other projects, I've come back to assembler projects and had to struggle to get back to flank speed on development.

Comments are neither time nor space wasted. IBM used to say, "one line of comments per line of code." That's good, but should be considered a *minimum* for assembly-language work. A better course (that I will in fact follow in the more complicated examples later on) is to use one short line of commentary to the right of each line of code, along with a *comment block* at the start of each sequence of instructions that work together in accomplishing some discrete task.

Here's the program. Read it carefully:

```
;-------------------------------------------------------------
;                             EAT.ASM
;                  Backhanded advertising program
;
;                                    by Jeff Duntemann
;                                    MASM/TASM
;                                    Last update 2/5/92
;-------------------------------------------------------------


;---------------------------|
;    BEGIN STACK SEGMENT     |
;---------------------------|
MyStack    SEGMENT STACK          ; STACK word ensures loading of SS by DOS

           DB   64 DUP ('STACK!!!') ; This reserves 512 bytes for the stack

MyStack    ENDS
;---------------------------|
;     END STACK SEGMENT      |
;---------------------------|


;---------------------------|
;    BEGIN DATA SEGMENT      |
;---------------------------|
MyData     SEGMENT

Eat1       DB       "Eat at Joe's...",'$'
CRLF       DB       0DH,0AH,'$'

MyData     ENDS
;---------------------------|
;      END DATA SEGMENT      |
;---------------------------|


;---------------------------|
;    BEGIN CODE SEGMENT      |
;---------------------------|
MyProg     SEGMENT
```

```
                assume CS:MyProg,DS:MyData
Main            PROC

Start:          ; This is where program execution begins:

                mov   AX,MyData     ; Set up our own data segment address in DS
                mov   DS,AX         ; Can't load segment reg. directly from memory

                lea   DX,Eat1       ; Load offset of Eat1 message string into DX
                mov   AH,09H        ; Select DOS service 09H: Print String
                int   21H           ; Call DOS

                lea   DX,CRLF       ; Load offset of CRLF string into DX
                mov   AH,09H        ; Select DOS service 09H: Print String
                int   21H           ; Call DOS

                mov   AH,4CH        ; Terminate process DOS service
                mov   AL,0          ; Pass this value back to ERRORLEVEL
                int   21H           ; Control returns to DOS

Main            ENDP

MyProg          ENDS

;--------------------------|
;     END CODE SEGMENT     |
;--------------------------|

                END Start
```

Three Segments

Useful assembly-language programs must contain at least three segments: one for code, one for data, and one for the stack. Larger programs may contain more than one code segment and more than one data segment, but 8086/8088 programs may contain only *one* stack segment at a time.

EAT.ASM has those three necessary segments. Each segment has a name: **MyStack**, **MyData**, and **MyCode**. Note that I've set off the three segments with comment blocks. This is a good idea when you're starting out, since separating a program's complexity into three compartments is a good first step in managing that complexity.

The code segment, pretty obviously, contains the machine instructions that do the program's work. The data segment contains *variables*, which are storage cubbyholes for information. Variables can be defined as having some particular value when the program begins running (as with the **Eat1** and **CRLF** variables defined in EAT.ASM's data segment), or they may simply be defined as empty boxes that can be filled at any point after the program begins operation.

The stack segment contains the program's stack. I haven't explained stacks just yet, and because you don't really need to understand stacks in order to understand how EAT.ASM works, I'm going to hold off just a little while longer. In short, a stack is simply an ordered place to stash things for the short term—and that will have to do until we cover the concept in depth in Section 7.2.

Labels

A segment is defined in a program by associating a label with the assembler directive **SEGMENT**. Labels are just identifiers that name something, like **MyStack**. The type of a label refers to the sort of creature the label identifies. For example, in EAT.ASM, the labels **MyStack**, **MyData**, and **MyCode** are **SEGMENT** labels. The *value* of a **segment** label is the segment address of the named segment. This is why the instruction **MOV AX,MyData** moves the segment address of segment **MyData** into register AX.

Notice that the label **MyData** is used twice in defining the data segment we're naming **MyData**. The **SEGMENT** directive begins the segment, and the **ENDS** directive, (think end segment) ends the directive. Everything between **MyData SEGMENT** and **MyData ENDS** belongs to the segment named **MyData**.

A label can be used to mark a location in the code segment. EAT1.ASM has one such label, **Start**:

```
Start:     ; This is where program execution begins
```

Start's value is the offset of its location into the code segment. The way you can spot a label used to mark a code address is by the colon used after the label. The colon, in a sense, is the sign reading "you are *here*" in the code, where "here" has a name given in the label.

The label **Start** has a special job: it specifies the point in the program where execution is to begin when the program starts running. You'll see in the program listing that the label **Start** is repeated in the very last line of the file:

```
END Start
```

The label following the **END** directive is the address of the first instruction to be executed when DOS loads and runs the program. The label used to specify the execution starting point does not have to be "**Start**," but there must be *some* label chosen as the starting point, and it must follow the **END** directive for your program to assemble and link without errors.

Later on, we'll see such labels used as the targets of jump instructions. For example, the following machine instruction transfers the flow of instruction execution to the location marked by the label **GoHome**:

```
JNE GoHome
```

Notice that in both the instructions above, the colon is *not* used. The colon is only placed where the label is *defined*, not where it is *referenced*. Think of it this way: use the colon when you are *marking* a location, not when you are *going* there.

Variables

The labels **Eat1** and **CRLF** define *variables*. A variable is defined by associating a label with a *data definition directive*. You've seen these used informally earlier in this book, and there are two in EAT.ASM. Data definition directives look like this:

```
MyByte    DB 07H                          ; 8 bits in size
MyWord    DW 0FFFFH                       ; 16 bits in size
MyDouble  DD 0B8000000H                   ; 32 bits in size
MyString  DB "I was born on a pirate ship.","$"
MyData    DB ?                            ; Uninitialized storage
MyQuery   DB '?'                          ; Contains a question mark
```

Think of the **DB** directive as "**D**efine **B**yte." **DB** sets aside one byte of memory for data storage. Think of the **DW** directive as "**D**efine **W**ord." **DW** sets aside one word of memory for data storage. Think of the **DD** directive as "**D**efine **D**ouble." **DD** sets aside a double word in memory for storage, typically for full 32-bit addresses.

All of the variable definitions shown above except for **MyData** both set aside memory for storage and then place some specific value in storage at that location. **MyData** simply sets aside storage and leaves the storage undefined, or empty. The undefined storage is indicated by the presence of a question mark after the directive.

If you really want to leave the defined variable empty, make sure you don't place the question mark in quotation marks. If you place the question mark in quotation marks, the assembler will set aside storage and then place a question mark character (ASCII character 63, or 03FH) in that storage.

You may at some point want to create a variable with a question mark in it, for this variable you'll need the quotation marks.

I find it useful to put some recognizable value in a variable whenever I can. It helps to be able to spot a variable in a DEBUG dump of memory rather than have to find it by "dead reckoning"—that is, by spotting the closest known location to the variable in question and counting bytes to determine where it is.

String Variables

String variables are an interesting case. A *string* is just that: a sequence or string of characters, all in a row in memory. A string is defined in EAT.ASM:

```
Eat1    DB "Eat at Joe's!","$"
```

Strings are a slight exception to the rule that a data definition directive sets aside a particular quantity of memory. The **DB** directive ordinarily sets aside one byte only. However, a string may be any length you like, as long as it remains on a single line of your source-code file. Because there is no data directive that sets aside 16 bytes, or 42 bytes, strings are defined simply by associating a label with the place where the string *starts.* The **Eat1** label and its **DB** directive specify one byte in memory as the string's starting point. The number of characters in the string is what tells the assembler how many bytes of storage to set aside for that string.

You can use either single quotation marks (') or double quotation marks (") to delineate a string—the choice is up to you—*unless* you are defining a string value that itself contains one or more quotation mark characters. Notice in EAT.ASM the string variable **Eat1** contains a single quotation mark character used as an apostrophe. Because the string contains this character, you *must* delineate it with double quotation marks. The reverse is also true: if you define a string that contains one or more double quotation mark characters, you must delineate it with single quotation mark characters:

```
Yukkh   DB 'He said, "How disgusting!" and threw up.',"$"
```

You may combine several separate substrings into a single string variable by separating the substrings by commas. Both **Eat1** and **Yukkh** do this, indicated by the dollar sign ($) in quotation marks at the end of the main string data. The dollar sign is used to mark the end of the string for the mechanism that displays the string to the screen. More on that mechanism and marking string lengths in Section 7.3.

Directives vs. Instruction Mnemonics

Data definition directives look a little like machine instruction mnemonics, but they are emphatically *not* machine instructions. One very common mistake made by beginners is looking for the binary opcode represented by a directive such as **DB** or **DW**. There is no binary opcode for **DW**, **DB**, and the other directives. Machine instructions, as the name implies, are instructions to the CPU itself. Directives, by contrast, are instructions to the *assembler.*

Understanding directives is easier when you understand the nature of the assembler's job. (Look back to Chapter 3 for a detailed refresher if you've gotten fuzzy on what the assembler and linker do.) The assembler scans your source-code file, and as it scans this file it builds an object-code file on disk. It builds this object-code file step by step, one byte at a time, starting at the beginning of the file and working its way through to the end. When it encounters a machine instruction mnemonic, it figures out what binary opcode is represented by that mnemonic and writes that binary opcode (which may be anywhere from one to six actual bytes) to the object-code file.

When the assembler encounters a directive like **DW**, it does not write any opcode to the object-code file. If the **DW** directive specifies an empty variable, the assembler just leaves two bytes of space in the next available slot in the data segment and moves on. If the **DW** directive specifies an initial value for the variable, the assembler writes the bytes corresponding to that value in the slot it set aside. The assembler writes the address of the allocated space into a table, beside the label that names the variable. *Then* the assembler moves on, to the next directive (if there are further directives) or on to whatever comes next in the source-code file.

When you write the following statement in your assembly language program:

```
MyVidOrg   DW 0B800H
```

What you are really doing is instructing the assembler to set aside two bytes of data (Define Word, remember) and place the value 0B800H in those two bytes. The assembler writes the label **MyVidOrg** and the label's address into a table it builds of labels in the program for later use by the linker.

This is true for all kinds of directives, not simply data definition directives. An assembler directive is just that: your walking orders handed to the assembler. There are numerous assembler directives other than **DB**, **DW**, and **DD**. The **SEGMENT** and **ENDS** directives are instructions to the assembler to consider the definitions they surround as belonging to a single segment. We'll take up the **PROC** and **ENDP** directives in Section 8.1, and the **ASSUME** directive shortly.

The Difference Between a Variable's Address and Its Contents

When you use a variable's label in a **MOV** instruction, you are accessing the *value* stored in that variable. Suppose you had defined a variable in the data segment called **MyData** this way:

```
MyData   DW 0744H
```

The label **MyData** represents some address within the data segment, and at that address the assembler places the value 0744H. Now, if you want to copy the value contained in **MyData** to the **AX** register, you would use the following **MOV** instruction:

```
MOV      AX,MyData
```

After this instruction, **AX** would contain 0744H.

Now, there are many situations where you need to move the *address* of a variable into a register rather than the *contents* of the variable. In fact, you may find yourself moving the addresses of variables around more than the contents of the variables, especially if you make a lot of calls to DOS and BIOS services. (For more on that, see Section 7.4.) The 8086/8088 instruction set contains an instruction for moving the address of a variable into a register. The instruction is **LEA**, which stands for **L**oad **E**ffective **A**ddress. **LEA** is used twice in EAT.ASM. Here's a typical example:

```
LEA     DX,Eat1
```

All this instruction does is take the offset address of the string variable **Eat1** in the data segment and place the offset address into register DX.

If you've used higher-level languages like BASIC and Pascal, this distinction may seem inane. After all, who would mistake the contents of a variable for its location? Well, that's easy for you to say—in BASIC and Pascal you rarely, if ever, even *think* about where a variable is. The language handles all that rigmarole for you. In assembler, knowing where a variable is located is essential to perform lots of important things.

The ASSUME Directive

Within the code segment of EAT.ASM, there is another directive, **ASSUME**:

```
ASSUME CS:MyProg,DS:MyData
```

Of all the directives a newcomer is likely to need to make a simple program work, **ASSUME** is almost certainly the toughest to understand. **ASSUME** has to do with labels and the way labels are used by the 8086/8088 CPU.

Recall that all memory addresses have two components: a segment address and an offset address. Furthermore, every label in an assembly-language program (with the single exception of labels used before the **SEGMENT** directive) represents some offset address from a segment address.

But which segment address?

Aye, that's the rub. Look at the data segment block named **MyData**:

```
;----------------------------|
;    BEGIN DATA SEGMENT       |
;----------------------------|
MyData      SEGMENT

Eat1        DB      "Eat at Joe's!","$"    ; Strings are terminated by "$"
CRLF        DB      ODH,OAH,'$'            ;  for printing by DOS service 9

MyData      ENDS
;----------------------------|
;    END DATA SEGMENT         |
;----------------------------|
```

Everything between the two directives **SEGMENT** and **ENDS** is the program's data segment. It says so (as they say) right on the label. But the label (by which I mean the comment blocks) is for *our* eyes only. The assembler ignores comments. *There is nothing in this segment definition to tell the assembler that it is a data segment.* You can define variables in the code segment or in the stack segment if you want, even though it's customary and more correct programming practice to keep variables in the data segment. Segment **MyData** could be just as easily considered a code segment, though not a stack segment. (Stack segments are a special case because, like Tigger, there can only be one. I'll speak of stacks, the stack segment, and the **STACK** directive in Section 7.2.)

We have the problem of indicating to the assembler which segment is the data segment. This might seem like an easy one, but rather than a single problem it is actually two problems: one is that the assembler needs to know which segment address to put into the Data Segment (**DS**) register; and the other problem is which form of memory-addressing machine instructions to use.

The first problem is easily addressed. Notice these two lines in EAT.ASM:

```
MOV  AX,MyData    ; Set up our own data segment address in DS
MOV  DS,AX        ; Can't load segment reg. directly from memory
```

MyData, if you recall, contains the segment address of a segment defined using the **SEGMENT** and **ENDS** directives. That address is first loaded into **AX**, and then from **AX** the address is loaded into **DS**. This roundabout path is necessary because the DS register cannot be loaded with either immediate data or memory data; it *must* be loaded from one of the other registers.

The end result is that the segment address represented by the label **MyData** is loaded into **DS**. This neatly solves the first problem of specifying the address of the data segment. We simply load the data segment's address into **DS**. Now **Mydata** can be considered a real data segment because its segment address is in the data segment register, **DS**.

That, however, doesn't solve the second problem. Although we wrote two instructions that moved the address of our data segment into **DS**, *the assembler doesn't "know" that this move took place.* Never forget that the assembler follows its orders without understanding them. It doesn't make inferences based on what you do to addresses or the segment registers. It must be *told* which segment is to be used as the data segment, the code segment, and the stack segment. Somewhere inside the assembler program is a little table where the assembler "remembers" that segment **MyData** is to be considered the data segment, and that segment **MyCode** is to be considered the code segment, and that segment **MyStack** is to be considered the stack segment. It can't remember these relationships, however, unless you first tell the assembler what they are somehow.

This somehow (for the data, code, and extra segments, at least) is the **ASSUME** directive. The **ASSUME** directive in EAT.ASM tidily specifies that **MyData** is the data segment and **MyCode** is the code segment.

Why is this important? It has to do with the way the assembler creates the binary opcodes for a given instruction. When you write an instruction that addresses memory data like this

```
MOV     AX,MyWord
```

the assembler must put together the series of binary values that will direct the CPU to perform this action. What that series of binary values turns out to be depends on what segment the label **MyWord** resides in. If **MyWord** is in the data segment, the binary opcodes will be one thing, but if **MyWord** resides in the code segment, stack segment, or extra segment, the binary opcodes will be something else again. The assembler must know whether any label indicates an address within the data segment, code segment, stack segment, or extra segment. The assembler knows that **MyWord** indicates an address within the segment **MyData**, but you must tell the assembler that **MyData** is in fact the data segment.

This is what **ASSUME** is for. As I've said before and will say again: *knowing where things are is the greatest part of all your work in assembly language.* Understand addresses and memory addressing (which includes telling the assembler how to find things, as we've done here with **ASSUME**), and the rest is easy.

The Main Program as a Procedure

All of the machine instructions in EAT.ASM are found between this pair of assembly-language statements:

```
Main PROC
```

```
Main ENDP
```

Just as the **SEGMENT** and **ENDS** directives frame a segment, the **PROC** and **ENDP** directives frame what we call a *procedure.* A procedure is just a group of machine instructions that is given a name. This is almost entirely what a procedure is: a name. Unlike Pascal or C, there is no necessary structure to a procedure in assembly language.

Making the main program portion of an assembly-language program a procedure is strictly optional, *until* you must begin dividing your program up into modules to keep it manageable. Then every executable component *must* be a procedure with a name, so that the linker can properly link the different modules together into the final executable program. If you're the least bit serious about assembly language, that will happen sooner than later, so I think it's a good idea to get in the habit of considering your main program a procedure at the outset.

In the next chapter I will explain the process of cutting a program up into procedures, and how the procedures work together to comprise a complete assembly-language program. Until then I won't have a lot more to say about procedures. The **Main** procedure defined in EAT.ASM is not germane to understanding the program's operation. Consider it a gesture to future expansion of the program, as we'll see in Chapter 8.

Choosing a Starting Point

There are no jumps, loops, or subroutines in EAT.ASM. If you've a smattering of assembly-language smarts you may wonder if the **Start:** label following the **ASSUME** directive is unnecessary except for readability purposes. After all, **Start** is not referenced anywhere within the program, so one would think it's an ornament, like **MyStack**, the name of the stack segment. On the contrary— EAT.ASM will not assemble without it.

The issue is this: DOS needs to know at what address to begin execution when it loads and runs the program. You might think DOS could assume that execution would begin at the start of the code segment, but not so—there may be more than one code segment, and under most circumstances the programmer does not specify the order of multiple code segments within a single program. (The linker has its own reasons for arranging them as it does.) Better to have no doubt about it, and for that reason you the programmer are required to pick a starting point and tell the assembler what it is.

The starting point may be any label that specifies an address within a code segment. Once you choose it, you inform the assembler of your choice by putting the chosen label at the very end of the source-ode file, following the **END** directive. Note that you must put the colon after the label when you define its location in its code segment, but you *cannot* use the colon when you place the starting point label after **END.**

END does multiple service for the assembler. Its most obvious job is to tell the assembler, "That's all, folks—the source-code file is finished—no further machine instructions or assembler directives will be forthcoming." Any text placed after the **END** directive will be ignored by the assembler. You can put comment blocks there if you like, but don't forget that any instructions or directives you place after **END** will simply be ignored, and *the assembler will not tell you that it is ignoring them.* Best, I think, not to put anything at all after **END.**

Why specify the starting point after the **END** directive? Very simply: the assembler can, with confidence, assume that the starting point cannot be redefined. There can be more than one of most everything else in an assembly-language program (including stack segments—you just can't *use* more than one at a time) but there must be only *one* starting point for execution. Putting the starting label after **END** ensures that this will be the case,

7.2 First In, First Out via the Stack

One problem with assembly language is that it's tough knowing where to put things. There are only so many registers to go around. Having variables in a data segment is helpful, but it isn't the whole story. People who come to assembler from higher-level languages like Pascal and BASIC find this particularly jarring, since they're used to being able to create new variables at any time as needed.

The 8086/8088 CPU contains the machinery to create and manage a vital storage area called the *stack*. The name is appropriate, and for a usable metaphor I can go back to my high school days, when I was a dishwasher for Resurrection Hospital on Chicago's Northwest side.

Five Hundred Plates an Hour

What I did most of the time was pull clean plates from a moving conveyor belt of little prongs that emerged endlessly from the steaming dragon's mouth of a 180° dishwashing machine. This was hot work, but it was a lot less slimy than stuffing the dirty plates into the other end of the machine.

When you pull five hundred plates an hour out of a dishwashing machine, you had better have some place efficient to stash them. Obviously you could simply stack them on a table, but stacked ceramic plates in any place habituated by rowdy teenage boys is asking for fragments. What the hospital had instead was an army of little wheeled stainless steel cabinets equipped with one or more spring-loaded circular plungers accessed from the top. When you had a handful of plates, you pushed them down into the plunger. The plunger's spring was adjusted such that the weight of the added plates pushed the whole stack of plates down just enough to make the new top plate flush with the top of the cabinet.

Each plunger held about fifty plates. We rolled one up next to the dragon's mouth, filled it with plates, and then rolled it back into the kitchen where the clean plates were used at the next meal shift to set patients' trays.

It's instructive to follow the path of the first plate out of the dishwashing machine on a given shift. That plate got into the plunger first, and was subsequently shoved down into the bottom of plunger by the remaining 49 plates that the cabinet could hold. After the cabinet was rolled into the kitchen, the kitchen girls pulled plates out of the cabinet one by one as they set trays. The *first* plate out of the cabinet was the *last* plate in. The *last* plate out of the cabinet had been the *first* plate to go in.

The 8086/8088 stack is like that. We call it a Last In, First Out, or LIFO stack.

An Upside-Down Segment

Two of the 8086/8088 registers team up to create and maintain the stack. Like everything else in 86 land, the stack must exist within a segment. The Stack Segment (**SS**) register holds the segment address of the segment chosen to be the stack segment, and the Stack Pointer (**SP**) register points to locations within the stack segment. As with all other segments, the stack segment can be as much as 65,536 bytes long, although you'll find in practice that the stack rarely needs to be larger than a thousand bytes or so unless you're doing some really peculiar things.

The stack segment begins at SS:0, but the truly odd thing about it is that all the stack action happens at the *opposite* end of the stack segment. When a stack segment is set up, the **SS** register points to the base or beginning of the stack segment, and the **SP** register is set to point to the end of the stack segment. To store something in the stack segment (which we usually call "pushing something on the stack"), we move the **SP** "down the stack" (closer to **SS**) and then copy the item to the memory location pointed to by **SS:SP**.

This takes some getting used to. Figure 7.1 provides the big picture of the stack segment and the two pointers that give it life. **SS** is set to the base of the stack segment by DOS when the program is loaded and begins running. **SP** is set to the far end of the stack segment, again by DOS when your program is loaded.

You can place data onto the stack in numerous ways, but the most straightforward way involves a pair of related machine instructions; **PUSH** and **PUSHF**. The two are identical except that **PUSHF** pushes the Flags register onto the stack, while **PUSH** pushes a register that is specified by you in your source-code file onto the stack, like so:

```
PUSHF             ; Push the Flags register

PUSH AX           ; Push the AX register
PUSH [BX]         ; Push the word stored in memory at DS:BX
PUSH DI           ; Push the DI register
PUSH ES           ; Push the ES register
```

Note that **PUSHF** takes no operands. You'll generate an assembler error if you try to hand it an operand; **PUSHF** pushes the Flags register and that's all it is capable of doing.

Both **PUSH** and **PUSHF** work this way: first **SP** is decremented by one word (two bytes) so that it points to an empty area of the stack segment that is two bytes long. Then whatever is to be pushed onto the stack is written to memory in the stack segment at the offset address in **SP**. Voila! The data is safe on the stack, and SP has crawled two bytes closer to **SS**. We call the word of memory pointed to by **SP** the *top of the stack*.

Figure 7.1. The big picture of the 8086/8088 stack

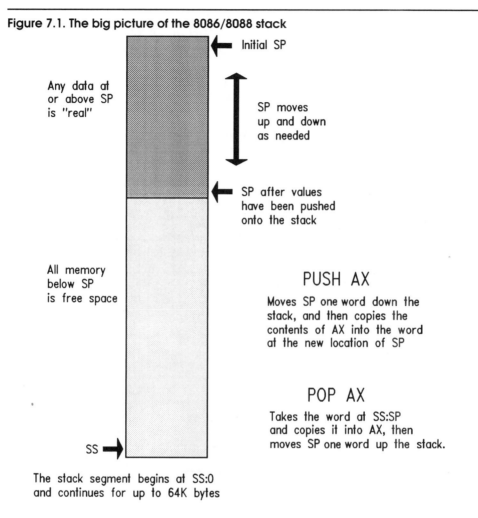

Initial SP

Any data at
or above SP
is "real"

SP moves
up and down
as needed

SP after values
have been pushed
onto the stack

All memory
below SP
is free space

PUSH AX

Moves SP one word down the
stack, and then copies the
contents of AX into the word
at the new location of SP

POP AX

Takes the word at SS:SP
and copies it into AX, then
moves SP one word up the stack.

SS ➡

The stack segment begins at SS:0
and continues for up to 64K bytes

All memory between **SP's** initial position and its current position (the top of the stack) contains real data that was explicitly pushed on the stack and will presumably be fetched from the stack (we say *popped* from the stack) later on. Memory between **SS** and **SP**, however, is considered free and available, and is used to store new data that is to be pushed onto the stack.

All memory between **SS:0** and **SS:SP** is considered free and available for the use of the stack.

Don't forget one important fact: the 8086/8088 pushes *only* word-sized items on the stack. You can't push **AL** or **BH** or any other of the 8-bit registers. Nor can you push immediate data. Registers and memory are legal for pushing onto the stack, but immediate data will generate an assembler error. (There is, in fact, a variant of **PUSH** that *will* push immediate data on the stack, but it's only available on the 286, 386, and 486 CPUs. I'll take up the issue of the more advanced CPUs in Chapter 11.)

Your morbid curiosity may be wondering what happens when **SP** runs out of room in its downward crawl and collides with **SS**. Nothing good, certainly—it depends heavily on how your program is laid out, but I would lay money on your program crashing hard and probably taking the system with it. *Stack crashes are serious business*—in part because there is only one stack in action at a time in the 8086/8088. It's a little hard to explain (especially at this stage in our discussion) but this means that the stack you set up for your own program must be large enough to support the needs of DOS and any interrupt-driven code (typically in the BIOS) that may be active while your program is running. Even if you don't fully understand how someone else may be using your program's stack at the same time you are, give those other guys some extra room—and keep an eye on the proximity of **SS** and **SP** while you trace a program in DEBUG. I'll explain how to allocate space for your stack a little later in this section.

POP Goes the Opcode

In general, what gets pushed must get popped, or you can end up in any of several different kinds of trouble. Getting a word of data *off* the stack is done with another two instructions, **POP** and **POPF**. As you might expect, **POP** is the general-purpose popper, while **POPF** is dedicated to popping the the Flags register off of the stack:

```
POPF            ; Pop the top of the stack into Flags

POP SI          ; Pop the top of the stack into SI
POP CS          ; Pop the top of the stack into CS
POP [BX]        ; Pop the top of the stack into memory at DS:BX
```

As with **PUSH**, **POP** only operates on word-sized operands. Don't try to pop data from the stack into an 8-bit register like AH or CL.

The **PUSH** and **POP** stack instructions work *only* on word-sized operands.

POP works pretty much the way **PUSH** does, but in reverse: first the word of data at **SS:SP** is copied from the stack and placed in **POP**'s operand, whatever you specified that to be. Then, **SP** is incremented (rather than decremented) by two bytes, so that in effect it moves two bytes up the stack, away from **SS.**

It's significant that **SP** is decremented *before* placing a word on the stack at push time, but incremented *after* removing a word from the stack at pop time. Certain other CPUs work in the opposite manner, which is fine—just don't get confused. *Unless the stack is empty,* **SP** *points to real data, not empty space.*

Ordinarily, you don't have to remember that fact, as **PUSH** and **POP** handle it all for you and you don't have to manually keep track of what **SP** is pointing to. If you decide to manipulate the stack pointer directly, it helps to know the sequence of events behind **PUSH** and **POP**.

Figure 7.2 shows the stack's operation in a little more detail. The values of the four "X" registers at some hypothetical point in a program's execution are shown at the top of the figure. **AX** is pushed first on the stack. Its least significant byte is at **SS:SP**, and its most significant byte is at SS:SP+1. (Remember that both bytes are pushed onto the stack at once, as a unit!)

Each time one of the registers is pushed onto the stack, SP is decremented two bytes down toward **SS**. The first three columns show **AX**, **BX**, and **CX** being pushed onto the stack, respectively. But note what happens in the fourth column, when the instruction **POP DX** is executed. The stack pointer is incremented by two bytes and moves away from **SS**. **DX** now contains a copy of the contents of **CX**. In effect, **CX** was pushed onto the stack, and then immediately popped off into **DX**.

That's a roundabout way to copy the value of **CX** into **DX**. **MOV DX,CX** is lots faster and more straightforward. However, *MOV will not operate on the Flags register.* If you want to load a copy of Flags register into another register, you must first push the flags register onto the stack with **PUSHF**, then pop the same word off the stack into the register of your choice. Getting the Flags register into **BX** is done like this:

```
PUSHF          ; Push the flags register onto the stack..
POP BX         ; ..and pop it immediately into BX
```

Storage for the Short Term

The stack should be considered a place to stash things for the short term. Items stored on the stack have no names, and in general must be taken off the stack in the reverse order that they were put on.

One excellent use of the stack allows the all-too-few registers to do multiple duty. If you need a register to temporarily hold some value to be operated on by the CPU and all the registers are in use, push one of the "busy" registers onto the stack. Its value will remain safe on the stack while you use the register for other things. When you're finished using the register, pop its old value off the stack—and you've gained the advantages of an additional register without

Figure 7.2. How the stack works

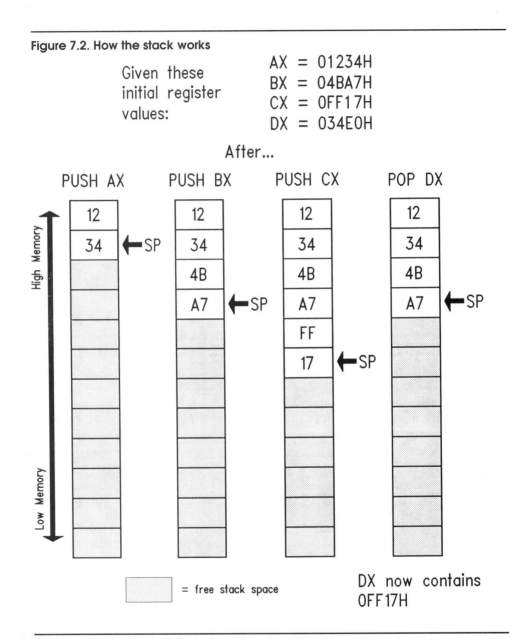

Given these initial register values:

AX = 01234H
BX = 04BA7H
CX = 0FF17H
DX = 034E0H

After...

PUSH AX   PUSH BX   PUSH CX   POP DX

= free stack space

DX now contains 0FF17H

really having one. (The cost, of course, is the time you spend moving that register's value onto and off of the stack. It's not something you want to do in the middle of an often-repeated loop!)

Specifying the Size of the Stack

The size of your program's code segment is dictated by the number of machine instructions you write into your program. Similarly, the size of your data segment is dictated by the number and sizes of the variables you define in your data segment. You might well ask: how do you specify the size of your stack segment when, until the program begins running, there's nothing in it?

The answer, quite simply, is to define the stack segment as one enormous variable without a name.

Look back at the EAT.ASM program, which has a stack segment allocated this way. Note that the stack segment contains a single **DB** directive with no label associated with it. The stack segment's **DB** is a little different from the ones in the data segment. It contains an additional directive, **DUP** (for Duplicate), that is the key to the whole mystery. Here's the **DB** instruction in its entirety:

```
DB 64 DUP ('STACK!!!')  ; This reserves 512 bytes for the stack
```

As the comment indicates, this statement somehow allocates 512 bytes for the stack. The **DB** directive by itself ordinarily allocates only a single byte within a segment. **DB**, however, can also mark the first byte of multi-byte strings and buffers. A *buffer* is nothing more than an area of memory set aside for later use with nothing particular inside it. The stack segment in EAT.ASM is really just a buffer without a name, addressed by **SS** and **SP**.

The "Eat at Joe's!" string (including the "$" at the end) is 14 bytes long, yet is defined by a **DB** directive. Really large variables and most buffers, however, must be allocated with the help of the **DUP** directive. **DUP** <u>must be followed by</u> <u>some sort of expression in parentheses, and preceded by a number indicating</u> <u>how many times that expression is to be duplicated in memory.</u>

An *expression* is a collection of values that ultimately "cooks down" (we say *evaluates*) to some specific value. In EAT.ASM, the stack segment's **DB** directive doesn't really contain an expression—its value is already "cooked down" as far as it will go. Later on we'll look at some more complex expressions that will need some cooking.

The stack segment's **DB** takes the short string of characters '**STACK!!!**' from within the parentheses and replicates the string into memory 64 times. The total size of the buffer is 64 multiplied by 8, (which is the length of the string 'STACK!!!' shorn of its quotation marks), for a total of 512 bytes. By this we accomplish two things: we set aside a buffer 512 bytes in size for the use of the stack, and we mark this buffer unmistakably so that we can spot it in memory and see how much of the buffer has actually been used by the stack.

The marking is indeed unmistakable. Assemble and link EAT.ASM, and then invoke DEBUG on EAT.EXE. Do a memory dump at SS:0. You should see this:

```
-d ss:0
19AA:0000  53 54 41 43 4B 21 21 21-53 54 41 43 4B 21 21 21   STACK!!!STACK!!!
19AA:0010  53 54 41 43 4B 21 21 21-53 54 41 43 4B 21 21 21   STACK!!!STACK!!!
19AA:0020  53 54 41 43 4B 21 21 21-53 54 41 43 4B 21 21 21   STACK!!!STACK!!!
19AA:0030  53 54 41 43 4B 21 21 21-53 54 41 43 4B 21 21 21   STACK!!!STACK!!!
19AA:0040  53 54 41 43 4B 21 21 21-53 54 41 43 4B 21 21 21   STACK!!!STACK!!!
19AA:0050  53 54 41 43 4B 21 21 21-53 54 41 43 4B 21 21 21   STACK!!!STACK!!!
19AA:0060  53 54 41 43 4B 21 21 21-53 54 41 43 4B 21 21 21   STACK!!!STACK!!!
19AA:0070  53 54 41 43 4B 21 21 21-53 54 41 43 4B 21 21 21   STACK!!!STACK!!!
-
```

There should be four blocks marked like this, as DEBUG's dump routine displays 128 bytes at a time. If any bytes in any of those four blocks get written over, you'll see it immediately. Certainly the last few bytes will be written over during the normal course of the program, but if something else in your program or your machine is clobbering your stack, this is one way to start the search for the alien menace.

Nothing, of course, *requires* that you use the **STACK!!!** string to allocate space in the stack segment. The simplest way is to use **DUP** with the undefined space symbol (?):

```
DB 512 DUP (?)
```

All this statement does is set aside 512 bytes of memory. *Nothing* is stored in that memory initially to mark it as belonging to the stack or anything else. The (?) simply reserves memory but does not otherwise touch it. Note here that the question mark is *not* in quoteation marks. Putting it in quotation marks will fill your stack segment with 512 question mark characters, which may be useful but is not the same as undefined space!

7.3 Using DOS Services through INT

I think of EAT.ASM as something of a Tom Sawyer program. It doesn't do much, and it does what it does in time-honored Tom Sawyer fashion—by getting somebody else to do all the work. All that EAT does is display two character strings on your screen. One is the advertising slogan "Eat at Joes!" The other is the EOL marker—the pair of "invisible" characters that signal the end of a line: carriage return (0DH) followed by line feed (0AH). (For more on EOL markers and how they interact with text, see Section 3.2.) The EOL marker does nothing more than return the display cursor to the left margin of the next screen line, so that any subsequent text displayed will begin at the left margin and not nipping at the heels of the slogan.

Invisible though it may be, the carriage return-line feed combination is still considered a text string, and is sent to the display in exactly the same way: through a *DOS service*.

As I explained in Chapter 3, DOS is both a god and a troll. DOS controls all the most important elements of the machine in godlike fashion, including the disk drives, the printer, and (to some extent) the display. At the same time, DOS is like a troll living under a bridge to all those parts of your machine: you tell the troll what you want done, and the troll will go out and do it for you.

There is another troll guarding the bridges to other components of your machine called the BIOS, to which we'll return in a little while. DOS and BIOS both offer *services*, which are simple tasks that your programs would have to do themselves if the services were not provided. Quite apart from saving you, the programmer, a lot of work, having DOS and BIOS services helps guarantee that certain things will be done in identical fashion on all machines. This uniformity (especially in terms of disk storage) is a major reason software written for DOS runs on so many different machines: all the machine-dependent stuff is done the same way.

One of the services DOS provides is simple (far too simple, actually) access to your machine's display. For the purposes of EAT.ASM (which is just a lesson in getting your first assembly-language program written and operating) simple services are enough.

So, how do we use DOS and BIOS services? The way is as easy to use as it is tricky to understand: through software interrupts.

An Interrupt That Doesn't Interrupt Anything

As one new to the 8086/8088 family of processors, the notion of a software interrupt drove me nuts. I kept looking and looking for the interrupter and interruptee. Nothing was getting interrupted.

The name is unfortunate, even though I admit that there was some reason for calling software interrupts what they are. They are, in fact, courteous interrupts—if you can still call an interrupt an interrupt when it is so courteous that it does no interrupting at all.

The nature of software interrupts and DOS services is best explained by a real example illustrated twice in EAT.ASM. As I hinted above, DOS keeps little sequences of machine instructions tucked away within itself. Each sequence does something useful—read something from a disk file, display something on the screen, send something to the printer. DOS uses them to do its own work, and it also makes them available (with its troll hat on) to you, the programmer, to access from your programs.

Well, there is the critical question: how do you find something tucked away inside of DOS? All code sequences, of course, have addresses, and Microsoft or IBM could publish a booklet of addresses indicating where all the code is hidden. There are numerous good reasons, however, not to pass out the addresses of the code. DOS is evolving and (we should hope) being repaired on an ongoing basis. Repairing and improving code involves adding, changing, and removing machine instructions, which changes the size of those hidden code sequences—and also, in consequence, changes their location. Add a dozen instructions to one sequence, and all the other sequences up memory from that one sequence will have to "shove over" to make room. Once they shove over, they'll be at different addresses, so instantly the booklets are obsolete. Even *one byte* added to or removed from a code sequence in DOS could change *everything*. (Suppose the first code sequence has a bug that must be repaired.)

The solution is ingenious. At the very start of memory, down at segment 0, offset 0, is a special table with 256 entries. Each entry is a complete address, including segment and offset portions, for a total of four bytes per entry. The first 1024 bytes of memory in *any* 8086/8088 machine are reserved for this table, and no code or data may be placed there.

Each of the addresses in the table is called an *interrupt vector*. The table as a whole is called the *interrupt vector table*. Each vector has a number, from 0 to 255. The vector occupying bytes 0 through 3 in the table is vector 0. The vector occupying bytes 4 through 7 is vector 1, and so on, as shown in Figure 7.3.

None of the addresses are burned into permanent memory the way BIOS routines are. When your machine starts up, DOS and BIOS fill many of the slots in the interrupt vector table with addresses of certain service routines within themselves. Each version of DOS knows the location of its innermost parts, and when you upgrade to a new version of DOS, that new version will fill the appropriate slots in the interrupt vector table with upgraded and accurate addresses.

What *doesn't* change with each new version of DOS is the *number* of the interrupt that holds a particular address. In other words, since the PC first began, interrupt 21H has pointed the way into DOS's *services dispatcher*, a sort of multiple-railway switch with spurs heading out to the many (over 50) individual DOS service routines. The address of the dispatcher has changed with every DOS version, but regardless of version, programs can find the address of the dispatcher in slot 21H of the interrupt vector table.

Furthermore, programs don't have to go snooping the table for the address themselves. The 8086/8088 CPU includes a machine instruction that makes use of the interrupt vector table. The INTerrupt (**INT**) instruction is used by EAT.ASM to request the services of DOS in displaying two strings on the screen. At two places EAT.ASM has an **INT 21H** instruction. When an **INT 21H** instruction is executed, the CPU goes down to the Interrupt Vector Table, fetches the address from slot 21H, and then jumps execution to the address stored in slot 21H. Since the DOS services dispatcher lies at the address in slot 21H, the dispatcher gets control of the machine and does the work that it knows how to do.

The process is shown in Figure 7.4. When DOS loads itself at boot time, one of the many things it does to prepare the machine for use is to put correct

Figure 7.3. The Interrupt Vector Table

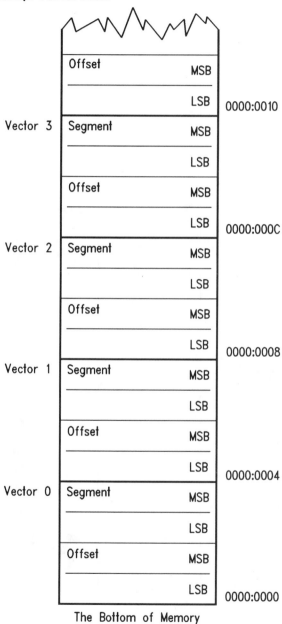

The Bottom of Memory

Figure 7.4. Riding the interrupt vector into DOS

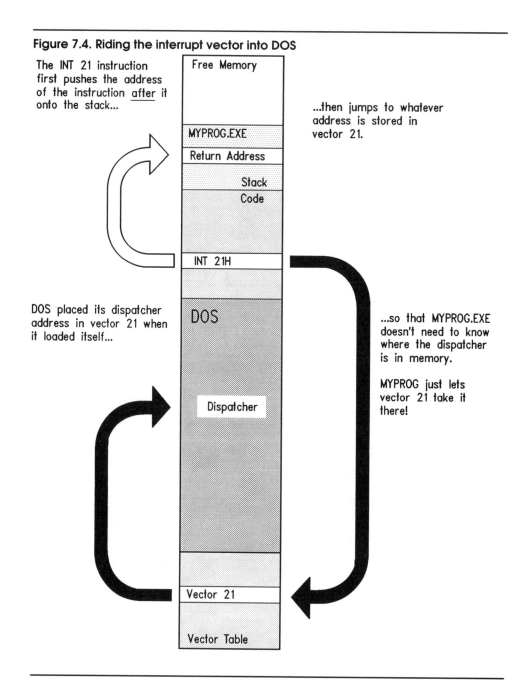

The INT 21 instruction first pushes the address of the instruction <u>after</u> it onto the stack...

...then jumps to whatever address is stored in vector 21.

DOS placed its dispatcher address in vector 21 when it loaded itself...

...so that MYPROG.EXE doesn't need to know where the dispatcher is in memory.

MYPROG just lets vector 21 take it there!

Free Memory

MYPROG.EXE

Return Address

Stack

Code

INT 21H

DOS

Dispatcher

Vector 21

Vector Table

addresses in several of the vectors in the interrupt vector table. One of these addresses is the address of the dispatcher, which goes into slot 21H.

Later on, when you type the name of your program MYPROG on the DOS command line, DOS loads MYPROG.EXE into memory and gives it control of the machine. MYPROG.EXE does *not* know the address of the DOS dispatcher. MYPROG *does* know that the dispatcher's address will always be in slot 21H of the interrupt vector table, so it executes an **INT 21H** instruction. The correct address lies in vector 21H, and MYPROG is content to remain ignorant and simply let the **INT 21H** instruction and vector 21H take it where it needs to go.

Back on the Northwest Side of Chicago, where I grew up, there was a bus that ran along Milwaukee Avenue. All Chicago bus routes had numbers, and the Milwaukee Avenue route was #56. It started somewhere in the tangled streets just north of Downtown, and ended up in a forest preserve just inside the city limits. The Forest Preserve district ran a swimming pool called Whelan Pool in that forest preserve. Kids all along Milwaukee Avenue could not necessarily have told you the address of Whelan Pool. But come summer, they'd tell you in a second how to get there: just hop bus #56 and take it to the end of the line. It's like that with software interrupts. Find the number of the vector that reliably points to your destination, and ride that vector to the end of the line, without worrying about the winding route or the address of your destination.

Note that the **INT 21H** instruction does something else: it pushes the address of the *next* instruction (that is, the instruction immediately following the **INT 21H** instruction) on the stack before it follows vector 21H into the depths of DOS. Like Hansel and Gretel, the **INT 21H** was pushing some breadcrumbs onto the stack as a way of helping execution find its way back to MYPROG.EXE after the excursion down into DOS—but more on that later.

Now, the DOS dispatcher controls access to dozens of individual service routines. How does it know which one to execute? You have to tell the dispatcher which service you need, and you do so by placing the service's number in 8-bit register **AH**. The dispatcher may require other information as well, and will expect you to provide that information in the correct place before executing **INT 21**.

Look at the following three lines of code from EAT.ASM:

```
lea DX,Eat1     ; Load offset of Eat1 message string into DX
mov AH,09H      ; Select DOS service 09H: Print String
int 21H         ; Call DOS
```

This sequence of instructions requests that DOS display a string on the screen. The first line sets up a vital piece of information: the offset address of the string to be displayed on the screen. Without that, DOS will not have any way to know what it is that we want to display. The dispatcher expects the offset address to be in **DX**, and assumes that the segment address will be in **DS**. The address of the data segment was loaded into DS earlier in the program by these two instructions:

```
mov AX,MyData        ; Set up our own data segment address in DS
mov DS,AX            ; Can't load segment reg. directly from memory
```

Once loaded, **DS** is not disturbed during the full run of the program, so the DOS dispatcher's assumption is valid even though **DS** is loaded early in the program and *not* each time we want to display a string.

In moving 09H into register **AH**, we tell the dispatcher which service we want performed. Service 09H is DOS's Print String service. This is not the fastest nor in other ways the best way to display a string on the PC's screen, but it is most certainly the *easiest*.

DOS service 09H has a slightly odd requirement: that the end of the string be marked with a dollar sign ($). This is the reason for the dollar signs hung incongruously on the ends of both of EAT.ASM's strings. Given that DOS does not ask us to pass it a value indicating how long the string is, the end of the string has to be marked somehow, and the dollar sign is DOS's chosen way. It's a lousy way, unfortunately, because with the dollar sign acting as a marker, *there is no way to display a dollar sign.* If you intend to talk about money on the PC's screen, don't use DOS service O9H! As I said, this is the easiest, but certainly not the best way to display text on the screen.

With the address of the string in **DS:DX** and service number 09H in **AH**, we take a trip to the dispatcher by executing **INT 21H**. The **INT** instruction is all it takes—*boom!*—and DOS has control, reading the string at **DS:DX** and sending it to the screen through mechanisms it keeps more or less to itself.

Getting Home Again

So much for getting into DOS. How do we get home again? The address in vector 21H took control into DOS, but how does DOS know where to go to pass execution back into EAT.EXE? Half of the cleverness of software interrupts is knowing how to get there, and the other half—just as clever—is knowing how to get back.

To get into DOS, a program looks in a completely reliable place for the address of where it wants to go: the address stored in vector 21H. This address takes execution deep into DOS, leaving the program sitting above DOS. To continue execution where it left off prior to the **INT 21** instruction, DOS has to look in a completely reliable place for the return address, and that completely reliable place is none other than the top of the stack.

I mentioned earlier (without much emphasis) that the **INT 21** instruction pushes an address to the top of the stack before it launches off into the unknown. This address is the address of the *next* instruction in line for execution: the instruction immediately following the **INT 21H** instruction. This location is completely reliable because, just as there is only one interrupt vector table in the machine, there is only one stack in operation at any one time. This means that there is only one top of the stack—that is, SS:SP—and DOS can always send execution back to the program that called it by popping the address off the top of the stack and jumping to that address.

The process is shown in Figure 7.5, which is the continuation of Figure 7.4. Just as the **INT** instruction pushes a return address onto the stack and then jumps to the address stored in a particular vector, there is a "combination" instruction that pops the return address off the stack and then jumps to the address. The instruction is Interrupt RETurn (**IRET**) and it completes this complex but reliable system of jumping to an address when you really don't know the address. The trick, once again, is knowing where the address can reliably be found. (There's actually a little more to what the software interrupt mechanism pushes onto and pops from the stack, but it happens transparently enough so that I don't want to complicate the explanation at this point.)

This should make it clear by now what happens when you execute the **INT 21H** instruction. EAT.ASM uses DOS services to save it the trouble of writing its string data to the screen a byte at a time. The address into DOS is at a known location in the Interrupt Vector Table, and the return address is at a known location on the stack.

All other software interrupts—and there are many—operate in the same fashion. In the next chapter, we'll use a few more, and explore some of the many services available through the BIOS interrupts that control your video display and printer.

Software Interrupts vs. Hardware Interrupts

Software interrupts evolved from an older mechanism that *did* involve some genuine interrupting: hardware interrupts. A hardware interrupt is your CPU's mechanism for paying attention to the world outside itself.

There is a fairly complex electrical system built into your PC that allows circuit boards to send signals to the CPU. An actual metal pin on the CPU chip is moved from one voltage level to another by a circuit board device like a disk drive controller or a serial port board. Through this pin the CPU is "tapped on the shoulder" by the external device. The CPU recognizes this tap as a *hardware interrupt.* Like software interrupts, hardware interrupts are numbered, and for each interrupt number there is a slot reserved in the interrupt vector table. In this slot is the address of an *interrupt service routine* (ISR) that performs some action relevant to the device that tapped the CPU on the shoulder. For example, if the interrupt signal came from a serial port board, the CPU would then allow the serial port board to transfer a character byte from itself into the CPU.

Figure 7.5. Returning home from an interrupt

To find the way home, the IRET instruction need only fetch the address at the top of the stack...

...and jump to that address. Execution then resumes at the instruction just after the INT 21 that started the journey!

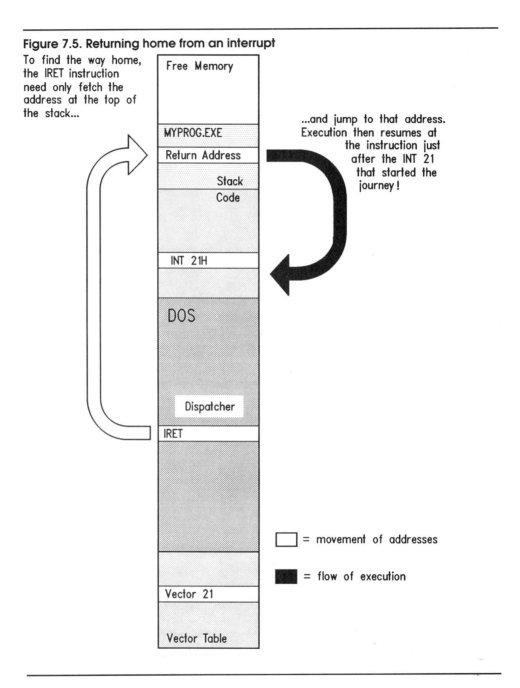

Most properly, any routine that lies at the end of a vector address in the interrupt vector table is an ISR, but the term is usually reserved for hardware interrupt service routines.

The only difference between hardware and software interrupts is the event that triggers the trip to the interrupt vector table. With a software interrupt, the triggering event is part of the software; that is, an **INT** instruction; with a hardware interrupt, the triggering event is an electrical signal applied to the CPU chip—without any **INT** instruction taking a hand in the process. The CPU itself pushes the return address on the stack when it recognizes the electrical pulse that triggers the interrupt; however, when the ISR is done, an **IRET** instruction sends execution home, just as it does for a software interrupt.

Hardware ISRs can be (and usually are) written in assembly language. It's a difficult business, because the negotiations between the hardware and software must be done just *so*, or the machine may lock up or go berserk. This is no place for beginners, and I would advise you to develop some skill and obtain some considerable knowledge of your hardware setup before attempting to write a hardware ISR.

7.4 Summary: EAT.ASM on the Dissection Table

Let's recap our disassembly of EAT.ASM by putting it back together again, with commentary. I should point out that this is one way to write an assembly-language program, but it isn't the only way by any means. I'm outlining what I feel is an ideal organization for short, assembly-language programs containing less than a thousand lines or so of source code assembled and linked *as one piece*. The essential structure of this organization is shown in Figure 7.6. Past that thousand lines, an assembly-language program *must* be broken up into modules or the program will collapse into an undecipherable black hole into which any quantity of effort may be poured without any improvement in the program. (We'll begin talking about modularizing programs in Chapter 8.)

Segment Definition and Segment Order

An assembly-language program of any usefulness must consist of at least three segments: a data segment, for variables used by the program; a stack segment, containing the program's stack; and a code segment, containing the program's machine instructions. These segments are defined using the two directives: **SEGMENT**, which marks the start of the segment, and **ENDS** which marks the end of the segment.

Each segment must have a name, and the name must be used *twice* in the definition of a segment: once before the **SEGMENT** directive and again before the **ENDS** directive. A segment must be named even though the name may not

Figure 7.6. The structure of a simple program

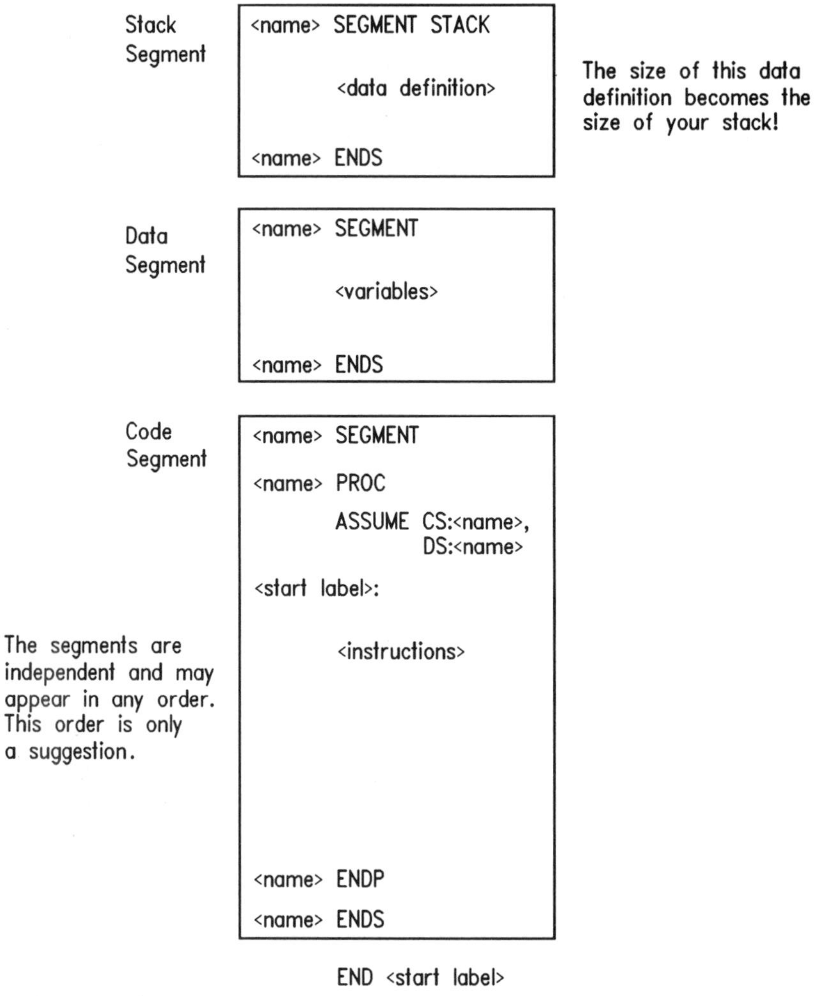

Stack
Segment
	`<name> SEGMENT STACK`
	
	    `<data definition>`
	
	`<name> ENDS`

The size of this data definition becomes the size of your stack!

Data
Segment
	`<name> SEGMENT`
	
	    `<variables>`
	
	`<name> ENDS`

Code
Segment
	`<name> SEGMENT`
	
	`<name> PROC`
	
	    `ASSUME CS:<name>,`
	            `DS:<name>`
	
	`<start label>:`
	
	    `<instructions>`
	
	`<name> ENDP`
	`<name> ENDS`

The segments are independent and may appear in any order. This order is only a suggestion.

`END <start label>`

be referenced anywhere in the program. Note that in EAT.ASM, the stack segment *is* named **MyStack** even though nothing in the program ever needs to reference **MyStack** by name.

The stack segment must be defined with the **STACK** directive following the **SEGMENT** directive. This definition tells DOS which segment address to load into the **SS** (Stack Segment) register.

The size of the stack segment is dictated by the definition of some data within the segment. You must define enough stack space to cover any possible need the program may have, *plus* the needs of DOS and any interrupt service routines (including loaded TSRs) that may be active while your program is running. If you don't define enough space, you may have a stack crash, which will definitely terminate your program and very possibly crash the machine as well. Decide how much stack space you may realistically need, and allocate twice as much. Use the **DB** and **DUP** directives to allocate space.

The segments are order independent, that is, you may place the segments in any order without changing the way the segments work together, nor the way the assembler treats them. My own custom is to define the stack segment first, followed by the data segment, followed by the code segment.

Data Definitions for Variables and Stack Space

Variables and space for the stack must be allocated during assembly. The **DB**, **DW**, **DD** and **DUP** directives are the most common means to do this. **DW** allocates word-sized (16-bit) variables, typically to contain register-sized values. **DD** allocates double word-sized (32-bit) variables, typically for full addresses containing both segment and offset.

These definitions have a form like the examples shown below:

```
MyWord    DW  0FFFFH
MyAddress DD  0B8000000H
```

The **DB** directive was designed to allocate byte-sized (8 bit) quantities like characters and register halves, but it has the special property of being able to allocate strings as well. Elements of the string may be numbers, characters, or quoted strings, separated by commas. The following are all legal **DB** variable definitions:

```
MyByte    DB   042H                  ; Using hex notation
Counter   DB   17                    ; Decimal!
Eat1      DB   "Eat at Joe's!","$"   ; Character string
CRLF      DB   0DH,0AH,'$'           ; Numbers separated by commas
```

If you need to allocate a variable or a buffer without specifying any initial values, use the **DUP** directive with a question mark (?) as the value:

```
MyBuffer  DB   1024 DUP (?)
```

The question mark value simply sets memory aside but stores nothing in it. Do not put the question mark in quotation marks, or the assembler will store the question mark character (ASCII 3FH) into every byte of the buffer.

The **DUP** directive can also be used to store repeated patterns into larger variables and buffers. This can make the buffers and variables easy to spot when you perform a hex dump from DEBUG:

```
Marked    DB 10 DUP ('Zorro!!!')
Table1    DB 5 DUP (02H,04H,06H,08H)
          DB 64 DUP ('STACK!!!')
```

The last example allocates space for the stack segment in EAT.ASM. Although this statement illustrates the fact that you don't have to name a buffer that simply exists to take up space (as in allocating space for the stack segment), I recommend that you name all variables and buffers.

Setting Up the Code Segment

Like any segment, the code segment must have a name, and the name must be given at the start and end of the segment definition, before the **SEGMENT** and **ENDS** directives. Although the name is unimportant and probably won't be referenced anywhere in the code, it must be there, or you will receive an assembler error.

An **ASSUME** directive must be included in the program. Its purpose is to tell the assembler which of the segments you have defined is to be used for the code segment, and which segment is to be used for the data segment. Unlike the stack segment, which has the directive **STACK** to tell the assembler what sort of segment it is, nothing in the code or data segments specifies which sort of segment they are. It isn't enough that there are variables defined in the data segment or machine instructions in the code segment. The assembler will allow you put variable definitions in the code segment and machine instructions in the data segment, regardless of whether that makes sense or not. (It may, in certain *extremely* advanced techniques.)

In EAT.ASM, the **ASSUME** directive tells the assembler that the code segment will be the segment named **MyCode**, and that the data segment will be named **MyData**.

EAT.ASM has its machine instructions grouped together in a procedure named **Main** with the **PROC** directive. This is not strictly necessary unless you have broken down your program into procedures or modules, and EAT.ASM will assemble and run correctly without the **Main PROC** and **Main ENDP** statements. I would advise you to get in the habit of placing the main program portion of any assembly-language program into a procedure called **Main** to help make the program more readable.

What *is* essential, however, is to provide a label that marks the place where program execution is to begin. I recommend the label **Start:** as a convention, but the label can be any legal identifier. Whatever label you choose, mark the main program's starting point with the label and a colon. Then, place the same label *minus* the colon after the **END** directive, which marks the end of the source-code file. Placing the "start" label after the **END** directive tells the assembler that there is no more source code, and that the label is the point at which execution is to begin.

What EAT.ASM's Machine Instructions Do

From the top:

```
mov  AX,MyData      ; Set up our own data segment address in DS
mov  DS,AX          ; Can't load segment reg. directly from memory
```

Before your program can access any of its variables in the data segment, it must have the segment address of the data segment in the **DS** register. The **ASSUME** directive tells the assembler to assemble any instruction referencing an identifier in the **MyData** segment under the assumption (hence the name of the directive) that **MyData** is to be a data segment. **ASSUME**, however, *does not load the data segment address into* **DS**!

You must do that yourself, which is the purpose of the two instructions shown above. This seemingly simple operation takes two instructions rather than one because **MOV** cannot move memory data directly into a segment register like **DS**. To load the address of memory data into a segment register, you must first load the address into one of the general-purpose registers and *then* load the general-purpose register into the segment register:

```
lea DX,Eat1         ; Load offset of Eat1 message string into DX
mov AH,09H          ; Select DOS service 09H: Print String
int 21H             ; Call DOS
```

Here's where the first real work of EAT.ASM gets done. The load effective address instruction (**LEA**) puts the offset address of variable **Eat1** into the **DX** register. Keep in mind that the segment address of **Eat1** is already in **DS**—loaded by the first two instructions in the program. **MOV AH,09H** loads the number of DOS service 09H (Print String) into register half **AH**. The term "Print String" is a misnomer inherited from an ancient age when video terminals were considered exotic, and strings could *only* be printed—on (kerchunk-kerchunkity-chunk) Teletype terminals!

Finally, **INT 21H** transfers control to the DOS services dispatcher by way of software interrupt 21H. The dispatcher looks in **DS:DX** for the address of the string variable to be displayed, and then hands control over to the Print String service routine somewhere deep within DOS. When the string is displayed, execution returns to the instruction following the **INT 21H** instruction, which is possible because the **INT 21H** instruction pushed the address of the next instruction onto the stack before it passed execution to the DOS services dispatcher. The dispatcher simply popped that return address of the stack and resumed execution at that address. Again, here is an explanation of how interrupts work: the previous block of instructions were enough to display the string "Eat at Joe's!" on your video display. DOS leaves the hardware cursor on the character following the last character of the string, however, and any subsequent display output would follow "Eat at Joe's!" immediately. You may want this, and you may not—and if you don't, it would be a good idea to return the cursor to the left margin and bump it down to the next screen line. This is what's going on here:

```
lea DX,CRLF          ; Load offset of CRLF string into DX
mov AH,09H           ; Select DOS service 09H: Print String
int 21H              ; Call DOS
```

The **CRLF** variable contains the EOL marker, which includes the ASCII carriage return characters. EAT.ASM passes the string containing these two "invisible" characters to DOS in exactly the same way it passed the string "Eat at Joe's!", by loading **CRLF**'s address into **DS:DX** and selecting DOS service O9H before handing control to the DOS services dispatcher through software interrupt 21H.

Finally, the job is done. Joe's has been properly advertised, and it's time to let DOS have the machine back:

```
mov  AH,4CH          ; Terminate process DOS service
mov  AL,0            ; Pass this value back to ERRORLEVEL
int  21H             ; Control returns to DOS
```

Another DOS service, 4CH (Terminate Process) handles the mechanics of courteously disentangling the machine from EAT.ASM's clutches. The Terminate Process service doesn't need the address of anything, but it will take whatever value it finds in the AL register and place it in the DOS ERRORLEVEL variable. DOS batch programs can test the value of the ERRORLEVEL variable and branch on it, as I'll demonstrate in the next chapter.

EAT.ASM doesn't do anything worth testing in a batch program, but if ERRORLEVEL will be set anyway, it's a good idea to provide some reliable and harmless value for ERRORLEVEL to take. This is why 0 is loaded into **AL** prior to ending it all by the final **INT 21** instruction. If you were to test ERRORLEVEL after running EAT.EXE, you would find it set to 0 in every case.

Dividing and Conquering
Using Procedures and Macros to Battle Complexity

8.1 Programming in Martian

There is a computer language called APL (an acronym for "A Programming Language," how clever) that has more than a little Martian in it. APL was the first computer language I learned, (on a major IBM mainframe) and when I learned it I learned a little more than just APL.

APL uses a very compact notation, with dozens of odd little symbols, each of which is capable of some astonishing power like matrix inversion. You can do more in one line of APL than you can in one line of anything else I have learned since. The combination of the strange symbol set and the compact notation make it very hard to read and remember what a line of code in APL actually does.

So it was in 1977. Having mastered (or so I thought) the whole library of symbols, I set out to write a text formatter program. The program would justify right and left, center headers, and do a few other things that we take for granted today, but which were very exotic in the Seventies.

The program grew over a period of a week to about 600 lines of squirmy little APL symbols. I got it to work, and it worked fine—as long as I didn't try to format a column that was more than 64 characters wide. Then everything came out scrambled.

Whoops. I printed the whole thing out and sat down to do some serious debugging. Then I realized with a feeling of sinking horror that, having finished the last part of the program, *I had no idea how the first part worked.*

The APL symbol set was only part of the problem. I soon came to realize that the most important mistake I had made was writing the whole thing as one 600-line monolithic block of code lines. There were no functional divisions, nothing to indicate what any 10-line portion of the code was trying to accomplish.

The Martians had won. I did the only thing possible: I scrapped it. And I settled for ragged margins in my text.

8.2 Boxes Within Boxes

This sounds like Eastern mysticism, but it's just an observation from life: *Within any action is a host of smaller actions.* Look inside your common activities. When you "brush your teeth," what you're actually doing is:

- Picking up your toothpaste tube
- Unscrewing the cap
- Placing the cap on the sink counter
- Picking up your toothbrush
- Squeezing toothpaste onto the brush from the middle of the tube
- Putting your toothbrush into your mouth
- Working the brush back and forth vigorously

and so on. The original list went the entire page. When you brush your teeth, you perform every one of those actions. However, when you think about brushing your teeth, you don't consciously run through each action on the list. You bring to mind the simple concept "brushing teeth."

Furthermore, when you think about what's behind the action we call "getting up in the morning," you might assemble a list of activities like this:

- Shut off the clock radio
- Climb out of bed
- Put on your robe
- Let the dogs out
- Make breakfast
- Brush your teeth
- Shave
- Get dressed

Brushing your teeth is on the list, but within the "brushing your teeth" activity a whole list of smaller actions exist. The same can be said for most of the activities collectively called "getting up in the morning." How many individual actions, for example, does it take to put a reasonable breakfast together? And yet in one small, if sweeping, phrase, "getting up in the morning," you embrace that whole host of small and even smaller actions without having to laboriously trace through each one.

What I'm describing is the "Chinese boxes" method of fighting complexity. Getting up in the morning involves hundreds of little actions, so we divide the mass up into coherent chunks and set the chunks into little conceptual boxes. "Making breakfast" is in one box, "brushing teeth" is in another, and so on. Closer inspection of any box shows that its contents can also be divided into numerous boxes, and those smaller boxes into even smaller boxes.

This process doesn't (and can't) go on forever, but it should go on as long as it needs to in order to satisfy this criterion: *the contents of any one box should be understandable with only a little scrutiny.* No single box should contain anything so subtle or large and involved that it takes hours of hair pulling to figure it out.

Procedures as Boxes for Code

The mistake I made in writing my APL text formatter is that I threw the whole collection of 600 lines of APL code into one huge box marked "text formatter."

While I was writing it, I should have been keeping my eyes open for sequences of code statements that worked together at some identifiable task. When I spotted such sequences, I should have set them off as *procedures*. Each sequence would then have a name that would provide a memory-tag for the sequence's function. If it took ten statements to justify a line of text, those ten statements should have been named **JustifyLine**, and so on.

Xerox's legendary APL programmer, Jim Dunn, later told me that I shouldn't ever write a procedure that wouldn't fit on a single 25-line terminal screen. "More than 25 lines and you're doing too much in one procedure. Split it up," he said. Whenever I worked in APL after that, I adhered to that rather sage rule of thumb. The Martians still struck from time to time, but when they did, it was no longer a total loss.

All computer languages have procedures of one sort or another, and assembly language is no exception. You may recall from the previous chapter that the main program is in fact a procedure, and the only thing setting it apart as the main program is the fact that its name is specified after the **END** directive.

Your assembly-language program may have numerous procedures. There's no limit to the *number* of procedures, as long as the *total* number of bytes of code does not exceed 65,536 (one segment). Other complications arise at that point, but nothing that can't be worked around.

But that's a lot of code. You needn't worry for awhile, and certainly not while you're just learning assembly language. (I won't be treating the creation of multiple code segments in this book.) In the meantime, let's take a look at the "Eat at Joe's" program, expanded a little to include a couple of procedures:

```
;--------------------------------------------------------------
;                           EAT2.ASM
;             Backhanded advertising program, with procedures
;
;                                      by Jeff Duntemann
;                                      MASM/TASM
;                                      Last update 3/10/92
;--------------------------------------------------------------


;------------------------------|
;    BEGIN STACK SEGMENT        |
;------------------------------|
MyStack     SEGMENT STACK          ; STACK word ensures loading of SS by DOS

            DB    64 DUP ('STACK!!!') ; This reserves 512 bytes for the stack

MyStack     ENDS
;------------------------------|
;    END STACK SEGMENT          |
;------------------------------|


;------------------------------|
;    BEGIN DATA SEGMENT         |
;------------------------------|
```

```
MyData      SEGMENT

Eat1        DB        "Eat at Joe's...",'$'
Eat2        DB        "...ten million flies can't ALL be wrong!",'$'
CRLF        DB        0DH,0AH,'$'

MyData      ENDS
;---------------------------|
;      END DATA SEGMENT     |
;---------------------------|


;---------------------------|
;     BEGIN CODE SEGMENT     |
;---------------------------|
MyCode      SEGMENT

            assume CS:MyCode,DS:MyData
Main        PROC

Start:      ; This is where program execution begins:
            mov  AX,MyData    ; Set up our own data segment address in DS
            mov  DS,AX        ; Can't load segment reg. directly from memory

            lea  DX,Eat1      ; Load offset of Eat1 string into DX
            call Writeln      ;   and display it
            lea  DX,Eat2      ; Load offset of Eat2 string into DX
            call Writeln      ;   and display it

            mov  AH,4CH       ; Terminate process DOS service
            mov  AL,0         ; Pass this value back to ERRORLEVEL
            int  21H          ; Control returns to DOS


;-----------------------------------------|
;            PROCEDURE SECTION             |
;-----------------------------------------|

Write       PROC
            mov AH,09H        ; Select DOS service 9: Print String
            int 21H           ; Call DOS
            ret               ; Return to the caller
Write       ENDP


Writeln     PROC
            call Write        ; Display the string proper through Write
            mov DX,OFFSET CRLF ; Load address of newline string to DS:DX
            call Write        ; Display the newline string through Write
            ret               ; Return to the caller
Writeln     ENDP
```

```
;----------------------------------------|
;           END PROCEDURE SECTION         |
;----------------------------------------|

Main        ENDP

MyCode      ENDS

;-----------------------------------|
;        END CODE SEGMENT           |
;-----------------------------------|

            END Start    ; The procedure named Start becomes the main program
```

Calling and Returning

EAT2.ASM does about the same thing as EAT.ASM. It prints a two-line slogan, and that's all. The way the two lines of the slogan are displayed, however, bears examination:

```
lea DX,Eat1
call Writeln
```

Here's a new instruction: **CALL**. The label **Writeln** refers to a procedure. As you might have gathered, (especially if you've programmed in an older language like BASIC or FORTRAN) **CALL Writeln** simply tells the CPU to go off and execute a procedure named **Writeln**.

The means by which **CALL** operates may sound familiar: **CALL** first pushes the address of the *next* instruction after itself onto the stack. Then **CALL** transfers execution to the address represented by the name of the procedure. The instructions contained in the procedure execute. Finally, the procedure is terminated by **CALL**'s alter ego: **RET** (for RETurn.) The **RET** instruction pops the address off the top of the stack and transfers execution to that address. Since the address pushed was the address of the first instruction *after* the **CALL** instruction, execution continues as though **CALL** had not changed the flow of instruction execution at all. See Figure 8.1.

This should remind you strongly of how software interrupts work. The main difference is that the caller *does* know the exact address of the routine it wishes to call. Apart from that, it's very close to being the same process. (Also note that **RET** and **IRET** are *not* interchangeable. **CALL** works with **RET** just as **INT** works with **IRET**. Don't get those return instructions confused!)

The structure of a procedure is simple and easy to understand. Look at the **Write** procedure from EAT2.ASM:

Figure 8.1. Calling a procedure and returning

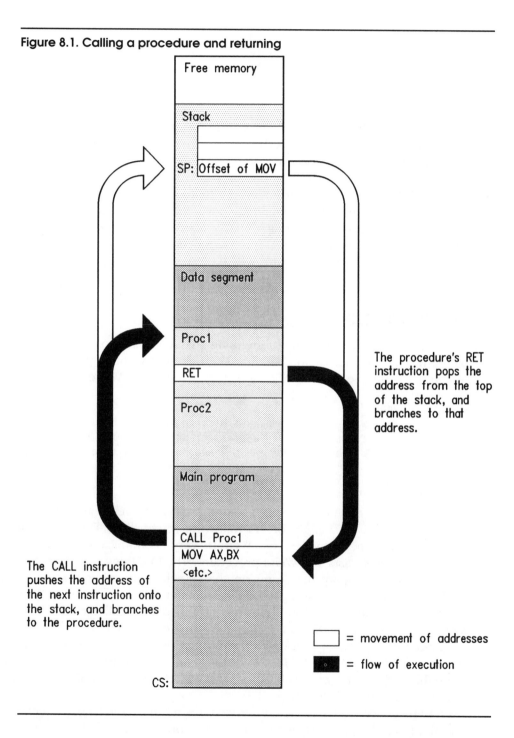

The procedure's RET instruction pops the address from the top of the stack, and branches to that address.

The CALL instruction pushes the address of the next instruction onto the stack, and branches to the procedure.

□ = movement of addresses

■ = flow of execution

```
Write       PROC
            mov AH,09H       ; Select DOS service 9: Print String
            int 21H          ; Call DOS
            ret              ; Return to the caller
Write       ENDP
```

The important points are these: a procedure must be bracketed by the **PROC/ENDP** directives, preceded in both cases by the name of the procedure. Also, somewhere within the procedure, and certainly as the last instruction in the procedure, there must be at least one **RET** instruction.

The **RET** instruction is the only way that execution can get back to the caller of the procedure. As I mentioned above, there can be more than one **RET** instruction in a procedure, although your procedures will be easier to read and understand if there is only one. Using more than one **RET** instruction requires the use of **JMP** (JuMP) instructions, which I haven't covered yet but will shortly in Chapter 9.

Calls Within Calls

Within a procedure you can do anything that you can do within the main program. This includes calling other procedures from within a procedure. Even something as simple as EAT2.ASM does that. Look at the **Writeln** procedure:

```
Writeln     PROC
            call Write       ; Display the string proper through Write
            lea DX,CRLF      ; Load address of newline string to DS:DX
            call Write       ; Display the newline string through Write
            ret              ; Return to the caller
Writeln     ENDP
```

The **Writeln** procedure displays a string on your screen, and then returns the cursor to the left margin of the following screen line. This procedure is actually two distinct activities, and **Writeln** very economically uses a mechanism that already exists: the **Write** procedure. The first thing that **Writeln** does is call **Write** to display the string on the screen. Remember that the caller loaded the address of the string to be displayed into DX before calling **Writeln**. Nothing has disturbed DX, so **Writeln** can immediately call **Write**, which will fetch the address from DX and display the string on the screen.

Returning the cursor is done by displaying the newline sequence, which is stored in a string named **CRLF**. **Writeln** again uses **Write** to display **CRLF**. Once that is done, the work is finished, and **Writeln** executes a **RET** instruction to return execution to the caller.

Calling procedures from within procedures requires you to pay attention to one thing: stack space. Remember that each procedure call pushes a return address onto the stack. This return address is not removed from the stack until the **RET** instruction for that procedure executes. If you execute another **CALL** instruction before returning from a procedure, the second **CALL** instruction pushes another return address onto the stack. If you keep calling procedures from within procedures, one return address will pile up on the stack for each **CALL** until you start returning from all those *nested* procedures.

If you run out of stack space, your program will crash and return to DOS, possibly taking DOS and the machine with it. This is why you should take care to allocate considerably more stack space than you think you might ever conceivably need. EAT2.ASM at most uses four bytes of stack space, because it nests procedure calls two deep—**Writeln** within itself calls **Write**. Nonetheless, I allocated 512 bytes of stack to get you in the habit of not being stingy with stack space. Obviously you won't always be able to keep a 128-to-1 ratio of "need to have," but consider 512 bytes a *minimum* for stack space allocation. If you need more, allocate it. Don't forget that there is only *one* stack in the system, and while your program is running, DOS and the BIOS and any active TSRs may well be using the same stack. If they fill it, you'll go down with the system—so leave room!

When to Make Something a Procedure

The single most important purpose of procedures is to manage complexity in your programs by replacing a sequence of machine instructions with a descriptive name. While this might seem to be overkill in the case of the **Write** procedure, which contains only two instructions apart from the structurally-necessary **RET** instruction.

True. But—the **Writeln** procedure hides two separate calls to **Write** behind itself: one to display the string, and another to return the cursor to the left margin of the next line.

If you look back to EAT.ASM, you'll see that it took six instructions to display both the slogan string and the newline string. What took six instructions now takes two, thanks to **Writeln**. Furthermore, the name **Writeln** is more readable and descriptive of what the sequence of six instructions do than the sequence of six instructions themselves.

Extremely simple procedures like **Write** don't themselves hide a great deal of complexity. They *do* give certain actions descriptive names, which is valuable in itself. They also provide basic building blocks for the creation of larger and more powerful procedures, as we'll see later on.

In general, when looking for some action to turn into a procedure, see what actions tend to happen a lot in a program. Most programs spend a lot of time displaying things on the screen. Procedures like **Write** and **Writeln** become general-purpose tools that may be used all over your programs. Furthermore, once you've written and tested them, they may be reused in future programs as well.

Try to look ahead to your future programming tasks and create procedures of general usefulness. (Tool-building is a very good way to hone your assembly language skills.) I'll be showing you more of this type of procedure by way of examples as we continue.

On the other hand, a short sequence (five to ten instructions) that is only called once or perhaps twice within a middling program (i.e., over hundreds of machine instructions) is a poor candidate for a procedure.

You may find it useful to define *large* procedures that are called only once when your program becomes big enough to require breaking it down into functional chunks. A thousand-line assembly-language program might split well into a sequence of nine or ten largish procedures. Each is only called once from the main program, but this allows your main program to be very indicative of what the program is doing:

```
Start: call Initialize
       call OpenFile
Input: call GetRec
       call VerifyRec
       call WriteRec
       loop Input
       call CloseFile
       call CleanUp
       call ReturnToDOS
```

This is clean and readable, and provides a necessary "view from a height" when you begin to approach a thousand-line assembly-language program. Remember that the Martians are always hiding somewhere close by, anxious to turn your program into unreadable hieroglyphics.

There's no weapon against them with half the power of procedures.

8.3 Using BIOS Services

In the last chapter we looked closely at DOS services, which are accessed through the DOS services dispatcher. The DOS dispatcher lives at the other end of software interrupt 21H, and offers a tremendous list of services at the disposal of your programs. There's another provider of services in your machine that lives even deeper than DOS: the ROM BIOS. ROM (Read-Only Memory), indicates memory chips whose contents are burned into their silicon and do not vanish when power is turned off. BIOS (Basic Input/Output System) is a collection of fundamental routines for dealing with your computers input and output peripherals. These peripherals include disk drives, displays, printers, and the like. DOS uses BIOS services as part of some of the services that it provides.

Like DOS, BIOS services are accessed through software interrupts. Unlike DOS, which channels nearly all requests for its services through the single interrupt 21H, BIOS uses numerous interrupts (about 10) and groups similar categories of services beneath the control of different interrupts. For example, video display services are accessed through interrupt 10H, keyboard services are accessed through interrupt 16H, printer services are accessed through interrupt 17H, and so on.

The overall method for using BIOS services, however, is very similar to that of DOS. You load a service number and sometimes other initial values into the registers and then execute an **INT <n>** instruction, where the *n* depends on the category of services you're requesting.

Nothing difficult about that at all. Let's start building some tools.

Positioning the Hardware Cursor

So far, in writing to the screen, we've simply let the text fall where it may. In general, this means one line of text following another, and when the screen fills DOS *scrolls* the screen upward to make room on the bottom line for more text. This makes for dull programs, very similar to programming in the bad old days when everything was done on clunky mechanical printers called Teletypes. (Indeed, this kind of screen I/O is called *glass teletype* I/O, due to its similarity to a printer scrolling paper up one line at a time.)

Let's leave the glass teletypes behind, and take control of the cursor. BIOS service 10H (often nicknamed VIDEO, in uppercase, for reasons that are obscure) offers a simple service to position the hardware cursor on the text screen. The service number is loaded into **AH**, a common thread through all BIOS services. The value 0 must be placed in **BH** unless you intend to tinker with multiple display pages. That's a story for another time; while you're learning, assume **BH** should be set to 0 for cursor positioning.

The new position of the cursor must be loaded into the two halves of the **DX** register. Cursor positions are given as XY coordinate pairs. The X component of the cursor position is the number of character columns to the right of the left margin where you want the cursor to be positioned. The Y component is the number of lines down from the top of the screen where you want the cursor to be positioned. The X component is loaded into **DL**, and the Y component is loaded into **DH**. The routine itself is nothing more than this:

```
GotoXY     PROC
           mov AH,02H       ; Select VIDEO service 2: Position cursor
           mov BH,0         ; Stay with display page 0
           int 10H          ; Call VIDEO
           ret              ; Return to the caller
GotoXY     ENDP
```

Don't forget that the X and Y value must be loaded into **DX** *by the caller.* Using **GotoXY** is done this way:

```
mov DL,35      ; Pass 35 as X coordinate
mov DH,9       ; Pass 9 as Y coordinate
call GotoXY    ; Position the cursor
```

EAT3.ASM uses **GotoXY** to position the cursor, but it does something else as well: it clears the display. If you're going to be moving the cursor at will around the screen with **GotoXY**, it makes sense to start with a completely clear screen so the remains of earlier programs and DOS commands don't clutter up the view.

There's another VIDEO service that can do the job. VIDEO Service 6 is an interesting and powerful one: not only does it clear the screen, it can scroll the screen as well, by any specified number of lines. Furthermore, it can clear or scroll the entire screen, or only a rectangular portion of the screen, leaving the rest of the screen undisturbed.

If *scrolling* is unfamiliar to you, just press Enter repeatedly at the DOS prompt and watch what happens when you reach the bottom line of the screen. The displayed text on the screen jumps up by one line, and an empty line appears at the bottom of the screen. The DOS prompt is then redisplayed in the empty line. Scrolling is the process of making the screen jump up by one or more lines, and inserting one or more blank lines at the bottom as appropriate.

Using VIDEO Service 6

Understanding VIDEO service 6 involves learning a fair number of values that need to be passed to the service in registers. The one unchanging item is the service number itself, passed as 6 in register **AH** (as with all BIOS services).

Service 6 acts upon a rectangular region of the display. This may be the full screen, or it may be only part of the screen. You must pass the coordinates of the upper-left and lower-right corners of the region in registers **CX** and **DX**. Because screen coordinates are always smaller than 255 (which is the largest value that can be expressed in 8 bits) the register halves of **CX** and **DX** are used independently to carry the X and Y values.

The upper-left corner's X coordinate is passed in **CL**, and the upper-left corner's Y coordinate is passed in **CH**. These are *0-based* coordinates, meaning that they count from 0 rather than 1. Confusion is possible here, because most high-level languages like Turbo Pascal number coordinates on the screen from 1. In other words, the upper-left corner of the screen in Turbo Pascal is given by the coordinates 1,1. To the BIOS, however, that same corner of the screen is 0,0. The width and height of a typical screen to Turbo Pascal would be 80 × 25; the BIOS would use 79 × 24.

Similarly, the lower-right corner's X coordinate is passed in **DL**, and the lower-right corner's Y coordinate is passed in **DH**. (Again, counting from 0.)

Service 6 either scrolls or clears the region. It can scroll the screen upward by any arbitrary number of lines. This number is passed to service 6 in register **AL**. Clearing the region is a special case of scrolling it: when you specify that zero lines be scrolled, the entire region is cleared.

The full screen is actually a special case of a rectangular region. By passing the coordinates of the upper-left and lower-right corners of the screen (0,0 and 79,24) the full screen is cleared.

Procedures with Multiple Entry Points

This is a lot of versatility for one service to handle, and it brings up a couple of questions. First of all, how versatile should a single procedure be? Should there be one procedure to clear the whole screen, another procedure to clear part of a screen, and a third procedure to scroll part of the screen?

The answer is that one procedure can do all three, and not duplicate any code at all. The method involves writing a single procedure that has four different *entry points*. Each entry point is a label that is called with a **CALL** instruction. When a given entry point's label is called, execution begins at the instruction specified by that label. There is only one **RET** instruction, so the procedure is in fact one procedure. It's like a house with three front doors but only one back door; having three front doors does not make it three separate houses.

Here's what such a creature might look like:

```
ClrScr     PROC
           mov CX,0          ; Upper-left corner of full screen
           mov DX,LRXY       ; Load lower-right XY coordinates into DX
ClrWin:    mov AL,0          ; 0 specifies clear entire region
ScrlWin:   mov BH,07H        ; Specify "normal" attribute for blanked line(s)
VIDEO6:    mov AH,06H        ; Select VIDEO service 6: Initialize/Scroll
           int 10H           ; Call VIDEO
           ret               ; Return to the caller
ClrScr     ENDP
```

There's nothing much to this. What we have here is a collection of **MOV** instructions setting up values in registers before calling VIDEO through interrupt 10H. Note that all of the entry points, except the one (**ClrScr**) doing double duty as the procedure name, must be given with colons. The colon, as I pointed out earlier, is necessary after any label used to mark an address within a code segment.

The multiple entry points exist only to allow you to skip certain portions of the procedure that set up values that you don't want set. All the registers used by service 6 must be set up *somewhere*. However, they can either be set within the procedure or in the caller's code just before the procedure is called. If the procedure sets them, the # registers have to be set to some generally useful configuration (say, clearing the entire screen); if the caller sets them, the registers can be set to serve the caller's needs, making service 6 perform any of its varied combinations.

So it is with the **ClrScr** procedure. If you enter **ClrScr** through its main or top entry point, *all* of its internal code will be executed: **CX** and **DX** will be set to the upper-left and lower-right corner coordinates of the full screen; **AL** will be set to 0 to clear the full screen rather than scroll it, and **BH** will be loaded with the "normal," (blank, for white text on a black background) text display attribute. Then service 6 is called.

If you wish to clear only a rectangular area of the screen (a *window*), you would use the **ClrWin** entry point. This entry point starts executing the code *after* **CX** and **DX** are set to the corners of the full screen. This means that the caller must load **CX** and **DX** with the upper-left and lower-right corners of the screen region to be cleared. Calling **ClrWin** *without* setting **CX** and **DX** at all will execute service 6 with whatever leftover garbage values happen to be in **CX** and **DX**. Something will happen, for certain. Whether it's what you *want* to happen or not is far less certain.

Keeping in mind that for proper operation, all of service 6's required registers must be set, calling **ClrWin** would be done this way:

```
mov  CX,0422H  ; Set upper-left corner to  X=22H; Y=04H
mov  DX,093AH  ; Set lower-right corner to X=3AH; Y=09H
call ClrWin    ; Call the window-clear procedure
```

The two **MOV** instructions are worth a closer look. Rather than use a separate instruction to load each half of **DX** and **CX**, the two halves are loaded together by loading a 16-bit immediate data value into the full 16-bit register. Thus two **MOV** instructions can do the work that a first glance might think would take four **MOV** instructions. This is a good example of writing tight, efficient assembler code. The trick is to document it (as I've done above) to make sure you understand six weeks from now what the magic number 093AH means!

The first instruction at the label **ClrWin** sets **AL** to 0, indicating that the region is to be cleared, not scrolled. If in fact you *do* want to scroll the region, you need to skip the **MOV** instruction that loads 0 into **AL**. This is the purpose of the entry point labeled **ScrlWin**: it gets you into the procedure below the point where you select clearing over scrolling. This means that you not only have to set the corners of the region to be scrolled, but also the number of lines to scroll as well:

```
mov  CX,0422H  ; Set upper-left corner to  X=22H; Y=04H
mov  DX,093AH  ; Set lower-right corner to X=3AH; Y=09H
mov  AL,1      ; Set to scroll by one line
call ScrlWin   ; Call the window-scroll procedure
```

As you can see, more and more of the work is being done by caller and less and less within the procedure. How you arrange the entry points to the procedure depends on what operations get done most frequently. In my programs, I tend to clear the whole screen a lot, clear windows less frequently, and scroll windows less frequently still, and this is what I had in mind while arranging the code within **ClrScr**.

Note that there is no entry point to scroll the full screen. To scroll the full screen, you need to load the coordinates of the corners of the full screen into **CX** and **DX**, and then call **ClrWin** as though you were clearing just a portion of the screen. If you do a lot of screen-scrolling, you might define a separate routine for scrolling the full screen. As an interesting exercise, write such a routine and a program to test it.

As one more entry point, I included a label **VIDEO6**. This label short-circuits all of the register setups apart from loading the service number into AH. This allows you to do something odd and infrequently, like scrolling the entire screen by three lines.

Memory Data or Immediate Data?

You may have been wondering what the variable identifier **LRXY** is for and where it is defined. **LRXY** is simply used to hold the current X,Y coordinates for the lower-right corner of the screen. Where **LRXY** is defined is in the program's data segment, in the usual way variables are defined, as you'll see if you look ahead to the full listing of EAT3.ASM.

The more interesting question is *why*. Most of the time I've been showing you values loaded into registers from immediate data, which is often useful. The coordinates of the upper-left corner of the full screen, for example, are always going to be 0,0, and nothing will change that. The lower-right corner, however, is not necessarily always 79,24.

The original 1981-vintage IBM MDA and CGA graphics adapters are indeed capable of displaying only an 80 by 25 text screen and no more. However, with an EGA it is possible to have an 80 by either 25 or 43 text screen, and the VGA, introduced in 1987 with the PS/2 line, can display 25, 43, or 50 line screens, all 80 characters wide. The newer super VGA video boards are capable even more different text modes, some of them with more than 80 characters in a visible line. If your program can determine what size screen is in force when it is invoked, it can modify its displays accordingly.

Avoid dropping immediate values into code (we call this *hard-coding*) whenever you can. A better strategy, which I'll be following from now on, uses variables in the data segment initialized with currently correct values when the program begins running.

Use Comment Headers!

As time goes on, you'll find yourself creating dozens or even hundreds of procedures as a means of not reinventing the same old wheel. The libraries of available procedures that most high-level language vendors supply with their compilers just don't exist with assembly language. By and large, you create your own.

Keeping such a list of routines straight is no easy task, when you've written them all yourself. You *must* document the essential facts about each individual procedure or you'll forget them, or, worse yet, remember them incorrectly and act on bad information. (The resultant bugs are often very hard to find, because you're *sure* you remember everything there is to know about that proc! After all, you *wrote* it!)

I recommend adding a comment header to every procedure you write, no matter how simple. Such a header should contain the following information:

- **The name of the procedure**
- **The date it was last modified**
- **What it does**
- **What data items the caller must pass it to make it work correctly**
- **What data is returned by the procedure, if any, and where it is returned**. (For example, in register **CX**.)
- **What other procedures, if any, are called by the procedure**
- **Any "gotchas" that need to be kept in mind while writing code that uses the procedure**

A typical workable procedure header is shown below:

```
;-----------------------------------------------------------
;   WRITELN  --  Displays information to the screen via DOS
;                service 9 and issues a newline
;   Last update 3/5/89
;
;   1 entry point:
;
;   Writeln:
;       Caller must pass:
;       DS: The segment of the string to be displayed
```

```
;          DX: The offset of the string to be displayed
;              String must be terminated by "$"
;      Action:  Displays the string at DS:DX up to the "$"
;               marker, then issues a newline.  Hardware cursor
;               will move to the left margin of the following
;               line.  If the display is to the bottom screen
;               line, the screen will scroll.
;      Calls: Write
;-------------------------------------------------------------
```

A comment header does not relieve you of the responsibility of commenting the individual lines of code within the procedure. It's a good idea to put a short comment to the right of every line that contains a machine instruction mnemonic, and also (in longer procedures) a comment block describing every major functional block within the procedure.

Examine EAT3.ASM, and notice the various commenting conventions. For a very short program such as this, such elaborate internal documentation might seem overkill. Once your programs get serious, however, you'll be very glad you expended the effort.

```
;-------------------------------------------------------------
;                         EAT3.ASM
;        Backhanded advertising program, over the full screen
;
;                                    by Jeff Duntemann
;                                    MASM/TASM
;                                    Last update 3/09/92
;-------------------------------------------------------------


;----------------------------|
;   BEGIN STACK SEGMENT       |
;----------------------------|
MYSTACK     SEGMENT STACK           ; STACK word ensures loading of SS by DOS

            DB  64 DUP ('STACK!!!') ; This reserves 512 bytes for the stack

MYSTACK     ENDS
;----------------------------|
;   END STACK SEGMENT         |
;----------------------------|


;----------------------------|
;   BEGIN DATA SEGMENT        |
;----------------------------|
MyData      SEGMENT
```

```
        ; 18H = 24D; 4FH = 79D; Combined 0-based X,Y of 80 x 25 screen LR corner:
LRXY        DW      184FH

TextPos     DW      ?
Eat1        DB      "Eat at Joe's...",'$'
Eat2        DB      "...ten million flies can't ALL be wrong!",'$'
CRLF        DB      0DH,0AH,'$'

MyData      ENDS
;---------------------------|
;       END DATA SEGMENT    |
;---------------------------|


;---------------------------|
;      BEGIN CODE SEGMENT   |
;---------------------------|
MyProg      SEGMENT

            assume CS:MyProg,DS:MyData
Main        PROC

Start:      ; This is where program execution begins:
            mov  AX,MyData   ; Set up our own data segment address in DS
            mov  DS,AX       ; Can't load segment reg. directly from memory

            call ClrScr      ; Clear the full display

            mov  TextPos, 0914H   ; 0914H = X @ 20, Y @ 9

            mov  DX,TextPos  ; TextPos contains X,Y position values
            call GotoXY      ; Position cursor
            lea  DX,Eat1     ; Load offset of Eat1 string into DX
            call Write       ;   and display it

            mov  DX,TextPos  ; Reuse text position variable
            mov  DH,10       ; Put new Y value into DH
            call GotoXY      ; Position cursor
            lea  DX,Eat2     ; Load offset of Ear2 string into DX
            call Writeln     ;   and display it

            mov  AH,4CH      ; Terminate process DOS service
            mov  AL,0        ; Pass this value back to ERRORLEVEL
            int  21H         ; Control returns to DOS

;---------------------------|
;    PROCEDURE SECTION       |
;---------------------------|
```

```
;-----------------------------------------------------------------
;   GOTOXY   --  Positions the hardware cursor to X,Y
;   Last update 3/5/89
;
;   1 entry point:
;
;   GotoXY:
;     Caller must pass:
;     DL: X value    These are both 0-based; i.e., they
;     DH: Y value       assume a screen 24 x 79, not 25 x 80
;     Action:  Moves the hardware cursor to the X,Y position
;              loaded into DL and DH.
;-----------------------------------------------------------------
GotoXY    PROC
          mov AH,02H        ; Select VIDEO service 2: Position cursor
          mov BH,0          ; Stay with display page 0
          int 10H           ; Call VIDEO
          ret               ; Return to the caller
GotoXY    ENDP


;-----------------------------------------------------------------
;   CLRSCR   --  Clears or scrolls screens or windows
;   Last update 3/5/89
;
;   4 entry points:
;
;   ClrScr:
;     No values expected from caller
;     Action:  Clears the entire screen to blanks with 07H as
;              the display attribute
;
;   ClrWin:
;     Caller must pass:
;     CH: Y coordinate, upper-left corner of window
;     CL: X coordinate, upper-left corner of window
;     DH: Y coordinate, lower-right corner of window
;     DL: X coordinate, lower-right corner of window
;     Action:  Clears the window specified by the caller to
;              blanks with 07H as the display attribute
;
;   ScrlWin:
;     Caller must pass:
;     CH: Y coordinate, upper-left corner of window
;     CL: X coordinate, upper-left corner of window
;     DH: Y coordinate, lower-right corner of window
;     DL: X coordinate, lower-right corner of window
;     AL: number of lines to scroll window by (0 clears it)
;     Action:  Scrolls the window specified by the caller by
;              the number of lines passed in AL.  The blank
```

```
;                     lines inserted at screen bottom are cleared
;                     to blanks with 07H as the display attribute
;
;    VIDEO6:
;       Caller must pass:
;       CH: Y coordinate, upper-left corner of window
;       CL: X coordinate, upper-left corner of window
;       DH: Y coordinate, lower-right corner of window
;       DL: X coordinate, lower-right corner of window
;       AL: number of lines to scroll window by (0 clears it)
;       BH: display attribute for blanked lines (07H is "normal")
;       Action:  Generic access to BIOS VIDEO service 6.  Caller
;                     must pass ALL register parameters as shown above
;----------------------------------------------------------------

ClrScr     PROC
           mov CX,0       ; Upper-left corner of full screen
           mov DX,LRXY    ; Load lower-right XY coordinates into DX
ClrWin:    mov AL,0       ; 0 specifies clear entire region
ScrlWin:   mov BH,07H     ; Specify "normal" attribute for blanked line(s)
VIDEO6:    mov AH,06H     ; Select VIDEO service 6: Initialize/Scroll
           int 10H        ; Call VIDEO
           ret            ; Return to the caller
ClrScr     ENDP


;----------------------------------------------------------------
;   WRITE    --  Displays information to the screen via DOS
;                service 9: Print String
;   Last update 3/5/89
;
;   1 entry point:
;
;   Write:
;      Caller must pass:
;      DS: The segment of the string to be displayed
;      DX: The offset of the string to be displayed
;           String must be terminated by "$"
;      Action:  Displays the string at DS:DX up to the "$" marker
;----------------------------------------------------------------

Write      PROC
           mov AH,09H     ; Select DOS service 9: Print String
           int 21H        ; Call DOS
           ret            ; Return to the caller
Write      ENDP
```

```
;-------------------------------------------------------------
;   WRITELN  --  Displays information to the screen via DOS
;                service 9 and issues a newline
;   Last update 3/5/89
;
;   1 entry point:
;
;   Writeln:
;      Caller must pass:
;      DS: The segment of the string to be displayed
;      DX: The offset of the string to be displayed
;          String must be terminated by "$"
;      Action:  Displays the string at DS:DX up to the "$" marker,
;               then issues a newline.  Hardware cursor will
;               move to the left margin of the following line.
;               If the display is to the bottom screen line,
;               the screen will scroll.
;      Calls: Write
;-------------------------------------------------------------

Writeln    PROC
           call Write          ; Display the string proper through Write
           mov DX,OFFSET CRLF   ; Load address of newline string to DS:DX
           call Write          ; Display the newline string through Write
           ret                 ; Return to the caller
Writeln    ENDP

;---------------------------|
;   END PROCEDURE SECTION   |
;---------------------------|


Main       ENDP

MyProg     ENDS

;---------------------------|
;      END CODE SEGMENT     |
;---------------------------|

           END Start   ; The procedure named Start becomes the main program
```

8.4 Building External Libraries of Procedures

You'll notice that the EAT3.ASM program, listed at the end of the previous section devoted most of its bulk to procedures. This is as it should be. Notice, however, that the procedures EAT3.ASM uses are the kind you're likely to use in any and all of your assembly-language programs. When this is the case, break the utility procedures out into an external library that you can assemble only once, and then link into every program that uses its procedures without assembling the library every time you assemble the program. This is called *modular programming*, and it is an extremely effective tool for programming efficiently in any language, assembly language not excluded. (Keeping cursor movement and screen-clearing routines in source-code form in every single program you write is a waste of space, and can clutter up the program in a way that makes it less easy to understand.)

I described this process briefly back in Chapter 3, and showed it pictorially in Figures 3.4 and 3.5. A program might consist of three or four separate .ASM files, each of which is assembled separately to a separate .OBJ file. To produce the final executable .EXE file, the linker weaves all of the .OBJ files together, resolving all of the references from one to the other, finally creating an .EXE file.

Each .ASM file is considered a *module*, and each module contains one or more procedures and possibly some data definitions. When all the *declarations* are done correctly, all of the modules may freely call one another, and any procedure may refer to any data definition.

The trick, of course, is to get all the declarations right.

Public and External Declarations

If you reference a label in your program (by, say, including a **CALL** instruction to that label) without defining that label anywhere in the program, the assembler will gleefully give you an error message. (You've probably already experienced this if you've begun writing your own programs in assembler.) In modular programming, you're frequently going to be calling procedures that don't exist anywhere in your program. How to get past the assembler's watchdogs?

The answer is to declare a procedure *external*. This works very much like it sounds: the assembler is told that a given label will have to be found outside the program somewhere, in another module. Once told that, that assembler is happy to give you a pass on an undefined label. You've promised the assembler you'll provide it later, and the assembler accepts your promise and keeps going without flagging the undefined label.

The promise looks like this:

```
EXTRN ClrScr : PROC
```

Here, you've told the assembler that the label **ClrScr** represents a procedure, and that it will be found somewhere external to the current module. That's all the assembler needs to know to withhold its error message.

And having done that, the assembler's part is finished. It leaves in place an empty socket in your program where the external procedure can later be plugged in. I sometimes think of it as an eyelet where the external procedure will later hook in.

Over in the other module where procedure **ClrScr** exists, you not only have to define the procedure, you must give the eyelet a hook. That is, you have to warn the assembler that **ClrScr** will be referenced from outside the module. The assembler needs to forge the hook that will hook into the eyelet. You forge the hook by declaring the procedure **public**, meaning that other modules may freely reference the procedure. Declaring a procedure public is simplicity itself:

```
PUBLIC ClrScr
```

That done, who actually connects the hook and the eyelet? The linker does that during the link operation. After all, why call it a linker if it doesn't link anything? At link time, the linker takes the two .OBJ files generated by the assembler, one from your program and the other from the module containing **ClrScr**, and combines them into a single .EXE file. When the .EXE file is loaded and run, the program can call **ClrScr** as cleanly and quickly as though both had been declared in the same source-code file.

This process is summarized in Figure 8.2.

What works for procedures works for data as well, and it can work in either direction. Your program can declare a variable as public with the **PUBLIC** directive, and that variable can then be used by any module in which the same variable name is declared as external with the **EXTRN** directive.

We sometimes say that a program or module containing procedures or variables declared as public *exports* those items. Also, we say that a program or module that uses procedures or variables that are external to it *imports* those items.

The Mechanics of Publics and Externals

I've described the source-code mechanics of assembly-language programs in detail in the last few chapters. EAT1.ASM, EAT2.ASM, and EAT3.ASM are good examples. External modules are similar to programs. There are two major differences, concerning things that external modules lack:

- **External modules have no main program and hence no start address.** That is, no label is given after the **END** directive that concludes the source-code file. External modules are not intended to be run by themselves, so a start address is both unnecessary and (if one were added) a temptation to chaos.

- **External modules have no stack segment.** This is not an absolute requirement (there are few such requirements in assembler work), but for simple assembly-language programming it's true enough. Your stack segment should be defined in your main program module. External modules should have none—they use the one defined by the programs that call them.

Figure 8.2. Connecting publics and externals

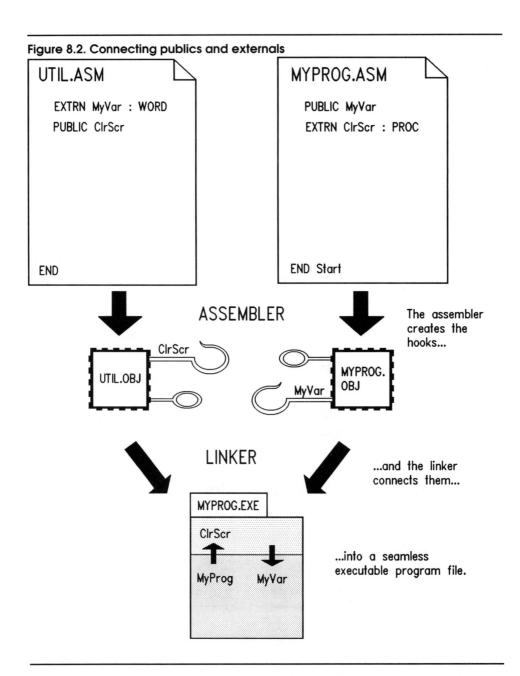

External modules can have a data segment. If the external module is to define a variable that is to be shared by the main program or by other externals, it obviously must have a data segment for that variable to reside in. But less obviously, if the external is to share a variable with another external or with the main program, it must *still* define a data segment, even if that data segment is empty except for the external declaration.

This is easier to demonstrate than to explain. Take a look at the following external module, which is a library containing all of the simple display control procedures introduced in EAT3.ASM:

```
;--------------------------------------------------------------
;                        VIDLIB.ASM
;                  Video Display Library
;
;                                 by Jeff Duntemann
;                                 MASM/TASM
;                                 Last update 3/7/92
;--------------------------------------------------------------

MyData      SEGMENT PUBLIC

            EXTRN   CRLF:BYTE,LRXY:WORD

MyData      ENDS


MyCode      SEGMENT PUBLIC

            PUBLIC GotoXY,ClrScr,ClrWin,ScrlWin,VIDEO6
            PUBLIC Write,Writeln

            ASSUME CS:MyCode,DS:MyData


;--------------------------------------------------------------
;   GOTOXY    --  Positions the hardware cursor to X,Y
;   Last update 3/5/89
;
;   1 entry point:
;
;   GotoXY:
;     Caller must pass:
;     DL: X value    These are both 0-based; i.e., they
;     DH: Y value      assume a screen 24 x 79, not 25 x 80
;     Action: Moves the hardware cursor to the X,Y position
;             loaded into DL and DH.
;--------------------------------------------------------------
GotoXY      PROC
            mov AH,02H         ; Select VIDEO service 2: Position Cursor
            mov BH,0           ; Stay with display page 0
            int 10H            ; Call VIDEO
            ret                ; Return to the caller
GotoXY      ENDP
```

```
;--------------------------------------------------------------
;   CLRSCR    --  Clears or scrolls screens or windows
;   Last update 3/5/89
;
;   4 entry points:
;
;   ClrScr:
;      No values expected from caller
;      Action:  Clears the entire screen to blanks with 07H as
;               the display attribute
;
;   ClrWin:
;      Caller must pass:
;      CH: Y coordinate, upper-left corner of window
;      CL: X coordinate, upper-left corner of window
;      DH: Y coordinate, lower-right corner of window
;      DL: X coordinate, lower-right corner of window
;      Action:  Clears the window specified by the caller to
;               blanks with 07H as the display attribute
;
;   ScrlWin:
;      Caller must pass:
;      CH: Y coordinate, upper-left corner of window
;      CL: X coordinate, upper-left corner of window
;      DH: Y coordinate, lower-right corner of window
;      DL: X coordinate, lower-right corner of window
;      AL: number of lines to scroll window by (0 clears it)
;      Action:  Scrolls the window specified by the caller by
;               the number of lines passed in AL.  The blank
;               lines inserted at screen bottom are cleared
;               to blanks with 07H as the display attribute
;
;   VIDEO6:
;      Caller must pass:
;      CH: Y coordinate, upper-left corner of window
;      CL: X coordinate, upper-left corner of window
;      DH: Y coordinate, lower-right corner of window
;      DL: X coordinate, lower-right corner of window
;      AL: number of lines to scroll window by (0 clears it)
;      BH: display attribute for blanked lines (07H is "normal")
;      Action:  Generic access to BIOS VIDEO service 6.  Caller
;               must pass ALL register parameters as shown above
;--------------------------------------------------------------

ClrScr    PROC
          mov CX,0      ; Upper-left corner of full screen
          mov DX,LRXY   ; Load lower-right XY coordinates into DX
ClrWin:   mov AL,0      ; 0 specifies clear entire region
```

```
ScrlWin:    mov BH,07H      ; Specify "normal" attribute for blanked line(s)
VIDEO6:     mov AH,06H      ; Select VIDEO service 6: Initialize/Scroll
            int 10H         ; Call VIDEO
            ret             ; Return to the caller
ClrScr      ENDP



;----------------------------------------------------------------
;   WRITE    --  Displays information to the screen via DOS
;                    service 9: Print String
;   Last update 3/5/89
;
;   1 entry point:
;
;   Write:
;     Caller must pass:
;     DS: The segment of the string to be displayed
;     DX: The offset of the string to be displayed
;         String must be terminated by "$"
;     Action:  Displays the string at DS:DX up to the "$" marker
;----------------------------------------------------------------

Write       PROC
            mov AH,09H      ; Select DOS service 9: Print String
            int 21H         ; Call DOS
            ret             ; Return to the caller
Write       ENDP



;----------------------------------------------------------------
;   WRITELN  --  Displays information to the screen via DOS
;                    service 9 and issues a newline
;   Last update 3/5/89
;
;   1 entry point:
;
;   Writeln:
;     Caller must pass:
;     DS: The segment of the string to be displayed
;     DX: The offset of the string to be displayed
;         String must be terminated by "$"
;     Action:  Displays the string at DS:DX up to the "$" marker,
;                 then issues a newline.  Hardware cursor will
;                 move to the left margin of the following line.
;                 If the display is to the bottom screen line,
;                 the screen will scroll.
;     Calls: Write
;----------------------------------------------------------------
```

```
Writeln      PROC
             call Write           ; Display the string proper through Write
             mov DX,OFFSET CRLF   ; Load address of newline string to DS:DX
             call Write           ; Display the newline string through Write
             ret                  ; Return to the caller
Writeln      ENDP


MyCode       ENDS

             END
```

VIDLIB.ASM has both a code segment and a data segment. Note well that both segments are declared with the **PUBLIC** keyword. A common mistake made by beginners is to declare the procedures and variables public, but not the segments that they reside in. Non obvious it may be, but essential nonetheless: make your module segments public if they contain any public declarations!

The code segment contains all the procedures. The data segment, on the other hand, contains only the following statement:

```
EXTRN  CRLF:BYTE,LRXY:WORD
```

VIDLIB.ASM declares no variables of its own. Instead, it uses two variables declared within the main program module EAT4.ASM. (EAT4.ASM is identical to EAT3.ASM, save that it has had its procedures removed and declared as external, and two of its variables declared public. The program's function is exactly the same as that of EAT3.ASM.)

The **EXTRN** statement above indicates that two variables referenced within the module are to be imported from somewhere. *You don't have to specify from where.* The names of the variables and their types have to be there. The linker and assembler are not case sensitive.

The directives following the colons in the **EXTRN** statement are type specifiers. The assembler builds hooks into the .OBJ it creates from the external module's source file. These hooks will then mate with the appropriate hooks in the .OBJ file that exports the imported variables. To get the hooks right, however, the assembler needs to know what kind of item is being imported. The name of the variable is just a label and gives no information about the type or size of data being imported. The type specifier must match the definition of the variable being imported. Table 8.1 summarizes what commonly used type specifiers correspond to what data declaration directives.

The most important piece of information contained in the type specifier is the size of the item being imported. Machine instructions assemble to different binary opcodes depending on the size of their memory data operands. An

Table 8.1. Type specifiers for external declarations

Specifier	Use with directive	Specifies
PROC	PROC	Procedure
BYTE	DB	Byte or string
WORD	DW	Word-sized data
DWORD	DD	Double word-sized data

opcode that acts on byte-sized data in memory will be different from an opcode that acts on word-sized data. To get the hooks right, then, the assembler has to know the size of the imported item *at assembly time*.

Dividing a Segment Across Module Boundaries

Note that the names of the code segment and data segment in the external module are the same as the names of the code segment and data segment in the main program module. The data segment is **MyData** in both, and the code segment is **MyCode** in both. This is not an absolute requirement, but it simplifies things greatly and is a good way to set things up while you're just learning your way around in assembly language. Regardless of the number of external modules that link with your main program, the program as a whole contains only one code segment and one data segment. Until your data requirements and code size get *very* large, you won't need more than a single code and data segment.

As long as the code and data segments are declared with the **PUBLIC** directive in all the modules sharing the segments, the linker will consider all to be part of the same code and data segments.

It is also necessary to have an **ASSUME** statement in every module sharing segments in this fashion. Furthermore, it should be the same **ASSUME** statement as the one in the main program, with CS associated with your single code segment and DS associated with your single data segment:

```
ASSUME CS:MyCode,DS:MyData
```

This ensures that the assembler does not get confused as it puts together references to the two segments in the .OBJ files it builds.

Your Main Program Module

Below is our backhanded advertising program, which has been modified for use with an external display control module:

```
;-----------------------------------------------------------------
;                            EAT4.ASM
;     Backhanded advertising program, with external references
;
;                                    by Jeff Duntemann
;                                    MASM/TASM
;                                    Last update 3/7/92
;-----------------------------------------------------------------


;---------------------------|
;    BEGIN STACK SEGMENT     |
;---------------------------|
MYSTACK     SEGMENT STACK         ; STACK word ensures loading of SS by DOS

            DB  64 DUP ('STACK!!!') ; This reserves 512 bytes for the stack

MYSTACK     ENDS
;---------------------------|
;    END STACK SEGMENT       |
;---------------------------|


;---------------------------|
;    BEGIN DATA SEGMENT      |
;---------------------------|
MyData      SEGMENT PUBLIC
            PUBLIC LRXY,CRLF

LRXY        DW      184FH ; 18H = 24D; 4FH = 79D; 0 based XY of LR screen corner

TextPos     DW      ?
Eat1        DB      "Eat at Joe's...",'$'
Eat2        DB      "...ten million flies can't ALL be wrong!",'$'
CRLF        DB      0DH,0AH,'$'

MyData      ENDS
;---------------------------|
;    END DATA SEGMENT        |
;---------------------------|


;---------------------------|
;    BEGIN CODE SEGMENT      |
;---------------------------|

; Note that the following items are external to EAT4.ASM, and must
;   be linked from the external file VIDLIB.OBJ.  Assemble VIDLIB.ASM
;   first to VIDLIB.OBJ before attempting the link.

        EXTRN GotoXY:PROC,Write:PROC,Writeln:PROC,ClrScr:PROC
```

```
MyCode    SEGMENT PUBLIC


          assume CS:MyCode,DS:MyData
Main      PROC

Start:    ; This is where program execution begins:
          mov  AX,MyData   ; Set up our own data segment address in DS
          mov  DS,AX       ; Can't load segment reg. directly from memory

          call ClrScr      ; Clear the full display

          mov  TextPos, 0914H   ; 0914H = X @ 20, Y @ 9

          mov  DX,TextPos  ; TextPos contains X,Y position values
          call GotoXY      ; Position cursor
          lea  DX,Eat1     ; Load offset of Eat1 string into DX
          call Write       ;   and display it

          mov  DX,TextPos  ; Reuse text position variable
          mov  DH,10       ; Put new Y value into DH
          call GotoXY      ; Position cursor
          lea  DX,Eat2     ; Load offset of Eat2 string into DX
          call Writeln     ;   and display it

          mov  AH,4CH      ; Terminate process DOS service
          mov  AL,0        ; Pass this value back to ERRORLEVEL
          int  21H         ; Control returns to DOS

Main      ENDP

MyCode    ENDS

;---------------------------|
;      END CODE SEGMENT     |
;---------------------------|

          END Start  ; The procedure named Start becomes the main program
```

EAT4.ASM differs in only a few ways from EAT3.ASM. First of all, the data and code segment declarations now include the **PUBLIC** directive:

```
MyData SEGMENT PUBLIC

MyCode SEGMENT PUBLIC
```

This is easy to forget but you must keep it in mind: the segments containing imported or exported items *as well as the imported or exported items themselves* must be declared as public.

Take note of the declaration of two of the variables in the data segment declared as public:

```
PUBLIC LRXY,CRLF
```

The **PUBLIC** directive allows external modules to use these two variables. The other variables declared in the main program, **Eat1**, **Eat2**, and **TextPos**, are not declared as public and are inaccessible from external modules. We would say that those three variables are *private* to the main program module EAT4.ASM.

EAT4.ASM contains no procedure declarations of its own. All the procedures it uses are imported from VIDLIB.ASM, and all are therefore declared as external in the code segment, using this statement:

```
EXTRN GotoXY:PROC,Write:PROC,Writeln:PROC,ClrScr:PROC
```

Something to keep in mind is that while VIDLIB.ASM exports seven procedures (seven labels, actually, since four are entry points to the **ClrScr** procedure) EAT4.ASM only imports four. The **ClrWin**, **ScrlWin**, and **VIDEO6** entry points to procedure **ClrScr** are declared as public in VIDLIB.ASM, but they are not declared as external in EAT4.ASM. EAT4.ASM only uses the four it imports. The other three are available, but the EAT4.ASM does not call them and therefore does not bother declaring them as external. If you were to expand EAT4.ASM to use one of the three other entry points to **ClrScr**, you would have to add the entry point to the **EXTRN** list.

Once all the external and public declaration are in place, your machine instructions may reference procedures and variables across module boundaries as though they were all within the same large program. No special qualifiers have to be added to the instructions. This **CALL ClrScr** instruction is written the same way, whether **ClrScr** is declared in the main program module or in an external module like VIDLIB.ASM.

Linking Multiple Modules

The linker hasn't had to do much linking so far. Once you have multiple modules, however, the linker begins to earn its keep. To link multiple modules, you must specify the name of the .OBJ file for each module on the linker command line.

Up until now, the linker command line contained only the name of the main program module:

```
TLINK EAT3
```

Now you must add the names of all external modules to the linker command line:

```
TLINK EAT4 VIDLIB
```

If you're using JED, display the Commands screen by pressing F4 and edit the linker command line. For example, to use TASM to link EAT4.OBJ and VIDLIB.OBJ, the linker command line would be the following:

```
TLINK ~ VIDLIB
```

Remember that the tilde character (~) stands for the currently loaded file in JED.

Pretty obviously, if you forget to name an external module on the linker command line, the linker will not be able to resolve the external references involving the missing .OBJ file, and you will get linker error messages like this one, one for each unresolved external reference:

```
Undefined symbol 'CLRSCR' in module EAT4.ASM
```

External Module Summary

Here are some points to keep in mind when you're faced with splitting a single program up into a main program and one or more external modules:

- **Declare the code segments public in all modules, and give them all the same name.**
- **Declare the data segments public in all modules, and give them all the same name.**
- **Declare all exported procedures, entry points, and variables as Public.** Place the **PUBLIC** directive *inside* the segment where the exported items are declared.
- **Declare all imported procedures, entry points, and variables as external.** Put the external directive *inside* the segment where the imported items are to be used. Data is used in the data segment, code in the code segment.
- **Make sure that there is a common ASSUME statement in the *code segment* of every module associating the CS register with the shared code segment and the DS register with the shared data segment.**
- **Finally, don't forget to add the names of all external modules to the linker command line in the link step.**

If this still seems fuzzy to you, follow VIDLIB.ASM and EAT4.ASM as a model. You will certainly find it useful to beef up VIDLIB.ASM by adding more screen control procedures.

8.5 Creating and Using Macros

Procedures are the easiest way to split an assembly-language program into more manageable chunks. The mechanism for calling and returning from procedures is built right into the CPU, and is independent of any given assembler product.

Today's two major assemblers (Microsoft's MASM and Borland's TASM) provide another complexity-management tool that works a little differently: *macros*. They're hardly a minor feature; their name is built right into Microsoft's product, which after all is the Microsoft Macro Assembler.

Macros are a different breed of cat entirely. Whereas procedures are implemented by the use of **CALL** and **RET** instructions built right into the instruction set, macros are a trick of the assembler, and do not depend on any particular instruction or group of instructions.

Most simply put, a macro is a label that stands for some sequence of text lines. This sequence of text lines can be (but does not have to be) a sequence of instructions. When the assembler encounters the macro label in a source code file, it replaces the macro label with the text lines that the macro label represents. This is called *expanding* the macro, because the name of the macro (occupying one text line) is replaced by several lines of text, which are then assembled just as though they had appeared in the source-code file all along.

Macros bear some resemblance to Include files in high-level languages like Pascal. In Turbo Pascal, an include command might look like this:

```
{$I ENGINE.DEF}
```

When this include command is encountered, the compiler goes out to disk and finds the file named ENGINE.DEF. It then opens the file and starts "feeding" the text contained in that file into the source-code file at the point where the include command was placed. The compiler then processes those lines as though they had always been in the source-code file.

You might think of a macro as an include file that's built right into the source-code file. It's a sequence of text lines that is defined once and given a name. The Macro can then be dropped into the source code again and again by simply using the name.

This process is shown in Figure 8.3. The source code stored on disk contains a macro definition, bracketed between **MACRO** and **ENDM** directives. Later in the file, the name of the macro, Clr Scr, appears several times. When the assembler processes this file, it copies the macro definition into a buffer somewhere in memory. As it assembles the text read from disk, the assembler "drops" the statements contained in the macro into the text wherever the macro name appears. The disk file is not affected; the expansion of the macros occurs *only* in memory.

Figure 8.3. How macros work

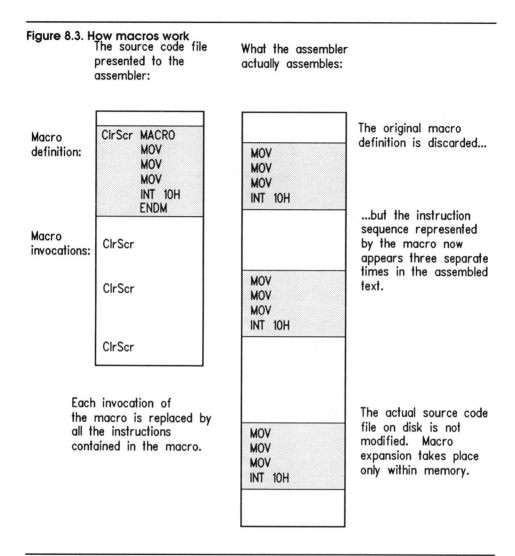

The source code file
presented to the
assembler:

What the assembler
actually assembles:

Macro
definition:

| ClrScr MACRO |
| MOV |
| MOV |
| MOV |
| INT 10H |
| ENDM |

The original macro
definition is discarded...

| MOV |
| MOV |
| MOV |
| INT 10H |

Macro
invocations:

ClrScr

ClrScr

ClrScr

...but the instruction
sequence represented
by the macro now
appears three separate
times in the assembled
text.

| MOV |
| MOV |
| MOV |
| INT 10H |

Each invocation of
the macro is replaced by
all the instructions
contained in the macro.

The actual source code
file on disk is not
modified. Macro
expansion takes place
only within memory.

| MOV |
| MOV |
| MOV |
| INT 10H |

Macros vs. Procedures: Pro and Con

There are advantages to using macros rather than procedures. One of them is speed. It takes time4 to execute the **CALL** and **RET** instructions that control entry to and exit from a procedure. In a macro, neither instruction is used. Only the instructions that perform the actual work of the macro are executed, so the macro's work is performed as quickly as possible.

There is a cost to this speed, and the cost is in extra memory used, especially if the macro is invoked a number of times. Notice in Figure 8.3 that three invocations of the macro generate a total of twelve instructions in memory. If the macro had been set up as a procedure, only the four instructions in the body of the procedure, plus one **RET** instructions and three **CALL** instructions would be required to do the same work. This would give you a total of eight instructions for the procedure and twelve for the macro. Each additional time the macro was invoked, the difference would grow.

> Every time a macro is invoked, all of its instructions are duplicated in the program again.

In short programs, this may not be a problem, and in situations where the code must be as fast as possible—as in graphics drivers—macros have a lot going for them.

By and large, think macros for speed and procedures for compactness.

The Mechanics of Macro Definition

A macro definition looks a lot like a procedure definition, with a slightly different pair of directives: **MACRO** and **ENDM**. One other crucial difference is that the name of the macro *cannot* be repeated in front of the **ENDM** directive. I'm not sure why this must be so, but it confuses the assembler to no end.

Don't put a **RET** instruction at the end of the macro! Executing a **RET** without a previous **CALL** will corrupt your stack and probably crash your program.

One important shortcoming of macros vis-a-vis procedures is that macros can have only *one* entry point. The **ClrScr** procedure described in the last section cannot be converted into a macro without splitting it up into four separate invocations of VIDEO interrupt 10H. If the **ClrScr** function (clearing the full screen to blanks for the normal video attribute) alone were written as a macro, it would look like this:

```
ClrScr    MACRO
          mov CX,0        ; Upper left corner of full screen
          mov DX,LRXY     ; Load lower-right XY coordinates into DX
          mov AL,0        ; 0 specifies clear entire region
          mov BH,07H      ; Specify "normal" attribute for blanked line(s)
          mov AH,06H      ; Select VIDEO service 6: Initialize/Scroll
          int 10H         ; Call VIDEO
          ENDM
```

You can see that **ClrScr** has shed its **RET** instruction and its additional entry points, but apart from that it's exactly the same sequence of instructions.

Functionally it works the same way, except that every time you clear your screen, **ClrScr**'s six instructions are dropped into the source code.

Macros are invoked simply by naming them. Don't use the **CALL** instruction! Just place the macro name on a line:

```
ClrScr
```

The assembler will handle the rest.

Defining Macros with Parameters

So far, macros may seem useful but perhaps not especially compelling. What makes macros really sing is their ability to mimic high-level language subroutines and accept arguments through parameters. For example, if you were to define a macro named **GotoXY** to position the hardware cursor, you could pass it the X and Y values as arguments:

```
GotoXY 17,3        ; Move the cursor to the Name field
```

You'd have to pinch yourself to be sure you weren't working in BASIC, no?

Macro parameters are, again, artifacts of the assembler. They are not pushed on the stack or set into COMMON or anything like that. The parameters are simply placeholders for the actual values (called *arguments*) that you pass to the macro.

I've converted the **GotoXY** procedure to a macro to show you how this works. Here's the macro:

```
GotoXY    MACRO NewX,NewY
          mov DH,NewY      ; The NewY parameter loads into DH
          mov DL,NewX      ; The NewX parameter loads into DL
          mov AH,02H       ; Select VIDEO service 2: Position Cursor
          mov BH,0         ; Stay with display page 0
          int 10H          ; Call VIDEO
          ENDM
```

The two parameters are **NewX** and **NewY**. Parameters are a kind of label, and they may be referenced anywhere *within* the macro. Here, the parameters are referenced as operands to a couple of **MOV** instructions. The arguments passed to the macro in **NewX** and **NewY** are thus loaded into **DL** and **DH**.

Don't confuse the arguments (actual values) with the parameters. If you understand Pascal, it's *exactly* like the difference between formal parameters and actual parameters. A macro's parameters correspond to Pascal's formal parameters, whereas a macro's arguments correspond to Pascal's actual parameters. *The macro's parameters are the labels following the **MACRO** directive* *where the macro is defined. The arguments are the values specified on the line where the macro is invoked.*

The Mechanics of Macro Parameters

A macro may have as many parameters as will fit on one line. This is a rather arbitrary restriction, leaving you no recourse but to use short parameters names if you need lots of parameters for a single macro.

Arguments are dropped into parameters in order, from left to right. If you pass only two arguments to a macro with three parameters, you're likely to get an error message from the assembler, depending on how you've referenced the unfilled parameter. The assembler builds opcodes based on the types of operands passed as arguments; if you don't pass an argument for a given parameter, any instructions that reference that parameter won't be constructable by the assembler, hence the errors.

If you pass more arguments to a macro than there are parameters to receive the arguments, the extraneous arguments will be ignored.

Local Labels within Macros

I haven't really gone into labels and branches yet, but there's an important problem with labels used inside macros. Labels in assembly-language programs must be unique, and yet a macro is essentially duplicated in the source code as many times as it is invoked. This means there will be error messages flagging duplicate labels...unless you declare a macro's labels as *local*.

Local labels are declared with the **LOCAL** directive. Here's an example; don't worry if you don't fully understand all of the instructions it uses:

```
UpCase     MACRO Target,Length   ; Target is a string; Length its length
           LOCAL Tester,Bump
           mov CX,Length         ; CX is acting as length counter for loop
           lea BX,Target         ; String will be at DS:BX
Tester:    cmp BYTE PTR [BX],'a' ; Is string character below 'a'?
           jb Bump               ; If so, leave character alone
           cmp BYTE PTR [BX],'z' ; Is string character above 'z'?
           ja Bump               ; If so, leave character alone
           and BYTE PTR [BX],11011111b  ; Char is lc alpha,
                                 ;   so force bit 5 to 0
Bump:      inc BX                ; Bump BX to point to next char in string
           loop Tester           ; And go back and do it again!
           ENDM
```

The important thing to understand is that unless the labels **Tester** and **Bump** are declared local to the macro, there will be multiple instances of a label in the program and the assembler will generate a duplicate label error.

The only thing to remember about declaring local labels within macros is that the **LOCAL** directive must immediately follow the macro header. Don't put anything—not even a comment line—between the two.

Macro Libraries

Just as procedures can be gathered in libraries external to your program, so can macros be gathered into *macro libraries*. A macro library is really nothing but a text file that contains the source code for the macros in the library. Unlike a procedures module, macro libraries are not separately assembled. Macro libraries must be passed through the assembler each time the program is assembled. This is a problem with macros in general, not only with macros that are gathered into libraries. Programs that manage complexity by dividing code up into macros will assemble more slowly than programs that have been divided up into separately assembled modules.

Macro libraries are used by including them into your program's source-code file. The means to do this is the **INCLUDE** directive. The **INCLUDE** directive precedes the name of the macro library:

```
INCLUDE MYLIB.MAC
```

This statement may be anywhere in your source-code file, but you must keep in mind that all macros must be fully defined before they are invoked. For this reason, it's a good idea to use the **INCLUDE** directive near the top of your source-code file, before any possible invocation of one of the library macros could occur.

The following is a macro library containing macro versions of all the procedures we discussed in the previous section:

```
;-----------------------------------------------------------------
;                          MYLIB.MAC
;         Macro library from ASSEMBLY LANGUAGE STEP BY STEP
;
;                                      by Jeff Duntemann
;                                      MASM/TASM
;                                      Last update 11/25/91
;-----------------------------------------------------------------


;-----------------------------------------------------------------
;   CLEAR    -- Clears the entire visible screen buffer
;   Last update 3/16/89
;
;       Caller must pass:
;       In VidAddress:  The address of the video refresh buffer
```

```
;       In ClearAtom:   The character/attribute pair to fill the
;                       buffer with.  The high byte contains the
;                       attribute and the low byte the character.
;       In BufLength:   The number of *characters* in the visible
;                       display buffer, *not* the number of bytes!
;                       This is typically 2000 for a 25-line screen
;                       or 4000 for a 50-line screen.
;       Action:         Clears the screen by machine-gunning the
;                       character/attribute pair in AX into the
;                       display buffer beginning at VidAddress.
;-----------------------------------------------------------------
Clear      MACRO VidAddress,ClearAtom,BufLength
           les   DI,DWORD PTR VidAddress
           mov   AX,ClearAtom
           mov   CX,BufLength
           rep   stosw
           GotoXY 0,0
           ENDM


;-----------------------------------------------------------------
;   RULER   --  Displays a "1234567890"-style ruler on screen
;   Last update 11/25/91
;
;       Caller must pass:
;       In VidAddress: The address of the start of the video buffer
;       In Length:  The length of the ruler to be displayed
;       In ScreenW: The width of the current screen (usually 80)
;       In ScreenY: The line of the screen where the ruler is
;                   to be displayed (0-24)
;       In ScreenX: The row of the screen where the ruler should
;                   start (0-79)
;       Action:     Displays an ASCII ruler at ScreenX,ScreenY.
;-----------------------------------------------------------------
Ruler      MACRO VidAddress,Length,ScreenW,ScreenX,ScreenY
           les   DI,DWORD PTR VidAddress
           mov   AL,ScreenY   ; Move Y position to AL
           mov   AH,ScreenW   ; Move screen width to AH
           imul  AH           ; Do 8-bit multiply AL*AH to AX
           add   DI,AX        ; Add Y offset into vidbuff to DI
           add   DI,ScreenX   ; Add X offset into vidbuf to DI
           shl   DI,1         ; Multiply by 2 for final address
           mov   CX,Length    ; CX monitors the ruler length
           mov   AH,07        ; Attribute 7 is "normal" text
           mov   AL,'1'       ; Start with digit "1"

DoChar:    stosw             ; Note that there's no REP prefix!
           add   AL,'1'       ; Bump the character value in AL up by 1
           aaa               ; Adjust AX to make this a BCD addition
           add   AL,'0'       ; Basically, put binary 3 in AL's high nybble
```

```
        mov     AH,07       ; Make sure our attribute is still 7
        loop    DoChar      ; Go back & do another char until BL goes to 0

        ENDM


;-------------------------------------------------------------
;   GOTOXY    --  Positions the hardware cursor to X,Y
;   Last update 3/5/89
;
;       Caller must pass:
;       In NewX: The new X value
;       In NewY: The new Y value
;         These are both 0-based; they assume a screen
;         whose dimensions are 24 by 79, not 25 by 80.
;       Action:  Moves the hardware cursor to the X,Y position
;                passed as NewX and NewY.
;-------------------------------------------------------------
GotoXY      MACRO NewX,NewY
            mov DH,NewY
            mov DL,NewX
            mov AH,02H      ; Select VIDEO service 2: Position Cursor
            mov BH,0        ; Stay with display page 0
            int 10H         ; Call VIDEO
            ENDM


;-------------------------------------------------------------
;   NEWLINE  --  Sends a newline sequence to DOS Standard Output
;                via DOS service 40H
;   Last update 3/16/89
;
;       Caller need not pass any parameters.
;       Action:  Sends a newline sequence DOS Standard Output
;-------------------------------------------------------------

Newline     MACRO
            Write CRLF,2
            ENDM


;-------------------------------------------------------------
;   POKECHAR    --  Inserts a single character into a string
;   Last update 3/16/89
;
;       Caller must pass:
;       In Target:  The name of the string to be poked at
;       In TheChar: The character to be poked into the string
;       In ToPos:   The 0-based position in the string to poke to
;       Action:     Pokes character passed in TheChar into string
;                   passed in Target to position passed in ToPos.
```

```
;                      The first character in the string is 0, etc.
;-------------------------------------------------------------------
PokeChar    MACRO Target,TheChar,ToPos
            lea  BX,Target   ; Load the address of target string into BX
            mov  BYTE PTR [BX+ToPos],TheChar  ; Move char into the string
            ENDM


;-------------------------------------------------------------------
;   WRITE    --  Displays information to the screen via DOS
;                    service 40: Print String to Standard Output
;   Last update 3/16/89
;
;      Caller must pass:
;      In ShowIt:     The name of the string to be displayed
;      In ShowLength: The length of the string to be displayed
;      Action:  Displays the string to DOS Standard Output
;-------------------------------------------------------------------
Write       MACRO ShowIt,ShowLength
            mov BX,1          ; Selects DOS file handle 1: Standard Output
            mov CX,ShowLength ; Length of string passed in CX
            lea DX,Showit     ; Offset address of string is passed in DX
            mov AH,40H        ; Select DOS service 40: Print String
            int 21H           ; Call DOS
            ENDM


;-------------------------------------------------------------------
;   WRITELN  --  Displays information to the screen via DOS
;                    service 40: Display to Standard Output, then
;                    issues a newline
;   Last update 3/16/89
;
;      Caller must pass:
;      In ShowIt: The name of the string to be displayed
;      In ShowLength: The length of the string to be displayed
;      Action:  Displays the string in ShowIt, then issues a
;               newline.  Hardware cursor will move to the
;               left margin of the following line.  If the
;               display is to the bottom screen line, the
;               screen will scroll.
;      Calls: Write
;-------------------------------------------------------------------

Writeln     MACRO ShowIt,ShowLength
            Write ShowIt,ShowLength   ; Display the string proper
                                      ;  through Write
            Write CRLF,2              ; Display the newline string
                                      ;  through Write
        ENDM
```

And, finally, yet another version of EAT.ASM, this time rearranged to make use of the macros in MYLIB.MAC. The macro library is included by way of the **INCLUDE** directive immediately following the comment header at the top of the file.

```
;-------------------------------------------------------------
;                          EAT5.ASM
;      Backhanded advertising program, full screen, with macros
;
;                                    by Jeff Duntemann
;                                    MASM/TASM
;                                    Last update 12/27/89
;-------------------------------------------------------------


INCLUDE MYLIB.MAC                  ; Load in screen control macro library


;----------------------------|
;    BEGIN STACK SEGMENT      |
;----------------------------|
MYSTACK      SEGMENT STACK         ; STACK word ensures loading of SS by DOS

            DB      64 DUP ('STACK!!!') ; This reserves 512 bytes for the stack

MYSTACK     ENDS
;----------------------------|
;    END STACK SEGMENT        |
;----------------------------|



;----------------------------|
;    BEGIN DATA SEGMENT       |
;----------------------------|
MyData      SEGMENT

LRXY        DW  184FH ; 18H = 24D; 4FH = 79D; 0-based XY of LR screen corner

VidOrigin DD  0B8000000H    ; Change to 0B0000000H if you have a mono CRT!
Eat1        DB   "Eat at Joe's..."
Eat1Length EQU $-Eat1
Eat2        DB   "...ten million flies can't ALL be wrong!"
Eat2Length EQU $-Eat2
CRLF        DB   0DH,0AH

MyData      ENDS
;----------------------------|
;    END DATA SEGMENT         |
;----------------------------|
```

```
;----------------------------|
;     BEGIN CODE SEGMENT     |
;----------------------------|

MyProg      SEGMENT

            assume CS:MyProg,DS:MyData
Main        PROC

Start:      ; This is where program execution begins:
            mov  AX,MyData   ; Set up our own data segment address in DS
            mov  DS,AX       ; Can't load segment reg. directly from memory

            Clear VidOrigin,07B0H,4000 ; Replace B0 with 20 for space clear

            GotoXY 14H,09H              ; Position cursor
            Write Eat1,Eat1Length      ; and display first text line

            GotoXY 14H,0AH             ; Position cursor
            Writeln Eat2,Eat2Length    ; and display second text line

            mov  AH,4CH     ; Terminate process DOS service
            mov  AL,0       ; Pass this value back to ERRORLEVEL
            int  21H        ; Control returns to DOS

Main        ENDP

MyProg      ENDS

;----------------------------|
;      END CODE SEGMENT      |
;----------------------------|

            END Start    ; The procedure named Start becomes the main program
```

You'll spot something odd in EAT5.ASM: instead of using **ClrScr** to clear the screen as I have been for the last several incarnations of EAT, I've replaced **ClrScr** with a new macro called **Clear**. **Clear** (defined in VIDLIB.MAC) uses some technology I haven't explained yet, but will return to in Chapter 10. The lesson is that there are numerous ways to skin a screen, and we've moved here from having the BIOS do it for us to doing it all on our own. Take it on faith for now, until I come back to it. More to the point for the current discussion is the use of the **GotoXY** and **Write** and **Writeln** macros.

Additionally, if you look closely at the main program procedure in EAT5.ASM, something odd may occur to you: It's starting to look like something other than an assembly-language program. This is true, and it's certainly possible to create so many macros that your programs will begin to look like some odd high-level language.

The danger there is that unless you name your macros carefully, and document them both in their macro-library files and on the lines where they are invoked, your programs will not be any more comprehensible for their presence. Dividing complexity into numerous compartments is only half the job—labeling the compartments is just as (or more) important!

Bits, Flags, Branches, and Tables

Easing into Mainstream Assembly Programming

You don't take off until *all* your flight checks are made.

That's the reason that we haven't done a lot of instruction arranging in this book up until now, here that we are on the third-to-last chapter. I've found that machine instructions aren't the most important part of assembly-language programming. What's most important is understanding your machine and your tools, and how everything fits together. Higher-level languages like Pascal and Modula-2 hide much of those essential details from you. In assembler you must see to them yourself. For some reason, authors of previous "beginner" books on assembly language haven't caught on to this fact.

This fact (in fact) was the major motivation for my writing this book.

If you've digested everything I've said so far, however, you're ready to get in and understand the remainder of the 8086/8088 instruction set. I won't teach it all in this book, but the phrase "ready to understand" is germane. You can now find yourself a reference and learn what instructions I don't cover on your own. The skills you need to build programming skills are now yours, and if this book has accomplished that much, I'd say it's accomplished a lot.

So let the fun begin.

9.1 Bits is Bits (and Bytes is Bits)

Assembly language is big on bits.

Bits, after all, are what bytes are made of, and one essential assembly-language skill is building bytes and taking them apart again. A technique called *bit mapping* is widely used in assembly language. Bit mapping assigns special meanings to individual bits within a byte to save space and squeeze the last little drop of utility out of a given amount of memory.

There is a family of instructions in the 8086/8088 instruction set that allow you to manipulate the bits within the bytes by applying Boolean logical operations to the bytes on a bit-by-bit basis. These *bitwise logical instructions* are: **AND**, **OR**, **XOR**, and **NOT**. Another family of instructions allows you to slide bits back and forth within a single byte or word. The most commonly used *shift/rotate instructions* are: **ROL**, **ROR**, **RCL**, **RCR**, **SHL**, and **SHR**. (There are a few others that I will not be discussing in this book.)

Bit Numbering

Dealing with bits requires that we have a way of specifying which bits we're dealing with. By convention, bits in assembly language are numbered, starting from 0, at the *least significant bit* in the byte, word, or other item we're using as a bit map. The least significant bit is the one with the least value in the binary number system. (Return to Chapter 1 and reread the material on base 2 if that seems fuzzy to you.) It's also the bit on the far right, if you write the value down as a binary number.

Figure 9.1. Bit numbering
Bits are numbered from right to left,
starting from 0:

Byte value:

7	6	5	4	3	2	1	0

Word value:

15	14	13	12	11	10	9	8	7	6	5	4	3	2	1	0

Most significant
bit (MSB)

Least significant
bit (LSB)

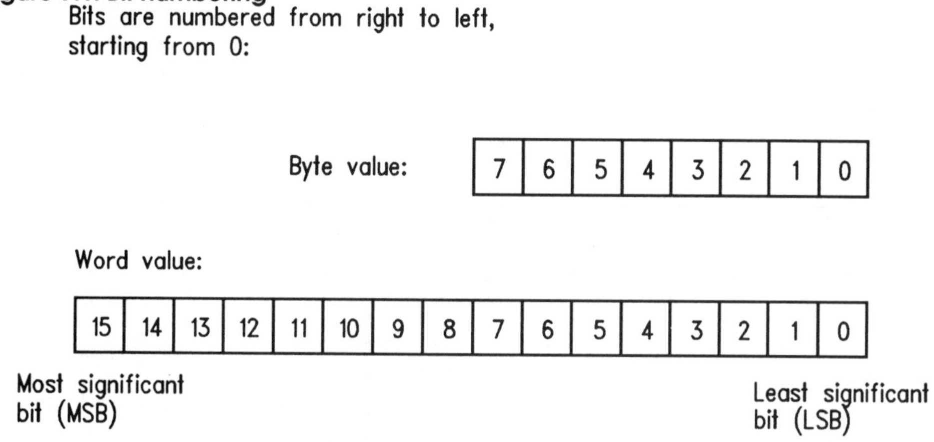

It works best as a visual metaphor. See Figure 9.1.

When you count bits, start with the bit on the right, and number them from 0.

"It's the Logical Thing to Do, Jim ..."

Boolean logic sounds arcane and forbidding, but remarkably, it reflects the realities of ordinary thought and action. The Boolean operator AND, for instance, pops up in many of the decisions you make every day of your life. For example, to write a check that doesn't bounce, you must have money in your checking account AND checks in your checkbook. Neither alone will do the job. ("How can I be overdrawn?" goes the classic question, "I still have checks in my checkbook!") You can't write a check you don't have, and a check without money behind it will bounce. People who live out of their checkbooks (and they always end up ahead of me in the checkout line at Safeway) must use the AND operator frequently.

When mathematicians speak of Boolean logic, they manipulate abstract values called *true* and *false*. The AND operator works like this. Condition1 AND Condition2 will be considered true if *both* Condition1 and Condition2 are true. If either condition is false, the result will be false.

There are in fact four different combinations of the two input values, so logical operations between two values are usually summarized in a form called a *truth table*. The truth table for the AND operator is shown in Table 9.1.

There's nothing mysterious about the truth table. It's just a summary of all possibilities of the AND operator as applied to two input conditions. The

Table 9.1. The AND truth table for Boolean logic

Condition 1	Operator	Condition 2		Result
False	AND	False	=	False
False	AND	True	=	False
True	AND	False	=	False
True	AND	True	=	True

important thing to remember is that *only* when both input values are true will the result also be true.

That's the way mathematicians see AND. In assembly-language terms, the **AND** instruction looks at two bits and yields a third bit based on the values of the first two bits. By convention, we consider a 1 bit to be true and a 0 bit to be false. The *logic* is identical; we're just using different symbols to represent true and false. Keeping that in mind, we can rewrite the truth table for the **AND** instruction to make it more meaningful for assembly-language work (see Table 9.2).

The AND Instruction

The **AND** instruction embodies this concept in the 8086/8088 instruction set. The **AND** instruction performs the AND logical operation on two bytes or two words (depending on how you write the instruction) and replaces its *first* operand with the result of the operation. (By first, I mean the operand closest to the mnemonic.) In other words, if you write this instruction

```
AND AL,BL
```

the CPU will perform a gang of eight bitwise AND operations on the 8 bits in **AL** and **BL**. Bit 0 of **AL** is ANDed with bit 0 of **BL**, bit 1 of **AL** is ANDed with bit 1 of **BL**, and so on. Each AND operation generates a result bit, and that bit is placed in the first operand (here, **AL**) *after all eight* AND operations occur. This is a common thread among machine instructions that perform some operation on two operands and produce a result: *the result replaces the first operand.*

Table 9.2. The AND truth table for assembly language

Bit 1	Operator	Bit 2		Result bit
0	AND	0	=	0
0	AND	1	=	0
1	AND	0	=	0
1	AND	1	=	1

Masking Out Bits

A major use of the **AND** instruction is to isolate one or more bits out of a byte value or a word value. The term isolate here simply means to set all *unwanted* bits to a reliable 0 value. As an example, suppose we are interested in testing bits 4 and 5 of a value to see what those bits are. To do that, we have to be able to ignore the other bits (bits 0 through 3 and 6 through 7) and the only way to safely ignore bits is to set them to 0.

AND is the way to go. We set up a *bit mask* in which the bit numbers that we want to inspect and test are set to 1, and the bits we wish to ignore are set to 0. To mask out all bits but bits 4 and 5, we must set up a mask in which bits 4 and 5 are set to 1, with all other bits at 0. This mask in binary is 00110000B, or 30H in hex. (To verify it, count the bits from the right hand end of the binary number, starting with 0.) This bit mask is then ANDed against the value in question. Figure 9.2 shows this operation in action, with the 30H bit mask just described, and an initial value of 9DH.

Figure 9.2. The Anatomy of an AND instruction

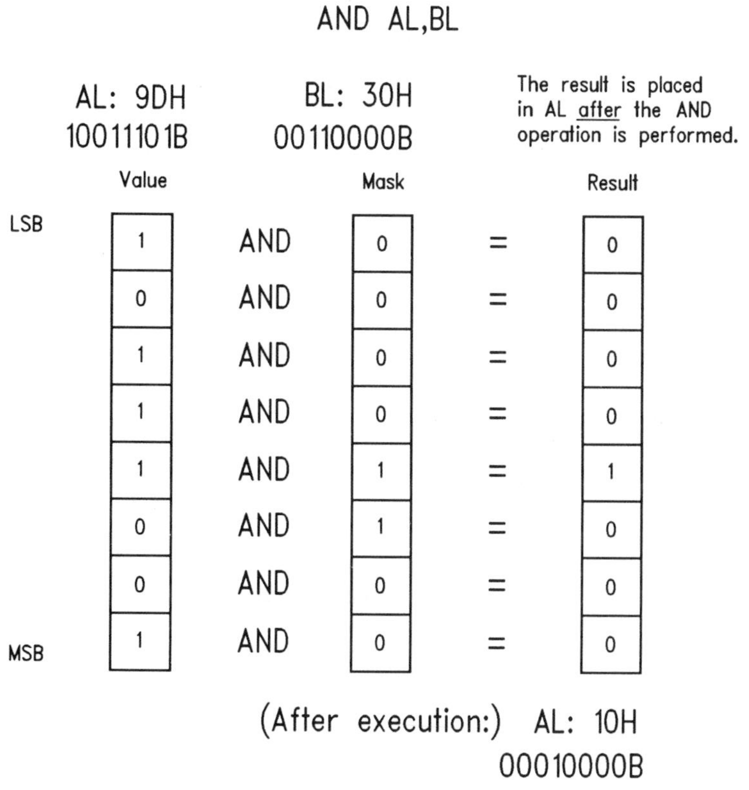

AND AL,BL

AL: 9DH   BL: 30H   The result is placed
10011101B   00110000B   in AL <u>after</u> the AND
                          operation is performed.

	Value		Mask		Result
LSB	1	AND	0	=	0
	0	AND	0	=	0
	1	AND	0	=	0
	1	AND	0	=	0
	1	AND	1	=	1
	0	AND	1	=	0
	0	AND	0	=	0
MSB	1	AND	0	=	0

(After execution:) AL: 10H
                    00010000B

The three binary values involved are shown laid out vertically, with the LSB (the right-hand end) of each value at the top. You should be able to trace each AND operation and verify it by looking at Table 9.2.

The end result is that all bits except 4 and 5 are *guaranteed* to be 0 and can thus be safely ignored. Bits 4 and 5 could be either 0 or 1. (That's why we need to test them; we don't *know* what they are.) With the initial value of 9DH, bit 4 turns out to be a 1, and bit 5 turns out to be a 0. If the initial value were something else, bits 4 and 5 could both be 0, both 1, or some combination of the two.

Don't forget: the result of the AND operation replaces the first operand after the operation is complete.

For an example of the **AND** instruction in operation isolating bits in a word, look ahead to the **Byte2Str** procedure on page XXX.

The OR Instruction

Closely related to the AND logical operation is OR, which, like the AND logical operation, has an embodiment with the same name in the 86-family instruction set. Structurally, the **OR** instruction works identically to **AND**. Only its truth table is different: while **AND** requires that both its operands be 1 for the result to be 1, **OR** is satisfied that at least *one* operand has a 1 value. The truth table for **OR** is shown in Table 9.3.

Because it's unsuitable for isolating bits, **OR** is used much more rarely than **AND**.

The XOR Instruction

In a class by itself is the exclusive OR operation, embodied in the **XOR** instruction. **XOR**, again, does in broad terms what **AND** and **OR** do: it performs a logical operation on two operands, and the result replaces the first operand. The logical operation, however, is *exclusive or,* meaning that the result is 1 only if the two operands are *different.* (1 and 0 or 0 and 1.) The truth table for **XOR** should make this slippery notion a little clearer (see Table 9.4).

Table 9.3. The OR truth table for assembly language

Bit 1	Operator	Bit 2		Result bit
0	OR	0	=	0
0	OR	1	=	1
1	OR	0	=	1
1	OR	1	=	1

Table 9.4. The XOR truth table for assembly language

Bit 1	Operator	Bit 2		Result bit
0	XOR	0	=	0
0	XOR	1	=	1
1	XOR	0	=	1
1	XOR	1	=	0

Look this over carefully! In the first and last cases, where the two operands are the *same*, the result is 0. In the middle two cases, where the two operands are *different*, the result is 1.

Some interesting things can be done with **XOR**, but most of them are a little arcane for a beginner's book. I will show you one handy **XOR** trick, however: "XORing" any value against itself yields 0. Furthermore, putting 0 in a register by XORing the register against itself is *faster* than putting a 0 in the register by MOVing in a 0 as immediate data.

That is, both of these instructions accomplish the same thing:

```
mov AL,0
xor AL,AL
```

However, if you're running an 8086 or 8088 processor, the first instruction uses four machine cycles, while the second uses only three. That's not a tremendous difference (though purists will argue that it represents a 25% improvement) but there are times in assembly language where every machine cycle counts!

How this trick works should be clear from reading the truth table, but to drive it home I've laid it out in Figure 9.3.

Follow each of the individual XOR operations across the figure to its result value. Because each bit in AL is XORed against itself, in every case the XOR operations happen between two operands that are identical. Sometimes both are 1, sometimes both are 0, but in every case the two are the same. With the XOR operation, when the two operands are the same, the result is always 0. Voila! 0 in a register in three cycles flat.

The NOT Instruction

Easiest to understand of all the bitwise logical instructions is NOT. The truth table for the **NOT** instruction (Table 9.5) is pretty simple because **NOT** only takes one operand. And what it does is simple as well: **NOT** takes the state of each bit in its single operand and changes it to its opposite state. What was 1 becomes 0 and what was 0 becomes 1.

Figure 9.3. Using XOR to zero a register

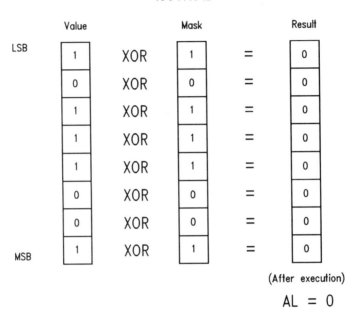

(After execution)

AL = 0

Segment Registers Don't Respond to Logic!

One limitation of the segment registers **CS**, **DS**, **SS**, and **ES** is that they cannot be used with any of the bitwise logical instructions. If you try, the assembler will hand you an "Illegal use of segment register" error. If you need to perform a logical operation on a segment register, you must first copy the segment register's value into one of the nonsegment registers (**AX**, **BX**, **CX**, **DX**, **BP**, **SI**, and DI); perform the logical operation on the new register, and then copy the result back into the segment register.

Table 9.5. The NOT truth table

Bit	Operator	Result bit
0	XOR	1
1	XOR	0

9.2 Shifting Bits

The other way of manipulating bits within a byte is a little more straightforward: you *shift* the bits to one side or the other. There are a few wrinkles to the process, but the simplest shift instructions are pretty obvious: the **SHL** instruction Shifts its operand Left, whereas the **SHR** instruction Shifts its operand Right.

All of the shift instructions (including the slightly more complex ones I'll describe a little later) have the same general form, illustrated here by the **SHL** instruction:

```
SHL <register/memory>,<count>
```

The first operand is the target of the shift operation; that is, the value that you're going to be shifting. It can be register data or memory data, but not immediate data. The second operand specifies the number of bits by which to shift.

Shift by What?

The **<count>** operand is a little peculiar. It can be one of two things: the literal digit 1, or else the register **CL**. (*Not* **CX**!) If you specify the count as 1, then the shift will be by one bit. If you wish to shift by more than one bit at a time, you must load the shift count into register **CL**. Counting things is **CX**'s (and hence **CL**'s) hidden agenda; it counts shifts, loops, string elements, and a few other things. That's why it's sometimes called the *count register* ("C" for "count").

Although you can load a number as large as 255 into CL, it really only makes sense to use count values up to 16. If you shift any bit in a word by 16, you shift it completely out of the word!

Something to keep in mind: moving an immediate count value into CL takes some time. Furthermore, executing a shift instruction that takes its count value from **CL** takes more time to execute than executing a shift instruction that uses the literal 1 as its count value. These two facts conspire to make it faster to use successive shift-by-1 instructions unless you need to shift by 5 or more bits.

As an example, consider the following instruction sequence, which is what must be done to use **CL** to shift a word by 3 bits:

```
MOV CL,3
SHL SI,CL
```

Most remarkably, it is faster to accomplish the same shift this way:

```
SHL SI,1
SHL SI,1
SHL SI,1
```

The rule of thumb is this: unless you need to shift by more than *4* bits, use consecutive shift-by-1 instructions rather than shifting via the **CL** register.

How Bit Shifting Works

Understanding the shift instructions requires that you think of the numbers being shifted as *binary* numbers, and not hexadecimal or decimal numbers. (If you're fuzzy on binary notation, again, take another slip through Chapter 1.) A simple example would start with register **AX** containing a value of 0B76FH. Expressed as a binary number (and hence as a bit pattern) 0B76FH is

```
1011011101101111
```

Keep in mind that each digit in a binary number is 1 bit. If you execute an **SHL AX,1** instruction, what you'd find in **AX** after the shift is the following:

```
0110111011011110
```

A 0 bit has been inserted at the right hand end of the number, and the whole shebang has been bumped toward the left by one digit. Notice that a 1 bit has been bumped off the left end of the number into nothingness.

Bumping Bits into the Carry Flag

Well, not exactly nothingness. The last bit shifted out is bumped into a temporary bucket for bits the *Carry flag* (**CF**). The Carry flag is one of those odd bits lumped together as the Flags register, which I described in Section 6.4. You can test the state of the Carry flag with a branching instruction, as I'll explain in Section 9.3.

Keep in mind when using shift instructions, however, that, in addition to the Shift instructions, a *lot* of different instructions, including the bitwise logical instructions and the arithmetic instructions, use the Carry flag. If you bump a bit into the Carry flag with the intent of testing that bit to see what it is, test it *before* you execute another instruction that affects the Carry flag.

If you shift a bit into the Carry flag and then immediately execute another shift instruction, the first bit *will* be bumped off the end of the world and into nothingness.

The Byte2Str Procedure: Converting Numbers to Displayable Strings

As we've seen, DOS has a fairly convenient method for displaying text on your screen. The problem is that it only displays *text*—if you want to display a numeric value from a register as a pair of digits, DOS won't help. You first have to convert the numeric value into its string representation, and then display the string representation through DOS.

Converting hexadecimal numbers to hexadecimal digits isn't difficult, and the routine to do the job demonstrates several of the new concepts we're exploring in this chapter. Read the **Byte2Str** procedure carefully:

```
;-------------------------------------------------------------
;   Byte2Str  --  Converts a byte passed in AL to a string at
;                   DS:SI
;   Last update 3/8/89
;
;   1 entry point:
;
;   Byte2Str:
;       Caller must pass:
;       AL : Byte to be converted
;       DS : Segment of destination string
;       SI : Offset of destination string
;
;       This routine converts 8-bit values to 2-digit hexadecimal
;       string representations at DS:SI.  The "H" specifier is
;       *not* included.  Four separate output examples:
;       02   B7   FF   6C
;-------------------------------------------------------------

Byte2Str    PROC
            mov DI,AX               ; Duplicate byte in DI
            and DI,000FH            ; Mask out high 12 bits of DI
            mov BX,OFFSET Digits    ; Load offset of Digits into DI
            mov AH,BYTE PTR [BX+DI] ; Load digit from table into AH
            mov [SI+1],AH           ;   and store digit into string
            xor AH,AH               ; Zero out AH
            mov DI,AX               ; And move byte into DI
            shr DI,1                ; Shift high nybble of byte to
            shr DI,1                ;   low nybble
            shr DI,1
            shr DI,1
            mov AH,BYTE PTR [BX+DI] ; Load digit from table into AH
            mov [SI],AH             ;   and store digit into string
            ret                     ; We're done--go home!
Byte2Str    ENDP
```

To call **Byte2Str** you must pass the value to be converted to a string in **AL**, and the address of the string into which the string representation is to be stored as **DS:SI**. Typically, **DS** will already contain the segment address of your data segment, so you most likely will only need to pass the offset of the start of the string in **SI**.

In addition to the code shown here, **Byte2Str** requires the presence of a second string in the data segment. This string, whose name must be **Digits**, contains all 16 of the digits used to express hexadecimal numbers. The definition of **Digits** looks like this:

```
Digits  DB '0123456789ABCDEF'
```

The important thing to note about **Digits** is that each digit occupies a position in the string whose offset from the start of the string is the value it represents. In other words, '0' is at the start of the string, zero bytes offset from the string's start. The character "7" lies seven bytes from the start of the string, and so on. **Digits** is what we call a *look up table* and it represents (as I'll explain below) an extremely useful mechanism in assembly language.

Splitting a Byte into Two Nybbles

Displaying the value stored in a byte requires two hexadecimal digits. The bottom four bits in a byte are represented by one digit (the least significant, or rightmost digit) and the top four bits in the byte are represented by another digit (the most significant, or leftmost digit.) Converting the two digits must be done one at a time, which means that we have to separate the single byte into two four-bit quantities, which are often called *nybbles*.

To split a byte in two, we need to *mask out* the unwanted half. This is done with an **AND** instruction. Note in the **Byte2Str** procedure that the first instruction, **MOV DI,AX**, copies the value to be converted (which is in **AL**) into **DI**. You don't need to move AH into DI here, but there is no instruction to move an 8-bit register-half like **AL** into a 16-bit register like **DI**. AH comes along for the ride, but we really don't need it. The second instruction masks out the high twelve bits of **DI** using **AND**. This eliminates what had earlier been in free-rider **AH**, as well as the high four bits of **AL**. What's left in **DI** is all we want: the lower four bits of what was originally passed to the routine in **AL**.

Using a Lookup Table

The low nybble of the value to be converted is now in **DI**. The address of **Digits** is loaded into **BX**. Then the appropriate digit character is copied from **Digits** into **AH**. The whole trick of using a lookup table lies in the way the character in the table is addressed:

```
mov AH,BYTE PTR [BX+DI]
```

DS:BX points to the start of **Digits**, so [**BX**] would address the *first* character in digits. To get at the desired digit, we must *index* into the lookup table by adding the offset into the table to **BX**. There is an 8086/8088 addressing mode intended precisely for use with lookup tables, called *base indexed addressing.* That sounds more arcane than it is; what it means is that instead of specifying a memory location at [**BX**], we add an index to **BX**, and address a memory location at [**BX+DI**].

If you recall, we masked out all of **DI** except the four lowest bits of the byte we are converting. These bits will contain some value from 0 through 0FH. **Digits** contains the hexadecimal digit characters from 0 through F. By using **DI** as the index, the value in **DI** will select its corresponding digit character in **Digits**. We are using the value in **DI** to look up its equivalent hexadecimal digit character in the lookup table **(Digits)**. See Figure 9.4.

So far, we've read a character from the lookup table into AH. Now, we use yet another addressing mode to move the character from **AX** back into the second character of the destination string, whose address was passed to **Byte2Str** in **DS:SI**. This addressing mode is called *indirect displacement addressing,*

Figure 9.4. Using a lookup table

MOV AH,BYTE PTR [BX+DI]

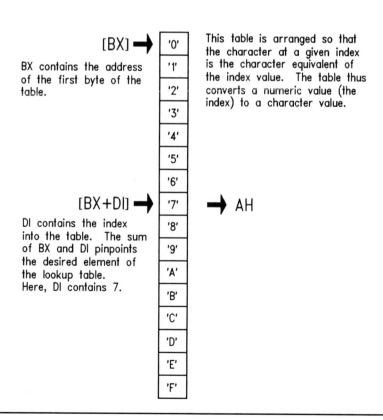

[BX] ➡

BX contains the address of the first byte of the table.

This table is arranged so that the character at a given index is the character equivalent of the index value. The table thus converts a numeric value (the index) to a character value.

[BX+DI] ➡ '7' ➡ AH

DI contains the index into the table. The sum of BX and DI pinpoints the desired element of the lookup table. Here, DI contains 7.

'0'
'1'
'2'
'3'
'4'
'5'
'6'
'7'
'8'
'9'
'A'
'B'
'C'
'D'
'E'
'F'

though I question the wisdom of memorizing that term. The mode is nothing more than indirect addressing (addressing the contents of memory at [SI]) with the addition of a literal displacement:

```
mov [SI+1],AH
```

This looks a lot like base indexed addressing (which is why the jargon may not be all that useful) with the sole exception that what is added to **SI** is not a *register* but a *literal constant*.

Once this move is done, the first of the two nybbles passed to **Byte2Str** in **AL** has been converted to its character equivalent and stored in the destination string variable at DS:SI.

Now we have to do it again, this time for the high nybble.

Shifting the High Nybble into the Low Nybble

The high nybble of the value to be converted has been waiting patiently all this time in **AL**. We didn't mask out the high nybble until we moved **AX** into **DI**, and did our masking on **DI** instead of **AX**. So **AL** is still just as it was when **Byte2Str** began.

The first thing to do is clear **AH** to 0. **Byte2Str** uses the **XOR AH,AH** trick I described in the last section. Then we move **AX** into **DI**.

All that remains to be done is to somehow move the high nybble of the low byte of **DI** into the position occupied by the low nybble. The fastest way to do this is simply to shift **DI** to the right—four times in a row. This is what the four **SHR** instructions in **Byte2Str** do. The low nybble is simply shifted off the edge of **DI**, into the Carry flag, and then out into nothingness. After the four shifts, what was the high nybble is now the low nybble, and once again, **DI** can be used as an index into the **Digits** lookup table to move the appropriate digit into **AH**.

Finally, there is the matter of storing the digit into the target string at **DS:SI**. Notice that *this* time, there is no +1 in the **MOV** instruction:

```
mov [SI],AH
```

Why not? The high nybble is the digit on the left, so it must be moved into the first byte in the target string. Earlier, we moved the low nybble into the byte on the right. String indexing begins at the left and works toward the right, so if the left digit is at index 0 of the string, the right digit must be at index 0+1.

Byte2Str does a fair amount of data fiddling in only a few lines. Read it over a few times while following the above discussion through its course until the whole thing makes sense to you.

Converting Words to Their String Form

Having converted a byte-sized value to a string, it's a snap to convert 16-bit words to their string forms. In fact, it's not much more difficult than calling **Byte2Str** twice:

```
;----------------------------------------------------------------
;   Word2Str  --  Converts a word passed in AX to a string at
;                 DS:SI
;   Last update 3/8/89
;
;   1 entry point:
;
;   Word2Str:
;      Caller must pass:
;      AX : Word to be converted
;      DS : Segment of destination string
;      SI : Offset of destination string
;----------------------------------------------------------------

Word2Str    PROC
            mov   CX,AX       ; Save a copy of convertee in CX
            xchg  AH,AL       ; Swap high and low AX bytes to do high first
            call  Byte2Str    ; Convert AL to string at DS:SI
            add   SI,2        ; Bump SI to point to second 2 characters
            mov   AX,CX       ; Reload convertee into AX
            call  Byte2Str    ; Convert AL to string at DS:SI
            ret               ; And we're done!
Word2Str    ENDP
```

The logic here is fairly simple—if you understand how **Byte2Str** works. Moving **AX** into **CX** simply saves an unmodified copy of the word to be converted in CX. Something to watch out for here: if **Byte2Str** were to use **CX** for something, this saved copy would be mangled, and you might be caught wondering why things weren't working correctly. This is a common enough bug for the following reason: you create **Byte2Str**, and then create **Word2Str** to call **Byte2Str**. The first version of **Byte2Str** does not make use of **CX**, so it's safe to use **CX** as a storage bucket.

However—later on you beef up **Byte2Str** somehow, and in the process add some instructions that use **CX**. You plum fergot that **Word2Str** stored a value in **CX** *while Word2Str was calling Byte2Str*. It's pointless arguing whether the bug is that **Byte2Str** uses **CX**, or that **Word2Str** assumes that no one else is using **CX**. To make things work again, you would have to stash the value somewhere other than in **CX**. Pushing it onto the stack is your best bet if you run out of registers. (You might hit on the idea of stashing it in an unused segment register like **ES**—but I warn against it! Later on, if you try to use these utility routines in a program that makes use of **ES**, you'll be in a position to mess over your memory addressing royally. Let segment registers hold segments. Use the stack instead.)

Virtually everything that **Word2Str** does involves getting the converted digits into the proper positions in the target string. A word requires four hexadecimal digits altogether. In a string representation, the high byte occupies the left two digits, and the low byte occupies the right two digits. Since strings are indexed from the left to the right, it makes a certain sense to convert the left end of the string first.

This is the reason for the **XCHG** instruction. It swaps the high and low bytes of **AX**, so that the *first* time **Byte2Str** is called, the high byte is actually in **AL** instead of **AH**. (Remember that **Byte2Str** converts the value passed in **AL**.) **Byte2Str** does the conversion and stores the two converted digits in the first two bytes of the string at **DS:SI**.

For the second call to **Byte2Str**, **AH** and **AL** are not exchanged. Therefore the low byte will be the one converted. Notice the following instruction:

```
add SI,2
```

This is not heavy-duty math, but it's a good example of how to add a literal constant to a register in assembly language. The idea is to pass the address of the *second* two bytes of the string to **Byte2Str** as though they were actually the start of the string. This means that when **Byte2Str** converts the low byte of **AX**, it stores the two equivalent digits into the second two bytes of the string.

For example, if the high byte was 0C7H, the digits C and 7 would be stored in the first two bytes of the string, counting from the left. Then, if the low byte were 042H, the digits 4 and 2 would be stored at the third and fourth bytes of the string, respectively. The whole string would read C742 when the conversion was complete.

As I've said numerous times before: understand memory addressing and you've got the greater part of assembly language in your hip pocket. Most of the trick of **Byte2Str** and **Word2Str** lies in the different ways they address memory. As you study them, focus on the machinery behind the lookup table and target string addressing. The logic and shift instructions are pretty obvious and easy to figure out by comparison.

9.3 Flags, Tests, and Branches

Those assembler-knowledgeable folk who have stuck with me this long may be wondering why I haven't covered conditional jumps until this late in the book. I mean, we've explained procedures already, and haven't even gotten to jumps yet.

Indeed. That's the whole point. I explained procedures before jumps because when people learn those two concepts the other way around, they have a tendency to use jumps for *everything*, even when procedures are called for. Unlike some high-level languages like Pascal and Modula-2, there is no way around jumps—what they so derisively call "GOTOs"—in assembly language. Sadly, some people then assume that jumps are "it," and don't bother imposing any structure at all on their assembly-language programs. By teaching procedures first, I feel that I've at least made possible a more balanced approach on the part of the learner.

Besides, I felt it wise to teach how to *manage* complexity before teaching the number one means of *creating* complexity.

Unconditional Jumps

A *jump* is just that: an abrupt change in the flow of instruction execution. Ordinarily, instructions are executed one after the other, in order, moving from low memory toward high memory. *Jump instructions* alter the address of the next instruction to be executed. Execute a jump instruction, and *zap!*—all of a sudden you're somewhere else in the code segment. A jump instruction can move execution forward in memory, or backward. It can bend execution back into a loop. (And it can tie your program logic in knots ....)

There are two kinds of jumps: *conditional* and *unconditional*. An unconditional jump is a jump that *always* happens. It takes this form:

```
jmp <label>
```

When this instruction executes, the sequence of execution moves to the instruction located at the label specified by the **<label>** operand. It's just that simple.

The unconditional **JMP** instruction is of limited use by itself. It almost always works in conjunction with the conditional jump instructions that test the state of the various 8086/8088 flags. You'll see how this works in just a little while, once we've gone through conditional jumps too.

Conditional Jumps

A conditional **JMP** instruction is one of those fabled tests I introduced in Chapter 0. When executed, a conditional jump tests something, usually one of the flags in the Flags register. If the flag being tested happens to be in a particular state, execution may jump to a label somewhere else in the code segment, or it may simply "fall through" to the next instruction in sequence.

This either/or nature is important. A conditional jump instruction either jumps, or it falls through. Jump, or no jump. It can't jump to one of two places, or three. Whether it jumps or not depends on the current value of one single bit within the CPU.

For example, the Zero flag (**ZF**) is set to 1 by certain instructions when the result of that instruction is 0. The decrement (**DEC**) instruction is one of these instructions. **DEC** subtracts 1 from its operand. If by that subtraction the operand becomes 0, ZF is set to 1. One of the conditional jump instructions, Jump if Zero (**JZ**) tests **ZF**. If **ZF** is found set to 1, a jump occurs, and execution transfers to a label. If **ZF** is found to be 0, execution falls through to the next instruction in line.

Here's a simple (and non optimal) example, using instructions you should already understand:

```
          mov   Counter,17   ; We're going to do this 17 times
WorkLoop: call  DoWork       ; Process the data
          dec   Counter      ; Subtract 1 from the counter
          jz    AllDone       ; If the Counter is 0, we're done!
          jmp   WorkLoop     ; Otherwise, go back and execute the loop again
```

The label **AllDone** isn't shown in the example because it's somewhere else in the program, maybe a long way off. The important thing is that the **JZ** instruction is a two-way switch. If **ZF** is equal to 1, execution moves to the location marked by the label **AllDone**. If **ZF** is equal to 0, execution falls through to the next instruction in sequence. Here, that would be the unconditional jump instruction **JMP WorkLoop**.

This simple loop is one way to perform a call to a procedure some set number of times. A count value is stored in a variable named **Counter**. The procedure is called. After control returns from the procedure, **Counter** is decremented by one. If that drops the counter to 0, the procedure has been called the full number of times, and the loop sends execution elsewhere. If the counter still has some count in it, execution loops back to the procedure call and begins the loop again.

Note the use of an unconditional jump instruction to "close the loop."

Beware Endless Loops!

This is a good place to warn you of a common sort of bug that produces the dreaded *endless loop*, which locks up your machine and forces you to reboot to get out. Suppose the code snippet shown above were instead done the following way:

```
WorkLoop: mov   Counter,17   ; We're going to do this 17 times
          call  DoWork       ; Process the data
          dec   Counter      ; Subtract 1 from the counter
          jz    AllDone       ; If the counter is 0, we're done!
          jmp   WorkLoop     ; Otherwise, go back and execute the loop again
```

This becomes a pretty obvious endless loop. (However, you'll be appalled at how often such an obvious bug will dance in your face for hours without being recognized as such ....) The key point is that the instruction that loads the initial value to the counter is *inside* the loop! Every time the loop happens, the counter is decremented by one ... and then immediately reloaded with the original count value. The count value thus never gets smaller than the original value minus 1, and the loop (which is waiting for the counter to become 0) never ends.

You're unlikely to do something like this deliberately, of course. But it's *very* easy to type a label at the wrong place, or (easier still) to type the name of the wrong label, a label that might be at or before the point where a counter is loaded with its initial value.

Assembly-language programming requires concentration and endless attention to detail. If you pay attention to what you're doing, you'll make fewer "stupid" errors like the one above.

But I can promise you that you'll still make a few.

Jumping on the Absence of a Condition

There are a fair number of conditional jump instructions, of which I'll discuss only the most common in this book. Their number is increased by the fact that every conditional jump instruction has an alter ego: a jump when the specified condition is *not* set to 1.

The **JZ** instruction provides a good example. **JZ** jumps to a new location in the code segment if ZF is set to 1. **JZ**'s alter ego is the Jump if Not Zero (**JNZ**). **JNZ** jumps to a label if **ZF** is 0, and falls through if **ZF** is 1.

This may be confusing at first, because **JNZ** jumps when **ZF** is equal to 0. Keep in mind that the name of the instruction applies to the *condition* being tested, and not necessarily the binary bit value of the flag. In the previous code example, **JZ** jumped when the **DEC** instruction decremented the Counter to 0. The condition being tested is something connected with an earlier instruction, *not* simply the state of **ZF**.

Think of it this way: a condition raises a flag. "Raising a flag" means setting the flag to 1. When one of numerous instructions forces an operand to a value of 0, (which is the condition) the Zero flag is raised. The logic of the instruction refers to the condition, *not* to the flag.

As an example, let's improve our little loop. I should caution you that its first implementation, while correct and workable in the strictest sense, is awkward and not the best way to code that kind of thing. It can be improved in several ways. Here's one:

```
          mov   Counter,17    ; We're going to do this 17 times
WorkLoop: call  DoWork         ; Process the data
          dec   Counter        ; Subtract 1 from the Counter
          jnz   WorkLoop       ; If the Counter is 0, we're done!
          < more code >
```

The **JZ** instruction has been replaced with a **JNZ** instruction. That makes much more sense, since to close the loop we have to jump, and we only close the loop while the **Counter** is greater than 0. The jump back to label **WorkLoop** will happen only while the counter is greater than 0.

Once the counter decrements to 0, the loop is considered finished. **JNZ** falls through, and the code that follows the loop (which I don't show here) executes. The next instruction could be a **JMP** to label **AllDone**, as shown earlier, or it could be the next bit of work that the assembly-language program has to do. The point is that if you can position the program's next task immediately after the **JNZ** instruction, you don't need to use the **JMP** instruction *at all*. Instruction execution will just flow naturally into the next task that needs performing. The program will have a more natural and less tangled top-to-bottom flow, and will be easier to read and understand.

Flags

Back in Section 6.4 I explained the Flags register and briefly described the purposes of all the flags it contains. Most flags are not terribly useful, especially when you're first starting out as a programmer. The Carry flag (**CF**) and the Zero flag (**ZF**) will be 90% of your involvement in flags as a beginner, with the Direction flag (**DF**), Sign flag (**SF**) and Overflow flag (**OF**) together making up an additional 9.998%. It might be a good idea to reread Section 6.4 now, just in case your grasp of flag etiquette has gotten a little rusty.

As explained a few pages ago, **JZ** jumps when ZF is 1, whereas **JNZ** jumps when **ZF** is 0. Most instructions that perform some operation on an operand (like **AND**, **OR**, **XOR**, **INC**, **DEC** and all arithmetic instructions) set **ZF** according to the results of the operation. On the other hand, instructions that simply move data around (such as **MOV**, **XCHG**, **PUSH**, and **POP**) do not affect ZF or any of the other flags. (Obviously, **POPF** affects the flags by popping the top-of-stack value into them.) One irritating exception is the **NOT** instruction, which performs a logical operation on its operand but does *not* set any flags— even when it causes its operand to become 0. Before you write code that depends on flags, *check your instruction reference* (one is almost certainly provided with your assembler) to make sure you have the flag etiquette down correctly.

Comparisons with CMP

One major use of flags is in controlling loops. Another is in comparisons between two values. Your programs will often need to know whether a value in a register or memory is equal to some other value. Further, you may want to know if a value is greater than a value or less than a value if it is not equal to that value. There is a jump instruction to satisfy every need, but something has to set the flags for the benefit of the jump instruction. The compare (**CMP**) instruction is what sets the flags for comparison tasks.

CMP's use is straightforward and intuitive. The second operand is compared with the first, and several flags are set accordingly:

```
cmp <op1>,<op2>  ; Sets OF, SF, ZF, AF, PF, and CF
```

The sense of the comparison can be remembered if you simply recast the comparison in arithmetic terms:

```
Result = <op1> - <op2>
```

CMP is a subtraction operation where the result of the subtraction is thrown away, and only the flags are affected. The second operand is subtracted from the first. Based on the results of the subtraction, the flags are set to appropriate values.

After a **CMP** instruction, you can jump based on several arithmetic conditions. People who have a fair grounding in math, or are FORTRAN or Pascal programmers will recognize the conditions: *equal, not equal, greater than, less than, greater than or equal to,* and *less than or equal to.* The sense of these operators follows from their names, and is exactly like the sense of the equivalent operators in most high-level languages.

A Jungle of Jump Instructions

There is a bewildering array of jump instruction mnemonics, but those dealing with arithmetic relationships sort out well into just six categories, one category for each of the six conditions listed above. Complication arises out of the fact that there are *two* mnemonics for each machine instruction, for example, **JLE** (Jump if Less than or Equal) and **JNG** (Jump if Not Greater than). These two mnemonics are *synonyms,* in that the assembler generates the identical binary opcode when it encounters either mnemonic. The synonyms are a convenience to you the programmer, in that they provide two alternate ways to think about a given jump instruction. In the above example, *jump if less than or equal to* is logically identical to *jump if not greater than.* (Think about it!) If the importance of the preceding compare was to see if one value is less than or equal to another, you'd use the **JLE** mnemonic. On the other hand, if you were testing to be sure one quantity was not greater than another, you'd use **JNG**. The choice is yours.

Another complication is that there is a separate set of instructions for signed and unsigned comparisons. I haven't spoken much about assembly-language math in this book, and thus haven't said much about the difference between signed and unsigned quantities. A *signed* quantity is one in which the high bit of the quantity is considered a built-in flag that indicates whether or not the quantity is negative. If that bit is 1, the quantity is considered negative; if that bit is 0, the quantity is considered positive.

Signed arithmetic in assembly language is complex and subtle, and not as useful as you might immediately think. I won't be covering it in detail in this book, though most all assembly language books treat it to some extent. All you need know to get a high-level understanding of signed arithmetic is that in signed arithmetic, negative quantities are legal. Unsigned arithmetic, on the other hand, does not recognize negative numbers.

Greater Than vs. Above

To tell the signed jumps apart from the unsigned jumps, the mnemonics use two different expressions for the relationships between two values:

- *Signed values* **are thought of as being** *greater than* **or** *less than*. For example, to test whether one signed operand is greater than another, you would use the **JG** (Jump if Greater) mnemonic after a **CMP** instruction.
- *Unsigned values* **are thought of as being** *above* **or** *below*. For example, to tell whether one unsigned operand is greater (above) another, you would use the **JA** (Jump if Above) mnemonic after a **CMP** instruction.

Table 9.6 summarizes the arithmetic jump mnemonics and their synonyms. Any mnemonics containing the words above or below are for unsigned values, while any mnemonics containing the words greater or less are for signed values. Compare the mnemonics with their synonyms and see how the two represent opposite viewpoints from which to look at identical instructions.

Table 9.6. Arithmetic jump mnemonics and their synonyms

Mnemonics		**Synonyms**	
JA	Jump if Above	JNBE	Jump if Not Below or Equal
JAE	Jump if Above or Equal	JNB	Jump if Not Below
JB	Jump if Below	JNAE	Jump if Not Above or Equal
JBE	Jump if Below or Equal	JNA	Jump if Not Above
JE	Jump if Equal	JZ	Jump if result is Zero
JNE	Jump if Not Equal	JNZ	Jump if result is Not Zero
JG	Jump if Greater	JNLE	Jump if Not Less than or Equal
JGE	Jump if Greater or Equal	JNL	Jump if Not Less
JL	Jump if Less	JNGE	Jump if Not Greater or Equal
JLE	Jump if Less or Equal	JNG	Jump if Not Greater

Table 9.6 simply served to expand the mnemonics into a more comprehensible form and associate a mnemonic with its synonym. Table 9.7, on the other hand, sorts the mnemonics out by logical condition and according to their use with signed and unsigned values. Also listed in Table 9.7 are the flags whose values are considered in each jump instruction. Notice that some of the jump instructions require one of two possible flag values in order to take the jump, while others require both of two flag values.

Several of the signed jumps compare two of the flags against one another. **JG**, for example, will jump when either **ZF** is 0, or when the Sign flag (**SF**) is equal to the Overflow flag (**OF**). I won't spend any further time explaining the nature of the Sign flag or Overflow flag. As long as you have the sense of each instruction under your belt, understanding exactly how the instructions test the flags can wait until you've gained some programming experience.

Some people have trouble understanding how it is that the **JE** and **JZ** mnemonics are synonyms, as are **JNE** and **JNZ**. Think again of the way a comparison is done within the CPU: the second operand is subtracted from the first, and if the result is 0 (indicating that the two operands were in fact equal), **ZF** is set to 1. That's why **JE** and **JZ** are synonyms: both are simply testing the state of **ZF**.

Table 9.7. Arithmetic tests useful after a CMP instruction

Condition	Pascal Operator	Unsigned Values	Jumps When	Signed Values	Jumps When
Equal	=	JE	ZF=1	JE	ZF=1
Not equal	<>	JNE	ZF=0	JNE	ZF=0
Greater than Not less than or equal to	>	JA JNBE	CF=0 and ZF=0	JG JNLE	ZF=0 or SF=OF
Less than Not greater than or equal to	<	JB JNAE	CF=1	JL JNGE	SF<>OF
Greater than or equal to Not less than	>=	JAE JNB	CF=0	JGE JNL	SF=OF
Less than or equal to Not greater than	<=	JBE JNA	CF=1 or ZF=1	JLE JNG	ZF=1 and SF<>OF

Detecting the Installed Display Adapter

A useful example of **CMP** and the conditional **JMP** instructions in action involves detecting the installed display adapter. Five different mainstream IBM display adapters that can be installed in a PC (from the first generation introduced with the original PC in 1981 to the VGA and MCGA introduced with the PS/2 series in 1987) are currently available. (I don't consider the PGC and the XGA to be mainstream—although the XGA will almost certainly get there in time.) Each adapter has certain unique features, and if you intend to use some of the (rather nifty) hardware assistance offered by the more advanced video boards like the EGA and VGA, you had better be prepared to tell which board is in a given machine. Then your program must decide what special features can and cannot be used.

It isn't quite enough to know which board is installed in a given machine. The way a certain board operates can change severely depending on whether a monochrome or color monitor is attached to the board. The most obvious difference (and the one of most interest to the programmer) is that the memory address of the video display buffer is different for color and monochrome monitors. This schizophrenic quality of the EGA, VGA, and MCGA is so pronounced that it makes sense to consider the EGA/color monitor combination an entirely separate display adapter from the EGA/monochrome monitor combination.

In my method, I use a separate numeric code to represent each legal adapter/monitor combination. There are nine possibilities in all, summarized in Table 9.8.

The codes are not consecutive; note that there is no code 3, 6 or 9. I didn't make these codes up arbitrarily. They are in fact the display adapter/monitor combination codes returned by one of the VGA/MCGA BIOS services.

The **DispID** procedure given below determines which display adapter is installed in the machine in which **DispID** is running. **DispID** then returns one

Table 9.8. Legal PC display adapter/monitor combinations

Code	Adapter/Monitor	Segment of Display Buffer
00	None	None
01H	MDA/Monochrome	0B000H
02H	CGA/Color	0B800H
04H	EGA/Color	0B800H
05H	EGA/Monochrome	0B000H
07H	VGA/Monochrome	0B000H
08H	VGA/Color	0B800H
0AH	MCGA/Color (digital)	0B800H
0BH	MCGA/Monochrome	0B000H
0CH	MCGA/Color (analog)	0B800H

of the codes listed in Table 9.8. I recommend that your programs define a byte-sized variable in their data segments where this code can be stored throughout the program's duration. If you detect the adapter with **DispID** immediately on program startup, your program can inspect the code any time it needs to make a decision as to which video features to use.

Given what I've told you about **CMP** and conditional jump instructions so far, see if you can follow the logic in **DispID** before we go through it blow by blow:

```
;------------------------------------------------------------------
;   DispID  --  Identifies the installed display adapter
;   Last update 3/12/92
;
;   1 entry point:
;
;   DispID:
;       Caller passes no parameters
;       Routine returns a code value in AX.
;       The codes are these:
;       0 : Adapter is unknown; recommend aborting
;       1 : MDA (Monochrome Display Adapter)
;       2 : CGA (Color Graphics Adapter)
;
;------------------------------------------------------------------

DispID      PROC
            mov  AH,1AH    ; Select PS/2 Identify Adapter Service
            xor  AL,AL     ; Select Get Combination Code subservice (AL=0)
            int  10H       ; Call VIDEO
            cmp  AL,1AH    ; If AL comes back with 1AH, we have a PS/2
            jne  TryEGA    ; If not, jump down to test for the EGA
            mov  AL,BL     ; Put Combination Code into AL
            ret            ;   and go home!
TryEGA:     mov  AH,12H    ; Select EGA Alternate Function
            mov  BX,10H    ; Select Get Configuration Information subservice
            int  10H       ; Call VIDEO
            cmp  BX,10H    ; If BX comes back unchanged, EGA is *not* there
            je   OldBords  ; Go see whether it's an MDA or CGA
            cmp  BH,0      ; If BH = 0, it's an EGA/color combo
            je   EGAColor  ;   otherwise it's EGA/mono
            mov  AL,5      ; Store code 5 for EGA mono
            ret            ;   and go home!
EGAColor:   mov  AL,4      ; Store code 4 for EGA color
            ret            ;   and go home!
OldBords:   int  11H       ; Call Equipment Configuration interrupt
            not  AL        ; Flip all bits in AL to opposite states
            test AL,30H    ; If bits 4 & 5 are both = 0, it's an MDA
```

```
              jne   CGA        ;   otherwise it's a CGA
              mov   AL,1        ; Store code 1 for MDA
              ret              ;   and go home!
    CGA:      mov   AL,2        ; Store code 2 for CGA
              ret              ;   and go home!
    DispID    ENDP
```

DispID is the most complex piece of code shown so far in this book. The overall strategy is not obvious and bears some attention.

IBM's standard display boards appeared in three generations. The first generation consisted of the original Color Graphics Adapter (CGA) and Monochrome Display Adapter (MDA). The second generation consisted of the Enhanced Graphics Adapter (EGA.) Finally, the third generation came in with the PS/2 in April of 1987 and provided the Video Graphics Array (VGA) and Multi-Color Graphics Array (MCGA).

The simplest way to find out what display board is installed in a machine is to "ask the machine" by querying BIOS services. There are BIOS services specific to each generation of display board, and by some quirk of fate all such services are well behaved, by which I mean that querying a service that doesn't exist (because an older generation of video board is installed) will not crash the system. (IBM's BIOS standard is extremely "downward compatible" in that newer generations all contain everything the older generations do.) Furthermore, if a BIOS service specific to a generation of boards is found *not* to exist, that tells us that the installed board is not a member of that generation or a newer generation.

Assuming that the target machine could have any of the standard IBM display boards in it, it makes sense to test for the presence of the newest boards first. Then, through a process of elimination, we move to the older and older boards.

The first test that **DispID** makes, then, is for the VGA or MCGA generation. The PS/2 machines contain in their ROM BIOS a service (VIDEO Service 1AH) specifically to identify the installed display adapter. **DispID** calls VIDEO service 1AH, having cleared **AL** to 0 via **XOR**. As it happens, if a PS/2 BIOS is present on the bus, the 1AH service number is returned in register **AL**. On return from the **INT 10H** call, we test **AL** for 1AH using **CMP**. If 1AH is *not* found in **AL**, we know up front that there is no PS/2 BIOS in the system, and therefore no VGA or MCGA.

After the **CMP** instruction is the **JNE TryEGA** conditional branch. If the **CMP** finds that **AL** is *not* equal to 1AH, then control jumps down to the code that tests for the next older generation of video boards: the EGA. If **AL** *is* equal to 1AH, then the PS/2 BIOS has placed the display adapter code in **BL**. **DispID** then copies **BL** into **AL** (which is where **DispID** returns the display code) and executes a **RET** instruction to pass control back to the caller.

Testing for the EGA is done a little differently, but the same general idea holds: we call an EGA-specific VIDEO service not present in the oldest generation of boards. The key test, again, is whether a certain register comes back unchanged. There is a twist, however: if **BX** comes back with the *same* value it held when the VIDEO call was made, (here, 10H) then an EGA BIOS does *not* exist in the machine. (Isn't the PC wonderful?) Here, after the **CMP BX,10H** instruction, we do a **JE OldBords** and not a **JNE** as we did when testing for the PS/2 generation. If **BX** comes back in an altered state, we assume an EGA is present, and that **BX** contains information on the display configuration.

If an EGA BIOS is found, a value in **BH** tells us whether the EGA is connected to a monochrome or color monitor. (Remember, there is a different code for each.) The value in **BH** is not the code itself, as it was with the PS/2 BIOS, so we have to do a little more testing to get the right code into **AL**. If **BH** contains 0, then the attached monitor is color. Any other value in **BH** indicates a monochrome system. The following sequence of instructions from **DispID** takes care of loading the proper EGA-specific code into AL:

```
          cmp   BH,0        ; If BH = 0, it's an EGA/color combo
          je    EGAColor     ;   otherwise it's EGA/mono
          mov   AL,5         ; Store code 5 for EGA mono
          ret                ;   and go home!
EGAColor: mov   AL,4         ; Store code 4 for EGA color
          ret                ;   and go home!
```

You'll find yourself writing sequences like this a lot when a single test decides between one of two courses of action. One course here is to load the value 5 into **AL**, and the other course is to load 4 into **AL**. Notice that after the appropriate **MOV** instruction is executed, a **RET** takes care of passing execution back to the caller. If **DispID** were not a procedure, but simple a sequence coded into the main line of instructions, you would need an unconditional **JMP** after each **MOV** to continue on with instruction execution somewhere else in the program. Using **RET** is much neater—which is yet another reason to explore small tasks like display adapter identification in a procedure wrapper.

Finally, if neither PS/2 nor EGA are present, **DispID** realizes that, by default, one of the original generation of display boards is on the bus. Telling MDA from CGA is not done with a BIOS call at all, because the first generation BIOS did not know which display board was present. (That was a feature instituted with the EGA in 1984.) Instead, there is a separate software interrupt, 11H, that returns machine configuration information.

Testing Bits with TEST

Service 11H returns a word's worth of bits in **AX**. Singly or in twos or threes, the bits tell a tale about specific hardware options on the installed PC. These hardware options are summarized in Figure 9.5.

Figure 9.5. Interrupt 11H configuration information

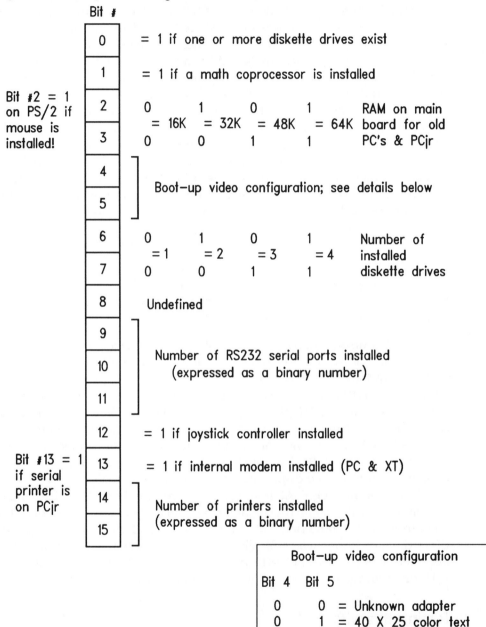

The bits we need to examine are bits 4 and 5. If both are set to 1, then we know we have a Monochrome Display Adapter. If the two bits are set to any other combination, the adapter must be a Color Graphics Adapter; all other alternatives have by this time been eliminated.

Testing for two 1 bits in a byte is an interesting exercise. The 86-family instruction set recognizes that assembly-language programmers do a lot of bit testing, and provides what amounts to a **CMP** instruction for bits: **TEST**.

The Phantoms of the Opcodes

TEST performs an AND logical operation between two operands, and then sets the flags as **AND** would, *without* altering the destination operation, as **AND** would. Here's the **TEST** instruction syntax:

```
TEST <operand>,<bit mask>
```

The bit mask operand should contain a 1 bit in each position where a 1-bit is to be sought in the operand, and 0 bits in all the other bits.

TEST ANDs the operand against the bit mask, and set the flags as **AND** would. The operand doesn't change. For example, if you want to determine if bit 3 of **AX** is set to 1, you would use this instruction:

```
TEST AX,3    ; 3 in binary is 00001000B
```

AX doesn't change as a result of the operation, but the AND truth table is asserted between **AX** and the binary pattern 00001000. If bit 3 in **AX** is a 1 bit, then **ZF** is cleared to 0. If bit 3 in **AX** is a 0 bit, then **ZF** is set to 1. Why? If you AND 1 (in the bit mask) with 0 (in **AX**) you get 0. (Look it up in the AND truth table.) And if all 8 bitwise AND operations come up 0, the result is 0, and **ZF** is raised to 1, indicating that the result is 0.

Key to understanding **TEST** is thinking of **TEST** as a sort of "Phantom of the Opcode," where the opcode is **AND**. **TEST** pretends it is **AND**, but doesn't follow through with the results of the operation. It simply sets the flags *as though* an AND operation had occurred.

CMP is another "Phantom of the Opcode," and bears the same relation to **SUB** as **TEST** bears to **AND**. **CMP** subtracts its second operand from its first, but doesn't follow through and store the result in the first operand. It just sets the flags *as though* a subtraction had occurred.

TEST Pointers

Here's something important to keep in mind: **TEST** is only useful for *finding 1 bits*. If you need to identify 0 bits, you must first flip each bit to its opposite state with the logical **NOT** instruction, as I explained in Section 9.1. **NOT** changes all 1 bits to 0 bits, and all 0 bits to 1 bits. Once all 0 bits are flipped to 1 bits, you can test for a 1 bit where you need to find a 0 bit. (Sometimes it helps to map it out on paper to keep it all straight.)

Also, **TEST** will *not* reliably test for two or more 1 bits in the operand at one time. **TEST** doesn't check for the presence of a bit pattern; *TEST checks for the presence of a single 1 bit.* In other words, if you need to check to make sure that *both* bits 4 and 5 are set to 1, **TEST** won't hack it.

And unfortunately, that's what we have to do in **DispID**.

What we're looking for in the last part of **DispID** is the monochrome code in bits 4 and 5, which is the value 30 (both bits 4 and 5 set to 1). Don't make the mistake (as I did once) of assuming that you can use **TEST** to spot the two 1 bits in bits 4 and 5:

```
test AL,30H      ; If bits 4 & 5 are both =1, it's an MDA
jnz  CGA         ;    otherwise it's a CGA
```

This doesn't work! The Zero flag will be set *only* if both bits are 0. If either bit is 1, **ZF** will become 0, and the branch will be taken. However, we *only* want to take the branch if *both* bits are 1.

Here's where your right brain can sometimes save both sides of your butt. **TEST** only spots a single 1 bit at a time. We need to detect a condition where two 1 bits are present. So let's get inspired and flip the state of all bits in the Equipment Identification Byte with **NOT**, and then look at the byte with **TEST**. After using **NOT**, what we need to find are two 0 bits, not two 1 bits. And if the two bits in question (4 and 5) are now both 0, the whole byte is 0, and **ZF** will be set and ready to test via **JNZ**:

```
not AL           ; Invert all bits in the equipment ID byte
test AL,30H      ; See if either of bits 4 or 5 are 1-bits
jnz CGA          ; If both = 0, they originally were both 1's,
                 ;  and the adapter is a monochrome
```

Tricky, tricky. But as you get accustomed to the instruction set and its quirks, you'll hit upon lots of non-obvious solutions to difficult problems of that kind.

So get that right brain working: how would you test for a specific pattern that was a *mix* of 0 bits and 1 bits?

9.4 Assembler Odds'n'Ends

Practice is the word.

You can do a lot with what you've learned so far, and certainly, you've learned enough to be able to figure out the rest with the help of an assembly-language reference and perhaps a more advanced book on the subject. For the remainder of this chapter we're going to do some practicing, flexing some assembly-language muscles and picking up a few more instructions in the process.

Yet Another Lookup Table

The DIGITS lookup table (used by **Byte2Str** and **Word2Str** in the previous section) is so obvious that it didn't need much in the line of comments or explanations. **Digits** simply converted the table's index into the ASCII character equivalent to the value of the index. **Digits** is only 16 bytes long, and its contents pretty much indicate what it's for:

```
Digits    DB    '0123456789ABCDEF'
```

Most of the time, your lookup tables will be a little less obvious. A lookup table does *not* have to be one single **DB** variable definition. You can define it pretty much as you need to, either with all table elements defined on a single line (as with **Digits**) or with each table element on its own line.

Consider the lookup table below:

```
OriginTbl    DW    0B000H    ; Code 0: No adapter identified
             DW    0B000H    ; Code 1: MDA
             DW    0B800H    ; Code 2: CGA
             DW    0B000H    ; Undefined
             DW    0B800H    ; Code 4: EGA/color
             DW    0B000H    ; Code 5: EGA/mono
             DW    0B000H    ; Undefined
             DW    0B000H    ; Code 7: VGA/mono
             DW    0B800H    ; Code 8: VGA/color
             DW    0B000H    ; Undefined
             DW    0B800H    ; Code 0AH: MCGA/color (digital)
             DW    0B000H    ; Code 0BH: MCGA/mono
             DW    0B800H    ; Code 0CH: MCGA/color (analog)
```

Here's a table where each table element has its own **DW** definition statement on its own line. This table treats a problem connected with the numerous different kinds of display adapters installable in a PC. There are two different addresses where the video refresh buffer begins. On boards connected to color or color/greyscale monitors, the address is B800:0, whereas on monochrome monitors the address is B000:0. (Refer back to Figure 5.4 and the accompanying text if you've forgotten what the video refresh buffer is.)

If you intend to address video memory directly (and doing so is much faster than working through DOS as we have been) then you have to know at which address the video refresh buffer lies. Knowing which display adapter is installed is the hardest part—and the **DispID** procedure described in the previous section answers that question. Each of the nine codes returned by **DispID** has a video refresh buffer address associated with it. But which goes with which? You could use a long and interwoven series of **CMP** and **JE** tests, but that's the hard road, and grossly wasteful of memory and machine cycles. A lookup table is simpler, faster in execution, and much easier to read.

The routine below returns the segment portion of the video refresh buffer address in **AX**. The display adapter code must be passed to **VidOrg** in **AL**:

```
;-------------------------------------------------------------
;   VidOrg  --  Returns origin segment of video buffer
;   Last update 3/8/89
;
;   1 entry point:
;
;   VidOrg:
;      Caller must pass:
;      AL : Code specifying display adapter type
;      VidOrg returns the buffer origin segment in AX
;-------------------------------------------------------------

VidOrg     PROC
           xor   AH,AH          ; Zero AH
           mov   DI,AX          ; Copy AX (with code in AL) into DI
           shl   DI,1           ; Multiply code by 2 to act as word index
           lea   BX,OriginTbl   ; Load address of origin table into BX
           mov   AX,[BX+DI]     ; Index into table using code as index
           ret                  ; Done; go home!
VidOrg     ENDP
```

This works a lot like the lookup table mechanism in **Byte2Str**. There's an important difference, however: each entry in the **OriginTbl** lookup table is *two* bytes in size, whereas each entry in **Digits** was *one* byte in size.

Using Shift Instructions to Multiply by Powers of 2

To use the **Digits** lookup table, we simply used the value to be converted as the index into the table. Because each element in the table was one byte in size, this worked. When table elements are more than one byte long, you have to multiply the index by the number of bytes in each table element, or the lookup won't find the correct table element.

OriginTbl is a good working example. Suppose you get a code 2 back from **DispID**, indicating that you have a CGA in the system. Adding the 2 code to the starting address of the table (as we did with **Digits**) takes us to the start of the second element in the table. Read across to the comment at the right of that second element and see which code it applies to: Code 1, the MDA! Not cool.

If you scan down to find the table element associated with the CGA, you'll find that it starts at an offset of *4* from the start of the table. To index into the table correctly, you have to add 4, not 2, to the offset address of the start of the table. This is where multiplication comes in.

There is a general-purpose multiply instruction in the 8086/8088 CPU, but **MUL** is outrageously slow as machine instructions go. Even in its fastest case on the 8086/8088 (multiplying an 8-bit register by some value) **MUL** takes 77 machine cycles to do its work. Considering that most of the instructions we've discussed complete their jobs in 4 to 10 cycles, that's slow indeed.

There's a better way—in some cases. When you need to multiply a value by some power of 2 (that is, 2, 4, 8, 16, 32, and so on) you can do it by using the **SHL** instruction. Shifting a value to the left by one bit multiplies the value by 2. Shifting a value to the left by two bits multiplies the value by 4. Shifting a value to the left by three bits multiplies the value by 8, and so on.

Magic? Not at all. Work it out on paper by expressing a number as a bit pattern (in binary form), shifting the bit pattern one bit to the right, and then converting the binary form back to decimal or hex. Like so:

```
00110101  Binary equivalent of 35H, 53 decimal
<-- by one bit yields
01101010  Binary equivalent of 6AH, 106 decimal
```

Sharp readers may have guessed that shifting to the right *divides* by powers of two—and that's also correct. Shifting right by one bit divides by 2; shifting right by two bits divides by 4, and so on.

The advantage to multiplying with shift instructions is that it's *fast*. Shifting a byte-sized value in a register to the left by one bit *takes only 2 machine cycles*. 2…as opposed to 77 with **MUL**.

As we say, no contest.

Once the index is multiplied by 2 using **SHL**, the index is added to the starting address of the table, just as with **Digits**. A word-sized **MOV** then copies the correct segment address from the table into **AX**, for return to the caller.

This illustrates how you can realize enormous speed advantages by structuring your tables properly. Even if it means leaving some wasted space at the end of each element, do your best to make the length of your table elements equal to some power of 2. That means making each element 1, 2, 4, 8, 16, 32, or some larger power of two in size, but not 3, 7, 12, 20, or 25 bytes in size.

Tables Within Tables

Tables are about the handiest means at your disposal for grouping together and organizing data. Sometimes tables can be as simple as those I've just shown you, which are simply sequences of single values.

In most cases, you'll need something a little more sophisticated. Sometimes you'll need a table of tables, and (surprise!) the 8086/8088 has some built-in machinery to handle such nested tables quickly and easily.

Let's continue on with the issue of video support. In the previous section we looked a table containing the display buffer addresses for each of the display adapters identified by **DispID**. This is good, but not enough: each adapter has a name, a display buffer address, and a screen size dictated by the size of the current character font. These items comprise a table of information about a display adapter, and if you wanted to put together a summary of all that information about all legal display adapters, you'd have to create such a table of tables.

Below is such a two-level table:

```
;-------------------------------------------------------------
; DISPLAY ADAPTER INFORMATION LOOKUP TABLE
;
; This is the lookup table containing information on all legal
; display adapters.  The first field in each element is a 27-
; character string containing a brief description of the
; adapter.  The next field is the segment of the video refresh
; buffer.  The last three fields are the number of screen lines
; an adapter displays when the 8-pixel, 14-pixel, and 16-pixel
; fonts are loaded, respectively.  Note that not all adapters
; support all fonts, but a screen line count is given for all
; three fonts for all adapter types.  Illegal combinations will
; not be accessed.
;-------------------------------------------------------------
VidInfoTbl DB      'No adapter identified     '   ; Code 0
           DW      0B000H
           DB      25,25,25
           DB      'Monochrome Display Adapter '  ; Code 1
           DW      0B000H
           DB      25,25,25
           DB      'Color Graphics Adapter     '  ; Code 2
           DW      0B800H
           DB      25,25,25
           DB      'Code 3: Undefined          '  ; Code 3
           DW      0B000H
           DB      25,25,25
           DB      'EGA with color monitor     '  ; Code 4
           DW      0B800H
           DB      43,25,25
           DB      'EGA with mono monitor      '  ; Code 5
           DW      0B000H
           DB      43,25,25
           DB      'Code 6: Undefined          '  ; Code 6
```

```
        DW      0B000H
        DB      25,25,25
        DB      'VGA with mono monitor      '    ; Code 7
        DW      0B000H
        DB      50,27,25
        DB      'VGA with color monitor     '    ; Code 8
        DW      0B800H
        DB      50,27,25
        DB      'Code 9: Undefined          '    ; Code 9
        DW      0B000H
        DB      25,25,25
        DB      'MCGA with digital color    '    ; Code 0AH
        DW      0B800H
        DB      25,25,25
        DB      'MCGA with monochrome       '    ; Code 0BH
        DW      0B000H
        DB      25,25,25
        DB      'MCGA with analog color     '    ; Code 0CH
        DW      0B800H
        DB      25,25,25
```

The table consists of twelve subtables, one for each possible code returned by **DispID** as well as a subtable for several undefined codes. Why a subtable for undefined codes? We're going to follow the same general strategy of indexing into the table based on the value of the code. In other words, to get the information for code 4, we have to look at the fifth table (counting from zero) which requires that tables 0 through 4 already exist. Code 3 is undefined, yet something must hold its place in the table for our indexing scheme to work.

Each subtable occupies three lines, for clarity's sake. Here's a typical subtable:

```
        DB      'EGA with color monitor     '    ; Code 4
        DW      0B800H
        DB      43,25,25
```

The first line is a 27-character quoted string containing the name of the display adapter. The second line is a word-sized address, the segment address of the visible display buffer corresponding to that name. The third line contains three numeric values. These are screen sizes, in lines, relating to the font sizes currently in force. The first value is the number of lines on the screen with the 8-pixel font in force. The second value is the number of lines on the screen with the 14-pixel font in force. The third value is the number of lines on the screen with the 16-pixel font in force. The items stored in the subtables give you just about everything you'd really need to know about a given display adapter to do useful work with it.

When your assembly-language program begins executing, it should inspect such a table and extract the values pertinent to the currently installed display adapter. These extracted values should be ordinary variables in the data segment, easily accessible without further table searching. These variables should be defined together, as a block, with comments explaining how they are related:

```
;-------------------------------------------------------------
; DISPLAY INFORMATION VARIABLES
;
; The following block of variables all relate to the video
; system and are initialized by the VidCheck procedure:
;-------------------------------------------------------------
DispType    DB    0       ; Code for display adapter type
VidOrigin   DW    0       ; Offset for FAR pointer to refresh buffer
VidSegment  DW    0B000H  ; Segment of installed display buffer
VisibleX    DB    80      ; Number of columns on screen
VisibleY    DB    25      ; Number of lines on screen
VidBufSize  DW    4000    ; Default to 25 x 80 x 2 (char & attribute)
FontSize    DB    8       ; Either 8, 14, or 16; default to 8
BordName    DW    ?       ; NEAR pointer to name string of installed board
; 18H = 24D; 4FH = 79D; Combined 0-based X,Y of 80 x 25 screen LR corner:
LRXY        DW    184FH
```

As the comments indicate, a single procedure named **VidCheck** reads values from the two-level lookup table **VidInfoTbl** and loads those values into the variables shown above.

VidCheck is an interesting creature, and demonstrates the way of dealing with two-level tables. Read it over:

```
;-------------------------------------------------------------
;   VidCheck  --  Identifies display board & display parameters
;   Last update 3/16/89
;
;   1 entry point:
;
;   VidCheck:
;       Caller passes no parameters.
;       VidCheck identifies the installed display board by
;       calling DispID.  It then calculates numerous display
;       information values, which it then stores in the block
;       of display information variables in the data segment.
;-------------------------------------------------------------

VidCheck    PROC
            ; First task is to figure out which board is on the bus:
            call DispID        ; Ask BIOS for adapter code; returns in AL
            mov  DispType,AL   ; Store display adapter code in DispType
```

```
                ; Next we determine the font size currently in force:
                cmp   AL,0AH          ; See if board is an MCGA
                jl    TryOld          ; If less than code 0AH, it's not an MCGA
                mov   FontSize,16     ; MCGA supports *only* 16-pixel text font
                jmp   GetName         ; Jump ahead to look up adapter name string
TryOld:         cmp   DispType,1      ; Is the display adapter code 1, for MDA?
                jne   TryCGA          ; If not, go test for CGA code 2
                mov   FontSize,14     ; MDA uses *only* 14-pixel text font
                jmp   GetName         ; Jump ahead to look up adapter name string
TryCGA:         cmp   DispType,2      ; Is the display adapter code 2, for CGA?
                jne   TryVGA          ; If not, go test for EGA/VGA font size
                mov   FontSize,8      ; CGA uses *only* 8-pixel text font
                jmp   GetName         ; Jump ahead to look up adapter name string
TryVGA:         mov   AH,11H          ; Select VIDEO Get Font Information subservice
                mov   AL,30H          ;   requires AH = 11H and AL = 30H
                mov   BH,0            ; 0 = Get info about current font
                int   10H             ; Call VIDEO
                mov   FontSize,CL     ; Font size in pixels is returned in CL

                ; Next we get the name string for the board from the info table:
GetName:        mov   AL,DispType     ; Load display adapter code into AL
                xor   AH,AH           ; Zero AH so we don't copy trash into DI
                mov   DI,AX           ; Copy AX (with code in AL) into DI
                mov   CL,5            ; We must shift the code 5 bits to mult. by 32
                shl   DI,CL           ; Multiply code by 32 to act as table index
                lea   BX,VidInfoTbl   ; Load address of info. table into BX
                mov   BordName,BX     ; Save pointer to video info. table in BordName
                add   Bordname,DI     ; Add offset into table to right element

                ; Next we get the refresh buffer segment from the table:
                mov   AX,[BX+DI+27]   ; Index into table past name string to segment
                mov   VidSegment,AX   ; Store segment from table to VidSegment variable

                ; Here we calculate the number of screen lines from font size:
                xor   AH,AH           ; Make sure AH has no trash in it
                mov   AL,FontSize     ; Load the font size in pixels into AL
                cmp   AL,8            ; Is it the 8-pixel font?
                jne   Try14           ; If not, try the 14-pixel font
                mov   AL,1            ; The 8-pixel font is table offset 1
                jmp   ReadLns         ; Jump ahead to read screen lines from table
Try14:          cmp   AL,14           ; Is it the 14-pixel font?
                jne   Do16            ; If not, it has to be the 16-pixel font
                mov   AL,2            ; The 14-pixel font is table offset 2
                jmp   ReadLns         ; Jump ahead to read screen lines from table
Do16:           mov   AL,3            ; The 16-pixel font is table offset 3
ReadLns:        add   DI,AX           ; Add font size offset to table element offset
                mov   AL,[BX+DI+28]   ; Load the screen lines value from the table
                mov   VisibleY,AL     ;  and store it in the VisibleY variable
```

```
        mov  AH,VisibleX   ; Load the screen columns value to AH
        xchg AH,AL         ; Exchange AH & AL for 0 basing
        dec  AL            ; Subtract one from column count for 0 basing
        dec  AH            ; Subtract one from line count for 0 basing
        mov  LRXY,AX       ; And store 0-based X,Y word into LRXY variable

        ; Finally, we calculate the size of the refresh buffer in bytes:
        mov  AL,VisibleY   ; We multiply screen lines by screen columns
        mul  VisibleX      ;  times 2 (for attributes) to get buffer size
        shl  AX,1          ; Multiply lines * columns by 2
        mov  VidBufSize,AX ; Store refresh buffer size in VidBufSize

        ret                ; Return to caller
VidCheck ENDP
```

The first thing **VidCheck** does is call **DispID** to determine the installed display adapter. Build on your own tools—there's no need to duplicate logic if you can avoid it. The adapter ID code is stored in the variable **DispType**.

It's possible to use the table to look up the number of lines on the screen from the current text font size, but to do that you have to determine the font size. Determining the font size is a good exercise in the use of the **CMP** instruction and conditional jumps. Certain adapters support only one font size. The MCGA has only the 16-pixel font. The CGA has only the 8-pixel font. The MDA has only the 14-pixel font. A series of compares and jumps selects a font size based on the display adapter ID code. The trickiness comes in with the EGA and VGA, versatile gentlemen capable of using more than one font size. Fortunately, BIOS has a service that reports the size, in pixels, of the text font currently being used, and this service is used to query the font size. Whatever it turns out to be, the font size is stored in the **FontSize** variable in the data segment.

Base-Indexed-Displacement Memory Addressing

So far, we haven't dealt with the **VidInfoTbl** table at all. This changes when we want to look up the string containing the English-language description of the installed display adapter. There are three general steps to reading *any* two-level lookup table:

- **Derive the offset of the subtable from the beginning of the larger table**
- **Derive the offset of the desired information within the subtable**
- **Read the information from the subtable.**

Each of the subtables is 32 bytes in size. To move from the start of the **VidInfoTbl** to a desired subtable, we multiply the index of the subtable by 32, just as we did in the previous section, in reading one single value from

OriginTbl. The index, here, is the display adapter ID code. We multiply the index by 32 by loading it into register **DI**, and then shifting **DI** to the left by 5 bits. (Shifting left by 5 bits multiplies the shifted quantity by 32.) We use the form

```
mov CL,5
shl DI,CL
```

because it is shorter and faster to shift by **CL** than to shift by using five **SHL DI,1** instructions in sequence.

Because the display adapter description is the first item in every subtable, no offset into the subtable is necessary. (The offset, if you must think of an offset, is 0.) The shifted quantity in **DI** is added to the address of the larger table, and the sum becomes the 16-bit address to the display adapter description string. This address is saved in the **BordName** variable.

At this point within **VidCheck**, we have the address of the **VidInfoTbl** table itself in **BX**, and the offset of the desired subtable in DI. Now we want to fetch the segment address of the display buffer from the middle of the subtable. The segment address is at some fixed offset from the start of the subtable. I say "fixed" because it never changes, and will be the same regardless of which subtable is selected by the adapter ID code. In the case of the segment address, the offset is 27, since the segment address is 27 bytes from the start of the subtable.

Expressed as a sum, the segment address is at the following offset from the start of **VidInfoTbl**: DI+27. Since **BX** contains the offset of **VidInfoTbl** from the start of the data segment, we can pin down the segment address in the data segment with this sum: BX+DI+27.

Is there a way to address memory using this three-part sum?

There is indeed, and it is the most complex of the numerous 8086/8088 addressing modes: *base-indexed-displacement addressing*, a term you probably can't memorize and shouldn't try. Specifically to serve two-level lookup tables like this one, the CPU understands **MOV** statements like the following:

```
mov AX,[BX+DI+27]
```

Here, the *base* is the address of the larger table in BX; the *index* is the offset of the subtable within the larger table, stored in **DI**; and the *displacement* is the fixed distance between the start of the subtable and the data we wish to address.

You can't just use any registers in building a memory address using based-indexed-displacement addressing. The base register can be *only* **BP** or **BX**. (Think of general-purpose register **BX**'s hidden agenda as that of *base register*; the "B" is your memory hook.) The index register can be *only* **SI** or **DI**. These registers' names, *Source Index* and *Destination Index*, should provide you with their own memory hooks.

Finally, the displacement can not be a register at all, but only a literal value like 27 or 14 or 3.

Finding the Number of Lines in the Screen

Reading the screen line count from the subtable is the trickiest part of the whole process. In one sense, the list of three different line count values is a table within a table within a table, but 8086/8088 addressing only goes down two levels. What we must do is point **BX** and **DI** plus a displacement to the first of the three values, and then add a second index to **DI** that selects one of the three line counts.

This second index is placed into **AL**, which is eventually (as part of AX) added to **DI**. The line count is read from the table with the following instruction:

```
mov AL,[BX+DI+28]
```

with the second index already built into DI.

The rest of **VidCheck** fills a few other video-related variables like **LRXY**, which bundles the X,Y position of the lower-right corner of the screen into a single 16-bit quantity. The size of the video buffer in bytes is calculated as the X size of the screen multiplied by the Y size of the screen multiplied by 2, and stored in **VidBufSize**.

A Program to Report on the Current Display Adapter

To make **VidCheck** show its stuff, I've written a short program called INFO.ASM that reports certain facts about the installed display controller.

As a program, INFO.ASM doesn't present anything we haven't used before, except in one respect: string lengths.

To display a string, you have to tell DOS just how long the string is, in characters. Counting characters is difficult, and if you get it wrong you'll either display too much string or not enough.

The solution is simple: let the assembler do the counting. Here's the notation:

```
VidIDStr   DB '  The installed video board is: '
LVidIDStr EQU  $-VidIDStr
```

The first statement is nothing more than a simple string constant definition that we've been using all along. The second statement is a new kind of statement, an *equate*, which looks a lot like a data definition but is not.

A data definition sets aside and optionally initializes an area of memory to some value. An equate, by contrast, generates a value similar to a simple constant in languages like Pascal. An equate allocates no memory, but instead generates a value that is stored in the assembler's symbol table. This value can then be used anywhere a literal constant of that type can be used.

Here, we're using an equate to generate a value giving us the length of the string defined immediately before the equate. The expression **$-VidIDStr** resolves to the difference between two addresses: one is the address of the first byte of the string variable **VidIDStr**, and the other is the *current location counter*, the assembler's way of keeping track of the code and data it's generating. (The current location counter bears *no relation* to **IP**, the instruction pointer!) When the assembler is generating information (either code or data) inside a segment, it begins with a counter set to zero for the start of the segment. As it works its way through the segment, generating code or allocating data, it increments this value by one for each byte of generated code or allocated data.

The expression **$-VidIDStr** is evaluated immediately after the string **VidIDStr** is allocated. This means the assembler's current location counter is pointing to the first byte *after* **VidIDStr**. Because the variable name **VidIDStr** itself resolves to the address of **VidIDStr**, and **$** resolves to the location counter immediately after **VidIDStr** is allocated, **$-VidIDStr** evaluates to the length of **VidIDStr**. Even if you add or delete characters to the contents of **VidIDStr**, the length count will always come out correct, because the calculation always subtracts the address of the beginning of the string from the address just past the end of the string.

```
;-------------------------------------------------------------
;                         INFO.ASM
;      Utility to determine and report system parameters
;
;                                    by Jeff Duntemann
;                                    MASM/TASM
;                                    Last update 12/26/89
;-------------------------------------------------------------

INCLUDE MYLIB.MAC               ; Load in macro library

;----------------------------|
;    BEGIN STACK SEGMENT      |
;----------------------------|
MYSTACK     SEGMENT STACK       ; STACK word ensures loading of SS by DOS

            DB  64 DUP ('STACK!!!') ; This reserves 512 bytes for the stack

MYSTACK     ENDS
;----------------------------|
;    END STACK SEGMENT        |
;----------------------------|
```

```
;---------------------------|
;    BEGIN DATA SEGMENT     |
;---------------------------|
MyData      SEGMENT

;-----------------------------------------------------------------
; DISPLAY INFORMATION VARIABLES
;
; The following block of variables all relate to the video
; system and are initialized by the VidCheck procedure:
;-----------------------------------------------------------------
DispType    DB      0        ; Code for display adapter type
VidOrigin   DW      0        ; Offset for FAR pointer to refresh buffer
VidSegment  DW      0B000H   ; Segment of installed display buffer
VisibleX    DB      80       ; Number of columns on screen
VisibleY    DB      25       ; Number of lines on screen
VidBufSize  DW      4000     ; Default to 25 X 80 X 2 (char & attribute)
FontSize    DB      8        ; Either 8, 14, or 16; default to 8
BordName    DW      ?        ; NEAR pointer to name string of installed board
; 18H = 24D; 4FH = 79D; Combined 0-based X,Y of 80 x 25 screen LR corner:
LRXY        DW      184FH


;-----------------------------------------------------------------
; DISPLAY ADAPTER INFORMATION LOOKUP TABLE
;
; This is the lookup table containing information on all legal
; display adapters.  The first field in each element is a 26-
; character string containing a brief description of the
; adapter.  The next field is the segment of the video refresh
; buffer.  The last three fields are the number of screen lines
; an adapter displays when the 8-pixel, 14-pixel, and 16-pixel
; fonts are loaded, respectively.  Note that not all adapters
; support all fonts, but a screen line count is given for all
; three fonts for all adapter types.  Illegal combinations will
; not be accessed.
;-----------------------------------------------------------------
VidInfoTbl  DB      'No adapter identified    '   ; Code 0
            DW      0B000H
            DB      25,25,25
            DB      'Monochrome Display Adapter '  ; Code 1
            DW      0B000H
            DB      25,25,25
            DB      'Color Graphics Adapter    '   ; Code 2
            DW      0B800H
            DB      25,25,25
            DB      'Code 3: Undefined         '   ; Code 3
            DW      0B000H
            DB      25,25,25
            DB      'EGA with color monitor    '   ; Code 4
```

```
            DW        0B800H
            DB        43,25,25
            DB        'EGA with mono monitor      '   ; Code 5
            DW        0B000H
            DB        43,25,25
            DB        'Code 6: Undefined          '   ; Code 6
            DW        0B000H
            DB        25,25,25
            DB        'VGA with mono monitor      '   ; Code 7
            DW        0B000H
            DB        50,27,25
            DB        'VGA with color monitor     '   ; Code 8
            DW        0B800H
            DB        50,27,25
            DB        'Code 9: Undefined          '   ; Code 9
            DW        0B000H
            DB        25,25,25
            DB        'MCGA with digital color    '   ; Code 0AH
            DW        0B800H
            DB        25,25,25
            DB        'MCGA with monochrome       '   ; Code 0BH
            DW        0B000H
            DB        25,25,25
            DB        'MCGA with analog color     '   ; Code 0CH
            DW        0B800H
            DB        25,25,25

Digits      DB        '0123456789ABCDEF' ; Lookup table for
                                         ;  numeric/string conv.


;-----------------------------------------------------------------
; These two variables are screen-clear "atoms" useable by the
; Clear macro.  The high byte is the display attribute, while
; the low byte is the character with which Clear fills the
; video refresh buffer to clear the screen.
;-----------------------------------------------------------------
HToneAtom   DW        07B0H             ; Clears screen to halftone pattern
ClearAtom   DW        0720H             ; Clears screen to blanks


;-----------------------------------------------------------------
; This is where all predefined string variables are stored.
;-----------------------------------------------------------------
CRLF        DB        0DH,0AH           ; Newline string
IDString    DB        '>>>INFO V1.0'
LIDString   EQU       $-IDString
AuthorStr   DB        '   by Jeff Duntemann'
LAuthorStr  EQU       $-AuthorStr
VidIDStr    DB        '   The installed video board is: '
LVidIDStr   EQU       $-VidIDStr
```

```
OrgIDStr     DB          '   The segment of the video refresh buffer is: '
LOrgIDStr    EQU     $-OrgIDStr
FontSzStr    DB          '   The size of the current text font is: '
LFontSzStr   EQU     $-FontSzStr
ScrnLnStr    DB          '   The number of lines currently on the screen is: '
LScrnLnStr   EQU     $-ScrnLnStr
BufSizStr    DB          '   The size of the refresh buffer in bytes is: '
LBufSizStr   EQU     $-BufSizStr
DigitStr     DB          '       '
LDigitStr    EQU     $-DigitStr


MyData       ENDS
;---------------------------|
;        END DATA SEGMENT   |
;---------------------------|


;---------------------------|
;      BEGIN CODE SEGMENT   |
;---------------------------|
MyProg       SEGMENT

             ASSUME CS:MyProg,DS:MyData
Main         PROC

Start:       ; This is where program execution begins:
             mov  AX,MyData  ; Set up our own data segment address in DS
             mov  DS,AX      ; Can't load segment reg. directly from memory

             call VidCheck   ; Initialize all video information variables

             Clear VidOrigin,ClearAtom,VidBufSize  ; Clear the screen

             ; Here we display the name of the program and its author:
             Writeln IDString,LIDString      ; Display the program name
             Writeln AuthorStr,LAuthorStr    ; display the author name
             Newline

             ; Here we display the name of the installed video board:
             Write VidIDStr,LVidIDStr        ; Display the intro string
             mov BX,1        ; Select DOS file handle 1: Standard Output
             mov CX,27       ; The name strings are 27 bytes long
             mov DX,BordName ; The string address is stored in BordName
             mov AH,40H      ; Service 40H: Write string to file
             int 21H         ; Call DOS to display to Standard Output
             Newline

             ; Here we display the segment address of the refresh buffer:
             Write OrgIDStr,LOrgIDStr     ; Display the intro string
             mov  AX,VidSegment ; AX gets the value to convert to a string
```

```
            lea  SI,DigitStr   ; String equivalent is written to DigitStr
            call Word2Str       ; Do the actual string conversion
            PokeChar DigitStr,'H',4  ; Append 'H' on the end of the string
            Writeln DigitStr,5 ;  and display the string equivalent

            ; Here we display the size of the current text font:
            Write FontSzStr,LFontSzStr   ; Display the intro string
            mov  AL,FontSize   ; AL gets the value to convert to a string
            lea  SI,DigitStr   ; String equivalent is written to DigitStr
            call Byte2Str       ; Do the actual string conversion
            PokeChar DigitStr,'H',2   ; Append 'H' on the end of the string
            Writeln DigitStr,3 ;  and display the string equivalent

            ; Here we display the number of lines on the screen:
            Write ScrnLnStr,LScrnLnStr
            mov  AL,VisibleY   ; AL gets the value to convert to a string
            lea  SI,DigitStr   ; String equivalent is written to DigitStr
            call Byte2Str       ; Do the actual string conversion
            PokeChar DigitStr,'H',2   ; Append 'H' on the end of the string
            Writeln DigitStr,3 ;  and display the string equivalent

            ;Finally, we display the size of the video refresh buffer:
            Write BufSizStr,LBufSizStr     ; Display the intro string
            mov  AX,VidBufSize ; AX gets the value to convert to a string
            lea  SI,DigitStr   ; String equivalent is written to DigitStr
            call Word2Str       ; Do the actual string conversion
            PokeChar DigitStr,'H',4   ; Append 'H' on the end of the string
            Writeln DigitStr,5 ;  and display the string equivalent
            Newline

            mov  AH,4CH        ; Terminate process DOS service
            mov  AL,0          ; Pass this value back to ERRORLEVEL
            int  21H           ; Control returns to DOS

Main        ENDP


;-----------------------------------------------------------------
;   Byte2Str  --  Converts a byte passed in AL to a string at
;                 DS:SI
;   Last update 3/8/89
;
;   1 entry point:
;
;   Byte2Str:
;      Caller must pass:
;      AL : Byte to be converted
;      DS : Segment of destination string
;      SI : Offset of destination string
```

```
;
;       This routine converts 8-bit values to 2-digit hexadecimal
;       string representations at DS:SI.
;-----------------------------------------------------------------

Byte2Str   PROC
           mov DI,AX                  ; Duplicate byte in DI
           and DI,000FH               ; Mask out high 12 bits of DI
           mov BX,OFFSET Digits       ; Load offset of Digits into DI
           mov AH,BYTE PTR [BX+DI]     ; Load digit from table into AH
           mov [SI+1],AH              ;   and store digit into string
           xor AH,AH                  ; Zero out AH
           mov DI,AX                  ; And move byte into DI
           shr DI,1                   ; Shift high nybble of byte to
           shr DI,1                   ;   low nybble
           shr DI,1
           shr DI,1
           mov AH,BYTE PTR [BX+DI]     ; Load digit from table into AH
           mov [SI],AH                ;   and store digit into string
           ret                        ; We're done--go home!
Byte2Str   ENDP


;-----------------------------------------------------------------
;   Word2Str  --  Converts a word passed in AX to a string at
;                 DS:SI
;   Last update 3/8/89
;
;   1 entry point:
;
;   Word2Str:
;     Caller must pass:
;     AX : Word to be converted
;     DS : Segment of destination string
;     SI : Offset of destination string
;-----------------------------------------------------------------

Word2Str   PROC
           mov  CX,AX                 ; Save a copy of convertee in CX
           xchg AH,AL                 ; Swap high and low AX bytes to do high first
           call Byte2Str              ; Convert AL to string at DS:SI
           add  SI,2                  ; Bump SI to point to second 2 characters
           mov  AX,CX                 ; Reload convertee into AX
           call Byte2Str              ; Convert AL to string at DS:SI
           ret                        ; And we're done!
Word2Str   ENDP
```

```
        ;-----------------------------------------------------------------
        ;   VidCheck  --  Identifies display board & display parameters
        ;   Last update 3/16/89
        ;
        ;   1 entry point:
        ;
        ;   VidCheck:
        ;       Caller need pass no parameters.
        ;       VidCheck identifies the installed display board by
        ;       calling DispID.  It then calculates numerous display
        ;       information values, which it then stores in the block
        ;       of display information variables in the data segment.
        ;-----------------------------------------------------------------

VidCheck    PROC
                    ; First task is to figure out which board is on the bus:
                    call DispID         ; Ask BIOS for adapter code; returns in AL
                    mov  DispType,AL     ; Store display adapter code in DispType

                    ; Next we determine the font size currently in force:
                    cmp  AL,0AH          ; See if board is an MCGA
                    jl   TryOld          ; If less than code 0AH, it's not an MCGA
                    mov  FontSize,16     ; MCGA supports *only* 16 pixel text font
                    jmp  GetName         ; Jump ahead to look up adapter name string
TryOld:             cmp  DispType,1      ; Is the display adapter code 1, for MDA?
                    jne  TryCGA          ; If not, go test for CGA code 2
                    mov  FontSize,14     ; MDA uses *only* 14-pixel text font
                    jmp  GetName         ; Jump ahead to look up adapter name string
TryCGA:             cmp  DispType,2      ; Is the display adapter code 2, for CGA?
                    jne  TryVGA          ; If not, go test for EGA/VGA font size
                    mov  FontSize,8      ; CGA uses *only* 8-pixel text font
                    jmp  GetName         ; Jump ahead to look up adapter name string
TryVGA:             mov  AH,11H          ; Select VIDEO Get Font
                                         ;   Information subservice
                    mov  AL,30H          ;   requires AH = 11H and AL = 30H
                    mov  BH,0            ; 0 = Get info about current font
                    int  10H             ; Call VIDEO
                    mov  FontSize,CL     ; Font size in pixels is returned in CL

                    ; Next we get the name string for the board from the info table:
GetName:            mov  AL,DispType     ; Load display adapter code into AL
                    xor  AH,AH           ; Zero AH so we don't copy trash into DI
                    mov  DI,AX           ; Copy AX (with code in AL) into DI
                    mov  CL,5            ; We must shift the code 5 bits to mult.
                                         ;   by 32
                    shl  DI,CL           ; Multiply code by 32 to act as table index
                    lea  BX,VidInfoTbl   ; Load address of origin table into BX
                    mov  BordName,BX     ; Save pointer to video info. table in
                                         ;   BordName
```

```
                add   Bordname,DI    ; Add offset into table to right element

                ; Next we get the refresh buffer segment from the table:
                mov   AX,[BX+DI+27]  ; Index into table past name string
                                     ;  to segment
                mov   VidSegment,AX  ; Store segment from table to
                                     ;  VidSegment variable

                ; Here we calculate the number of lines on-screen from font size:
                xor   AH,AH          ; Make sure AH has no trash in it
                mov   AL,FontSize    ; Load the font size in pixels into AL
                cmp   AL,8           ; Is it the 8-pixel font?
                jne   Try14          ; If not, try the 14-pixel font
                mov   AL,1           ; The 8-pixel font is table offset 1
                jmp   ReadLns        ; Jump ahead to read screen lines from table
Try14:          cmp   AL,14          ; Is it the 14-pixel font?
                jne   Do16           ; If not, it has to be the 16-pixel font
                mov   AL,2           ; The 14-pixel font is table offset 2
                jmp   ReadLns        ; Jump ahead to read screen lines from table
Do16:           mov   AL,3           ; The 16-pixel font is table offset 3
ReadLns:        add   DI,AX          ; Add font size offset to table
                                     ;  element offset
                mov   AL,[BX+DI+28]  ; Load the screen lines value from the table
                mov   VisibleY,AL    ;  and store it in the VisibleY variable
                mov   AH,VisibleX    ; Load the screen columns value to AH
                xchg  AH,AL          ; Exchange AH & AL for 0-basing
                dec   AL             ; Subtract one from column count
                                     ;  for 0-basing
                dec   AH             ; Subtract one from line count for 0-basing
                mov   LRXY,AX        ; And store 0-based X,Y word into LRXY
                                     ;  variable

                ; Finally, we calculate the size of the refresh buffer in bytes:
                mov   AL,VisibleY    ; We multiply screen lines time screen
                                     ;  columns
                mul   VisibleX       ;  times 2 (for attributes) to get
                                     ;  buffer size
                shl   AX,1           ; Multiply lines * columns by 2
                mov   VidBufSize,AX  ; Store refresh buffer size in VidBufSize

                ret                  ; Return to caller
VidCheck        ENDP


;------------------------------------------------------------------
;   DispID  --  Identifies the installed display adapter
;   Last update 3/8/89
;
;   1 entry point:
```

```
;    DispID:
;       Caller passes no parameters
;       Routine returns a code value in AX.
;       The codes are these:
;       0 : Adapter is unknown; recommend aborting
;       1 : MDA (Monochrome Display Adapter)
;       2 : CGA (Color Graphics Adapter)
;
;----------------------------------------------------------------

DispID     PROC
           mov   AH,1AH      ; Select PS/2 Identify Adapter Service
           xor   AL,AL       ; Select Get Combination Code
                             ;  Subservice (AL=0)
           int   10H         ; Call VIDEO
           cmp   AL,1AH      ; If AL comes back with 1AH, we have a PS/2
           jne   TryEGA      ; If not, jump down to test for the EGA
           mov   AL,BL       ; Put Combination Code into AL
           ret               ;   and go home!
TryEGA:    mov   AH,12H      ; Select EGA Alternate Function
           mov   BX,10H      ; Select Get Configuration Information
                             ;  subservice
           int   10H         ; Call VIDEO
           cmp   BX,10H      ; If BX comes back unchanged, EGA is
                             ;  *not* there
           je    OldBords    ; Go see whether it's an MDA or CGA
           cmp   BH,0        ; If BH = 0, it's an EGA/color combo
           je    EGAColor    ;   otherwise it's EGA/mono
           mov   AL,5        ; Store code 5 for EGA mono
           ret               ;   and go home!
EGAColor:  mov   AL,4        ; Store code 4 for EGA color
           ret               ;   and go home!
OldBords:  int   11H         ; Call Equipment Configuration interrupt
           and   AL,30H      ; Mask out all but bits 4 & 5
           cmp   AL,30H      ; If bits 4 & 5 are both =1, it's an MDA
           jne   CGA         ;   otherwise it's a CGA
           mov   AL,1        ; Store code 1 for MDA
           ret               ;   and go home!
CGA:       mov   AL,2        ; Store code 2 for CGA
           ret               ;   and go home!
DispID     ENDP

MyProg     ENDS

;---------------------------|
;      END CODE SEGMENT     |
;---------------------------|

           END Start   ; The procedure named Start becomes the main program
```

Stringing Them Up

Those Amazing String Instructions

311

Most people, having learned a little assembly language, grumble about the seemingly huge number of instructions it takes to do anything useful. By and large, this is a legitimate gripe—and the major reason there are things like Turbo Pascal and Microsoft BASIC.

The 8086/8088 instruction set, on the other hand, is full of surprises, and the surprise most likely to make apprentice assembly-language programmers gasp is the instruction group we call the *string instructions*.

They alone of all the instructions in the 8086/8088 instruction set have the power to deal with long sequences of bytes or words at one time. (In assembly language, any contiguous sequence of bytes or words in memory may be considered a string.) More amazingly, they deal with these large sequences of bytes or words in an extraordinarily compact way: by executing an instruction loop entirely *inside* the CPU! A string instruction is, in effect, a complete instruction loop baked into a single instruction.

The string instructions are subtle and complicated, and I won't be able to treat them exhaustively in this book. Much of what they do qualifies as an advanced topic. Still, you can get a good start on understanding the string instructions by using them to build some simple tools to add to your video toolkit.

Besides, for my money, the string instructions are easily the single most fascinating aspect of assembly-language work.

10.1 The Notion of an Assembly-Language String

Words fail us sometimes by picking up meanings as readily as a magnet picks up iron filings. The word *string* is a major offender here. It means roughly the same thing in all computer programming, but there are a multitude of small variations on that single theme. If you learned about strings in Turbo Pascal, you'll find that what you know isn't totally applicable when you program in C, or BASIC, or assembly.

So here's the big view: a string is any contiguous group of bytes, of any arbitrary size up to the size of a segment. The main concept of a string is that its component bytes are right there in a row, with no interruptions.

That's pretty fundamental. Most higher-level languages build on the string concept, in several ways.

Turbo Pascal treats strings as a separate data type, limited to 255 characters in length, with a single byte at the start of the string to indicate how many bytes are in the string. In C, a string can be longer than 255 bytes, and it has no "length byte" in front of it. Instead, a C string is said to end when a byte with a binary value of 0 is encountered. In BASIC, strings are stored in something called *string space*, which has a lot of built-in code machinery associated with it.

When you begin working in assembly, you have to give all that high-level language stuff over. Assembly strings are just contiguous regions of memory. They start at some specified segment:offset address, go for some number of bytes, and stop. There is no "length byte" to tell how many bytes are in the string, and no standard boundary characters like binary 0 to indicate where a string starts or ends.

You can certainly write assembly-language routines that allocate Turbo Pascal-style strings or C-style strings and manipulate them. To avoid confusion, however, you must think of the data operated on by your routines to be Pascal or C strings rather than assembly strings.

Turning Your "String Sense" Inside-Out

As I mentioned above, assembly strings have no boundary values or length indicators. They can contain any value at all, including binary 0. In fact, you really have to stop thinking of strings in terms of specific regions in memory. You should instead think of strings in much the same way you think of segments: in terms of the register values that define them.

It's slightly inside-out compared to how you think of strings in languages like Pascal, but it works: *you've got a string when you set up a pair of registers to point to one.* And once you point to a string, the length of that string is defined by the value you place in register **CX**.

This is key: assembly strings are wholly defined by values you place in registers. There is a set of assumptions about strings and registers baked into the silicon of the CPU. When you execute one of the string instructions, (as I'll describe a little later) the CPU uses those assumptions to determine what area of memory it reads from or writes to.

Source Strings and Destination Strings

There are two kinds of strings in assembly work: *source strings* are strings that you read from, and *destination strings* are strings that you write to. The difference between the two is *only* a matter of registers. Source strings and destination strings can overlap; in fact, the very same region of memory can be *both* a source string and a destination string, all at the same time.

Here are the assumptions the CPU makes about strings when it executes a string instruction:

- **A source string is pointed to by DS:SI.**
- **A destination string is pointed to by ES:DI.**
- **The length of both kinds of string is the value you place in CX.**
- **Data coming from a source string or going to a destination string must pass through register AX.**

The CPU can recognize both a source string and a destination string simultaneously, because DS:SI and ES:DI can hold values independent of one another.

However, because there is only one **CX** register, the length of source and destination strings must be identical when they are used simultaneously, as in copying a source string to a destination string.

One way to remember the difference between source strings and destination strings is by their offset registers. SI means "source index," and DI means "destination index."

10.2 REP STOSW: The Software Machine Gun

The best way to cement all that string background information in your mind is to see a string instruction at work. In this section, I'm going to lay out a very useful video display tool that makes use of the simplest string instruction, **STOSW** (STOre String by Word). The discussion involves something called a *prefix*, which I haven't gone into yet. Bear with me for now. We'll discuss prefixes in a little while.

Machine Gunning the Video Display Buffer

The **ClrScr** procedure we discussed earlier relied on BIOS to handle the actual clearing of the screen. BIOS is very much a black box, and we're not expected to know how it works. (IBM would rather we didn't, in fact....) The trouble with BIOS is that it only knows how to clear the screen to blanks. Some programs (such as Turbo Pascal 6.0) give themselves a stylish, sculpted look by clearing the screen to one of the PC's "halftone" characters, which are character codes 176-178. BIOS can't do this. If you want the halftone look, you'll have to do it yourself. It doesn't involve anything more complex than replicating a single word value (two bytes) into every position in your video refresh buffer.

Such things should always be done in tight loops. The obvious way would be to put the video refresh buffer segment into the extra segment register **ES**, the refresh buffer offset into **DI**, the number of words in your refresh buffer into **CX**, the word value to clear the buffer to into **AX**, and then code up a tight loop this way:

```
Clear:   MOV  ES:[DI],AX    ; Copy AX to ES:DI
         INC  DI            ; Bump DI to next *word* in buffer
         INC  DI
         DEC  CX            ; Decrement CX by one position
         JNZ  Clear         ; And loop again until CX is 0
```

This will work. It's even tolerably fast. But *all* of the above code is equivalent to this one single instruction:

```
REP STOSW
```

Really. *Really.*

There's two parts to this instruction, actually. As I said, **REP** is a new type of critter, called a *prefix*. We'll get back to it. Right now let's look at **STOSW**. Like all the string instructions, **STOSW** makes certain assumptions about some CPU registers. It works only on the destination string, so **DS** and **SI** are not involved. However, these assumptions must be respected and dealt with:

- **ES must be loaded with the segment address of the destination string**. (That is, the string into which the data will be stored.)
- **DI must be loaded with the offset address of the destination string**.
- **CX (the Count register) must be loaded with the number of times the copy of AX is to be stored into the string**. Note that this does *not* mean the size of the string in bytes!
- **AX must be loaded with the word value to be stored into the string**.

Executing the STOSW Instruction

Once you set up these four registers, you can safely execute a **STOSW** instruction. When you do, this is what happens:

- **The word value in AX is copied to the word at ES:DI**.
- **DI is incremented by 2, such that ES:DI now points to the next word in memory following the one just written to**.

Note that we're *not* machine gunning here. *One* copy of **AX** gets copied to *one* word in memory. The **DI** register is adjusted so that it'll be ready for the *next* time **STOSW** is executed.

One important point to remember is that **CX** is *not* automatically decremented by **STOSW**. **CX** is decremented automatically *only* if you put the **REP** prefix in front of **STOSW**. Lacking the **REP** prefix, you have to do the decrementing yourself, either explicitly through **DEC** or through the **LOOP** instruction, as I'll explain a little later in this chapter.

So you can't make **STOSW** run automatically without **REP**. However, you can if you like execute other instructions before executing another **STOSW**. As long as you don't disturb **ES**, **DI**, or **CX**, you can do whatever you wish. Then when you execute **STOSW** again, another copy of **AX** will go out to the location pointed to by **ES:DI**, and **DI** will be adjusted yet again. (You have to remember to decrement **CX** somehow.) Note that you can change **AX** if you like, but the changed value will be copied into memory. (You may want to do that—there's no law saying you have to fill a string with only one single value.)

However, this is like the difference between a semiautomatic weapon (which fires one round every time you press and release the trigger) and a fully automatic weapon, which fires rounds continually as long as you hold the trigger down. To make **STOSW** fully automatic, just hang the **REP** prefix ahead of it. What **REP** does is beautifully simple: it sets up the tightest of all tight loops completely *inside* the CPU, and fires copies of **AX** into memory repeatedly (hence its name), incrementing **DI** by 2 each time and decrementing **CX** by 1, until **CX** is decremented down to 0. Then it stops, and when the smoke clears you'll see that your whole destination string, however large, has been filled with copies of **AX**.

Man, now *that's* programming!

The following macro sets up and triggers **REP STOSW** to clear the video refresh buffer. The **Clear** macro was designed to be used with the block of video information variables initialized by the **VidCheck** procedure I described in Chapter 9. It needs to be passed a far pointer (which is nothing more than a a full 32-bit address consisting of a segment and an offset laid end to end) to the video refresh buffer, the word value to be blasted into the buffer, and the size of the buffer in bytes.

```
;----------------------------------------------------------------
;   CLEAR    --   Clears the entire visible screen buffer
;   Last update 11/23/91
;
;       Caller must pass:
;       In VidAddress:  A far pointer to the video refresh buffer
;       In ClearAtom:   A word containing the video attribute to be
;                       used in the high byte, and the fill character
;                       to be used in the low byte.
;       In BufLength:   The size of the refresh buffer in bytes
;       Action:     Blasts copies of ClearAtom into the refresh buffer
;                       until the buffer is filled.
;----------------------------------------------------------------
Clear   MACRO VidAddress,ClearAtom,BufLength
        LES  DI,DWORD PTR VidAddress  ; Load ES and DI from far pointer
        MOV  AX,ClearAtom     ; Load AX with word to blast into memory
        MOV  CX,BufLength     ; Load CX with length of buffer in bytes
        SHR  CX,1             ; Divide size of buffer by 2 for word count
        CLD                   ; Set direction flag so we blast up memory
        REP  stosw            ; Blast away!
        GotoXY 0,0            ; Move hardware cursor to UL corner of screen
        ENDM
```

Don't let the notion of a far pointer throw you. It's jargon you're going to hear again and again, and this was a good point to introduce it. A pointer is an address, quite simply. A *near pointer* is an offset address only, used in conjunction with some value in some segment register that presumably doesn't change. A *far pointer* is a pointer that consists of both a segment value and an offset value, both of which can be changed at any time, working together. The video refresh buffer is not usually part of your data segment, so if you're going to work with it, you're probably going to have to access it with a far pointer, as we're doing here.

Note that most of **Clear** is setup work. The **LES** instruction loads both **ES** and **DI** with the address of the destination string. The screen atom (display character plus attribute value) is loaded into **AX**.

The handling of **CX** deserves a little explanation. The value in **BufLength** is the size, *in bytes*, of the video refresh buffer. Remember, however, that **CX** is assumed to contain the number of times that **AX** is to be machine gunned into memory. **AX** is a word, and a word is two bytes. So each time **STOSW** fires, *two* bytes of the video refresh buffer will be written to. Therefore, in order to tell **CX** how many times to fire the gun, we have to divide the size of the refresh buffer (which is given in bytes) by 2, in order to express the size of the refresh buffer in words.

As I explained in Chapter 9, dividing a value in a register by 2 is easy. All you have to do is shift the value of the register to the right by one bit. This what the **SHR CX,1** instruction does: divides **CX** by 2.

STOSW and the Direction Flag DF

Note the **CLD** instruction in the **Clear** macro. I've avoided mentioning it until now to avoid confusing you. Most of the time you'll be using **STOSW**, you'll want to run it uphill in memory; that is, from a lower memory address to a higher memory address. In **Clear**, you put the address of the start of the video refresh buffer into **ES** and **DI**, and then blast character/attribute pairs into memory at successively higher memory addresses. Each time **STOSW** fires a word into memory, **DI** is incremented twice to point to the *next higher* word in memory.

This is the logical way to work it, but it doesn't have to be done that way. **STOSW** can just as easily begin at a high address and move downward in memory. On each store into memory, **DI** can be *decremented* by two instead.

Which way **STOSW** fires—uphill toward successively higher addresses, or downhill toward successively lower addresses, is governed by one of the flags in the Flags register. This is the *Direction flag* (**DF**). **DF**'s sole job in life is to control the direction of certain instructions that, like **STOSW**, can move in one of two directions in memory. Most of these (like **STOSW**) are string instructions.

The sense of **DF** is this: when **DF** is *set* (that is, when **DF** has the value 1) **STOSW** and its fellow string instructions work downhill, from higher to lower addresses; when **DF** is *cleared* (that is, when **DF** has the value 0) **STOSW** and its brothers work uphill from lower to higher addresses. This in turn is simply the direction in which the **DI** register is adjusted: when **DF** is set, **DI** is decremented; when **DF** is cleared, **DI** is incremented.

The Direction flag defaults to 0 when the CPU is reset. You can change the **DF** value in one of two ways: with the **CLD** instruction, or with the **STD** instruction. **CLD** clears **DF**, and **STD** sets **DF**. (You should keep in mind when debugging that the **POPF** instruction can also change **DF**, by popping an entire new set of flags from the stack into the Flags register.) It's always a good idea to place either **CLD** or **STD** right before a string instruction to make sure that your machine gun fires in the right direction!

People sometimes get confused and think that **DF** also governs whether **CX** is incremented or decremented by the string instructions. Not so! Nothing in a string instruction ever increments **CX**! You place a count in **CX** and it counts down, period. **DF** has nothing to say about it.

The **Clear** macro is part of the MYLIB.MAC macro library on the listings diskette for this book. As you build new macro tools, you might place them in MYLIB.MAC as well.

10.3 The Semiautomatic Weapon: STOSW without REP

I chose to show you **REP STOSW** first because it's dramatic in the extreme. But even more, it's actually simpler to use **REP** than not to use **REP**. **REP** simplifies string processing from the programmer's perspective, because it brings the instruction loop *inside* the CPU. You can also use the **STOSW** instruction without **REP**, but it's a little more work. The work involves setting up the instruction loop outside the CPU, and making sure it's correct.

Why bother? Simply this: with **REP STOSW**, you can only store the *same* value into the destination string. Whatever you put into **AX** before executing **REP STOSW** is the value that gets fired into memory **CX** times. **STOSW** can be used to store *different* values into the destination string, by firing it semiautomatically, and changing the value in **AX** between each squeeze of the trigger.

Also, by firing each character individually, you can change the value in DI periodically to break up the data transfer into separated regions of memory instead of one contiguous area as you must with **REP STOSW**. This may be hard to picture until you see it in action. The SHOWCHAR program listing I'll present a little later will give you a f'rinstance that will make it instantly clear what I mean.

You lose a little time in handling the loop yourself, outside the CPU. This is because there is a certain amount of time spent in fetching the loop's instruction bytes from memory. Still, if you keep your loop as tight as you can, you don't lose a *lot* of speed.

Who Decrements CX?

Early in my experience with assembly language, I recall being massively confused about where and when the **CX** register was decremented when using string instructions. It's a key issue, especially when you *don't* use the **REP** prefix.

When you use **REP STOSW** (or **REP** with any of the string instructions) **CX** is decremented automatically, by 1, for each memory access the instruction makes. And once **CX** gets itself decremented down to 0, **REP STOSW** detects that **CX** is now 0, and stops firing into memory. Control then passes down to the next instruction in line. But take away **REP**, and the automatic decrementing of **CX** stops. So, also, does the automatic detection of when **CX** has been counted down to 0.

Obviously, something has to decrement **CX**, since **CX** governs how many times the string instruction accesses memory. If **STOSW** doesn't do it—you guessed it—you have to do it somewhere else, with another instruction.

The obvious way to decrement **CX** is to use **DEC CX**. And the obvious way to determine if **CX** has been decremented to 0 is to follow the **DEC CX** instruction with a **JNZ** (Jump if Not Zero) instruction. **JNZ** tests the zero flag (**ZF**), and jumps back to the **STOSW** instruction until ZF becomes true. And **ZF** becomes true when a **DEC** instruction causes its operand (here, **CX**) to become 0.

The LOOP Instructions

With all that in mind, consider the following assembly-language instruction loop:

```
DoChar:   STOSW                 ; Note that there's no REP prefix!

          ADD     AL,'1'        ; Bump the character value in AL up by 1
          AAA                   ; Adjust AX to make this a BCD addition
          ADD     AL,'0'        ; Basically, put binary 3 in AL's high nybble
          MOV     AH,07         ; Make sure our attribute is still 7

          DEC     CX            ; Decrement the count by 1.
          JNZ     DoChar        ;Loop again if CX > 0
```

Ignore the block of instructions in the middle for the time being. What they do is what I suggested could be done a little earlier: change **AX** in between each store of **AX** into memory. I'll explain in detail shortly. Look instead (for now) to see how the loop runs. **STOSW** fires, **AX** is modified, and then **CX** is decremented. The **JNZ** instruction tests to see if the **DEC** instruction has forced **CX** to 0. If so, **ZF** is set, and the loop will terminate. But until **ZF** is set, the jump is made to the label **DoChar**, where **STOSW** fires yet again.

There is a simpler way, using a new instruction: **LOOP**. The **LOOP** instruction combines the decrementing of **CX** with a test and jump based on **ZF**. It looks like this:

```
DoChar:   STOSW                 ; Note that there's no REP prefix!

          ADD     AL,'1'        ; Bump the character value in AL up by 1
          AAA                   ; Adjust AX to make this a BCD addition
          ADD     AL,'0'        ; Basically, put binary 3 in AL's high nybble
```

```
        MOV    AH,07      ; Make sure our attribute is still 7

        LOOP   DoChar     ; Go back & do another char until CX goes to 0
```

The **LOOP** instruction first decrements **CX** by 1. It then checks **ZF** to see if the decrement operation forced **CX** to 0. If so, it falls through to the next instruction. If not (that is, if ZF remains 0, indicating that **CX** was still greater than 0) **LOOP** branches to the label specified as its operand.

So the loop keeps looping the **LOOP** until **CX** counts down to 0. At that point, the loop is finished, and execution continues with the next instruction following the loop.

Displaying a Ruler on the Screen

As a useful demonstration of when it makes sense to use **STOSW** without **REP** (but with **LOOP**) let me offer you another item for your video toolkit.

The **Ruler** macro shown below displays a repeating sequence of ascending digits, from 1, at some selectable location on your screen. In other words, you can display a string of digits like this at the top of a window:

```
12345678901234567890123456789012345678901234567890
```

allowing you to determine where in the horizontal dimension of the window a line begins or some character falls. The **Ruler** macro allows you to specify how long the ruler is, in digits, and where on the screen it will be displayed.

A call to **Ruler** would look like this:

```
Ruler VidOrigin,20,80,15,5
```

This invocation (assuming you had defined **VidOrigin** to be the address of the start of the video refresh buffer in your machine) places a 20-character long ruler at position 15,5. The 80 argument indicates to **Ruler** that your screen is 80 characters wide. If you had a wider or narrower text screen, you would have to change the argument to reflect the true width of your screen in text mode.

Don't just read the code inside **Ruler**! Load it up into a copy of EAT5.ASM, and display some rulers on the screen. You don't learn half as much by just reading assembly code as you do by loading and using it!

```
;--------------------------------------------------------------
;   RULER   -- Displays a "1234567890"-style ruler on screen
;   Last update 11/25/91
;
;       Caller must pass:
;       In VidAddress: The address of the start of the video buffer
;       In Length:  The length of the ruler to be displayed
```

```
;       In ScreenW: The width of the current screen (usually 80)
;       In ScreenY: The line of the screen where the ruler is
;                   to be displayed (0 through 24)
;       In ScreenX: The row of the screen where the ruler should
;                   start (0 through 79)
;       Action:     Displays an ASCII ruler at ScreenX,ScreenY.
;----------------------------------------------------------------
Ruler     MACRO VidAddress,Length,ScreenW,ScreenX,ScreenY
          LES   DI,DWORD PTR VidAddress
          MOV   AL,ScreenY    ; Move Y position to AL
          MOV   AH,ScreenW    ; Move screen width to AH
          IMUL  AH            ; Do 8-bit multiply AL*AH to AX
          ADD   DI,AX         ; Add Y offset into vidbuff to DI
          ADD   DI,ScreenX    ; Add X offset into vidbuf to DI
          SHL   DI,1          ; Multiply by two for final address
          MOV   CX,Length     ; CX monitors the ruler length
          MOV   AH,07         ; Attribute 7 is "normal" text
          MOV   AL,'1'        ; Start with digit "1"

DoChar:   STOSW               ; Note that there's no REP prefix!
          ADD   AL,'1'        ; Bump the character value in AL up by 1
          AAA                 ; Adjust AX to make this a BCD addition
          ADD   AL,'0'        ; Basically, put binary 3 in AL's high nybble
          MOV   AH,07         ; Make sure our attribute is still 7
          LOOP  DoChar        ; Go back & do another char until BL goes to 0

          ENDM
```

Over and above the **LOOP** instruction, there's a fair amount of new assembly technology at work here that could stand explaining. Let's detour from the string instructions for a bit and take a closer look.

Simple Multiplies with IMUL

Ruler can put its ruler anywhere on the screen, using the position passed as **ScreenX** and **ScreenY**. It's not using **GotoXY**, either. It's actually calculating a position in the video refresh buffer where the ruler characters must be placed—and then uses **STOSW** to place them there.

Locations in the video refresh buffer are always expressed as offsets from a single segment address that is either B000H or B800H. The algorithm for determining the offset in bytes for any given X and Y value looks like this:

Offset = ((Y × width in characters of a screen line) + X) × 2

Pretty obviously, you have to move Y lines down in the screen buffer, and then move X bytes over from the left margin of the screen to reach your X,Y position.

The trickiest part of implementing the algorithm lies in multiplying the Y value by the screen width. There is an instruction to do the job, **IMUL**, but it's a little quirky and (as assembly instructions go) not very fast.

It is, however, fast enough for what we're doing here, which is just positioning the ruler somewhere on the screen. The positioning only needs to be done once, not many times within a tight loop. So even if **IMUL** is slow as instructions go, when you only need to use it to set something else up, it's certainly fast enough.

IMUL *always* operates in conjunction with the AX register. In every case, the destination for the product value is AX, or else **AX** and **DX** for products larger than 32,767.

On the 8086/8088 there are basically two variations on **IMUL**, and the difference depends on the size of the operands. If you are multiplying two 8-bit quantities, you can put one in **AL** and the other in some 8-bit register or memory location. The product will be placed in **AX**. If you are multiplying two 16-bit quantities, one can be placed in **AX** and one in a 16-bit register or memory location. The product from multiplying two 16-bit quantities is too large to fit in a single 16-bit register, so the low-order 16 bits are placed in **AX**, and the high-order 16 bits are placed in **DX**. You have no control over the destination; it's either **AX** or **AX:DX**. Also, one of the operands *must* be in **AL** (for 8-bit multiplies) or **AX** (for 16-bit multiplies.) You have no control over that; it's impossible to multiply (for example) **CX** × **BX**, or **DX** × **DS:[BX]**.

One very common bug you may commit when using **IMUL** is simply forgetting that when given 16-bit operands, **IMUL** changes the value in **DX**. The easiest way to avoid this problem is to use **IMUL** in its 8-bit mode whenever possible, which is when *both* multiplier and multiplicand are less than 256. If either operand is 16 bits in size, **DX** will be altered.

Here are some examples of the various legal forms of IMUL:

```
IMUL    BYTE PTR [BX]   ; multiplies AL x byte at DS:[BX]
IMUL    BH              ; multiplies AL x BH

IMUL    WORD PTR [BX]   ; multiplies AX x word at DS:[BX]
IMUL    BX              ; multiplies AX x BX
```

In the first two lines, the destination for the product is **AX**. In the second two lines, the destination for the product is **DX:AX**

IMUL sets two flags in those cases where the product is larger than the two operands. The flags involved are the Carry flag (**CF**) and the Overflow flag (**OF**). For example, if you're multiplying two 8-bit operands and the product is larger than 8 bits, both **CF** and **OF** will be set. Otherwise, the two flags will be cleared.

Now, why the final multiplication by 2? Keep in mind that every character position in the screen buffer is represented by *two* bytes: One character byte and one attribute byte. So moving *X* characters from the left margin actually moves X × 2 bytes into the screen buffer. You might think of an 80-character line on the screen as being 80 characters long, but it's actually 160 characters long in the screen buffer, to account for the "invisible" attribute bytes. Multiplying by 2 is done using the **SHL** instruction (shift DI to the left by one bit). As I explained in Chapter 9, this is exactly the same as multiplying **DI** by 2.

The Limitations of Macro Arguments

There's another problem you will eventually run into if you're like most people. Given the macro header for **Ruler**

```
Ruler     MACRO VidAddress,Length,ScreenW,ScreenX,ScreenY
```

you might be tempted to write something like this:

```
MOV    AL,ScreenY
IMUL   ScreenW
```

No go! The assembler will call you on it, complaining of an *illegal immediate.* What went wrong? You can freely use constructions like these:

```
MOV    AL,ScreenY
ADD    DI,ScreenX
CMP    AL,Length
```

All of these use arguments from the macro header. So what's that assembler complaining about? The problem here is that the **IMUL** instruction cannot work with immediate operands. And this isn't just a problem with **IMUL**: *all* instructions that cannot work with immediate operands will reject a macro argument under these circumstances.

And "these circumstances" involve the way that the macro is invoked. In the test file RULER.ASM, you'll see the following line, which invokes the macro to display a ruler:

```
Ruler   VidOrigin,20,80,50,10   ; Draw ruler
```

Except for the video origin address argument, all of these arguments are numeric literals. A numeric literal, when used in an assembly-language instruction, is called *immediate data.* When the macro is expanded, the argument you pass to the macro is substituted into the actual instruction that uses a macro argument, just as you passed it to the macro.

In other words, if you pass the value 10 in the **ScreenY** argument of the instruction **MOV AL,ScreenY**, the instruction becomes **MOV AL,10** once the macro is expanded by the macro assembler. Now, **MOV AL,10** is a completely legal instruction. But if you pass the literal value 80 in the **ScreenW** argument, you cannot use **IMUL ScreenW**, because after expansion this becomes **IMUL 80**, which is not a legal instruction. **IMUL** does not operate on immediate data!

The problem is *not* that you're using macro arguments with **IMUL**. The problem is that you're passing a numeric literal in a macro argument to an instruction that doesn't work with immediate data.

What you have to remember (especially if you're familiar with languages like Pascal) is that macro arguments are *not* high-level language procedure parameters passed on the stack. They are simply text substitutions. If you had defined a variable in memory called **ScreenWidth** using **DB**, stored the value 80 in it, and then passed **ScreenWidth** to **Ruler** as a macro argument, things would be different:

```
Ruler  VidOrigin,20,ScreenWidth,50,10  ; Draw ruler
```

In this case, you *could* use the instruction **IMUL ScreenW** in Ruler, because **IMUL ScreenW** would be expanded to **IMUL ScreenWidth**, which is legal because **ScreenWidth** is a memory location.

I wrote **Ruler** as I did so that you *could* use numeric literals when invoking **Ruler.** Using literals saves memory by making memory variables unnecessary, and if you'd prefer to define a meaningful name for the screen width rather than hard coding the value 80 in the source (which is unwise) you can define a symbol called **ScreenWidth** as an *equate.* Equates are a little like miniature macros, and I'll deal with them a little later in this chapter.

Adding ASCII Digits

Once the correct offset is placed in the buffer for the ruler's beginning is calculated in **DI,** (and once we set up initial values for **CX** and **AX**) we're ready to start making rulers.

Immediately before the **STOSW** instruction, we load the ASCII digit '1' into **AL**. Note that the instruction **MOV AL,'1'** does *not* move the value 01 into **AL**! '1' is an ASCII character, and the character '1' (the "one" digit) has a numeric value of 31H, or 49 decimal.

This becomes a problem immediately after we store the digit '1' into video memory with **STOSW**. After digit '1' we need to display digit '2', and to do that we need to change the value stored in **AL** from '1' to '2'.

Ordinarily, you can't just add '1' to '1' and get '2'. Adding 31H and 31H will give you 62H, which (when seen as an ASCII character) is lowercase letter 'b', *not* '2'! However, in this case the 8086/8088 instruction set comes to the rescue, in the form of a somewhat peculiar instruction called **AAA,** (Adjust AL after BCD Addition).

What **AAA** does is allow us, in fact, to "add" ASCII character digits rather than numeric values. **AAA** is one of a group of instructions called the BCD instructions, so called because they support arithmetic with binary coded decimal (BCD) values. BCD is just another way of expressing a numeric value, somewhere between a pure binary value like 01 and an ASCII digit like '1'. A BCD value is a 4-bit value, occupying the low nybble of a byte. It expresses values between 0 and 9 *only*. It's possible to express values greater than 9 (from 9 through 15, actually) in four bits, but those additional values are not valid BCD values. See Figure 10.1.

The value 31H is a valid BCD value, because the low nybble contains 1. Because BCD is a 4-bit numbering system, the high nybble (which in the case of 31H contains a 3) is ignored. In fact, all of the ASCII digits from '0' through '9'

Figure 10.1. Unpacked BCD digits

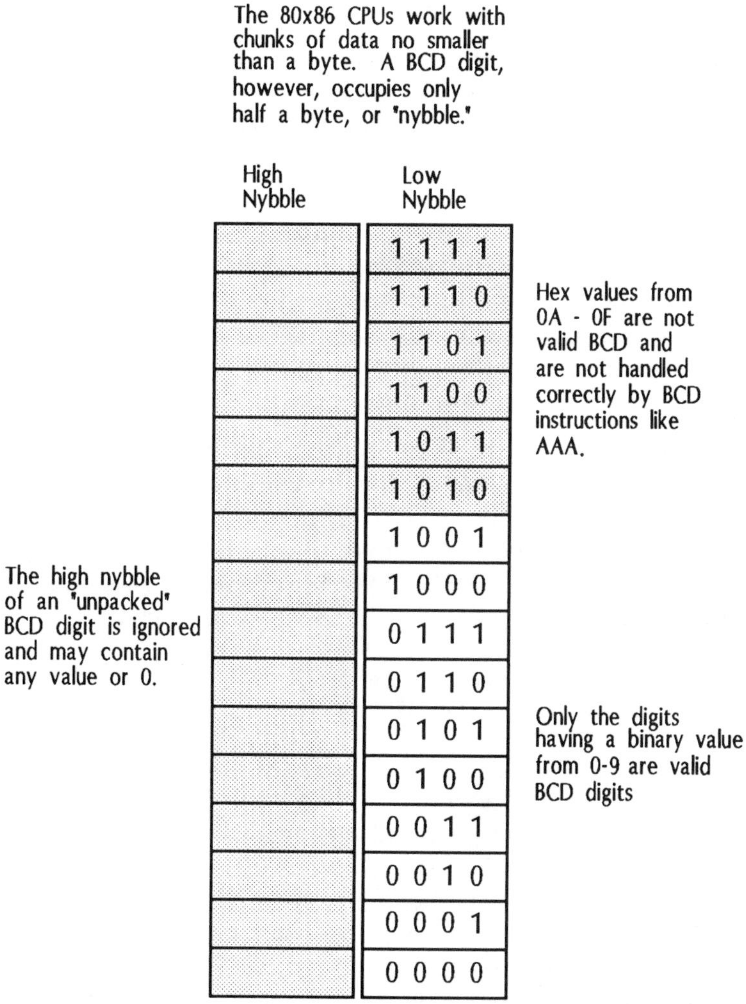

The 80x86 CPUs work with chunks of data no smaller than a byte. A BCD digit, however, occupies only half a byte, or "nybble."

High Nybble	Low Nybble	
	1 1 1 1	
	1 1 1 0	Hex values from 0A - 0F are not
	1 1 0 1	valid BCD and are not handled
	1 1 0 0	correctly by BCD instructions like
	1 0 1 1	AAA.
	1 0 1 0	
	1 0 0 1	
	1 0 0 0	
	0 1 1 1	
	0 1 1 0	
	0 1 0 1	Only the digits having a binary value
	0 1 0 0	from 0-9 are valid BCD digits
	0 0 1 1	
	0 0 1 0	
	0 0 0 1	
	0 0 0 0	

The high nybble of an "unpacked" BCD digit is ignored and may contain any value or 0.

can be considered legal BCD values, because in each case the characters' low four bits contain a valid BCD value. The 3 stored in the high four bits of each digit is ignored.

So if there were a way to perform BCD addition on the 86-family CPU, adding ASCII digits '1' and '1' would indeed give us '2' because '1' and '2' can be manipulated as legal BCD values.

AAA (and several other instructions I don't have room to discuss here) give us that ability to perform BCD math. The actual technique may seem a little odd, but it does work. **AAA** is a sort of a fudge factor, in that you execute **AAA** after performing an addition using the "normal" addition instruction **ADD**. **AAA** takes the results of the **ADD** instruction and forces them to "come out right" in terms of BCD math.

AAA basically does these two things:

- **It forces the value in the low four bits of AL (which could be any value from 0 through F) to a value between 0 and 9 *if* it was greater than 9.** This is done by adding 6 to **AL** and then forcing the high nybble of **AL** to 0. Obviously, if the low nybble of **AL** contains a valid BCD digit, the digit in the low nybble is left alone.

- **If the value in AL had to be adjusted, the adjustment indicates that there was a carry in the addition, and that AH was incremented.** Also, the Carry flag (**CF**) is set to 1, as is the Auxiliary carry flag (**AF**). Again, if the low nybble of **AL** contained a valid BCD digit when **AAA** was executed, **AH** is not incremented, and the two carry flags are cleared (forced to 0) rather than set.

AAA thus facilitates base 10 (decimal) addition on the low nybble of **AL**. After **AL** is adjusted by **AAA**, the low nybble contains a valid BCD digit and the high nybble is 0. (But note well that this will be true *only* if the addition that preceded **AAA** was executed on two valid BCD operands!)

This allows us to add ASCII digits like '1' and '2' using the **ADD** instruction. **Ruler** does this immediately after the **STOSW** instruction:

```
ADD    AL,'1'      ; Bump the character value in AL up by 1
AAA                ; Adjust AX to make this a BCD addition
```

If prior to the addition, the contents of **AL**'s low nybble were 9, adding '1' would make the value A, which is not a legal BCD value. **AAA** would then adjust **AL** by adding 6 to **AL** and clearing the high nybble. Adding 6 to 0A would give 10, so once the high nybble is cleared the new value in **AL** would be 00. Also, **AH** would have been incremented by 1.

In **Ruler** we're not adding multiple columns, but instead are simply "rolling over" a count in a single column, and displaying the number in that column to the screen. Therefore we just ignore the incremented value in **AH** and use **AL** alone.

Adjusting AAA's Adjustments

There is one problem: AAA clears the high nybble to 0. This means that adding ASCII digits '1' and '1' doesn't *quite* equal '2', the displayable digit. Instead, **AL** becomes 02, which in ASCII is the dark "smiley face" character. To make **AL** a displayable ASCII digit again, we have to add 30H to **AL**. This is easy to do: Just add '0' to AL. The ASCII digit '0' has a numeric value of 30H, so adding '0' takes 02H back up to 32H, which is the numeric equivalent of the ASCII digit '2'. This is the reason for the **ADD AL,'0'** instruction that immediately follows **AAA**.

There's a lot more to BCD math than what I've explained here. When you want to perform multiple-column BCD math, you have to take carries into account, which involves the Auxiliary Carry flag (**AF**). There are also the **AAD**, **AAM**, and **AAS** instructions for adjusting **AL** after BCD divides, multiplies, and substracts, respectively. The same general idea applies: all the BCD adjustment instructions force the standard binary arithmetic instructions to "come out right" for BCD operands.

And yet another problem: **AAA** increments **AH** whenever it finds a value in the low nybble of **AL** greater than 9. In **Ruler**, **AH** contains the text attribute we're using to display our ruler, and if **AH** is incremented, the attribute will change and we'll end up displaying parts of the ruler in different colors. This is why we have to do one last adjustment to **AAA**'s adjustments: we must reassert our desired text attribute in **AH**, each time we change the ASCII digit in **AL**.

An interesting thing to do is comment out the **ADD AL,'0'** instruction in the **Ruler** macro and then run the RULER.ASM test program. Another interesting thing to do (especially if you work on a color screen) is to comment out the **MOV AH,07** instruction in **Ruler** and then run RULER.ASM. Details count, big time!

Ruler's Lessons

The **Ruler** macro is a good example of using **STOSW** *without* the **REP** prefix. We have to change the value in **AX** every time we store **AX** to memory, and thus can't use **REP STOSW**. Note that nothing is done to **ES:DI** or **CX** while changing the digit to be displayed, and thus the values stored in those registers are held over for the next execution of **STOSW**. **Ruler** is a good example of how **LOOP** works with **STOSW** to adjust **CX** downward and return control to the top of the loop. **LOOP**, in a sense, does outside the CPU what **REP** does inside the CPU: adjust **CX** and close the loop. Try to keep that straight in your head when using any of the string instructions!

10.4 Storing Data to Discontinuous Strings

Sometimes you have to break the rules. Until now I've been explaining the string instructions under the assumption that the destination string is always one continuous sequence of bytes in memory. This isn't necessarily the case. In addition to changing the value in **AX** between executions of **STOSW**, you can change the *destination address* as well. The end result is that you can store data to several different areas of memory within a single very tight loop.

Displaying an ASCII Table in a Big Hurry

I've created a small demo program to show you what I mean. It's not as useful a tool as the **Ruler** macro, but it makes its point and is easy to understand. The SHOWCHAR program clears the screen and shows a table containing all 256 ASCII characters, neatly displayed in four lines of 64 characters each. The table includes the "undisplayable" ASCII characters corresponding to the control characters whose values are less than 32. They are displayable from SHOWCHAR because the program writes them directly into video memory. Neither DOS nor BIOS are "aware" of the display of the control characters, so they have no opportunity to interpret or filter out those characters with special meanings.

SHOWCHAR.ASM introduces a number of new concepts and instructions, all related to program loops. (String instructions like **STOSW** and program loops are intimately related.) Read over the main body of the SHOWCHAR.ASM program carefully. We'll go over it idea by idea through the next several pages.

```
;-----------------------------------------------------------------
;                            SHOWCHAR.ASM
;          Demonstration of STOSW to disjoint areas of memory
;          through the display of an ASCII table direct to the
;          video refresh buffer
;
;
;                                      by Jeff Duntemann
;                                      MASM/TASM
;                                      Last update 12/14/91
;
;-----------------------------------------------------------------

INCLUDE MYLIB.MAC                 ; Load in screen control macro library


;---------------------------|
;     BEGIN STACK SEGMENT    |
;---------------------------|
MyStack    SEGMENT STACK          ; STACK word ensures loading of SS by DOS

           DB      64 DUP ('STACK!!!') ; This reserves 512 bytes for the stack

MyStack    ENDS
;---------------------------|
;      END STACK SEGMENT     |
;---------------------------|
```

```
;---------------------------|
;     BEGIN DATA SEGMENT    |
;---------------------------|
MyData     SEGMENT

LRXY       DW    184FH ; 18H = 24D; 4FH = 79D; 0-based XY of LR screen corner

VidOrigin  DD    0B0000000H   ; Change to 0B0000000H if you have a mono CRT!
CRLF       DB    0DH,0AH

ScrnWidth  EQU   80           ; Width of the screen in characters
LineLen    EQU   64           ; Length of one line of the ASCII table
LinesDown  EQU   4            ; Number of lines down to start ASCII table

MyData     ENDS
;---------------------------|
;      END DATA SEGMENT     |
;---------------------------|


;---------------------------|
;     BEGIN CODE SEGMENT    |
;---------------------------|

MyProg     SEGMENT

           ASSUME CS:MyProg,DS:MyData
Main       PROC

Start:     ; This is where program execution begins:
           MOV    AX,MyData   ; Set up our own data segment address in DS
           MOV    DS,AX       ; Can't load segment reg. directly from memory

           Clear  VidOrigin,0720H,4000   ; Clear full video buffer to spaces

           LES    DI,DWORD PTR VidOrigin   ; Put vid seg in ES & offset in DI
           ADD    DI,ScrnWidth*LinesDown*2 ; Start table display down a ways
           MOV    CX,256      ; There are 256 chars in the ASCII set
           MOV    AX,0700H    ; Start with char 0, attribute 7

DoLine:    MOV    BL,LineLen  ; Each line will consist of 64 characters
DoChar:    STOSW              ; Note that there's no REP prefix!
           JCXZ   AllDone     ; When the full set is printed, quit
           INC    AL          ; Bump the character value in AL up by 1
           DEC    BL          ; Decrement the line counter by one
           LOOPNZ DoChar      ; Go back & do another char until BL goes to 0
           ADD    DI,(ScrnWidth - LineLen)*2 ; Move DI to start of next line
           JMP    DoLine      ; Start display of the next line
```

```
AllDone:   GotoXY  0,12        ; Move hardware cursor down below char. table
           MOV     AH,4CH      ; Terminate process DOS service
           MOV     AL,0        ; Pass this value back to ERRORLEVEL
           INT     21H         ; Control returns to DOS


Main       ENDP


MyProg     ENDS


;----------------------------|
;      END CODE SEGMENT      |
;----------------------------|

           END Start    ; The procedure named Start becomes the main program
```

The Nature of Equates

You might remember (and it wouldn't hurt to go back and take another look) how we calculated the offset from the beginning of the video refresh buffer to the memory location corresponding to an arbitrary X,Y position on the screen. We used the **ADD** instruction, along with the **SHL** instruction to multiply by 2.

There is another way to perform calculations of that general sort in assembly work: let the assembler do them, while the program is being assembled. Take a look at the line below, lifted from SHOWCHAR.ASM:

```
ADD    DI,ScrnWidth*LinesDown*2 ; Start table display down a ways
```

This is new indeed. What can we make of this? What sort of an operand is **ScrnWidth*LinesDown*2**? The answer is that it's a simple integer operand, no different from the value 12, 169, or 15324.

The key is to go back to SHOWCHAR and find out what **ScrnWidth** and **LinesDown** are. You might have thought that these were variables in memory, defined with the **DW** directive. Instead, they're something we haven't really discussed in detail until now: *equates*. Equates are defined with the **EQU** operator, and if you find yourself confused over the differences between **EQU** and **DW**, don't despair. It's an easy enough thing to do.

One road to understanding harkens back to the Pascal language. What is the difference between a variable and a simple constant? A variable is located at one and only one particular place in memory. A simple constant, on the other hand, is a value "dropped into" the program anywhere it is used, and exists at no particular place in memory. Simple constants are used mostly in expressions calculated by the compiler during compilation.

It's the same thing here. The **DW** and **DB** directives define and set aside areas of memory for storage of data. A **DW** exists somewhere at some address, and only exists in one place. The **EQU** directive, by contrast, is a symbol you define mostly for the assembler's use. It sets aside no memory and has no particular address. Consider this line from SHOWCHAR:

```
LinesDown  EQU   4    ; Number of lines down to start ASCII table
```

The value defined as **LinesDown** exists at no single place in the SHOWCHAR program. It allocates no storage. It's actually a notation in the assembler's symbol table, telling the assembler to substitute the value 4 for the symbol **LinesDown**, anywhere it encounters the symbol **LinesDown**. The same is true of the equates for **ScrnWidth** and **LineLen**.

When the assembler encounters equates in a program, it performs a simple textual substitution of the values assigned to the symbol defined in the equate. The symbol is dumped, and the value is dropped in. *Then* assembly continues, using the substituted values rather than the symbols. In a very real sense, the assembler is pausing to alter the source code when it processes an equate, then picks up its assembly task again. This is exactly what happens when the assembler processes a macro, by the way.

An example may help. Imagine that the assembler is assembling SHOWCHAR.ASM, when it encounters the following line:

```
ADD    DI,ScrnWidth*LinesDown*2 ; Start table display down a ways
```

It looks up **ScrnWidth** and **LinesDown** in its symbol table, and discovers that they are equates. It then calls time out from assembling, and processes the two equates by substituting their values into the line of source code for their text symbols. The line of source code changes to the following:

```
ADD    DI,80*4*2                ; Start table display down a ways
```

Assembly-Time Calculations

But in assembling the line shown above, the assembler has to pull another trick out of its hat. It has to be able to deal with the expression **80*4*2**. We've not seen this before in our discussions, but the assembler happily parses the expression and performs the math exactly as you would imagine: it cooks **80*4*2** down to the single integer value 640. It then performs another substitution on the line in question, which finally cooks down to this:

```
ADD    DI,640   ; Start table display down a ways
```

At last, the line becomes an utterly ordinary line of assembly-language code, which is turned to object code in a trice.

So the assembler can in fact do a little math on its own, quite apart from the arithmetic instructions supported by the CPU. This is called *assembly-time math*, and it has some very important limitations:

- **Assembly-time calculations can *only* be done on values that are fixed and unambiguous at assembly-time**. This most pointedly excludes the contents of variables. Equates are fine. **DB**s, **DW**s, and **DD**s are *not*. Variables are empty containers at assembly time; just buckets into which values will be thrown at runtime. You can't perform a calculation with an empty bucket!
- **Assembly-time calculations are performed *once*, at assembly-time, and cannot be recalculated at runtime for a different set of values**. This should be obvious, but it's easy enough to misconstrue the nature of assembly-time math while you're a beginner.

Let me point out an importance consequence of the use of assembly-time math in SHOWCHAR. In SHOWCHAR, the ASCII table is displayed four lines down from the top of the screen, at the left margin. Now, what do we need to do to allow the ASCII table to be moved around the screen at runtime?

Oh, not much, just rewrite the whole thing.

I'm not being trying to be funny. That's the price you pay for the convenience of assembly-time calculation. We baked the screen position of the ASCII table into the program at the source code level, and if we wanted to parameterize the position of the ASCII table we'd have to take a whole different approach, and do what we did with RULER.ASM: use the **IMUL** instruction to perform the multiplication that calculates the offset into the screen buffer, at runtime.

We can change the **LinesDown** equate in SHOWCHAR.ASM to have a value of 6 or 10—but we then have to reassemble and relink SHOWCHAR for the change to take effect. The calculation is done only once, at assembly time. Thereafter, as long as we use the resulting .EXE file, the ASCII table will be the number of lines down the screen that we defined in the **LinesDown** equate.

Assembly-time calculations may not seem as useful now, in the light of these restrictions. However, they serve a purpose that may not be immediately obvious: they make it a little easier for us to read the sense in our own source code. We could have just skipped the equates and the assembly-time math, done the math in our heads and written the line of code like this:

```
ADD    DI,640    ; Start table display down a ways
```

How obvious is it to you that adding 640 to DI starts the display of the table down the screen by four lines? Using equates and assembly-time math builds the screen-positioning algorithm into the source code, right there where it's used.

Equates and assembly-time math cost you *nothing* in terms of runtime speed or memory usage. They *do* slow down the assembly process a little, but the person who uses your programs never knows that—and it's the user that you want to wow with your assembly-language brilliance. And anything that makes your own source code easier to read and modify is well worth the minuscule extra time it takes to assemble.

Nested Instruction Loops

Once all the registers are set up correctly according to the assumptions made by **STOSW**, the real work of SHOWCHAR is performed by two instruction loops, one inside the other. The inner loop displays a line consisting of 64 characters. The outer loop breaks up the display into four such lines. The inner loop is by far the more interesting of the two. Here it is:

```
DoChar:   STOSW                   ; Note that there's no REP prefix!
          JCXZ    AllDone         ; When the full set is printed, quit
          INC     AL              ; Bump the character value in AL up by 1
          DEC     BL              ; Decrement the line counter by one
          LOOPNZ  DoChar          ; Go back & do another char until BL goes to 0
```

The work here (putting a character/attribute pair into the video buffer) is again done by **STOSW**. Once again, **STOSW** is working solo, without **REP**. Without **REP** to pull the loop inside the CPU, you have to set the loop up yourself.

Keep in mind what happens each time **STOSW** fires: the character in **AX** is copied to **ES:DI**, And **DI** is incremented by 2. At the other end of the loop, the **LOOPNZ** instruction decrements **CX** by 1 and closes the loop.

During register setup, we loaded **CX** with the number of characters we wanted to display—in this case, 256. Each time **STOSW** fires, it places another character on the screen, and there is one less character left to display. **CX** acts as the master counter, keeping track of when we finally display the last remaining character. When **CX** goes to 0, we've displayed the full ASCII character set and the job is done.

Jumping When CX Goes to 0

Hence the instruction **JCXZ**. This is a special branching instruction created specifically to help with loops like this. Back in Chapter 9, I explained how it's possible to branch using one of the many variations of the **JMP** instruction, based on the state of one of the machine flags. Earlier in this chapter, I explained the **LOOP** instruction, which is a special purpose sort of a **JMP** instruction, one combined with an implied **DEC CX** instruction. **JCXZ** is yet another variety of **JMP** instruction, but one that doesn't watch any of the flags or decrement any registers. Instead, **JCXZ** watches the **CX** register. When it sees that **CX** has just gone to 0, it jumps to the specified label. If **CX** does not contain an 0 value, execution falls through to the next instruction in line.

In the case of the inner loop shown above, **JCXZ** branches to the "close up shop" code when it sees that **CX** has finally gone to 0. This is how the SHOWCHAR program terminates.

Most of the other **JMP** instructions have "partners" that branch when the governing flag is *not* true. That is, **JC** (Jump on Carry) branches when the Carry flag equals 1. Its partner, **JNC** (Jump on Not Carry), jumps if the Carry flag is *not* 1.

However, **JCXZ** is a loner. There is *no* **JCXNZ** instruction, so don't go looking for one in the instruction reference!

Closing the Inner Loop

Assuming that **CX** has not yet been decremented down to 0 by the **STOSW** instruction, (a condition watched for by **JCXZ**) the loop continues, and **AL** is again incremented by 1. This is how the next ASCII character in line is selected. The value in **AX** is sent to the location at **ES:DI** by **STOSW**, and the character code proper is stored in **AL**. If you increment the value in **AL**, you change the displayed character to the next one in line. For example, if **AL** contains the value for the character A (65), incrementing **AL** changes the A character to a B (66) character. On the next pass through the loop, **STOSW** will fire a B at the screen instead of an A.

Why not just increment **AX**? The **AH** half of **AX** contains the attribute byte, and we do *not* want to change that. By explicitly incrementing **AL** instead of **AX**, we ensure that **AH** will never be altered.

After the character code in **AL** is incremented, **BL** is decremented. Now, **BL** is not directly related to the string instructions. Nothing in any of the assumptions made by the string instructions involves **BL**. We're using **BL** for something else entirely here; **BL** is acting as a counter that governs the length of the lines of characters shown on the screen. **BL** was loaded earlier with the value represented by **LineLen**; here, 64. On each pass through the loop, the **DEC BL** instruction decrements the value of **BL** by 1. Then the **LOOPNZ** instruction gets its moment in the sun.

LOOPNZ is a little bit different from our friend **LOOP** that we examined earlier. It's just different enough to get you into trouble if you don't truly understand how it works. Both **LOOP** and **LOOPNZ** decrement the **CX** register by 1: **LOOP** watches the state of the **CX** register, and closes the loop until **CX** goes to 0; **LOOPNZ** watches *both* the state of the CX register *and* the state of the Zero flag (**ZF**). (**LOOP** ignores **ZF**.) **LOOPNZ** will only close the loop if **CX** <> 0 *and* ZF = 0. In other words, **LOOPNZ** closes the loop only if CX still has something left in it, *and* if the **ZF** is not set.

So what exactly is **LOOPNZ** watching for here? Remember that immediately prior to the **LOOPNZ** instruction, we're decrementing **BL** by 1 through a **DEC BL** instruction. The **DEC** instruction always affects **ZF**. If **DEC**'s operand goes to 0 as a result of the **DEC** instruction, **ZF** goes to 1 (is set). Otherwise, **ZF** stays at 0 (remains cleared). So in effect, **LOOPNZ** is watching the state of the **BL** register. Until **BL** is decremented to 0 (setting **ZF**) **LOOPNZ** closes the loop. After BL goes to 0, the inner loop is finished and execution falls through **LOOPNZ** to the next instruction.

What about **CX**? Well, **LOOPNZ** is watching **CX**—but so is **JCXZ**. **JCXZ** is actually the switch that governs when the whole loop—both inner and outer portions—have done their work and must stop. So while **LOOPNZ** does watch **CX**, somebody else is doing that task, and that somebody else will take action on **CX** before **LOOPNZ** can. **LOOPNZ**'s job is thus to decrement **CX**, but to watch **BL**. It governs the inner of the two loops.

Closing the Outer Loop

But does that mean **JCXZ** closes the outer loop? No. **JCXZ** tells us when *both* loops are finished. Closing the outer loop is done a little differently from closing the inner loop. Take another look at the two nested loops:

```
DoLine:   MOV     BL,LineLen    ; Each line will consist of 64 characters
DoChar:   STOSW                 ; Note that there's no REP prefix!
          JCXZ    AllDone       ; When the full set is printed, quit
          INC     AL            ; Bump the character value in AL up by 1
          DEC     BL            ; Decrement the line counter by 1
          LOOPNZ  DoChar        ; Go back & do another char until BL goes to 0
          ADD     DI,(ScrnWidth - LineLen)*2 ; Move DI to start of next line
          JMP     DoLine        ; Start display of the next line
```

The inner loop is considered complete when we've displayed one full line of the ASCII table to the screen. **BL** governs the length of a line, and when **BL** goes to 0 (which the **LOOPNZ** instruction detects) a line is finished. **LOOPNZ** then falls through to the **ADD** instruction that modifies **DI**.

We modify **DI** to jump from the end of a completed line to the start of the next line at the left margin. This means we have to "wrap" by some number of characters from the end of the ASCII table line to the end of the visible screen. The number of bytes this requires is noted by the assembly-time expression **(ScrnWidth-LineLen)*2**. This expression is basically the difference between the length of one ASCII table line and the width of the visible screen. Remember that each character position is actually represented by both a character and an attribute byte in the video refresh buffer, thus the ***2** portion of the expression. The result of the expression is the number of bytes we must move into the video refresh buffer to come to the start of the next line at the left screen margin.

But after that "wrap" is accomplished by modifying **DI**, the outer loop's work is done, and we close the loop. This time, we do it *unconditionally*, by way of a simple **JMP** instruction. The target of the **JMP** instruction is the **DoLine** label. No ifs, no arguments. At the top of the outer loop, (represented by the **DoLine** label) we load the length of a line back into the now-empty **BL** register, and drop back into the inner loop. The inner loop starts firing characters at the screen again, and will continue to do so until **JCXZ** detects that **CX** has gone to 0.

At that point, both the inner and outer loops are finished, and the full ASCII table has been displayed. SHOWCHAR's work is done, and it terminates.

SHOWCHAR.ASM Recap

Let's look back at what we've just been through. SHOWCHAR.ASM contains two nested loops. The inner loop shoots characters at the screen via **STOSW**. The outer loop shoots *lines* of characters at the screen, by repeating the inner loop some number of times (here, 4).

The inner loop is governed by the value in the **BL** register, which is initially set up to take the length of a line of characters (here, 64). The outer loop is not explicitly governed by the number of lines to be displayed. That is, you don't load the number 4 into a register and decrement it. Instead, the outer loop continues until the value in CX goes to 0, indicating that the whole job is done.

Both the inner and outer loops modify the registers that **STOSW** works with. The inner loop modifies **AL** after each character is fired at the screen. This makes it possible to display a different character each time **STOSW** fires. The outer loop modifies **DI** (the destination index register) each time a *line* of characters is complete. This allows us to break the destination string up into four separate, non continuous lines.

The Other String Instructions

STOSW is only one of the several string instructions in the 86-family instruction set. I would have liked to cover the others here, but space won't allow, in this edition, at least. In particular, the **MOVSW** instruction (Move String by Word) is useful, because it allows you to copy entire regions of memory from one place to another, screamingly fast, and with only a single instruction:

```
REP MOVSW
```

You probably understand enough about string instruction etiquette now to pick up **MOVSW** yourself from an assembly-language reference. All of the same register conventions apply, only with **MOVSW** you're working with both the source and destination strings at the same time.

I felt it important to discuss not only the string instructions, but their supporting cast of characters: **LOOP**, **LOOPNZ**, and **JCXZ**. Individual instructions are important, but not nearly as important as the full context within which they work. Now that you've seen how **STOSW** is used in non **REP** loops, you should be able to apply the same knowledge to the other string instructions as well.

Further Research: Building Your Assembly-Language Video Toolkit

Video is important—it's the fundamental way your programs communicate with their users. *Fast* video is essential, and BIOS-based video fails in that regard. The **Clear** and **Ruler** macros are good examples of just how fast video routines can be made with solid knowledge of assembly language.

You have the fundamentals of a really good and extremely fast toolkit of video routines for your assembly-language programs. To get some serious practice in assembly-language design and implementation, it's up to you to fill that toolkit out.

Here's a list of some of the new routines you should design and perfect for your video toolkit:

- **WriteFast**   A routine to move a string of characters from your data segment to the visible display buffer. You can do this easily using instructions we've discussed so far. A suggestion: use the **LOOP** instruction for an easy time of it, or research the **MOVSW** instruction for a trickier—but much faster—routine.

- **WriteInFast**   Like **WriteFast**, but moves the hardware cursor to the beginning of the following line after the write. If the write is to the bottom line on the screen, scroll the screen using **INT 10** BIOS calls, or for more speed, **MOVSW**.

- **WriteDown**   A routine to move a string of characters from the data segment to the visible display buffer, only *vertically*. This is useful for displaying boxes for menus and other screen forms, using the PC's line drawing characters. SHOWCHAR.ASM gives you a hint as to how to approach this one.

- **DrawBox**   Using **WriteFast** and **WriteDown**, create a routine that draws a box on the screen. Allow the programmer to specify whether it is made of single-line or double-line line-drawing characters.

- **GetString**   A delimited field-entry routine. Delineate a field, by highlighting the background or framing a portion of a line with vertical bar characters, and allow the user to move the cursor and enter characters within the bounds of the field. When the user presses Enter, return the entered characters to a buffer somewhere in the data segment. This is ambitious and might require seventy or eighty instructions, but it's likely to be a lot of fun.

Getting your video tools in order will allow you to move on to other, more involved subjects like file I/O and interface to the serial and parallel ports. "Real" assembly-language programs require all these things, and you should strive to create them as small, easily read and understood toolkit-style procedures and macros. Create them so that they call one another rather than duplicating function—assembly language is difficult enough without creating routines that do the same old things over and over again.

O Brave New World!

The Complications of Assembly-Language Programming in the '90s

I sometimes think back with some wonderment at the fact that I replaced the carburetor of my first car (a 1968 Chevelle I called "Shakespeare") in front of my mother's house on a freezing, windy day in January of 1974. All this without shelter of any kind, with marginal tools, and with no light but the light from the sky. I had never done it before, but it worked right the first time, and I saved a bundle of money that I didn't have anyway.

One reason that I call my 1984 Plymouth Voyager the "Magic Van" is that, having looked carefully under the hood, I can only conclude that the damned thing runs by magic. I don't think I could replace the carburetor on the Magic Van. If pressed, I'm not even sure I could open the hood and show you where it was. (I'm not, in fact, quite certain that cars even *have* carburetors anymore!)

This is one reason that I bought a restorable 1969 Chevelle this past winter. I'm not an auto mechanic and have no desire to be, but I enjoyed repairing Shakespeare and tuning him up, because it was simple and straightforward and required no greater skill than I cared to learn.

The point I want to make here is that the game of repairing cars has changed drastically since 1968. What was once a simple matter of aligning a timing mark on a pulley with a scratch on the engine block has now become a coordinated effort of getting a half dozen embedded microcontrollers to send signals to complicated electromechanical components at all the correct times. It would take me years to learn how to do all that, and I'd really rather be programming or building radios.

Similarly, the game of programming has begun to change drastically since the end of the 1980s. What I've described in this book so far has been necessary groundwork that everyone should learn in becoming an effective PC programmer. However, until fairly recently, the situation I described in this book has been pretty much the whole story. There was the 8088/8086 CPU and its instruction set, segmented memory, and DOS. If you learned only that (and learned it completely and well, of course), you could write significant software in assembly that was the equal of what you could buy on the open market.

Times change. As with my poor Chevelle, the programs I wrote in the middle 1980s now seem modest to the point of being quaint. Big things have been happening to the PC since 1989 or so, and those changes are by no means complete. They involve both hardware and software, and extend to the core of the assumptions we make when we place machine instructions together on the screen.

This is the final chapter in this book, and I did not want to leave you with a false impression of having "learned it all." There is more, *much* more to be done. The topics I'll mention here could be addressed in whole volumes. At best, I can give you your bearings. Hold on to your chair—but let's go.

11.1 A Short History of the CPU Wars

I wrote most of the first edition of this book in 1988, which (as I've suggested above) was a much simpler time. The 80286 microprocessor was the standard CPU, but almost nobody used its special features. It was (and is) used almost exclusively as a fast 8088. The 80386 was around (I jumped in quick and have had one since the end of 1986), but it was still considered a little exotic and was usually pretty expensive. Like the 286, the 386 sat on most people's desks as an even faster 8088.

All this changed in 1990. The most signficant event of that year was the appearance of a second source for Intel's 80386 CPU chip. American Micro Devices (AMD) announced a 386 clone, under a contract with Intel that allowed them to second source Intel CPUs. Intel claimed the contract didn't apply to the 386. They sued—and lost. AMD's 386 didn't hit the market in quantity until early 1991, but its effect on Intel was immediate: they started cutting prices on the 386 to make AMD's clone less profitable.

Free Fall

Suddenly, prices on 386 machines went into free fall. Intel's low-cost 386SX chip appeared in quantity (it was designed as a "286 killer" to take the profit out of AMD's 286 product line), accelerating the plunge in prices. CPU speeds, which had initially been stuck at 16 or 20 Mhz, suddenly started creeping up, first to 25 Mhz, and then to 33 Mhz. RAM prices, which had been high at the end of the 1980s, started to plunge as well. By the beginning of 1991, the standard business desktop machine was a 25 Mhz 386 with four megabytes of RAM—often more. The somewhat slower 386SX machines muscled into the "home and personal use" niche previously held by the 80286, and the 80286 came to be seen as a "kiddie" machine—probably because America's dads gave their 286s to Junior when their Taiwan 386SX boxes arrived.

What happened to the 8088s? I'm not sure. I suspect a lot of them are in closets, up there on the second shelf with a busted VCR atop them, and the ratty guest quilt thrown over the pile until Uncle Mack pays another visit.

It may be true that you still have one, and are still using one—but this is getting less likely all the time. I've found that most people who have the will to try programming have long become impatient with the 8088 and moved on to something faster—especially now that you can buy a complete 386SX machine at Price Club for less than $1000.

Meet the New Boss

In late 1990, Intel finally turned loose their long-in-coming 80486 CPU, which was even faster than a fast 80386—and the newcomer initiated yet another shuffle down in prices and status. The 486 is now "The Boss" on corporate desktops, and more and more programmers are picking them up as well. The 386 and the 286 have taken a bump down in status, and the 8088—well, when you're on the bottom, how much farther down can you go? I've seen genuine IBM PC systems on sale for as little as $200 on the used market. The no-name, 8088-based XT clones are considered by most used office equipment dealers to have little if any value at all.

How long will the 486 stay on top? That depends on how quickly Intel perfects and releases their 80586 CPU chip. The process will proceed as it has proceeded since the early 1980s—only with less and less time between cycles.

So where are we today, in the early 1990s? Published figures indicate that there are about 70,000,000 "countable" PC-type machines in the world. By countable they mean manufactured by firms who are well-known in the industry and release figures on sales. There is, however, another component to the world PC marketplace: the uncounted and uncountable clone boxes assembled here in the US and elsewhere by small, often family firms and sold in small shops and through the mail. Anybody who scopes out the import process can boat in a container lot of motherboards, clone cabinets, and other parts, and be selling completed and tested systems at the next neighborhood "computer swap meet."

How many of these are there? Maybe 25,000,000 worldwide. Maybe more. Nobody has any way to be sure. Those who talk about the battle between the PC and other machines like the Macintosh or Amiga are thinking most wishfully. The battle is over. The PC won by *at least* 80,000,000 votes.

11.2 Opening Up the Far Horizon

I've gone through this exercise to point up a fact few people ponder much: the 8088 is now the minority player in the PC world. Absolutely no more than a third of the world's PCs sport 8088 CPUs, and the proportion is probably closer to 20% or 25%. Again, because of the nature of the PC business, nobody has any way to be sure. (And the proportion of *active* 8088 PCs is even smaller—don't forget what's under the busted VCR on the closet shelf!)

DOS Extenders

Something else that came into its own in 1990 was the *DOS extender*. DOS extenders are extremely clever programs that place the "extra" features of the 286, 386, and 486 at the disposal of DOS programs. By necessity, DOS extenders exclude machines based on the 8086 and 8088.

What the more advanced processors bring to the table is more memory (*lots* more) and something called *protected mode*, which radically alters the programmer's view of the memory system. It won't be possible for me to explain in detail the mechanics of extended memory or protected mode in this book. The important thing to understand now is that with DOS extenders, the 286, 386, and 486 CPUs are no longer just faster 8088s. Once you understand what they have to offer, you can do some amazing things at an assembly-language level.

Most amazing is release from the tyranny of the 64K segment. A segment in 386 protected mode can be as large as 4 gigabytes—now *that's* a far horizon! This greatly simplifies dealing with really *big* data items, and also (because all of the code from a substantial program can exist in single moose of a code segment) simplifies program design and structure.

In short, when a DOS extender is in control of the machine, an application program can be *much* larger than the customary 640K of DOS memory, and can manipulate individual data items much larger than 64K.

Windows 3.0

1990's third and final blow to the past came in the form of Microsoft Windows 3.0 (Windows). Microsoft finally got both the big picture and the details right, and launched a graphics-oriented DOS shell that everyone seems to be able to agree on.

Windows is more than just a menuing replacement for the DOS prompt. Windows contains its own limited DOS extender technology, and programs written to make use of Windows' features can be much larger than ordinary DOS programs. Windows can also use the hardware multitasking features of the 386 to allow more than one program to run at once.

In a great many ways, Windows has changed the methodology of PC programming forever. Windows has an enormous influence over the shape of programs that run under it and use its services. This is in part because Windows defines literally hundreds of system calls to do all sorts of things, including graphics drawing, some file I/O, and nearly everything you would want to do to interface with the underlying machine.

This is good, because on the flipside, Windows *demands* that you use its services and not just go out to the hardware and grab whatever you want, whenever you want it. Nor is Windows just being snotty. Whenever you put two programs in a single machine (somewhat like two tomcats in a closet) there is the potential for some bloody fights. Two programs cannot write blithely to the same place in memory at the same time, and Windows, as reluctant referee, demands that both programs submit to its set of rules for peaceful global coexistance.

Event-Driven Programming

But probably the most significant effect Windows has on the nature of programming is that it lays out a whole new conceptual model for how a program should work. This new model is called *event-driven programming*, and while Windows certainly placed it most brightly in the spotlight, other programming systems (like Turbo Vision and Smalltalk) have been using it for some time.

Event-driven programming is a complicated subject, and I'm not going to be able to cover it in detail in this chapter. I would like to give you a flavor for it so that you can plan your future explorations as a programmer accordingly.

Event-driven programming is a consequence of our operating system getting smarter. DOS and Windows are gradually fusing into a new and more powerful operating system with *far* more capabilities than DOS's simple list of passive services that you call through a software interrupt. Most tellingly, Windows is now an active partner rather than a passive helper.

In the old world, your program was in the driver's seat, asking for assistance from DOS when in need. DOS remained passive but ready, not speaking until spoken to. In the old world, your program would go out and ask DOS, "Has the user pressed a key yet?" If a key had been pressed, DOS would meekly hand the key value up to your program and wait for further orders.

Windows, on the other hand, takes a far more active role. Although your program is still nominally calling the shots, Windows governs a lot more of the system, especially those parts of the system that interact with the user. Today, what Windows does is tap your program on the shoulder and say, "Hey boss, the user just pressed a key. What are you going to do about it?"

That press of a key or click of a mouse button is called an *event*, and the flow of control of the programs that run under Windows is dictated by the stream of events that the user sends from the keyboard and mouse to the program. The user has a lot more power under an event-driven system. No more is the user necessarily confined by a rigid menu structure within a single program. Now, with a single mouse click, the user can pre-emptively send the current program into the background and start up another one at will—and still return to the first program whenever he or she chooses.

In an event-driven program, the program and the *platform* (which is the new term for an operating system combined with a particular screen and keyboard management system like Windows) become nearly equal partners. The program calls on the platform for services, just as programs have been calling on DOS for years. But the platform also calls on the program to respond intelligently to things that happen within the platform, things like user-initiated events and critical errors. Program and platform thus speak back and forth continually, by way of a data-handling protocol called *message passing*.

It sounds complicated, and it is. On the other hand, event-driven programming makes things possible that simply can't be done using older programming models. With Windows acting as an intelligent proctor, multiple programs can operate at once within the same machine, some in the foreground, some in the background, freely passing data back and forth among them. Windows standardizes the protocol for this data transfer, so that the process (while tricky) becomes one that every program can understand if it was built along the Windows model.

Windows and Assembly Language

Can Windows programs be written in assembly language? Of course. Never forget: *assembly language is the language of the underlying machine*, and *any* program that can execute on the machine may be written in assembly language. The more important question is how much trouble that writing will be, and how much time it will take.

And that answer to that question is, a lot, and a long time. Higher-level languages like Pascal, Smalltalk, and C become a lot more compelling when you have to write complex code like that which speaks to platforms like Windows. An ambitious program like Word for Windows or Excel might take *years* to perfect in assembly language, even with a crack team of programmers sweating blood day and night over the project. And you just can't take years to write a program anymore. If you do, by the time your program is complete, the rules that you followed when you designed the program will no longer be valid when the program is ready to send to market. Your program will be obsolete before it's even finished.

That's the bad news. The good news is that *parts* of a Windows program can be written in assembly language, and the improved speed and compactness of the assembly portions may be able to give the program as a whole (which might have been written in Pascal or C) a serious competitive edge.

Windows includes support for a very handy feature called a *dynamic link library* (DLL), which is simply a collection of subroutines gathered into a file and loaded whenever they're needed. DLLs are vaguely similar to the overlays of times past, which were chunks of code left on disk because the whole program was too large to fit into memory at once. Just as the application would then load chunks of itself into a common area as it needed them (overwriting chunks in that area that it no longer needed), Windows loads a DLL into memory when the code inside the DLL is called. But unlike overlays, DLL code can be used by *any* Windows program that knows the standard Windows DLL calling conventions.

DLLs can be written in assembly language much more easily than entire Windows programs, and if you want to work under Windows but write assembly code, DLLs are a natural place to begin. Again, I can't explain how to write DLLs in this book (that's a fairly advanced topic), but I want to point out right now that it's certainly possible, and may be one way to make money programming in the Windows market. If you write a fast "engine" that accomplishes only one thing (say, data communications or database management) but accomplishes it *very* well, other Windows programmers may license the DLL containing your engine and use it to enhance their own Windows applications.

I do have some advice about Windows, however: learn to program it first from a higher-level language like Borland's Turbo Pascal for Windows. Learning assembly language is hard enough. Windows presents a lot of new concepts that are confusing enough without having to learn them at the very lowest level. Once you're fluent at creating Windows applications, use your assembly skills to replace time-critical portions of the code with optimized assembly-language DLLs.

11.3 Using the "New" Instructions in the 80286

This probably all sounds pretty grim from where you sit now, a novice assembly programmer with a desire to go further. Don't despair, though. It's not all bad news. Particularly, there are new registers and instructions in the 286, 386, and 486 that you can learn and use right now, without even going into protected mode. In the next several sections, I'll describe some of these new features and explain how you can use them.

Still 16 Bits

The 286 is a 16-bit processor. Inside of itself, it handles data in 16-bit chunks, and all of its registers are 16 bits wide, just like the 8086 and 8088. Furthermore, it can read and write data from and to the memory system 16 bits at a time. (To get 32-bit registers and 32-bit data transfers, you'll need to get a 386 or 486 machine.)

Now, people sometimes get confused about "how many bits" a processor "is." We call this value the *data width* of a CPU. Although I took up this issue briefly in Section 2.3, now might not be a bad time to expand on the question, because it will come up again with regard to the 386 and the 386SX. The answer is ... well, it depends on your point of view.

The 286 is a 16-bit processor, both inside and out. Inside the CPU, data can be processed 16 bits at a time. This is made possible by virtue of the 286's general-purpose registers, (**AX**, **BX**, **CX**, and **DX**) which are all 16 bits wide. You can access the general-purpose registers by 8-bit halves (that is, by using **CL** and **CH** rather than **CX**), but the *most* you can put in any one register is 16 bits.

There are people who define the data width of a CPU in terms of its general-purpose registers. In truth, however, this is a false indicator. What you *really* need to look for is the width of the data path that leads from inside the CPU out to the physical memory system.

The original CPU in the IBM PC was the 8088. Its general-purpose registers are all 16 bits wide. However, the 8088 can only move one byte at a time out to the memory system. The 8086 (which was never much of a player in the PC world) can move 16 bits out to the memory system in a single operation.

This is a lot more important, functionally. It's a little like building a big boat in your basement. It's nice to have a big boat, sure—but if you have to dismantle it into several pieces every time you want to take it out to sail, you'll eventually conclude that its bigness is more of a bother than an advantage. Sooner or later, you're going to get a canoe and enjoy it a lot more.

Moving memory into and out of the CPU is one of the most time-consuming things the CPU can do. If at all possible, you want to minimize the number of "fetches" that the CPU must perform. The best way to do this is to choose a CPU with the greatest available data width. The 8086 is inherently faster than the 8088 because it can move twice the data into or out of the CPU chip in one operation.

So why don't the CPU manufacturers just all make 128-bit CPUs (or wider!) and be done with it? Unfortunately, it's harder to manufacturer a "wide" CPU chip. Each of those bits has to go out to the outside world on a pin, (along with a great many other signals) and once you're into the 32-bit world, you're talking a *lot* of pins. The 8088 fits comfortably on a 40-pin IC (integrated circuit) package, but the 80386 has so many pins it looks like a bed of nails—a little ceramic square whose lower surface is nearly covered by gold pins. Inside the IC package, each pin has to be connected to the physical silicon chip by a minuscule gold wire, which is difficult enough to do once, let alone literally a hundred or more times.

Wide CPUs cost more to make than narrow ones, because they're physically more difficult to manufacture. There's also more complication on the computer motherboard to support wide CPU chips, which further adds to the cost of the computer.

386DX vs. 386SX

In the late '80s, Intel released its 80386SX chip. Internally, the 386SX was a genuine 386—it had all the registers and instructions supported by the original 386 CPU. However, the 386SX moved data into and out of itself only 16 bits at a time, just like the 8086 and 286. This lowered the cost of the 386SX, which made it cheaper to incorporate into an actual computer. (Intel then renamed the "big" 386 the 386DX to make sure no one got them mixed up.)

So while 386-specific software will run perfectly well on the 386SX, it runs more slowly, because the CPU can only move 16 bits at a time, rather than 32. The 386DX is a 32-bit CPU that moves 32 bits to or from memory in one crack.

At this writing, Intel has released very little information about its as-yet-unannounced 586 CPU. Will it be a 64-bit CPU? We don't know yet, but it's unlikely. People whose opinions I respect believe that 32 bits is the optimum data width for a practical CPU. I suspect they may be wrong—but we'll know soon enough.

Pushing and Popping All the Registers at Once

The 286 added a pair of new instructions to its repertoire: **PUSHA** and **POPA**. These instructions move *all* the general-purpose registers to or from the stack in one blistering operation. The registers affected are **AX, CX, DX, BX, SP, BP, SI**, and **DI**.

PUSHA pushes these registers on the stack. You should keep in mind that the registers go onto the stack in the order listed above.
DI is the last register pushed onto the stack, and therefore will be the first popped off the stack when you go back to pop what you pushed.

Something else to keep in mind: the value of **SP** that is pushed onto the stack is the value that **SP** held *before* the **PUSHA** instruction began pushing everything onto the stack. Don't forget this if you intend to pop registers from the stack piecemeal after pushing the whole crew with **PUSHA**. If you do something like this, you'll be in for a surprise:

```
POP DI
POP SI
POP BP
POP SP
```

Why? The last instruction pops the saved value of **SP** back into **SP**. That value, remember, was the value **SP** had *before* **PUSHA** started to work. Once you use an individual **POP** instruction to pop the **SP** value off the stack, *you'll no longer be able to pop AX, BX, CX, and DX*. The **SP** value pushed onto the stack points *above* the **AX** value pushed by **PUSHA**.

Most of the time, if you use **PUSHA** to push all the registers onto the stack, you'll use **POPA** to pop them off, again as one operation. **POPA** reverses what **PUSHA** did, and takes the values off the stack and plugs them into the registers in reverse order:

```
DI, SI, BP, SP, BX, DX, CX, AX
```

POPA does something interesting: it simply pops and discards the value pushed onto the stack for **SP**. This prevents the problem I mentioned above with popping registers piecemeal after using **PUSHA**. So why push **SP** at all? In the very peculiar way CPU chips operate internally, it was probably easier to push **SP** on the stack and ignore the popped value that might have gone into **SP** than to leave **SP** out of the process entirely. It's just that **PUSHA** and **POPA** "step through" the registers, and it's easier to step through them all than to try and skip one.

So what are **PUSHA** and **POPA** good for? You might use them to "frame" a subroutine that makes heavy use of registers. If you push all the registers on entry to a subroutine, you can use *all* of the registers from inside the subroutine, and not worry about trashing something that the caller will need after you return from the subroutine. By pushing all of the general-purpose registers, you needn't worry about forgetting to save one or another before using it within that subroutine. It's only one instruction, so it adds very little bulk to your code, and it's excellent bug insurance.

PUSHA and **POPA** are also useful when writing interrupt service routines.

More Versatile Shifts and Rotates

PUSHA and **POPA** are entirely new instructions, present in the 286 and newer CPUs, but not present at all in the 8086 and 8088. However, not everything that's new with the 286 is a whole new instruction. Some of the 286's enhancements are improvements to existing instructions.

For my money, the best of these are enhancements to the shift and rotate instructions. There are six such instructions: **SHL**, **SHR**, **ROL**, **ROR**, **RCL**, **RCR**. (The instructions **SAL** and **SAR** are just duplicate names for **SHL** and **SHR**.) I dealt with the shift instructions in Chapter 9, as they exist on the 8088 and 8086. If you'll recall from that chapter, you can express the number of bits by which to shift in one of two ways:

```
SHL AX,1   ; Shift left by 1
SHL AX,CL  ; Shift left by number in CL
```

(The **AX** register is just for example's sake; obviously, you can replace **AX** here with any legal operand. Furthermore, this dicussion applies to any of the six shift/rotate instructions.) To shift an operand by 1 bit, you specify the literal value 1. To shift by any greater number of bits greater than 1, you must first load a count value into the **CL** register, and then use **CL** as the second operand.

Well, this is how it is on the 8086/8088. Starting with the 286, you can drop the use of **CL** and use an immediate value (that is, a digit like 4 or 7) for shift values greater than 1. It becomes legal to use instructions that look like this:

```
SHL AX,4
SHL BX,7
```

It's more than just convenience. Having to load CL with a shift value not only takes time, but it eats up code space as well (the **MOV CL,4** or **MOV CL,7** instructions have to go somewhere).

Limiting the Shift Count

The 286 and newer CPUs put another, much subtler twist on the shift and rotate instructions: they limit the shift count to 31. This will take a little explaining; I recall having trouble with it when I first encountered the 86-family instruction set.

When you specify the shift count in **CL**, the assembler will permit you to use any value that will physically fit in **CL**. This means you can theoretically shift an operand by up to 255 bits, since the largest value you can load into 8-bit **CL** is 255, Aka 0FFH.

But think about that for a moment. What does it actually *mean* to shift an operand by 255 bits? The largest operand you can *ever* shift with *any x*86 CPU is only 32 bits wide. If you shift a 32-bit operand by 32 or more bits in either direction, you're left with nothing but 0s in the operand, because all significant bits will be shifted completely out of the operand into nothingness. So for the shift instructions, at least, shifting by more than 31 bits is meaningless.

It's a little trickier for the rotate instructions. The rotate instructions, if you recall, rotate bits off one end of the operand and then feed them back into the opposite end of the operand, to begin the trip again. Therefore, you could rotate a bit pattern in an operand by 255 and still have bits in the operand, because the bits never really leave the operand. They simply go out the front door and come back in immediately through the back door.

So rotating an operand by 255 could still be meaningful. The question is, is it uniquely meaningful? Or, is there some smaller rotation count that leaves the same pattern in the operand?

Figure 11.1 may help things become clear. Start with a single 1 bit in the very lowest position of a 32-bit wide operand. Figure 11.1 shows this operand as EAX, which is a 32-bit register found in the 386 and 486 CPUs. (I'll return to EAX later in this chapter. I only use it here because it's a convenient 32 bits wide.) Begin rotating to the left. Rotating the 1 bit 31 times will bring that single 1-bit to the opposite end of the operand, as shown in the figure. Rotate one more time. Shazam! Your 1-bit is back where it started, and the operand now contains a pattern identical to the pattern you had when you began.

In other words, given a 32-bit operand, rotating the operand by 32 bits is the same as not rotating it at all. Rotating it by 33 bits is the same as rotating it by 1 bit. Rotating it by 34 bits is the same as rotating it by 2 bits, and so on. So there's really no purpose to rotating an operand by more bits than the operand itself is wide. Doing so just wastes time inside the CPU. This is why, on the 286 and newer processors, the shift-by count is truncated to 5 bits: the largest value expressible in 5 bits is ... 32!

An Instruction You'll Probably Never Use

Not all of the new goodies introduced with the 286 are likely to be useful to you. One new instruction in particular has always puzzled me: **BOUND**.

The **BOUND** instruction was created to provide a way to test whether or not an array index was within two legal array bounds, and to do so quickly. The testing process helps prevent software from accidentally writing outside

Figure 11.1. Why shift/rotate counts are limited to 31

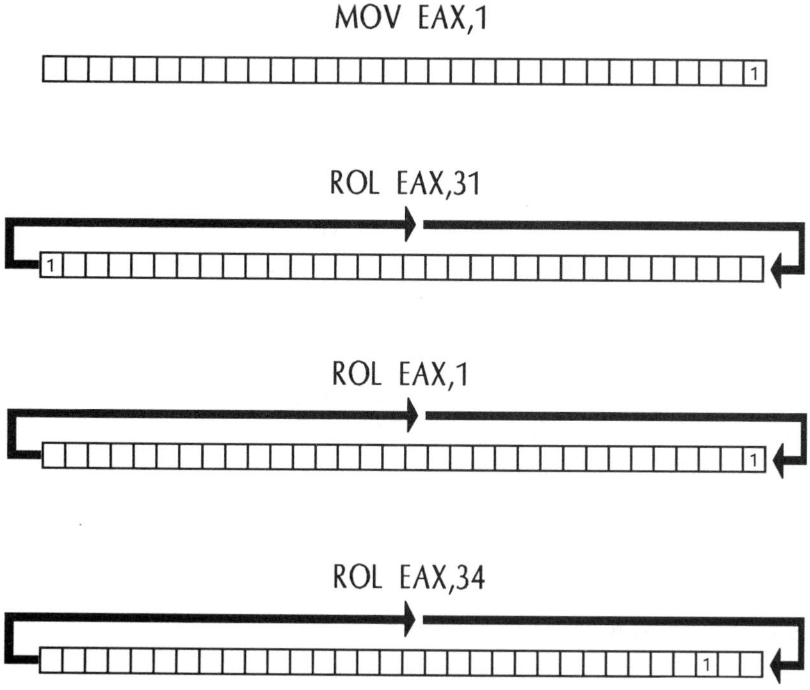

MOV EAX,1

ROL EAX,31

ROL EAX,1

ROL EAX,34

the bounds of the area currently being worked on, which is a major problem in advanced assembly-language work.

The **BOUND** instruction has a complicated set of operands that I won't try to explain here. I'll summarize its operation instead: **BOUND** takes the value given in its first operand and tests to see whether that operand is within the two values (the array bounds) pointed to by its second operand. If that first operand is within the bounds, everything is cool and nothing happens. (The flags are not affected.) However, if the first operand is discovered to be outside the bounds, the CPU triggers an interrupt 5. Interrupt 5 is hard baked into the silicon of the CPU. It's not something you can set, say, to interrupt 37 or 79 as needed. If an index fails **BOUND**'s test, it's interrupt 5, period.

This means that in order to use BOUND, you have to know how to create and install an interrupt service routine. That's OK; there's nothing hideously difficult about it once you've studied the ropes. *However....*

When IBM designed its original PC, somebody somewhere on the PC development team wasn't reading the fine print of Intel's documentation for the *x*86 family of CPUs. From the start, Intel has "reserved" a certain number of interrupts for the exclusive use of its CPUs. (Reserved means, "*This is ours! Don't use it for something else!*") Interrupt 5 was one of these.

Programmers don't like fine print. So one of IBM's guys needed an interrupt, and picked interrupt 5. He used it for the Print Screen mechanism in the original PC BIOS. When you press Shift+PrtSc on the PC keyboard, the BIOS issues an interrupt 5, and the interrupt service routine for interrupt 5 prints whatever is on the screen to your printer.

The Print Screen mechanism is in ROM, and exists in every PC and PC compatible ever built. This means that if you try to use BOUND without doing anything with the interrupt vector table, BOUND will trigger a Print Screen interrupt when a bound test fails. This, of course, is useless.

You can, in fact, jigger things in an interrupt service routine to "share" an interrupt between two or more interrupting entities. It's entirely possible for both BOUND and the Print Screen mechanism to coexist in using interrupt 5. It's plenty complicated, but it can be (and has been) done.

Still, there's one final fly in the tequila. For reasons unclear to me, the **BOUND** instruction, when it generates an interrupt 5, pushes *its own address* on the stack as the interrupt return address, rather than the address of the *next* instruction in line.

This is best explained just by describing what happens: **BOUND** triggers interrupt 5. The interrupt 5 service routine takes control and does what it must. Then the service routine pops the return address from the stack...and the **BOUND** instruction executes again! If neither the array index nor the bounds were changed by the interrupt service routine, **BOUND** will fail again, and trigger another interrupt 5, and so on without end.

Whew. And yes, by being *extraordinarily* clever, you can get around that as well, by reaching up onto the stack and goosing the return address a little. I've long since decided, however, that **BOUND** simply isn't worth the bother.

But I've told this story for a specific reason. Several times in my 10-year career as a PC programmer, I've seen my machine go into a peculiar sort of endless loop. The loop consists of repeated Print Screen operations, as though someone were repeatedly pressing Shift+PrtSc.

And someone was, of course: **BOUND**. I was accidentally executing a **BOUND** instruction, probably by trying to execute data as code, or by jumping into the middle of a multibyte instruction opcode. By rearranging things, I was always able to stop the problem from occurring, but it was *years* before I actually figured out who the culprit was.

Aren't bugs wonderful?

11.4 Moving to 32 Bits with the 386 and 486

The features that the 286 has over the 8088 are few and not outrageously useful. Mostly, the 286 had its day in the sun because (relative to an 8088) it was greased lightning. It obtains much of that relative speed by being a true 16-bit CPU, but more than that, most of its instructions also ran more quickly than the same instructions on the 8088. For example, the **MOV AX,1** instruction (which moves an immediate value into a register) takes four machine (clock) cycles to execute on the 8088, but only two clock cycles on the 286. Many of the other instructions are correspondingly faster as well.

This process of instruction speedup has continued with the advent of the 386 and 486 CPUs. The **MOV AX,1** instruction takes only *one clock cycle* to execute on the 486! Couple that with a 486 clock speed that *starts* at 33 Mhz and is now more and more commonly 50 Mhz, and we're talking some serious speed here. There was also another quantum leap in processor data width, from 16 bits to 32 bits. Both the 386 and 486 process data internally in 32-bit chunks, and also move data into and out of the CPU 32 bits at a time.

The 386SX chip, as I mentioned earlier, was sort of a throwback: it is only a 16-bit CPU in terms of moving data into and out of the CPU. (It does, however, process data internally 32 bits at a time.) It's cheaper, but the 16-bit data path also slows it down considerably over its big brothers, the 386 and 486.

The Extended General-Purpose Registers

So we come at last to the question of how the 386 and 486 (including the 386SX) process data internally in 32-bit chunks. The registers we've discussed in this book so far are only 16 bits wide. We need some new registers—or at least some wider ones.

And we've got both.

First of all, our seven familiar general-purpose registers and the stack pointer have been doubled in size, from 16 bits to 32 bits. The older 16-bit registers are still there; in fact, they're the same registers. But just as **AX**, **BX**, **CX**, and **DX** each contain a pair of 8-bit registers; so now do **EAX**, **EBX**, **ECX**, and **EDX** each contain a pair of 16-bit registers. You can still use the names **AX**, **BX**, **CX**, or **DX**, but when you do, you will only be addressing the lower 16 bits of the larger registers.

Figure 11.2 may make this a little clearer. In the 386 and 486, there are four general-purpose registers. Each is 32 bits wide. When you specify **EAX**, you're specifying the full 32-bit extended form of our familiar **AX** register. **EAX** *contains* **AX**, just as **AX** contains both **AL** and **AH**. Don't make the mistake (as some do) of thinking that there is a separate set of 16-bit registers inside the 386, in addition to the 32-bit registers. It's like a box within a box within a box, and with the 386/486 we've added an outer layer of box.

One unfortunate thing about the extended registers is that you can't separately manipulate their *high* 16 bits. In other words, you can separately access the low 16 bits of **EAX** by working with **AX**, and the high 16 bits of **EAX** will not be disturbed. You cannot, however, specify only the high 16 bits of EAX or

Figure 11.2. The 386/486 general purpose registers

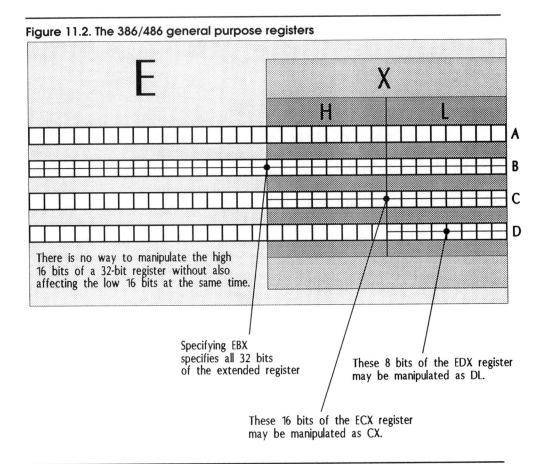

There is no way to manipulate the high 16 bits of a 32-bit register without also affecting the low 16 bits at the same time.

Specifying EBX specifies all 32 bits of the extended register

These 8 bits of the EDX register may be manipulated as DL.

These 16 bits of the ECX register may be manipulated as CX.

the other extended registers. There's simply no way to name those high 16 bits as a distinct group.

Similarly, there are extensions to **SI**, **DI**, **BP**, and **SP**. (See Figure 11.3.) Just as with the general-purpose registers, the extended index and pointer registers contain their familiar 16-bit counterparts as their low 16 bits. **ESI** contains **SI**, **EDI** contains **DI**, and so on. Again, there is no way to separately specify the high 16 bits of the extended index and pointer registers.

More Segment Registers

The whole issue of memory segments changes drastically when you move from real mode to protected mode, so drastically that I don't have much hope of explaining it usefully in this book. This seems all the more surprising, since our

Figure 11.3. The 386/486 extended pointer and index registers

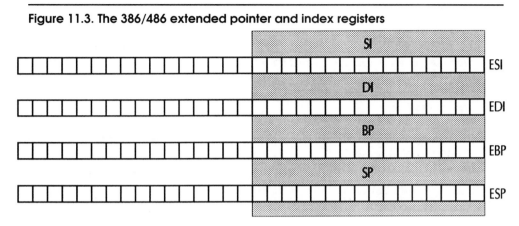

The lower 16 bits of these extended registers are the familiar 16-bit index and pointer registers from the 16-bit processors.

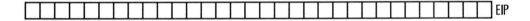

The 32-bit extended instruction pointer (EIP) allows a single code segment to be as large as 4 gigabytes.

familiar segment registers don't change at all, physically, in the move from the 286 to the 386. They are still 16 bits wide, and (in real mode at least) they still work exactly the same way.

Not only that, but there are two more of them.

With the 386 comes the **FS** and **GS** registers, so named (I suspect) because they follow the **ES** register. And, like the **ES** register, they are extra segment registers, allowing you to set up and retain more segments at a single time.

I hesitate (a little) at suggesting that an otherwise unused segment register can sometimes be a lifesaver when you need "just one more place" to put a value to make a fast assembly-language algorithm happen. In real mode you can do anything you want with the segment registers, including use them as general-purpose registers. (Keep in mind that the segment registers can't do everything that the general-purpose registers can do.) The problems begin when you try to run such code in protected mode, where the CPU is *very* fussy about what you do with segment registers. In protected mode, segment registers hold segment values and participate in memory addressing, and that's it. Do other things with them and you're asking for numerous kinds of trouble.

Using the new segment registers requires that you use their segment over-ride prefixes, as there are no "assumed" uses of **FS** and **GS** in the 386/486 instruction set. This isn't difficult. If you're still fuzzy on the notion of segment override prefixes, glance back at Section 6.2. It's simply a matter of putting **FS:** or **GS:** in front of a memory addressing operation:

```
MOV FS:[SI],AX
```

This instruction moves the 16-bit word at **FS:SI** into **AX**. The **GS:** prefix works exactly the same way.

In real mode, the **FS** and **GS** segment registers have no hidden agendas. They are truly extra segment registers, and you have to specify their use every time you use them.

Not Just in Protected Mode!

A common misconception is that the new segment registers and the 32-bit features of the 386 and 486 are available only in protected mode. Not so! There are in fact a number of instructions and special registers that can only be accessed from protected mode, but the 32-bit extended registers are not among them. **EAX**, **EBX**, **ECX**, **EDX**, **ESI**, **EDI**, and **EBP** are fully usable from real mode. **ESP** is usable, but only the lower 16 bits are meaningful unless you're in protected mode using segments larger than 64K.

Let Your Assembler Know What You Want

You should keep in mind, however, that you must tell your assembler that you want to use the extended registers and advanced CPU instructions. Otherwise, if you try to use the register name **EAX**, or the **PUSHA** instruction, the assembler will tell you it doesn't know what you're talking about.

This is actually a safety feature. Most people choose to program for the least common demoninator of the entire 80x86 series, which is the fundamental 8086/8088 instruction set that I've been discussing throughout the earlier portions of this book. Both MASM and TASM default to that common demoninator instruction and register set, and must be specifically told that you're "graduating" to the additional features of the 286/386/486.

There are commands you can give to MASM and TASM to tell them what set of advanced assembler features you wish to use. By including these commands at the top of your assembly-language source-code files, you can then use the advanced features throughout the remainder of those files. These commands are summarized in Tables 11.1 and 11.2.

One thing to remember when using these assembler commands is that older versions of both assemblers may have been released before the 486 was in general use, and thus your version of MASM or TASM may be too old to

Table 11.1. Using MASM and TASM in MASM mode

Command	Use
286	Allows assembly of all real mode 286 instructions
386	Allows assembly of all real mode 286 and 386 instructions, and use of 32-bit register names
486	Allows assembly of all real mode 286, 386, and 486 instructions, and use of 32-bit register names

Table 11.2. Using TASM in Ideal mode

Command	Use
P286N	Allows assembly of all real mode 286 instructions
P386N	Allows assembly of all real mode 286 and 386 instructions, and use of 32-bit register names
P486N	Allows assembly of all real mode 286, 386, and 486 instructions, and use of 32-bit register names

understand the 486-specific commands. TASM 2.0, for example, understands the 386 but not the 486.

The versions of both assemblers current in early 1992 provide full support for the 486-specific CPU features.

11.5 Additional 386/486 Instructions

You may be disappointed if you look for a host of marvelous new instructions in the 386 and 486 instruction set. There are new instructions there, but the most marvelous of them mostly serve the needs of operating system programming in protected mode.

Some instructions that exist in the earlier processors have been extended, with additional addressing or counting operands and modes. And there are (a few) valuable new instructions that I'll present in this section.

But the major change in the 386 and especially the 486 is that Intel has made many of the most-used instructions *faster.* Instruction speeds are measured by the number of ticks of the master system clock that it takes to execute a given instruction. Intel has done extensive studies of the "opcode mix" in typical applications, and has rearranged the internal structure of the newer CPUs to enable the most-used instructions to execute more quickly.

On some instructions, the process has reached its ultimate conclusion with the 486: the instructions execute in only one clock cycle. Most **MOV** instruction variations execute in one cycle on the 486, as do **TEST**, **SUB**, **NOT**, **INC**, **ADD**, **CMP**, and many other often-used instructions.

There's been some backsliding however: some instructions, including **DIV**, **ENTER**, **LEAVE** (none of which we've discussed in this book), and some others have actually gotten *slower* on the 486 (they take more machine cycles to execute than they did on the 386). And there are a significant number of instructions that are slower on the 386 than on the 286, including those marvelous string instructions we discussed in Chapter 10.

Why would Intel turn progress back and make an instruction *slower* than it once was? It's a question of chip "real estate" and a question of priorities. When Intel designs a new CPU, it decides about how many individual transistors it can successfully create on the *die* (the fresh, unaltered silicon chip), and then allocates them to individual instructions and other functions in order of importance.

In general, it takes more transistors to make an instruction execute quickly than it does to make an instruction execute slowly. Intel wants to make its CPUs the fastest on the market, and CPU speed is measured by executing a "mix" of instructions—that is, by executing real programs! Some instructions appear in the mix more frequently than others, so for *overall* CPU speed, it pays to throw transistors at the most frequently used instructions. Ideally, *all* the instructions would be made to execute in one cycle, but there aren't enough transistors on the finished chip to do that. So Intel made some hard decisions, and in some cases took some transistors from a seldom-used instruction like **ENTER** and gave them to a more-frequently used instruction like **ADD**.

This effect was most pronounced in the move from the 286 to the 386. The 486 gave back some of the speed to the seldom-used instructions, and there's every reason to expect that the process will continue until all instructions execute in a single clock cycle.

This, by the way, is the major reason that a 33 Mhz 486 seems faster than a 33 Mhz 386 ... it is! The individual instructions on the 486 execute more quickly than those of the 386, so even at identical clock rates, the 486 has a significant performance edge.

Obviously, get a 486 if you can.

Pushing and Popping All 32-Bit Registers

I presented the **PUSHA** and **POPA** instructions in the last section, and there are 32-bit equivalents available on the 386 and 486. **PUSHAD** pushes all of the 32-bit registers onto the stack, in this order:

```
EAX, ECX, EDX, EBX, ESP, EBP, ESI, EDI
```

Note that the value pushed for **ESP** is the value the stack pointer had *before* the first register was pushed onto the stack. The CPU makes a private copy of **ESP** before beginning execution of the instruction, and it is this private copy that is pushed onto the stack.

Similarly, **POPAD** pops the registers from the stack in reverse order:

```
EDI, ESI, EBP, ESP, EBX, EDX, ECX, EAX
```

The **ESP** value popped from the stack is *not* loaded into **ESP**; it's simply discarded.

As I explained with **PUSHA** and **POPA**, these instructions should be used as a pair; that is, what you push with **PUSHAD** you should pop with **POPAD**.

Looking for 0 Bits with BT

Back in Section 9.3 I introduced the **TEST** instruction, which allows you to determine if any given bit in a byte or word is set to 1. As I explained, **TEST** has its limits: it's not cut out for determining when a bit is set to 0.

The 386 and 486 have an instruction that allows you to test for either 0 bits or 1 bits. The Bit Test (**BT**) instruction performs a very simple task: it copies the specified bit into the Carry flag CF. In other words, if the selected bit is a 1 bit, **CF** is set. If the selected bit is a 0 bit, **CF** is cleared. You can then use any of the conditional jump instructions that examine and act on the state of **CF**.

BT is easy to use. It takes two operands: the first one is the value containing the bit in question; the second operand is the ordinal number of the bit you want to test, starting from 0. The syntax is shown below:

```
BT <value containing bit>,<bit number>
```

Once you execute a **BT** instruction, you should immediately test the value in **CF** and branch based on its value. Here's an example:

```
BT  AX,4  ; Test bit 4 of AX
JNC Quit  ; We're all done if bit 4 = 0
```

Note that we're branching if **CF** is *not* set; that's what **JNC** (Jump if Not Carry) does.

Use TEST to Test for 1-Bits!

One problem. As thankfully understandable as **BT** is, you must keep in mind that **TEST** is considerably faster than **BT**. If you're trying to write code that absolutely has to be fast, be aware that BT can be less than half as fast as **TEST**—if all you need to execute to test a bit is **TEST**.

Remember, however, that **TEST** requires additional code to look for 0 bits, so if you're looking for a 0 bit, **BT** is faster. **TEST**, furthermore, is available on *all* 80x86 CPUs, so you needn't be concerned with safe execution.

It's one of those little tradeoffs you'll be faced with time and again as you hone your skills in assembly.

11.6 Detecting Which CPU Your Code Is Running On

If you think about the notion of using the instructions present in the 286 or 386 but not the 8086/8088, the question very quickly arises: what happens when you try to execute a 386 instruction on an 8088 or a 286?

Simple answer: *nothing good.* On the 8088 and 8086, the response of the CPU to an undefined opcode is truly undefined, in that the instruction fetching mechanism simply hands the bogus opcode to the CPU's microcode circuitry, and then whatever happens, happens. Sometimes nothing, sometimes something defined but unexpected (like finding that a register is "magically" incremented or zeroed out), and sometimes the CPU will just hang. The worst of it is that you can never count on "undocumented instructions" to work consistently from one build of the CPU chip to another, so the best advice is, *don't do it!*

Things are both better and worse on the 286, 386, and 486. On these more advanced processors, the instruction fetching mechanism actually checks each fetched instruction against a valid opcode matrix to determine if the instruction is defined or not. If the CPU fetches an undefined opcode, it will generate an interrupt 6, which can be used to signal the error.

That's the good news—a *consistent* reaction to a bogus opcode. The bad news is that there's no standard for handing an interrupt 6. The CPU only knows how to generate the interrupt; once execution jets off to the address stored in the interrupt vector table for interrupt 6, things are out of the CPU's hands. It's the responsibility of the BIOS or of DOS to install handlers for "system" interrupts like interrupt 6.

Some do. Some (especially 8088-based, XT-class machines) don't. And of those that do, the action taken on an interrupt 6 is anything but consistent. Some machines ignore the interrupt and simply return control without taking action. On machines like that, nothing at all happens when an undefined opcode is fetched. Other machines may halt execution with a cryptic error message on the screen. Still other machines may just go nuts.

Again, *don't do it.* You'll generate bugs aplenty just arranging the multitude of perfectly legal opcodes in your programs. Don't complicate matters by forcing the target machine to digest and react to instructions it doesn't have.

Practicing Safe Execution

So, if you're going to use instructions that are defined on some PCs and not on others, you are going to have to build some machinery into your programs to detect what sort of CPU the programs are running on, and abort execution if an older machine is detected that can't run the software.

This sounds harder than it actually is. There are some well-defined differences among the various CPUs that do not involve defined or undefined instructions, and a very clever program can look for those differences and safely determine what sort of CPU is executing it. If your program requires a 386 and determines that it isn't running on one, it can abort back to DOS before anything untoward happens.

I've written such a routine, and it's given at the end of this section, in the listing WHATAMI.ASM. Read it through, and then we'll go through it, step by step. It's certainly the subtlest piece of code I've presented in this book, and if you can understand how it works, you're well on your way to being a competent journeyman assembly programmer.

The CPU Identifier from a Height

WHATAMI.ASM is a fully executable program that is a shell around the CPU detector procedure, **CPUID**. Nothing unusual has to be done to assemble and link it; create the executable file the same way you've been doing for all the listings in this book. The only caution, again, is to be sure the version of the assembler you're using is new enough to understand 386 instructions!

CPUID returns a value in **AL** that indicates what CPU is currently executing the program. A 0 value indicates the presence of either an 8086 or an 8088. (Because those two chips execute the same identical instruction set, there's very little point in looking further to see which one it actually is.) A 1 value indicates the presence of an 80286, a 2 value indicates any of the 80386 family, including the 386SX and 386DX, and a 3 value indicates the presence of a 486SX or 486DX.

Looking for an 8086 or 8088

We start at the bottom of the CPU totem pole, and assume that we have an 8088 or 8086. The first test is to eliminate the possibility of these CPUs. The test turns on a quirk of the 8086/8088 CPUs: the top four bits of the Flags register are forever stuck in the set state; that is, as 1 bits. Even if you try to force the Flags register to 16 0 bits, the top 4 bits will not change, and if you read back the Flags register after trying to set all 16 bits to 0, you'll find that the top 4 bits always come back as 1s.

That's how it is on the 8086 and 8088. However, things are different on the newer CPUs. More of the bits in the Flags register are meaningful, and therefore the top 4 bits are not left stuck at 1. So if you push 16 0 bits onto the stack and then read them back, any value *other* than 0F000H eliminates the 8086 and 8088 from the running.

There's no instruction that allows you to directly store a value into the Flags register. The only instruction that can affect the entire Flags register at once is **POPF**, which pops the word from the top of the stack into the Flags register.

In the test, we clear **DX** to 0, push **DX** onto the stack, and then pop the two 0 bytes from the top of the stack into the Flags register with **POPF**. That writes our test value to the Flags register; to read it back we simply use **PUSHF** to push the Flags register back onto the stack, and then pop the top of the stack into **AX** for inspection.

The test consists of a comparison of the value in **AX** (which used to be in the Flags register) against the literal value 0F000H:

```
CMP AX,0F000H
JE  Done
```

If the value in **AX** is in fact 0F000H, we're done—because we found that the top four bits of the flags register are stuck at 1, indicating an 8086 or 8088.

At the **Done** label, we copy the value in **DX** to **AX** and return to the caller. The value in **DX** is going to indicate which CPU we've found. Each time we eliminate the next higher CPU, we increment **DX** to the next higher code. **DX** was originally forced to 0, so we pass 0 back to the caller—indicating an 8086 or 8088.

Looking for a 286

Eliminating the 286 is similarly easy. The same general method is used, because the 286 has a quirk that is inside out from the 8088s: the top 4 bits of the stack are always forced to *0 bits* on the 286, *when the 286 is running in real mode.* If the 286 is running in protected mode, bits 12 through 14 of the Flags register are meaningful and can change, but in real mode (which is the only mode our code will be using in this book) bits 12 through 15 will always be 0. (Bit 15 is always 0 on the 286, regardless of real or protected mode.) So what we do is try to set the Flags register to 0F000H—and if the flags come back as something *other* than 0F000H, we can eliminate the 286 and know that we have at least a 386.

Before we do anything else, we increment **DX** to 1, since we now know that we have at least a 286 on the line. And because we know we have at least a 286 on the line, we can use an instruction introduced with the 286: **PUSH <immed>**, which can push an immediate value (like 0F000H) onto the stack. This makes it unnecessary to first load 0F000H into a register (as we did for the 8088 test) and then push the register's value onto the stack. On the 286 and newer processors, you can push a literal value directly.

Using the same general method we used in testing for the 8088, we push 0F000H onto the stack, pop it into the Flags register, push the Flags register back into the stack, and pop the value from the Flags register off the stack into **AX**. Then we check to see if **AX** still contains the 0F000H value we forced into the Flags register. If the value comes back as 0, we know we have a 286, so we exit to **Done** with 1 in **DX**.

Remember that the 286 forces the top 4 bits of the Flags register to 0. If something other than 0 comes back in those top 4 bits, we know we have at least a 386 and possibly a 486. So we increment **DX** again, to 2 (2 is the code for the 386).

Is It a 386 or a 486?

We now know we have either a 386 or a 486. Telling them apart isn't quite as easy as telling them from their less-powerful brothers, but once again, it's a matter of flags. The 486 has a flag that the 386 doesn't have, and by testing for this flag we can see whether we have a 486 on the line. If we don't, we know we have a 386 by elimination.

You'll notice in reading the 486 test that we're suddenly working with the extended registers introduced with the 386: **EAX**, **ESP**, and so on. Keep in mind that these are all 32 bits in size.

The 486 extended Flags register (**EFLAGS**) has a flagcalled the *alignment check* (**AC**) Flag. The **AC** Flag is used to detect *alignment faults*; that is, attempts to access memory from an address that is *not* evenly divisible by 4. Why 4? The 386 and 486 access memory 32 bits (4 bytes) at a time, every time they access memory at all. Because of the way that the CPU sends memory address information out on the memory address pins, memory accesses happen most quickly when the requested addresses are *aligned* on a *double word boundary*, that is, when the requested address is divisible by 4.

There are some truly arcane reasons why it is vitally important that memory accesses be aligned on a double word boundary sometimes, but you're unlikely to encounter them in normal work. (Mostly they come up when more than one processor must share the same address space, which is *mighty* unlikely on a PC-compatible machine!) The **AC** flag was added to the 486 to allow enforcement of double word alignment. If you set up some of the 486's special control registers just so, a nonaligned memory access can generate an error interrupt, and the **AC** flag is part of this enforcement machinery.

For our purposes, however, it's a handy feature that doesn't exist on the 386—so if we can spot the Alignment check flag in **EFLAGS**, we know we have a 486.

The first step in the test is to save the value in **ESP** into a register, because we're going to have to ensure that the stack pointer is double word aligned—which might change **ESP**'s value. Having the old value in a register will allow us to put things back the way they were before we started testing.

Aligning an Address to a Double Word Boundary

With **ESP's** original value safely tucked away, we force the stack pointer to be double word aligned. This is as simple as rounding the value of the stack pointer down to the next lowest memory address on a double word boundary. The way we do this may puzzle you:

```
AND ESP,NOT 3
```

What does **NOT 3** mean? **NOT** is an assembler operator that inverts all the bits of its operand, which in this case is 3. Because **ESP** is a 32-bit register, the **NOT 3** operand is also 32 bits in size. The full 32-bit expression of 3 (including all the leading zeroes) is 00000003H. If you invert the bits in every digit in that number (including those leading zeroes) you get FFFFFFFCH.

That's a big, ugly hex number, and all those Fs really aren't the point. The whole point lies in the lowest two bits of the last hex digit C, which are 0. When you **AND** two values bit by bit, any 0 bits in either operand will force those bits in the result to 0.

What we want to do is force the two lowest-order bits in **ESP** to 0. If we do that, regardless of what address was previously in **ESP**, the altered address will be aligned on a double word boundary. If this isn't immediately clear, think of it this way: every double word aligned address is four bytes greater than the one before it. Not one byte, or two bytes, or three bytes, but four bytes greater. You're essentially counting bytes by fours (0,4,8,12,16, etc.), which means that the bits that carry the "in between" values (5, 6, or 7, for example) must be zeroed out, or you're not really counting by fours at all.

AND ESP,NOT 3 simply forces the low two bits of ESP to 0, ensuring that **ESP** is aligned on a double word boundary. We need to do that because if ESP is *not* double word aligned and we attempt to use it, we may inadvertently set **AC** to 1, which would muddy the waters of the test we're trying to do.

The Last Test

And the test is this: we push **EFLAGS** onto the stack, and then save a copy of **EFLAGS** in both **EAX** and **EBX** by popping the flags value off the stack into **EAX** and then copying **EAX** into **EBX**. (Note that this use of the ESP could generate a flip in the **AC** flag if ESP were not double word aligned.) Then, we take the copy of **EFLAGS** in **EAX**, and try to flip the state of the **AC** flag. It's done this way:

```
XOR EAX,00040000H
```

Remember: XORing a bit against 0 leaves the bit in its current state. XORing a bit against 1 reverses the state of that bit. Only one bit in 00040000H is 1; all the others are 0. That single 1 bit is at the same ordinal position as the **AC** bit in the **EFLAGS** register. XORing 00040000H against **EFLAGS** will toggle the state of the **AC** bit.

We can't, of course, **XOR** against **EFLAGS** directly. So we do basically what we did in the previous two tests: manipulate a value in a register, and then push the value to the stack and pop it back into **EFLAGS**. We **XOR** a copy of **EFLAGS** against 00040000H to toggle the bit at position 18, then push the altered value from **EAX** onto the stack and pop it back into **EFLAGS**.

Having forced an altered value into **EFLAGS**, we then immediately copy it back for a look. Remember: the 386 doesn't define the **AC** bit, and on the 386 the bit at position 18 is stuck at 0. We attempted to flip the bit at position 18 in **EFLAGS**. On the 486 it will flip; on the 386 it's stuck. If we read back **EFLAGS** and find that bit 18 has changed, we have a 486. If the bit at position 18 has *not* changed, we have a 386.

If we find a 486, we increment **DX** to 3 and return. Otherwise, we simply return, leaving **DX** at 2, which is the code for the 386.

Many thanks to Robert Hummel of *PC Magazine* for explaining this algorithm to me.

The WHATAMI.ASM Utility

That's all there is to **CPUID**. WHATAMI.ASM does nothing more than call **CPUID** to determine the running CPU, and then use **CPUID**'s return code to index into a table of messages. The selected message indicates to the user (through DOS function 40H) which CPU is in the machine.

Only a little review on selecting items in a table: each text message in **MsgTbl** is exactly 16 bytes long. The first message is for the 8088, and to select it you need an offset into the table of 0. The second message, for the 286, is at an offset of 16 into the table—1 × 16, and the 286 ID code is 1. The third message, for the 386, is at an offset of 32 into the table—2 × 16, and the 386 ID code is 2.

Getting the idea?

We're basically multiplying the CPU ID code by 16 to create an offset to the correct message in the table. Multiplying by 16—a power of 2—is easy: you just shift left by four bits. That done, you add the offset to the starting address of the table, and pass the resulting address for DOS so that DOS can display the message with its function 40H.

As I've said before, it's a *very* good rule of thumb: *always* make items in a table come out to a length that's an even power of 2—2, 4, 8, 16, 32, or 64 bytes comprise a good assortment of lengths. Even if you have to pad the ends of data items with 0s or space characters, you will save a lot of fooling around if you can generate an offset by simple power-of-2 multiplies using **SHL**.

Passing a Value Back to ERRORLEVEL

You can use WHATAMI.EXE from a batch file, and it will pass the CPU ID code back to DOS for use in the batch ERRORLEVEL feature, allowing your batch files to test the value returned by WHATAMI and take action accordingly. All you have to do to pass a value back in ERRORLEVEL is to leave the value in **AL** when your program calls DOS service 4CH to return control to DOS. DOS takes care of the rest.

```
;----------------------------------------------------------------
;                         WHATAMI.ASM
;
; Program to demonstrate runtime detection of the installed CPU
;
; Many thanks to Nicholas Wilt for providing me the algorithm!
;
;                                        by Jeff Duntemann
;                                        MASM/TASM
;                                        Last update 2/9/92
;----------------------------------------------------------------


;----------------------------|
;    BEGIN STACK SEGMENT      |
;----------------------------|
MYSTACK     SEGMENT STACK           ; STACK word ensures loading of SS by DOS

            DB      64 DUP ('STACK!!!') ; This reserves 512 bytes for the
stack

MYSTACK     ENDS
;----------------------------|
;    END STACK SEGMENT        |
;----------------------------|


;----------------------------|
;    BEGIN DATA SEGMENT       |
;----------------------------|
MyData      SEGMENT

MsgTbl      DB        "You have an 88. "
            DB        "You have a 286. "
            DB        "You have a 386. "
            DB        "You have a 486. "

MyData      ENDS
;----------------------------|
;    END DATA SEGMENT         |
;----------------------------|


;----------------------------|
;    BEGIN CODE SEGMENT       |
;----------------------------|
```

```
MyProg      SEGMENT

            assume CS:MyProg,DS:MyData


; CPUID -- determines the installed CPU
;
;           Returns a value in AL that has the following meaning:
;           0 - 8086 or 8088
;           1 - 80286
;           2 - 80386, DX or SX
;           3 - 80486

CPUID       PROC
.386
            ; Assume we have an 8086/8088 for now...
            xor  DX,DX        ; Clear DX to 0
            push DX           ; Push 16 bits of 0's on the stack
            popf              ; Pop 16 bits of 0's off stack & into flags
            pushf             ; Push state of flags back onto stack..
            pop  AX           ; ..so that we can pop them off & look at them
            cmp  AX,0F000H    ; Test the high 4 bits of what was in flags
            je   Done         ; If top 4 bits are set, it's an 8086/8088
            inc  DX           ; Otherwise, we have at least a 286, so we can
                              ;   increment the ID code & keep on testing..
            push 0F000H       ; Push the value 0F000H on the stack
            popf              ; Pop 0F000H off stack into the flags
            pushf             ; Push state of flags back onto stack..
            pop  AX           ; ..so that we can pop them off & look at them
            and  AX,0F000H    ; Check to see if they still contain 0F000H
            jz   Done         ; This time, if the flags are *not* 0F000H,
                              ;   we have a 286
            inc  DX           ; Otherwise, we have at least a 386, so we can
                              ;   increment the ID code & keep on testing..

; Testing for the 486 -- algorithm from Hummel
            mov  ECX,ESP      ; Save the stack pointer in EDX
            and  ESP,NOT 3    ; Force stack pointer to align on a DWORD
            pushfd            ; Push extended flags register onto the stack
            pop  EAX          ; Pop extended flags values off stack into EAX
            mov  EBX,EAX      ; Save a copy of the extended flags for later
            xor  EAX,00040000H    ; Try to toggle AC bit in extended flags
            push EAX          ; Push flags test value from EAX onto stack..
            popfd             ; and pop it back into the extended flags reg.
            pushfd            ; Push extended flags value back onto stack..
            pop  EAX          ; and pop it back into EAX for inspection
            xor  EAX,EBX      ; Compare altered against unaltered
                              ; flags value
```

```
                jz   FixESP    ; If toggle of AC bit didn't "take," it's a 386..
                inc  DX        ; ..but if it did, we have a 486, so inc DX to 3

FixESP:         mov  ESP,ECX   ; Put the original stack pointer back into ESP
Done:           mov  AX,DX     ; Let's return the CPU code in AX
                ret            ; and go back to the caller

CPUID           ENDP


; BEGIN MAIN PROGRAM

Main            PROC

Start:          ; This is where program execution begins:
                mov  AX,MyData  ; Set up our own data segment address in DS
                mov  DS,AX      ; Can't load segment reg. directly from memory

                ; Identifying the CPU is just a matter of calling the CPUID proc:
                call CPUID      ; Go out and test for the installed CPU
                push AX         ; Save the return code on stack for ERRORLEVEL

                ; Now we print the message based on the CPU code:
                xor  AH,AH      ; Clear AH so the code stands alone
                mov  DI,AX      ; Put AL with CPU ID code value into DI
                mov  CL,4       ; Load shift count value into CL
                shl  DI,CL      ; Multiply code by 16 to get offset into table
                lea  DX,MsgTbl  ; Load address of start of message table into BX
                add  DX,DI      ; Add calculated offset to address
                mov  CX,16      ; All messages in table are 16 bytes long
                mov  BX,1       ; Selects DOS file handle #1: Standard Output
                mov  AH,40H     ; Select DOS service 40: Print String
                int  21H        ; Make the DOS call

                pop  AX         ; Make sure code is still in AL
                mov  AH,4CH     ; Terminate process DOS service
                int  21H        ; Control returns to DOS

Main            ENDP

MyProg          ENDS

;----------------------------|
;      END CODE SEGMENT      |
;----------------------------|

                END Start  ; The procedure named Start becomes the main program
```

Conclusion

Not the End, but Only the Beginning

You never really *learn* assembly language.

You can improve your skills over time, by reading good books on the subject, by reading good code that others have written, and most of all, by writing lots and lots of code yourself. But at no point will you be able to stand up and say, I *know* it.

You shouldn't feel bad about this. In fact, I take some encouragement from occasionally hearing that Michael Abrash, author of *Zen of Assembly Language*, has learned something new about assembly language. Michael has been writing high-performance assembly code for almost ten years, and has evolved into one of the five or six best assembly programmers in the Western Hemisphere.

If Michael is still learning, is there hope for the rest of us?

Wrong question. *Silly* question. If Michael is still learning, it means that *all* of us are students and will always be students. It means that the journey is the goal, and as long as we continue to probe and hack and fiddle and try things we never tried before, that over time we will advance the state of the art, and create programs that would have made the pioneers in our field catch their breath in 1977.

For the point is not to conquer the subject, but to live with it, and grow with your knowledge of it. The journey *is* the goal, and with this book I've tried hard to help those people who have been frozen with fear at the thought of starting the journey, staring at the complexity of it all and wondering where the first brick in that "yellow brick road" might be.

It's *here*, with nothing more than the conviction that you can do it.

I got out of school in recession year 1974 with a B.A. in English, Summa Cum Laude, and not much in reliable prospects outside of driving a cab. I finessed my way into a job with Xerox Corporation, repairing copy machines. Books were fun, but paperwork makes money—so I picked up a toolbag and had a fine old time for several years, before finessing my way into a computer-programming position.

But I'll never forget that first awful moment when I looked over the shoulder of an accomplished technician at a model 660 copier with its panels off. It looked like a bottomless pit of little cams and gears and drums and sprocket chains, turning and flipping and knocking switch actuators back and forth. Mesmerized by the complexity, I forgot to notice that a sheet of paper had been fed through the machine and turned into a copy of the original document. I was terrified of never learning what all the little cams did, and missed the comforting simplicity of the Big Picture—that a copy machine makes copies.

That's Square One—discover the big picture. Ignore the cams and gears for a bit. You can do it. Find out what's important in holding the big picture together (ask someone if it's not obvious), and study that before getting down to the cams and gears. Locate the processes that happen. Divide the Big Picture into sub pictures. See how things flow. Only then should you focus on something as small and as lost in the mess as an individual cam or switch.

That's how you conquer complexity, and that's how I've presented assembly language in this book. Some might say I've shorted the instruction set, but covering the instruction set was never the real goal here.

The real goal was to conquer your fear of the complexity of the subject, with some metaphors and some pictures and some funny stories to bleed the tension away.

Did it work? You tell me. I'd really like to know.

12.1 Where to Now?

If you've followed me so far, you've probably lost your fear of assembly language, picked up some skills and a good part of the instruction set, and are ready to move on. Here are some other good books to pick up:

Mastering Turbo Assembler
by Tom Swan
Howard W. Sams & Co., 1989
ISBN 0-672-48435-8
Tom's intermediate-level assembly volume is a natural next step if you're working with the Borland tools. There's no similarly good book on Microsoft's MASM, but much of what Tom discusses in his book applies to MASM as well.

Mastering Turbo Debugger
by Tom Swan
Howard W. Sams & Co, 1990
ISBN 0-672-48454-4
This is the only good book on debugging ever published, and for what I consider an advanced topic it's remarkably approachable. Again, it focuses on the Borland tools, but Tom's higher-level strategies for finding and nuking bugs in your code is absolutely essential reading, no matter *what* assembler you're using, now or at any time in the future.

PC Magazine Programmer's Technical Reference:
The Processor and Coprocessor
Robert L. Hummel
Ziff-Davis Press, 1992
ISBN 1-56276-016-5
This is not a tutorial but a reference on all of Intel's *x86* processors, and it's by far the best one ever written or likely to be written for some time. It has the best discussion of that mysterious protected mode that I've ever seen, and its

description of the individual assembly instructions is wonderfully crafted. I'm tempted to have my own copy taken apart and rebound as hardcover—if I don't, it's going to fall to pieces any day now!

PC TECHNIQUES
7721 E. Gray Road #204
Scottsdale AZ 85260
(602) 483-0192
This is the programmers' magazine that I own and publish, and we cover assembly language in every issue. Tom Swan writes a column on Windows programming, and Michael Abrash writes about high-performance C and assembly coding. Other industry powers write on their own areas of expertise, and there is probably something of interest to you in every issue.

But don't take my word for it. I only work here. Send the card from the back of this book in right now, and don't miss another issue!

12.2 Stepping Off Square One

OK—with a couple of new books in hand and good night's sleep behind you, strike out on your own a little. Set yourself a goal, and try to achieve it: something *tough*, say, an assembly-language utility that locates all files anywhere on a hard disk drive with a given ambiguous filename. That's ambitious, and will take some research and study and (perhaps) a few false starts. But you can do it, and once you do it you'll be a real journeyman assembly-language programmer.

Becoming a master takes work, and time. Michael Abrash's massive *Zen of Assembly Language* (now out of print but to be republished soon) is a compilation of the "secret" knowledge of a programming master. It's not easy reading, but it will give you a good idea where your mind has to be to consider yourself an expert assembly-language programmer.

Keep programming. Michael can show you things that would have taken you years to discover on your own, but they won't stick in your mind unless you *use* them. Set yourself a real challenge, something that has to be both correct and *fast*: rotate graphics objects in 3-D, transfer data through a serial port at 19,200 bits per second, things like that.

You can do it.

Coming to believe the truth in that statement is the essence of stepping away from Square One.

Partial 8086/8088 Instruction Set Reference

Instruction	Reference page	Text page
MOV	397	155
NEG	399	169
NOP	400	-----
NOT	401	178
OR	402	266
POP	403	196
POPA	404	348
POPF	405	196
PUSH	406	194
PUSHF	407	194
PUSHA	408	348
RET	409	220
ROL	410	-----
ROR	411	-----
SBB	412	-----
SHL	413	269
SHR	414	269
STC	415	-----
STD	416	317
STOS	417	314
SUB	418	289
XCHG	419	161
XOR	420	266

Notes on the Instruction Set Reference

Instruction operands

When an instruction takes two operands, the destination operand is the one on the *left*, and the source operand is the one on the *right*. In general, when a result is produced by an instruction, the result replaces the destination operand. For example, in this instruction:

```
ADD BX,SI
```

the BX register is added to the SI register, and the sum is then placed in the BX register, overwriting whatever was in BX before the addition.

Flag results

Each instruction contains a flag summary that looks like this (the asterisks will vary from instruction to instruction):

```
O D I T S Z A P C      OF: Overflow flag   TF: Trap flag   AF: Aux carry
F F F F F F F F F      DF: Direction flag  SF: Sign flag   PF: Parity flag
*         * * * * *    IF: Interrupt flag  ZF: Zero flag   CF: Carry flag
```

The nine flags are all represented here. An asterisk indicates that the instruction on that page affects that flag. If a flag is affected at all (that is, if it has an asterisk beneath it) it will be affected according to these rules:

OF: Set if the result is too large to fit in the destination operand.

DF: Set by the STD instruction; cleared by CLD.

IF: Set by the STI instruction; cleared by CLI.

TF: For debuggers; not used in normal programming and may be ignored.

SF: Set when the sign of the result forces the destination operand to become negative.

ZF: Set if the result of an operation is zero. If the result is non-zero, ZF is cleared.

AF: "Auxiliary carry" used for 4-bit BCD math. Set when an operation causes a carry out of a 4-bit BCD quantity.

PF: Set if the number of 1 bits in the low byte of the result is even; cleared if the number of 1 bits in the low byte of the result is odd. Used in data communications applications but little else.

CF: Set if the result of an add or shift operation "carries out" a bit beyond the destination operand; otherwise cleared. May be manually set by STC and manually cleared by CLC when CF must be in a known state before an operation begins.

Some instructions force certain flags to become undefined. When this is the case, it will be noted under "Notes." "Undefined" means *don't count on it being in any particular state.*

AAA Adjust AL after BCD addition

Flags affected:

```
O D I T S Z A P C     OF: Overflow flag   TF: Trap flag   AF: Aux carry
F F F F F F F F F      DF: Direction flag  SF: Sign flag   PF: Parity flag
            *   *      IF: Interrupt flag  ZF: Zero flag    CF: Carry flag
```

Legal forms:

AAA

Examples:

AAA

Notes:

AAA makes an addition "come out right" in AL when what you're adding are BCD values rather than ordinary binary values. Note well that AAA does *not* perform the arithmetic itself, but is a "postprocessor" after ADD or ADC. AL is an implied operand and may not be explicitly stated—so make sure that the preceding ADD or ADC instruction leaves its results in AL!

A BCD digit is a byte with the high 4 bits set to 0, and the low 4 bits containing a digit from 0 to 9. AAA will yield garbage results if the preceding ADD or ADC acted upon one or both operands with values greater than 09.

After the addition of two legal BCD values, AAA will adjust a non-BCD result (that is, a result greater than 09 in AL) to a value between 0 and 9. This is called a *decimal carry*, since it is the carry of a BCD digit and not simply the carry of a binary bit.

For example, if ADD added 08 and 04 (both legal BCD values) to produce 0C in AL, AAA will take the 0C and adjust it to 02. The decimal carry goes to AH, *not* to the upper 4 bits of AL, which are *always* cleared to 0 by AAA.

If the preceding ADD or ADC resulted in a decimal carry, (as in the example above) *both* CF and AF are set to 1 and AH is incremented by 1. Otherwise, AH is not incremented and CF and AF are cleared to 0.

This instruction is subtle. See the detailed discussion in Section 10.3.

```
r8 = AL AH BL BH CL CH DL DH    r16 = AX BX CX DX BP SP SI DI
sr = CS DS SS ES
m8 = 8-bit memory data          m16 = 16-bit memory data
i8 = 8-bit immediate data       i16 = 16-bit immediate data
d8 = 8-bit signed displacement  d16 = 16-bit signed displacement
```

ADC Arithmetic addition with carry

Flags affected:

```
O D I T S Z A P C    OF: Overflow flag   TF: Trap flag   AF: Aux carry
F F F F F F F F F    DF: Direction flag  SF: Sign flag   PF: Parity flag
*       * * * *      IF: Interrupt flag  ZF: Zero flag    CF: Carry flag
```

Legal forms:

```
ADC r8,r8
ADC m8,r8
ADC r8,m8
ADC r16,r16
ADC m16,r16
ADC r16,m16
ADC r8,i8
ADC m8,i8
ADC r16,i16
ADC m16,i16
ADC r16,i8
ADC m16,i8
ADC AL,i8
ADC AX,i16
```

Examples:

```
ADC BX,DI
ADC AX,0FFFFH                ;Uses single-byte opcode
ADC AL,42H                   ;Uses single-byte opcode
ADC BP,17H
ADC WORD PTR [BX+SI+Inset],5
ADC WORD PTR ES:[BX],0B800H
```

Notes:

ADC adds the source operand and the carry flag to the destination operand, and after the operation the result replaces the destination operand. The add is an arithmetic add, and the carry allows multiple-precision additions across several registers or memory locations. (To add without taking the carry flag into account, use the ADD instruction.) All affected flags are set according to the operation. Most importantly, if the result does not fit into the destination operand, the carry flag is set to 1.

```
r8 = AL AH BL BH CL CH DL DH    r16 = AX BX CX DX BP SP SI DI
sr = CS DS SS ES
m8 = 8-bit memory data          m16 = 16-bit memory data
i8 = 8-bit immediate data       i16 = 16-bit immediate data
d8 = 8-bit signed displacement  d16 = 16-bit signed displacement
```

ADD Arithmetic addition

Flags affected:

```
O D I T S Z A P C    OF: Overflow flag   TF: Trap flag   AF: Aux carry
F F F F F F F F F    DF: Direction flag  SF: Sign flag   PF: Parity flag
*       * * * *      IF: Interrupt flag  ZF: Zero flag   CF: Carry flag
```

Legal forms:

```
ADD r8,r8
ADD m8,r8
ADD r8,m8
ADD r16,r16
ADD m16,r16
ADD r16,m16
ADD r8,i8
ADD m8,i8
ADD r16,i16
ADD m16,i16
ADD r16,i8
ADD m16,i8
ADD AL,i8
ADD AX,i16
```

Examples:

```
ADD BX,DI
ADD AX,0FFFFH              ;Uses single-byte opcode
ADD AL,42H                 ;Uses single-byte opcode
ADD BP,17H
ADD WORD PTR [BX+SI+Inset],5
ADD WORD PTR ES:[BX],0B800H
```

Notes:

ADD adds the source operand to the destination operand, and after the operation the result replaces the destination operand. The add is an arithmetic add, and does *not* take the carry flag into account. (To add using the carry flag, use the ADC Add With Carry instruction.) All affected flags are set according to the operation. Most importantly, if the result does not fit into the destination operand, the carry flag is set to 1.

```
r8 = AL AH BL BH CL CH DL DH    r16 = AX BX CX DX BP SP SI DI
sr = CS DS SS ES
m8 = 8-bit memory data          m16 = 16-bit memory data
i8 = 8-bit immediate data       i16 = 16-bit immediate data
d8 = 8-bit signed displacement  d16 = 16-bit signed displacement
```

AND   Logical AND

Flags affected:

```
O D I T S Z A P C      OF: Overflow flag   TF: Trap flag   AF: Aux carry
F F F F F F F F F      DF: Direction flag  SF: Sign flag   PF: Parity flag
*       * * * *        IF: Interrupt flag  ZF: Zero flag   CF: Carry flag
```

Legal forms:

```
AND r8,r8
AND m8,r8
AND r8,m8
AND r16,r16
AND m16,r16
AND r16,m16
AND r8,i8
AND m8,i8
AND r16,i16
AND m16,i16
AND AL,i8
AND AX,i16
```

Examples:

```
AND BX,DI
AND AX,0FFFFH              ;Uses single-byte opcode
AND AL,42H                 ;Uses single-byte opcode
AND ES:[BX],0B800H
AND [BP+SI],DX
```

Notes:

AND performs the AND logical operation on its two operands. Once the operation is complete, the result replaces the destination operand. AND is performed on a bit-by bit basis, such that bit 0 of the source is ANDed with bit 0 of the destination, bit 1 of the source is ANDed with bit 1 of the destination, and so on. The AND operation yields a 1 if *both* of the operands are 1; and a 0 only if *either* operand is 0. Note that the operation makes the Auxiliary Carry flag undefined. CF and OF are cleared to 0, and the other affected flags are set according to the operation's results.

```
r8 = AL AH BL BH CL CH DL DH    r16 = AX BX CX DX BP SP SI DI
sr = CS DS SS ES
m8 = 8-bit memory data          m16 = 16-bit memory data
i8 = 8-bit immediate data       i16 = 16-bit immediate data
d8 = 8-bit signed displacement  d16 = 16-bit signed displacement
```

BT   Bit Test   386/486

Flags affected:

```
O D I T S Z A P C      OF: Overflow flag   TF: Trap flag   AF: Aux carry
F F F F F F F F F      DF: Direction flag  SF: Sign flag   PF: Parity flag
                *      IF: Interrupt flag  ZF: Zero flag    CF: Carry flag
```

Legal forms:

```
BT r16,r16
BT m16,r16
BT r32,r32
BT m32,r32
BT r16,i8
BT m16,i8
BT r32,i8
BT m32,i8
```

Examples:

```
BT AX,CX
BT [BX+DI],DX
BT AX,64
BT EAX,EDX
BT ECX,17
```

Notes:

BT copies a single specified bit from the left operand to the Carry flag, where it can be tested, or fed back into a quantity using one of the shift/rotate instructions. Which bit is copied is specified by the right operand. Neither operand is altered by BT.

When the right operand is an 8-bit immediate value, the value specifies the number of the bit to be copied. In BT AX,5 bit 5 of AX is copied into CF. When the immediate value exceeds size of the left operand, the value is expressed modulo the size of the left operand. That is, because there are not 66 bits in EAX, BT EAX,66 "pulls out" as many 32's from the immediate value as can be taken, and what remains is the bit number. (Here, 2.) When the right operand is *not* an immediate value, the right operand not only specifies the bit to be tested but also an offset from the memory reference in the left operand. This is complicated. See a detailed discussion in a full assembly language reference.

```
r8 = AL AH BL BH CL CH DL DH   r16 = AX BX CX DX BP SP SI DI
sr = CS DS SS ES
m8 = 8-bit memory data         m16 = 16-bit memory data
i8 = 8-bit immediate data      i16 = 16-bit immediate data
d8 = 8-bit signed displacement d16 = 16-bit signed displacement
```

`CALL` Call Procedure

Flags affected:

```
O D I T S Z A P C      OF: Overflow flag   TF: Trap flag   AF: Aux carry
F F F F F F F F F      DF: Direction flag  SF: Sign flag   PF: Parity flag
        <none>         IF: Interrupt flag  ZF: Zero flag   CF: Carry flag
```

Legal forms:

```
CALL <near label>
CALL <far label>
CALL r16
CALL m16
CALL m32
```

Examples:

```
CALL InsideMySegment        ;InsideMySegment is a Near label
CALL OutsideMySegment       ;OutsideMySegment is a Far label
CALL BX
CALL [BX+DI+17]             ;Calls Near address at [BX+DI+17]
CALL DWORD PTR [BX+DI+17]   ;Calls full 32-bit address at [BX+DI+17]
```

Notes:

CALL transfers control to a procedure address. Before transferring control, CALL pushes the address of the instruction immediately after itself onto the stack. This allows a RET instruction (see also) to pop the return address into either CS:IP or IP only (depending on whether it is a Near or Far call) and thus return control to the instruction immediately after the CALL instruction.

In addition to the obvious CALL to a defined label, CALL can transfer control to a Near address within a 16-bit general-purpose register, and also to an address located in memory. These are shown in the Legal Forms column as m16 and m32. m32 is simply a full 32-bit address stored at a location in memory that may be addressed through any legal 8086/8088 memory addressing mode. CALL m16 and CALL m32 are useful for creating jump tables of procedure addresses.

```
r8 = AL AH BL BH CL CH DL DH   r16 = AX BX CX DX BP SP SI DI
sr = CS DS SS ES               m32 = 32-bit memory data
m8 = 8-bit memory data         m16 = 16-bit memory data
i8 = 8-bit immediate data      i16 = 16-bit immediate data
d8 = 8-bit signed displacement d16 = 16-bit signed displacement
```

CLC Clear Carry flag (CF)

Flags affected:

```
O D I T S Z A P C    OF: Overflow flag   TF: Trap flag   AF: Aux carry
F F F F F F F F F    DF: Direction flag  SF: Sign flag   PF: Parity flag
              *      IF: Interrupt flag  ZF: Zero flag   CF: Carry flag
```

Legal forms:

CLC <none>

Examples:

CLC

Notes:

CLC simply sets the carry flag (CF) to the cleared (0) state. Use CLC in situations where the carry flag *must* be in a known cleared state before work begins, as when you are rotating a series of words or bytes using the rotate instructions RCL and RCR.

```
r8 = AL AH BL BH CL CH DL DH    r16 = AX BX CX DX BP SP SI DI
sr = CS DS SS ES
m8 = 8-bit memory data          m16 = 16-bit memory data
i8 = 8-bit immediate data       i16 = 16-bit immediate data
d8 = 8-bit signed displacement  d16 = 16-bit signed displacement
```

CLD   Clear Direction Flag (DF)

Flags affected:

```
O D I T S Z A P C    OF: Overflow flag   TF: Trap flag   AF: Aux carry
F F F F F F F F F    DF: Direction flag  SF: Sign flag   PF: Parity flag
    *                IF: Interrupt flag  ZF: Zero flag   CF: Carry flag
```

Legal forms:

```
CLD <none>
```

Examples:

```
CLD
```

Notes:

CLD simply sets the direction flag (DF) to the cleared (0) state. This affects the adjustment performed by repeated string instructions like STOS, SCAS, and MOVS. Typically, when DF=0, the destination pointer is increased, and decreased when DF=1. DF is set to one with the STD instruction.

```
r8 = AL AH BL BH CL CH DL DH    r16 = AX BX CX DX BP SP SI DI
sr = CS DS SS ES
m8 = 8-bit memory data          m16 = 16-bit memory data
i8 = 8-bit immediate data       i16 = 16-bit immediate data
d8 = 8-bit signed displacement  d16 = 16-bit signed displacement
```

CMP   Arithmetic subtraction

Flags affected:

```
O D I T S Z A P C     OF: Overflow flag    TF: Trap flag    AF: Aux carry
F F F F F F F F F     DF: Direction flag   SF: Sign flag    PF: Parity flag
*       * * * *       IF: Interrupt flag   ZF: Zero flag    CF: Carry flag
```

Legal forms:

```
CMP r8,r8
CMP m8,r8
CMP r8,m8
CMP r16,r16
CMP m16,r16
CMP r16,m16
CMP r8,i8
CMP m8,i8
CMP r16,i16
CMP m16,i16
CMP r16,i8
CMP m16,i8
CMP AL,i8
CMP AX,i16
```

Examples:

```
CMP BX,DI
CMP AX,0FFFFH                 ;Uses single-byte opcode
CMP AL,42H                    ;Uses single-byte opcode
CMP BP,17H
CMP WORD PTR [BX+SI+Inset],5
CMP WORD PTR ES:[BX],0B800H
```

Notes:

CMP compares its two operations, and sets the flags to indicate the results of the comparison. *The destination operand is not affected.* The operation itself is identical to subtraction of the source from the destination without borrow (SUB) save that the result does not replace the destination. Typically, CMP is followed by one of the conditional jump instructions; i.e., JE to jump if the operands were equal; JNE if they were unequal; etc.

```
r8 = AL AH BL BH CL CH DL DH    r16 = AX BX CX DX BP SP SI DI
sr = CS DS SS ES
m8 = 8-bit memory data          m16 = 16-bit memory data
i8 = 8-bit immediate data       i16 = 16-bit immediate data
d8 = 8-bit signed displacement  d16 = 16-bit signed displacement
```

DEC Decrement operand

Flags affected:

```
O D I T S Z A P C    OF: Overflow flag   TF: Trap flag   AF: Aux carry
F F F F F F F F F    DF: Direction flag  SF: Sign flag   PF: Parity flag
*         * * * *    IF: Interrupt flag  ZF: Zero flag   CF: Carry flag
```

Legal forms:

```
DEC m8
DEC m16
DEC AL
DEC CL
DEC DL
DEC BL
DEC AH
DEC DH
DEC CH
DEC BH
DEC AX
DEC BX
DEC CX
DEC DX
DEC SP
DEC BP
DEC SI
DEC DI
```

Examples:

```
DEC BYTE PTR [BP]  ; Decrements the BYTE at [BP]
DEC AL
DEC BX
DEC WORD PTR [BX]  ; Decrements the WORD at [BX]
```

Notes:

Remember that segment registers *cannot* be decremented with DEC. All register-half opcodes are *two* bytes in length, but all 16-bit register opcodes are *one* byte in length. If you can decrement an entire register of which only the lower half contains data, use the 16-bit opcode and save a byte.

Memory data forms *must* be used with BYTE PTR or WORD PTR!

```
r8 = AL AH BL BH CL CH DL DH    r16 = AX BX CX DX BP SP SI DI
sr = CS DS SS ES
m8 = 8-bit memory data          m16 = 16-bit memory data
i8 = 8-bit immediate data       i16 = 16-bit immediate data
d8 = 8-bit signed displacement  d16 = 16-bit signed displacement
```

IMUL Signed integer multiplication

Flags affected:

```
O D I T S Z A P C      OF: Overflow flag    TF: Trap flag    AF: Aux carry
F F F F F F F F F      DF: Direction flag   SF: Sign flag    PF: Parity flag
*               *      IF: Interrupt flag   ZF: Zero flag    CF: Carry flag
```

Legal forms:

```
IMUL r8
IMUL m8
IMUL r16
IMUL m16
```

Examples:

```
IMUL CH                  ; AL * CH —> AX
IMUL BX                  ; AX * BX —> DX:AX
IMUL WORD PTR [BX+DI]    ; AX * DS:[BX+DI] —> DX:AX
```

Notes:

IMUL multiplies its operand by AL or AX, and the result is placed in AX, or in DX:AX. Note that only *one* operand is choosable by the programmer; that is, you can't multiply DX by CX, or [BX] by DX. One operand is always AL or AX, and the result always affects AX.

If IMUL is given an 8-bit operand (either an 8-bit register or an 8-bit memory operand) the results will be placed in AX. This means that AH will be affected, even if the results will fit entirely in AL.

Similarly, if IMUL is given a 16-bit operand, the results will be placed in DX:AX, *even if the entire result will fit in AX!* It's easy to forget that IMUL affects DX on 16-bit multiplies. Keep that in mind!

The 286, 386, and 486 CPUs support enhancements to the IMUL instruction that I do not cover in this book and do not summarize on this page.

```
r8 = AL AH BL BH CL CH DL DH     r16 = AX BX CX DX BP SP SI DI
sr = CS DS SS ES
m8 = 8-bit memory data           m16 = 16-bit memory data
i8 = 8-bit immediate data        i16 = 16-bit immediate data
d8 = 8-bit signed displacement   d16 = 16-bit signed displacement
```

INC   Increment operand

Flags affected:

```
O D I T S Z A P C       OF: Overflow flag   TF: Trap flag   AF: Aux carry
F F F F F F F F F       DF: Direction flag  SF: Sign flag   PF: Parity flag
*         * * * *       IF: Interrupt flag  ZF: Zero flag   CF: Carry flag
```

Legal forms:

```
INC m8
INC m16
INC AL
INC CL
INC DL
INC BL
INC AH
INC DH
INC CH
INC BH
INC AX
INC BX
INC CX
INC DX
INC SP
INC BP
INC SI
INC DI
```

Examples:

```
INC BYTE PTR [BP]  ; Increments the BYTE at [BP]
INC AL
INC BX
INC WORD PTR [BX]  ; Increments the WORD at [BX]
```

Notes:

Remember that segment registers *cannot* be incremented with INC. All register-half opcodes are *two* bytes in length, but all 16-bit register opcodes are *one* byte in length. If you can increment an entire register of which only the lower half contains data, use the 16-bit opcode and save a byte.

Memory data forms *must* be used with BYTE PTR or WORD PTR!

```
r8 = AL AH BL BH CL CH DL DH    r16 = AX BX CX DX BP SP SI DI
sr = CS DS SS ES
m8 = 8-bit memory data          m16 = 16-bit memory data
i8 = 8-bit immediate data       i16 = 16-bit immediate data
d8 = 8-bit signed displacement  d16 = 16-bit signed displacement
```

INT Software interrupt

Flags affected:

```
O D I T S Z A P C      OF: Overflow flag   TF: Trap flag   AF: Aux carry
F F F F F F F F F       DF: Direction flag  SF: Sign flag   PF: Parity flag
      * *               IF: Interrupt flag  ZF: Zero flag   CF: Carry flag
```

Legal forms:

```
INT 3
INT i8
```

Examples:

```
INT 3        ;Uses single-byte opcode
INT 10H
```

Notes:

INT triggers a software interrupt to one of 256 vectors in the first 1024 bytes of memory. The operand specifies which vector, from 0-255. When an interrupt is called, the Flags register is pushed on the stack along with the return address. The IF flag is cleared, which prevents further interrupts (either hardware or software) from being recognized until IF is set again. TF is also cleared.

A special form of the instruction allows calling Interrupt 3 with a single-byte instruction. Debuggers use Interrupt 3 to set "breakpoints" in code by replacing an instruction with the single-byte opcode for calling Interrupt 3. Virtually all cases will use the other form, which takes an 8-bit immediate numeric value.

Always return from a software interrupt service routine with the IRET instruction. IRET restores the flags that were pushed onto the stack by INT, and in doing so clears IF, allowing further interrupts.

```
r8 = AL AH BL BH CL CH DL DH      r16 = AX BX CX DX BP SP SI DI
sr = CS DS SS ES
m8 = 8-bit memory data            m16 = 16-bit memory data
i8 = 8-bit immediate data         i16 = 16-bit immediate data
d8 = 8-bit signed displacement    d16 = 16-bit signed displacement
```

IRET Return from Interrupt

Flags affected:

```
O D I T S Z A P C     OF: Overflow flag   TF: Trap flag   AF: Aux carry
F F F F F F F F F     DF: Direction flag  SF: Sign flag   PF: Parity flag
* * * * * * * * *     IF: Interrupt flag  ZF: Zero flag   CF: Carry flag
```

Legal forms:

```
IRET
```

Examples:

```
IRET
```

Notes:

IRET *must* be used to exit from interrupt service routines called through INT or through interrupt hardware such as serial ports etc. IRET pops the return address from the top of the stack into CS and IP, and then pops the next word from the stack into the Flags register. *All flags are affected.*

If the interrupt was triggered by hardware, there may be additional steps to be taken to prepare the hardware for another interrupt before IRET is executed. Consult your hardware documentation.

```
r8 = AL AH BL BH CL CH DL DH    r16 = AX BX CX DX BP SP SI DI
sr = CS DS SS ES
m8 = 8-bit memory data          m16 = 16-bit memory data
i8 = 8-bit immediate data       i16 = 16-bit immediate data
d8 = 8-bit signed displacement  d16 = 16-bit signed displacement
```

J? Jump On Condition

Flags affected:

```
O D I T S Z A P C      OF: Overflow flag    TF: Trap flag    AF: Aux carry
F F F F F F F F F      DF: Direction flag   SF: Sign flag    PF: Parity flag
      <none>           IF: Interrupt flag   ZF: Zero flag    CF: Carry flag
```

Legal forms:	Descriptions:	Jump if flags are:
JA/JNBE d	Jump If Above/Jump If Not Below or Equal	CF=0 AND ZF=0
JAE/JNB d	Jump If Above or Equal/Jump If Not Below	CF=0
JB/JNAE d	Jump If Below/Jump If Not Above or Equal	CF=1
JBE/JNA d	Jump If Below or Equal/Jump If Not Above	CF=1 OR ZF=1
JE/JZ d	Jump If Equal/Jump If Zero	ZF=1
JNE/JNZ d	Jump If Not Equal/Jump If Not Zero	ZF=0
JG/JNLE d	Jump If Greater/Jump If Not Less or Equal	ZF=0 OR SF=OF
JGE/JNL d	Jump If Greater or Equal/Jump If Not Less	SF=OF
JL/JNGE d	Jump If Less/Jump If Not Greater or Equal	SF<>OF
JLE/JNG d	Jump If Less or Equal/Jump If Not Greater	ZF=1 OR SF<>OF
JC d	Jump If Carry flag set	CF=1
JNC d	Jump If Carry flag Not set	CF=0
JO d	Jump If Overflow flag set	OF=1
JNO d	Jump If Overflow flag Not set	OF=0
JP/JPE d	Jump If PF set/Jump if Parity Even	PF=1
JNP/JPO d	Jump If PF Not set/Jump if Parity Odd	PF=0
JS d	Jump If Sign flag set	SF=1
JNS d	Jump If Sign flag Not set	SF=0

Examples:

```
JB HalfSplit          ;Jumps if CF=1
JLE TooLow            ;Jumps if either ZF=1 or SF<>OF
```

Notes:

All these instructions make a short jump (127 bytes forward or 128 bytes back) if some condition is true, or fall through if the condition is not true. The conditions all involve flags, and the flag conditions in question are given to the right of the mnemonic and its description.

The mnemonics incorporating "above" or "below" are for use after unsigned comparisons, whereas the mnemonics incorporating "less" or "greater" are for use after signed comparisons. "Equal" and "Zero" may be used after unsigned or signed comparisons.

```
r8 = AL AH BL BH CL CH DL DH     r16 = AX BX CX DX BP SP SI DI
sr = CS DS SS ES                   d = short displacement; -128/+127 bytes
m8 = 8-bit memory data           m16 = 16-bit memory data
i8 = 8-bit immediate data        i16 = 16-bit immediate data
d8 = 8-bit signed displacement   d16 = 16-bit signed displacement
```

JCXZ Jump If CX = 0

Flags affected:

```
O D I T S Z A P C     OF: Overflow flag   TF: Trap flag   AF: Aux carry
F F F F F F F F F     DF: Direction flag  SF: Sign flag   PF: Parity flag
       <none>         IF: Interrupt flag  ZF: Zero flag   CF: Carry flag
```

Legal forms:

```
JCXZ <short displacement>
```

Examples:

```
JCXZ AllDone
```

Notes:

Many instructions use CX as a "count register", and JCXZ allows you to test to see if CX has become 0 and jump. The jump may only be a short jump (that is, no more than 127 bytes forward or 128 bytes back), and will be taken if CX=0 at the time the instruction is executed. If CX is any other value than 0, execution falls through to the next instruction. See also the **Jump on Condition** instructions on page 390.

```
r8 = AL AH BL BH CL CH DL DH    r16 = AX BX CX DX BP SP SI DI
sr = CS DS SS ES
m8 = 8-bit memory data          m16 = 16-bit memory data
i8 = 8-bit immediate data       i16 = 16-bit immediate data
d8 = 8-bit signed displacement  d16 = 16-bit signed displacement
```

JMP Unconditional Jump

Flags affected:

```
O D I T S Z A P C      OF: Overflow flag   TF: Trap flag    AF: Aux carry
F F F F F F F F F      DF: Direction flag  SF: Sign flag    PF: Parity flag
      <none>           IF: Interrupt flag  ZF: Zero flag     CF: Carry flag
```

Legal forms:

```
JMP <short displacement>
JMP <near label>
JMP <far label>
JMP r16
JMP m16
JMP m32
```

Examples:

```
JMP RightCloseBy            ;Plus or minus 128 bytes
JMP InsideMySegment        ;To 16-bit offset from CS
JMP OutsideMySegment       ;To immediate 32-bit address
JMP DX                     ;To 16-bit offset stored in GP register
JMP [BX+DI+17]             ;To Near address stored at [BX+DI+17]
JMP DWORD PTR [BX+DI+17]   ;To full 32-bit address stored at [BX+DI+17]
```

Notes:

JMP transfers control unconditionally to the destination given as the single operand. In addition to defined labels, JMP can transfer control to a 16-bit offset from CS stored in a general-purpose register, or to an address (either Near or Far) stored in memory and accessed through any legal 8086/8088 addressing mode. These m16 and m32 forms are useful for creating jump tables in memory, where a jump table is an array of addresses. For example, JMP [BX+DI+17] would transfer control to the 16-bit offset into CS found at the based-indexed-displacement address [BX+DI+17].

No flags are affected, and, unlike CALL, no return address is pushed onto the stack.

```
r8 = AL AH BL BH CL CH DL DH    r16 = AX BX CX DX BP SP SI DI
sr = CS DS SS ES                m32 = 32-bit memory data
m8 = 8-bit memory data          m16 = 16-bit memory data
i8 = 8-bit immediate data       i16 = 16-bit immediate data
d8 = 8-bit signed displacement  d16 = 16-bit signed displacement
```

LEA   Load Affective Address

Flags affected:

```
O D I T S Z A P C      OF: Overflow flag   TF: Trap flag    AF: Aux carry
F F F F F F F F F      DF: Direction flag  SF: Sign flag    PF: Parity flag
        <none>         IF: Interrupt flag  ZF: Zero flag    CF: Carry flag
```

Legal forms:

```
LEA r16,m<any size>
```

Examples:

```
LEA BX,MyByteVar        ;Loads offset of MyByteVar to BX
LEA BP,MyWordVar        ;Loads offset of MyWordVar to BP
```

Notes:

LEA derives the offset of the source operand from the start of its segment, and loads that offset into the destination operand. The destination operand must be a 16-bit register, and *cannot* be memory. The source operand must be a memory operand, but it can be any size. The address stored in the destination operand is the address of the first byte of the source in memory, and the size of the source in memory is unimportant.

This is a good, clean way to place the address of a variable into a register prior to a procedure or interrupt call.

```
r8 = AL AH BL BH CL CH DL DH    r16 = AX BX CX DX BP SP SI DI
sr = CS DS SS ES
m8 = 8-bit memory data          m16 = 16-bit memory data
i8 = 8-bit immediate data       i16 = 16-bit immediate data
d8 = 8-bit signed displacement  d16 = 16-bit signed displacement
```

LOOP   Loop until CX=0

Flags affected:

```
O D I T S Z A P C      OF: Overflow flag   TF: Trap flag   AF: Aux carry
F F F F F F F F F      DF: Direction flag  SF: Sign flag   PF: Parity flag
      <none>           IF: Interrupt flag  ZF: Zero flag    CF: Carry flag
```

Legal forms:

```
LOOP d8
```

Examples:

```
LOOP PokeValue
```

Notes:

LOOP is a combination decrement counter, test, and jump instruction. It simplifies code by acting as a DEC CX instruction, a CMP CX,0 instruction, and JZ instruction, all at once. A repeat count must be initially loaded into CX. When the LOOP instruction is executed, it first decrements CX. Then it tests to see if CX=0. If CX is *not* 0, LOOP transfers control to the displacement specified as its operand:

```
          MOV CX,17
DoIt:     CALL CrunchIt
          CALL StuffIt
          LOOP DoIt
```

Here, the two procedure CALLs will be made 17 times. The first 16 times through, CX will still be nonzero and LOOP will transfer control to DoIt. On the 17th pass, however, LOOP will decrement CX to 0, and then fall through to the next instruction in sequence when it tests CX.

LOOP does not alter any flags, even when CX is decremented to 0. *Warning*: If CX is initially 0, LOOP will decrement it to 65,535 (0FFFFH) and then perform the loop 65,535 times, which might take long enough to appear to be a system lockup.

```
r8 = AL AH BL BH CL CH DL DH      r16 = AX BX CX DX BP SP SI DI
sr = CS DS SS ES
m8 = 8-bit memory data            m16 = 16-bit memory data
i8 = 8-bit immediate data         i16 = 16-bit immediate data
d8 = 8-bit signed displacement    d16 = 16-bit signed displacement
```

LOOPZ Loop while CX>0 and ZF=1

Flags affected:

```
O  D  I  T  S  Z  A  P  C     OF: Overflow flag   TF: Trap flag   AF: Aux carry
F  F  F  F  F  F  F  F  F     DF: Direction flag  SF: Sign flag   PF: Parity flag
         <none>               IF: Interrupt flag  ZF: Zero flag   CF: Carry flag
```

Legal forms:

```
LOOPZ d8
LOOPE d8
```

Examples:

```
LOOPZ SenseOneShots
LOOPE CRCGenerate
```

Notes:

LOOPZ and LOOPE are synonyms. LOOPZ decrements CX and jumps to the location specified in the target operand if CX is not 0 and the zero flag ZF is 1. Otherwise, execution falls through to the next instruction.

What this means is that the loop is pretty much controlled by ZF. If ZF remains 1, the loop is looped until CX is decremented to 0. But as soon as ZF is cleared to 0, the loop terminates. Think of it as "Loop While Zero Flag."

Keep in mind that LOOPZ does not itself affect ZF. Some instruction within the loop (typically one of the string instructions) must do something to affect ZF to terminate the loop before CX counts down to 0.

```
r8 = AL AH BL BH CL CH DL DH     r16 = AX BX CX DX BP SP SI DI
sr = CS DS SS ES
m8 = 8-bit memory data           m16 = 16-bit memory data
i8 = 8-bit immediate data        i16 = 16-bit immediate data
d8 = 8-bit signed displacement   d16 = 16-bit signed displacement
```

LOOPNZ Loop while CX>0 and ZF=0

Flags affected:

```
O D I T S Z A P C     OF: Overflow flag   TF: Trap flag   AF: Aux carry
F F F F F F F F F     DF: Direction flag  SF: Sign flag   PF: Parity flag
      <none>          IF: Interrupt flag  ZF: Zero flag    CF: Carry flag
```

Legal forms:

```
LOOPNZ d8
LOOPNE d8
```

Examples:

```
LOOPNZ StartProcess
LOOPNE GoSomewhere
```

Notes:

LOOPNZ and LOOPNE are synonyms. LOOPNZ decrements CX and jumps to the location specified in the target operand if CX is not 0 and the zero flag ZF *is* 0. Otherwise, execution falls through to the next instruction.

What this means is that the loop is pretty much controlled by ZF. If ZF remains 0, the loop is looped until CX is decremented to 0. But as soon as ZF is set to 1, the loop terminates. Think of it as "Loop While Not Zero Flag."

Keep in mind that LOOPNZ does not itself affect ZF. Some instruction within the loop (typically one of the string instructions) must do something to affect ZF to terminate the loop before CX counts down to 0.

```
r8 = AL AH BL BH CL CH DL DH     r16 = AX BX CX DX BP SP SI DI
sr = CS DS SS ES
m8 = 8-bit memory data           m16 = 16-bit memory data
i8 = 8-bit immediate data        i16 = 16-bit immediate data
d8 = 8-bit signed displacement   d16 = 16-bit signed displacement
```

MOV   Move (copy) right operand into left operand

Flags affected:

```
O D I T S Z A P C      OF: Overflow flag   TF: Trap flag   AF: Aux carry
F F F F F F F F F      DF: Direction flag  SF: Sign flag   PF: Parity flag
        <none>         IF: Interrupt flag  ZF: Zero flag    CF: Carry flag
```

Legal forms:

```
MOV r8,r8
MOV m8,i8
MOV m16,i16
MOV m8,r8
MOV r16,r16
MOV m16,r16
MOV r8,m8
MOV r16,m16
MOV sr,r16
MOV sr,m16
MOV r16,sr
MOV m16,sr    ┐
MOV AL,a16    │
MOV AX,a16    │
MOV a16,AL    │
MOV a16,AX    │
MOV AL,i8     │
MOV CL,i8     │
MOV DL,i8     │
MOV BL,i8     │
MOV AH,i8     │
MOV CH,i8     ├─ Single-byte opcodes
MOV DH,i8     │
MOV BH,i8     │
MOV AX,i16    │
MOV CX,i16    │
MOV DX,i16    │
MOV BX,i16    │
MOV SP,i16    │
MOV BP,i16    │
MOV SI,i16    │
MOV DI,i16    ┘
```

Examples:

```
MOV AL,BH
MOV BX,DI
MOV BP,ES
MOV ES,AX
MOV AX,0B800H
```

```
MOV ES:[BX],0FFFFH
MOV CX,[SI+Inset]
```

Notes:

This is perhaps the most-used of all instructions. Note the large number of register-specific forms that resolve to single-byte opcodes. Use them when you can; smaller opcodes aid both speed and memory efficiency. The flags are not affected.

```
r8 = AL AH BL BH CL CH DL DH      r16 = AX BX CX DX BP SP SI DI
sr = CS DS SS ES
m8 = 8-bit memory data            m16 = 16-bit memory data
i8 = 8-bit immediate data         i16 = 16-bit immediate data
d8 = 8-bit signed displacement    d16 = 16-bit signed displacement
```

NEG   Negate (two's complement; i.e. multiply by -1)

Flags affected:

```
O D I T S Z A P C      OF: Overflow flag   TF: Trap flag   AF: Aux carry
F F F F F F F F F      DF: Direction flag  SF: Sign flag   PF: Parity flag
*       * * * *        IF: Interrupt flag  ZF: Zero flag   CF: Carry flag
```

Legal forms:

```
NEG r8
NEG m8
NEG r16
NEG m16
```

Examples:

```
NEG AL
NEG CX
NEG BYTE PTR [BX]   ; Negates byte quantity at DS:BX
NEG WORD PTR [DI]   ; Negates word quantity at DS:BX
```

Notes:

This is the assembly language equivalent of multiplying a value by -1. Keep in mind that negation is *not* the same as simply inverting each bit in the operand. (Another instruction, NOT, does that.) The process is also known as generating the *two's complement* of a value. The two's complement of a value added to that value yields zero. -1 = $FF; -2 = $FE; -3 = $FD; etc.

If the operand is 0, CF is cleared and ZF is set; otherwise CF is set and ZF is cleared. If the operand contains the maximum negative value (-128 for 8-bit or -32768 for 16-bit) the operand does not change, but OF and CF are set. SF is set if the result is negative, else SF is cleared. PF is set if the low-order 8 bits of the result contain an even number of set (1) bits; otherwise PF is cleared.

NOTE: You *must* use a type override specifier (BYTE PTR or WORD PTR) with memory data!

```
r8 = AL AH BL BH CL CH DL DH    r16 = AX BX CX DX BP SP SI DI
sr = CS DS SS ES
m8 = 8-bit memory data          m16 = 16-bit memory data
i8 = 8-bit immediate data       i16 = 16-bit immediate data
d8 = 8-bit signed displacement  d16 = 16-bit signed displacement
```

NOP No Operation

Flags affected:

```
O D I T S Z A P C     OF: Overflow flag   TF: Trap flag   AF: Aux carry
F F F F F F F F F     DF: Direction flag  SF: Sign flag   PF: Parity flag
      <none>          IF: Interrupt flag  ZF: Zero flag   CF: Carry flag
```

Legal forms:

```
NOP <none>
```

Examples:

```
NOP
```

Notes:

This, the easiest-to-understand of all 86-family machine instructions, simply does nothing. Its job is to take up space in sequences of instructions. When fetched by the CPU, NOP is simply ignored. IP is incremented by one, and the next instruction is fetched. NOP is used for "NOPping out" machine instructions during debugging, leaving space for future procedure or interrupt calls, or padding timing loops.

```
r8 = AL AH BL BH CL CH DL DH    r16 = AX BX CX DX BP SP SI DI
sr = CS DS SS ES
m8 = 8-bit memory data          m16 = 16-bit memory data
i8 = 8-bit immediate data       i16 = 16-bit immediate data
d8 = 8-bit signed displacement  d16 = 16-bit signed displacement
```

NOT Logical NOT (one's complement)

Flags affected:

```
O D I T S Z A P C      OF: Overflow flag   TF: Trap flag   AF: Aux carry
F F F F F F F F F      DF: Direction flag  SF: Sign flag   PF: Parity flag
      <none>           IF: Interrupt flag  ZF: Zero flag   CF: Carry flag
```

Legal forms:

```
NOT r8
NOT m8
NOT r16
NOT m16
```

Examples:

```
NOT CL
NOT DX
NOT WORD PTR [SI]
```

Notes:

NOT inverts each individual bit within the operand separately. I.e, every bit that was 1 becomes 0, and every bit that was 0 becomes 1. This is the "logical NOT" or "one's complement" operation. See also the NEG instruction for the negation, or "two's complement" operation.

The value FFH would become 0; the value AAH would become 55H.

```
r8 = AL AH BL BH CL CH DL DH    r16 = AX BX CX DX BP SP SI DI
sr = CS DS SS ES
m8 = 8-bit memory data          m16 = 16-bit memory data
i8 = 8-bit immediate data       i16 = 16-bit immediate data
d8 = 8-bit signed displacement  d16 = 16-bit signed displacement
```

OR Logical OR

Flags affected:

```
O D I T S Z A P C      OF: Overflow flag    TF: Trap flag    AF: Aux carry
F F F F F F F F F      DF: Direction flag   SF: Sign flag    PF: Parity flag
*       * * * * *      IF: Interrupt flag   ZF: Zero flag    CF: Carry flag
```

Legal forms:

```
OR r8,r8
OR m8,r8
OR r8,m8
OR r16,r16
OR m16,r16
OR r16,m16
OR r8,i8
OR m8,i8
OR r16,i16
OR m16,i16
OR AL,i8
OR AX,i16
```

Examples:

```
OR BX,DI
OR AX,0FFFFH          ;Uses single-byte opcode
OR AL,42H             ;Uses single-byte opcode
OR ES:[BX],0B800H
OR [BP+SI],DX
```

Notes:

OR performs the OR logical operation between its two operands. Once the operation is complete, the result replaces the destination operand. OR is performed on a bit-by bit basis, such that bit 0 of the source is ORed with bit 0 of the destination, bit 1 of the source is ORed with bit 1 of the destination, and so on. The OR operation yields a 1 if one of the operands is 1; and a 0 only if both operands are 0. Note that the operation makes the Auxiliary Carry flag undefined. CF and OF are cleared to 0, and the other affected flags are set according to the operation's results.

```
r8 = AL AH BL BH CL CH DL DH      r16 = AX BX CX DX BP SP SI DI
sr = CS DS SS ES
m8 = 8-bit memory data            m16 = 16-bit memory data
i8 = 8-bit immediate data         i16 = 16-bit immediate data
d8 = 8-bit signed displacement    d16 = 16-bit signed displacement
```

POP Pop top of stack into operand; increment SP by 2

Flags affected:

```
O D I T S Z A P C      OF: Overflow flag    TF: Trap flag    AF: Aux carry
F F F F F F F F F      DF: Direction flag   SF: Sign flag    PF: Parity flag
       <none>          IF: Interrupt flag   ZF: Zero flag    CF: Carry flag
```

Legal forms:

```
POP m16
POP AX
POP BX
POP CX
POP DX
POP BP
POP SP
POP SI
POP DI
POP CS
POP DS
POP SS
POP ES
```

Examples:

```
POP [BX]
POP AX
POP ES
```

Notes:

Note that it is impossible to pop a byte-sized item from the stack. It's words or nothing. Also remember that "the top of the stack" is defined as the word at address SS:SP, and there's no way to override that using prefixes. There is a separate pair of instructions, PUSHF and POPF, for pushing and popping the flags register.

All register forms are single-byte opcodes.

```
r8 = AL AH BL BH CL CH DL DH    r16 = AX BX CX DX BP SP SI DI
sr = CS DS SS ES
m8 = 8-bit memory data          m16 = 16-bit memory data
i8 = 8-bit immediate data       i16 = 16-bit immediate data
d8 = 8-bit signed displacement  d16 = 16-bit signed displacement
```

POPA Pop all general registers   286/386/486

Flags affected:

```
O D I T S Z A P C    OF: Overflow flag   TF: Trap flag   AF: Aux carry
F F F F F F F F F    DF: Direction flag  SF: Sign flag   PF: Parity flag
        <none>       IF: Interrupt flag  ZF: Zero flag   CF: Carry flag
```

Legal forms:

POPA

Examples:

POPA

Notes:

POPA pops all general registers off the stack. This instruction is present on the 286 and later CPUs, and is not available in the 8086/8088.

The registers are popped in this order:

```
 DI, SI, BP, SP, BX, DX, CX, AX
```

There's one wrinkle here; the SP value popped off the stack is *not* popped back into SP! (That would be insane, since we're using SP to manage the stack as we pop values off of it.) The value in SP's position on the stack is simply discarded when instruction execution reaches it.

POPA is usually used in conjunction with PUSHA, but nothing guarantees this. If you pop "garbage" values off the stack into the general registers, well, interesting things (in the sense of the old Chinese curse) can and probably will happen.

```
r8 = AL AH BL BH CL CH DL DH    r16 = AX BX CX DX BP SP SI DI
sr = CS DS SS ES
m8 = 8-bit memory data          m16 = 16-bit memory data
i8 = 8-bit immediate data       i16 = 16-bit immediate data
d8 = 8-bit signed displacement  d16 = 16-bit signed displacement
```

POPF Pop top of stack into Flags reg; increment SP by 2

Flags affected:

```
O D I T S Z A P C     OF: Overflow flag   TF: Trap flag   AF: Aux carry
F F F F F F F F F     DF: Direction flag  SF: Sign flag   PF: Parity flag
* * * * * * * * *     IF: Interrupt flag  ZF: Zero flag   CF: Carry flag
```

Legal forms:

```
POPF <none>
```

Examples:

```
POPF
```

Notes:

POPF pops the word at the top of the stack into the Flags register. "The top of the stack" is defined as the word at SS:SP, and there is no way to override that with prefixes.

SP is incremented *after* the word comes off the stack. Remember that SP always points to either an empty stack or else real data. There is a separate pair of instructions, PUSH and POP, for pushing and popping other register data and memory data.

PUSHF and POPF are most used in writing interrupt service routines, where you must be able to save and restore the "environment" i.e., all machine registers, to avoid disrupting machine operations while servicing the interrupt.

```
r8 = AL AH BL BH CL CH DL DH     r16 = AX BX CX DX BP SP SI DI
sr = CS DS SS ES
m8 = 8-bit memory data           m16 = 16-bit memory data
i8 = 8-bit immediate data        i16 = 16-bit immediate data
d8 = 8-bit signed displacement   d16 = 16-bit signed displacement
```

PUSH Push operand onto top of stack; decrement SP by 2

Flags affected:

```
O D I T S Z A P C    OF: Overflow flag   TF: Trap flag   AF: Aux carry
F F F F F F F F F    DF: Direction flag  SF: Sign flag   PF: Parity flag
      <none>         IF: Interrupt flag  ZF: Zero flag   CF: Carry flag
```

Legal forms:

```
POP m16
POP AX
POP BX
POP CX
POP DX
POP BP
POP SP
POP SI
POP DI
POP CS
POP DS
POP SS
POP ES
```

Examples:

```
POP [BX]
POP AX
POP ES
```

Notes:

Note that it is impossible to push a byte-sized item onto the stack. It's words or nothing. Also remember that "the top of the stack" is defined as the word at address SS:SP+1, and that there's no way to override that using prefixes. There is a separate pair of instructions, PUSHF and POPF, for pushing and popping the flags register.

Also remember that SP is decremented *before* the push takes place; SP points to either an empty stack or else real data.

```
r8 = AL AH BL BH CL CH DL DH   r16 = AX BX CX DX BP SP SI DI
sr = CS DS SS ES
m8 = 8-bit memory data         m16 = 16-bit memory data
i8 = 8-bit immediate data      i16 = 16-bit immediate data
d8 = 8-bit signed displacement d16 = 16-bit signed displacement
```

PUSHA   Push all general registers   286/386/486

Flags affected:

```
O D I T S Z A P C      OF: Overflow flag   TF: Trap flag   AF: Aux carry
F F F F F F F F F      DF: Direction flag  SF: Sign flag   PF: Parity flag
       <none>          IF: Interrupt flag  ZF: Zero flag   CF: Carry flag
```

Legal forms:

PUSHA

Examples:

PUSHA

Notes:

PUSHA pushes all general-purpose registers onto the stack. This instruction is present on the 286 and later CPUs, and is not available in the 8086/8088.

The registers are pushed in this order:

```
AX, CX, DX, BX, SP, BP, SI, DI
```

However, note that the value of SP pushed is the value SP had *before* the first register was pushed onto the stack. In the course of executing PUSHA, the stack pointer is decremented by 16 bytes.

The Flags register is not pushed onto the stack by PUSHA; see PUSHF.

```
r8 = AL AH BL BH CL CH DL DH    r16 = AX BX CX DX BP SP SI DI
sr = CS DS SS ES
m8 = 8-bit memory data          m16 = 16-bit memory data
i8 = 8-bit immediate data       i16 = 16-bit immediate data
d8 = 8-bit signed displacement  d16 = 16-bit signed displacement
```

PUSHF   Push Flags onto top of stack; decrement SP by 2

Flags affected:

```
O D I T S Z A P C      OF: Overflow flag    TF: Trap flag   AF: Aux carry
F F F F F F F F F      DF: Direction flag   SF: Sign flag   PF: Parity flag
        <none>         IF: Interrupt flag   ZF: Zero flag   CF: Carry flag
```

Legal forms:

PUSHF <none>

Examples:

PUSHF

Notes:

PUSHF simply pushes the current contents of the Flags register onto the top of the stack. "The top of the stack" is defined as the word at SS:SP, and there is no way to override that with prefixes.

SP is decremented *before* the word goes onto the stack. Remember that SP always points to either an empty stack or else real data. There is a separate pair of instructions, PUSH and POP, for pushing and popping other register data and memory data.

The Flags register is not affected when you *push* the flags, but only when you pop them back with POPF.

PUSHF and POPF are most used in writing interrupt service routines, where you must be able to save and restore the "environment" i.e., all machine registers, to avoid disrupting machine operations while servicing the interrupt.

```
r8 = AL AH BL BH CL CH DL DH     r16 = AX BX CX DX BP SP SI DI
sr = CS DS SS ES
m8 = 8-bit memory data           m16 = 16-bit memory data
i8 = 8-bit immediate data        i16 = 16-bit immediate data
d8 = 8-bit signed displacement   d16 = 16-bit signed displacement
```

RET Return from procedure

Flags affected:

```
O D I T S Z A P C      OF: Overflow flag   TF: Trap flag   AF: Aux carry
F F F F F F F F F      DF: Direction flag  SF: Sign flag   PF: Parity flag
      <none>            IF: Interrupt flag  ZF: Zero flag   CF: Carry flag
```

Legal forms:

```
RET
RETN
RETF
RET i8
RETN i8
RET i16
RETF i16
```

Examples:

```
RET
RET 12H
RETN
RETF 117H
```

Notes:

The RETF and RETN forms are *not* available in MASM prior to V5.0!

There are two kinds of returns: Near and Far, where Near is within the current code segment and Far is to some other code segment. Ordinarily the RET form is used, and the assembler resolves it to a Near or Far return opcode to match the procedure definition's use of the NEAR or FAR specifier. Specifying RETF or RETN may be done when necessary.

RET may take an operand indicating how many bytes of stack space are to be released on returning from the procedure. This figure is subtracted from the stack pointer to "erase" data items that had been pushed onto the stack for the procedure's use immediately prior to the procedure call.

```
r8  = AL AH BL BH CL CH DL DH    r16 = AX BX CX DX BP SP SI DI
sr  = CS DS SS ES
m8  = 8-bit memory data          m16 = 16-bit memory data
i8  = 8-bit immediate data       i16 = 16-bit immediate data
d8  = 8-bit signed displacement  d16 = 16-bit signed displacement
```

ROL Rotate Left

Flags affected:

```
O D I T S Z A P C      OF: Overflow flag   TF: Trap flag   AF: Aux carry
F F F F F F F F F      DF: Direction flag  SF: Sign flag   PF: Parity flag
*               *      IF: Interrupt flag  ZF: Zero flag    CF: Carry flag
```

Legal forms:

```
ROL r8,1
ROL m8,1
ROL r16,1
ROL m16,1
ROL r8,CL
ROL m8,CL
ROL r16,CL
ROL m16,CL
```

Examples:

```
ROL AL,1
ROL WORD PTR [BX+SI],CL
ROL BP,1
ROL BP,CL
```

Notes:

ROL rotates the bits within the destination operand to the left, where left is toward the most significant bit (MSB). A rotate is a shift (see SHL and SHR) that wraps around; the leftmost bit of the operand is shifted into the rightmost bit, and all intermediate bits are shifted one bit to the left. Except for the direction the shift operation takes, ROL is identical to ROR.

The number of bit positions shifted may either be specified as the literal 1, or by the value in CL. (*Not* CX!) It is usually faster to perform sequential shift-by-one instructions unless the number of bits shifted by exceeds four. Note that while CL may accept a value up to 255, it is meaningless to shift by any value larger than 16, *even though the shifts are actually performed on the 8086 and 8088.*

The leftmost bit is copied into the carry flag on each shift operation. OF is modified *only* by the shift-by-one forms of ROL; after shift-by-CL forms OF becomes undefined.

```
r8 = AL AH BL BH CL CH DL DH    r16 = AX BX CX DX BP SP SI DI
sr = CS DS SS ES
m8 = 8-bit memory data          m16 = 16-bit memory data
i8 = 8-bit immediate data       i16 = 16-bit immediate data
d8 = 8-bit signed displacement  d16 = 16-bit signed displacement
```

ROR Rotate Right

Flags affected:

```
O D I T S Z A P C      OF: Overflow flag   TF: Trap flag   AF: Aux carry
F F F F F F F F F      DF: Direction flag  SF: Sign flag   PF: Parity flag
*                 *    IF: Interrupt flag  ZF: Zero flag   CF: Carry flag
```

Legal forms:

```
ROR r8,1
ROR m8,1
ROR r16,1
ROR m16,1
ROR r8,CL
ROR m8,CL
ROR r16,CL
ROR m16,CL
```

Examples:

```
ROR AL,1
ROR WORD PTR [BX+SI],CL
ROR BP,1
ROR BP,CL
```

Notes:

ROR rotates the bits within the destination operand to the right, where right is toward the least significant bit (LSB). A rotate is a shift (see SHL and SHR) that wraps around; the rightmost bit of the operand is shifted into the leftmost bit, and all intermediate bits are shifted one bit to the right. Except for the direction the shift operation takes, ROR is identical to ROL.

The number of bit positions shifted may either be specified as the literal 1, or by the value in CL. (*Not* CX!) It is usually faster to perform sequential shift-by-one instructions unless the number of bits shifted by exceeds four. Note that while CL may accept a value up to 255, it is meaningless to shift by any value larger than 16, *even though the shifts are actually performed on the 8086 and 8088.*

The rightmost bit is copied into the carry flag on each shift operation. OF is modified *only* by the shift-by-one forms of ROR; after shift-by-CL forms OF becomes undefined.

```
r8 = AL AH BL BH CL CH DL DH    r16 = AX BX CX DX BP SP SI DI
sr = CS DS SS ES
m8 = 8-bit memory data          m16 = 16-bit memory data
i8 = 8-bit immediate data       i16 = 16-bit immediate data
d8 = 8-bit signed displacement  d16 = 16-bit signed displacement
```

SBB Arithmetic subtraction with borrow

Flags affected:

```
O D I T S Z A P C      OF: Overflow flag    TF: Trap flag    AF: Aux carry
F F F F F F F F F      DF: Direction flag   SF: Sign flag    PF: Parity flag
*       * * * * *      IF: Interrupt flag   ZF: Zero flag    CF: Carry flag
```

Legal forms:

```
SBB r8,r8
SBB m8,r8
SBB r8,m8
SBB r16,r16
SBB m16,r16
SBB r16,m16
SBB r8,i8
SBB m8,i8
SBB r16,i16
SBB m16,i16
SBB r16,i8
SBB m16,i8
SBB AL,i8
SBB AX,i16
```

Examples:

```
SBB BX,DI
SBB AX,0FFFFH                 ;Uses single-byte opcode
SBB AL,42H                    ;Uses single-byte opcode
SBB BP,17H
SBB WORD PTR [BX+SI+Inset],5
SBB WORD PTR ES:[BX],0B800H
```

Notes:

SBB performs a subtraction with borrow, where the source is subtracted from the destination, and then the carry flag is subtracted from the result. The result then replaces the destination. If the result is negative, the carry flag is set. To subtract without taking the carry flag into account (i.e., without borrowing) use the SUB instruction.

```
r8 = AL AH BL BH CL CH DL DH   r16 = AX BX CX DX BP SP SI DI
sr = CS DS SS ES
m8 = 8-bit memory data         m16 = 16-bit memory data
i8 = 8-bit immediate data      i16 = 16-bit immediate data
d8 = 8-bit signed displacement d16 = 16-bit signed displacement
```

SHL Shift Left

Flags affected:

```
O D I T S Z A P C      OF: Overflow flag   TF: Trap flag  AF: Aux carry
F F F F F F F F F      DF: Direction flag  SF: Sign flag  PF: Parity flag
*         * * * *      IF: Interrupt flag  ZF: Zero flag  CF: Carry flag
```

Legal forms:

```
SHL r8,1
SHL m8,1
SHL r16,1
SHL m16,1
SHL r8,CL
SHL m8,CL
SHL r16,CL
SHL m16,CL
```

Examples:

```
SHL AL,1
SHL WORD PTR [BX+SI],CL
SHL BP,1
SHL BP,CL
```

Notes:

SHL shifts the bits within the destination operand to the left, where left is toward the most significant bit (MSB). The number of bit positions shifted may either be specified as the literal 1, or by the value in CL. (*Not* CX!) It is usually faster to perform sequential shift-by-one instructions unless the number of bits shifted by exceeds four. Note that while CL may accept a value up to 255, it is meaningless to shift by any value larger than 16, *even though the shifts are actually performed on the 8086 and 8088.*

The leftmost bit of the operand is shifted into the carry flag; the rightmost bit is cleared to 0. The auxiliar carry flag (AF) becomes undefined after this instruction. OF is modified *only* by the shift-by-one forms of SHL; after shift-by-CL forms OF becomes undefined.

Except for the direction the shift operation takes, SHL is identical to SHR.

```
r8 = AL AH BL BH CL CH DL DH    r16 = AX BX CX DX BP SP SI DI
sr = CS DS SS ES
m8 = 8-bit memory data          m16 = 16-bit memory data
i8 = 8-bit immediate data       i16 = 16-bit immediate data
d8 = 8-bit signed displacement  d16 = 16-bit signed displacement
```

SHR Shift Right

Flags affected:

```
O D I T S Z A P C    OF: Overflow flag   TF: Trap flag   AF: Aux carry
F F F F F F F F F    DF: Direction flag  SF: Sign flag   PF: Parity flag
*       * * * * *    IF: Interrupt flag  ZF: Zero flag   CF: Carry flag
```

Legal forms:

```
SHR r8,1
SHR m8,1
SHR r16,1
SHR m16,1
SHR r8,CL
SHR m8,CL
SHR r16,CL
SHR m16,CL
```

Examples:

```
SHR AL,1
SHR WORD PTR [BX+SI],CL
SHR BP,1
SHR BP,CL
```

Notes:

SHR shifts the bits within the destination operand to the right, where right is toward the least significant bit (LSB). The number of bit positions shifted may either be specified as the literal 1, or by the value in CL. (*Not* CX!) It is usually faster to perform sequential shift-by-one instructions unless the number of bits shifted by exceeds four. Note that while CL may accept a value up to 255, it is meaningless to shift by any value larger than 16, *even though the shifts are actually performed on the 8086 and 8088.*

The rightmost bit of the operand is shifted into the carry flag; the leftmost bit is cleared to 0. The auxiliar carry flag (AF) becomes undefined after this instruction. OF is modified *only* by the shift-by-one forms of SHR; after shift-by-CL forms OF becomes undefined.

Except for the direction the shift takes, SHR is identical to SHL.

```
r8 = AL AH BL BH CL CH DL DH    r16 = AX BX CX DX BP SP SI DI
sr = CS DS SS ES
m8 = 8-bit memory data          m16 = 16-bit memory data
i8 = 8-bit immediate data       i16 = 16-bit immediate data
d8 = 8-bit signed displacement  d16 = 16-bit signed displacement
```

STC Set Carry flag (CF)

Flags affected:

```
O D I T S Z A P C     OF: Overflow flag   TF: Trap flag   AF: Aux carry
F F F F F F F F F     DF: Direction flag  SF: Sign flag   PF: Parity flag
              *       IF: Interrupt flag  ZF: Zero flag    CF: Carry flag
```

Legal forms:

STC <none>

Examples:

STC

Notes:

STC asserts the Carry flag (CF) to a known set state (1). Use it prior to some task that needs a bit in the Carry flag.

```
r8 = AL AH BL BH CL CH DL DH    r16 = AX BX CX DX BP SP SI DI
sr = CS DS SS ES
m8 = 8-bit memory data          m16 = 16-bit memory data
i8 = 8-bit immediate data       i16 = 16-bit immediate data
d8 = 8-bit signed displacement  d16 = 16-bit signed displacement
```

STD   Set Direction Flag (DF)

Flags affected:

```
O D I T S Z A P C    OF: Overflow flag   TF: Trap flag   AF: Aux carry
F F F F F F F F F    DF: Direction flag  SF: Sign flag   PF: Parity flag
    *                IF: Interrupt flag  ZF: Zero flag    CF: Carry flag
```

Legal forms:

STD <none>

Examples:

STD

Notes:

STD simply asserts the direction flag (DF) to the set (1) state. This affects the adjustment performed by repeated string instructions like STOS, SCAS, and MOVS. Typically, when DF=0, the destination pointer is increased, and decreased when DF=1. DF is set to 0 with the CLD instruction.

```
r8 = AL AH BL BH CL CH DL DH   r16 = AX BX CX DX BP SP SI DI
sr = CS DS SS ES
m8 = 8-bit memory data         m16 = 16-bit memory data
i8 = 8-bit immediate data      i16 = 16-bit immediate data
d8 = 8-bit signed displacement d16 = 16-bit signed displacement
```

STOS Store String

Flags affected:

```
O D I T S Z A P C     OF: Overflow flag   TF: Trap flag    AF: Aux carry
F F F F F F F F F     DF: Direction flag  SF: Sign flag    PF: Parity flag
      <none>           IF: Interrupt flag  ZF: Zero flag    CF: Carry flag
```

Legal forms:

```
STOS ES:m8
STOS ES:m16
STOSB
STOSW
```

Examples:

```
STOS ES:MyWordVar    ;Stores AX to ES:DI
STOS ES:MyByteVar    ;Stores AL to ES:DI
STOSB                ;Stores AL to ES:DI
STOSW                ;Stores AX to ES:DI
REP STOSW            ;Stores AX to ES:DI and following, for CX repeats
```

Notes:

Stores either AL (for 8-bit store operations) or AX to the location at ES:DI. ES must be the segment of the destination and cannot be overridden. Similarly, DI must always be the destination offset.

By placing an operation repeat count (not a byte or word count!) in CX and preceding the mnemonic with the REP prefix, STOS can do an automatic "machine-gun" store of AL/AX into successive memory locations beginning at the initial ES:DI. After each store, DI is adjusted (see next paragraph) by either by either 1 (for 8-bit store operations) or 2, and CX is decremented by 1.

"Adjusting" means incrementing if the direction flag is cleared (by CLD) or decrementing if the direction flag has been set.

```
r8 = AL AH BL BH CL CH DL DH    r16 = AX BX CX DX BP SP SI DI
sr = CS DS SS ES
m8 = 8-bit memory data          m16 = 16-bit memory data
i8 = 8-bit immediate data       i16 = 16-bit immediate data
d8 = 8-bit signed displacement  d16 = 16-bit signed displacement
```

SUB Arithmetic subtraction

Flags affected:

```
O D I T S Z A P C     OF: Overflow flag    TF: Trap flag    AF: Aux carry
F F F F F F F F F     DF: Direction flag   SF: Sign flag    PF: Parity flag
*       * * * *       IF: Interrupt flag   ZF: Zero flag    CF: Carry flag
```

Legal forms:

```
SUB r8,r8
SUB m8,r8
SUB r8,m8
SUB r16,r16
SUB m16,r16
SUB r16,m16
SUB r8,i8
SUB m8,i8
SUB r16,i16
SUB m16,i16
SUB r16,i8
SUB m16,i8
SUB AL,i8
SUB AX,i16
```

Examples:

```
SUB BX,DI
SUB AX,0FFFFH              ;Uses single-byte opcode
SUB AL,42H                 ;Uses single-byte opcode
SUB BP,17H
SUB WORD PTR [BX+SI+Inset],5
SUB WORD PTR ES:[BX],0B800H
```

Notes:

SUB performs a subtraction without borrow, where the source is subtracted from the destination, and the result replaces the destination. If the result is negative, the carry flag is set. Multiple-precision subtraction can be performed by following SUB with SBB (Subtract With Borrow) which takes the carry flag into account as a borrow.

```
r8 = AL AH BL BH CL CH DL DH    r16 = AX BX CX DX BP SP SI DI
sr = CS DS SS ES
m8 = 8-bit memory data          m16 = 16-bit memory data
i8 = 8-bit immediate data       i16 = 16-bit immediate data
d8 = 8-bit signed displacement  d16 = 16-bit signed displacement
```

XCHG   Exchange operands

Flags affected:

```
O D I T S Z A P C      OF: Overflow flag   TF: Trap flag   AF: Aux carry
F F F F F F F F F      DF: Direction flag  SF: Sign flag   PF: Parity flag
        <none>         IF: Interrupt flag  ZF: Zero flag    CF: Carry flag
```

Legal forms:

```
XCHG r8,r8
XCHG r8,m8
XCHG r16,r16
XCHG r16,m16
XCHG AX,CX
XCHG AX,DX
XCHG AX,BX        ─┐  Single-byte
XCHG AX,SP         │    special cases
XCHG AX,BP        ─┘
XCHG AX,SI
XCHG AX,DI
```

Examples:

```
XCHG AL,DH
XCHG BH,[SI]
XCHG SP,BP
XCHG DX,[DI]
XCHG AX,BX        ; Uses single-byte opcode
```

Notes:

XCHG exchanges the contents of its two operands. This is why there is no form of XCHG for identical operands; i.e., XCHG AX,AX is not a legal form since exchanging a register with itself makes no logical sense.

Exchanging an operand with AX may be accomplished with a single-byte opcode, saving fetch time and code space. All good assemblers recognize these cases and optimize for them, but if you are hand-assembling INLINE statements for Turbo Pascal or some other language, keep the single-byte special cases in mind.

```
r8 = AL AH BL BH CL CH DL DH   r16 = AX BX CX DX BP SP SI DI
sr = CS DS SS ES
m8 = 8-bit memory data         m16 = 16-bit memory data
i8 = 8-bit immediate data      i16 = 16-bit immediate data
d8 = 8-bit signed displacement d16 = 16-bit signed displacement
```

XOR Exclusive Or

Flags affected:

```
O D I T S Z A P C    OF: Overflow flag   TF: Trap flag   AF: Aux carry
F F F F F F F F F    DF: Direction flag  SF: Sign flag   PF: Parity flag
*       * * * *      IF: Interrupt flag  ZF: Zero flag    CF: Carry flag
```

Legal forms:

```
XOR r8,r8
XOR m8,r8
XOR r8,m8
XOR r16,r16
XOR m16,r16
XOR r16,m16
XOR r8,i8
XOR m8,i8
XOR r16,i16
XOR m16,i16
XOR AL,i8
XOR AX,i16
```

Examples:

```
XOR BX,DI
XOR AX,0FFFFH           ;Uses single-byte opcode
XOR AL,42H              ;Uses single-byte opcode
XOR ES:[BX],0B800H
XOR [BP+SI],DX
```

Notes:

XOR performs the exlsusive OR logical operation between its two operands. Once the operation is complete, the result replaces the destination operand. XOR is performed on a bit-by bit basis, such such that bit 0 of the source is XORed with bit 0 of the destination, bit 1 of the source is XORed with bit 1 of the destination, and so on. The XOR operation yields a 1 if the operands are different, and a 0 if the operands are the same. Note that the operation makes the Auxiliary Carry flag undefined. CF and OF are cleared to 0, and the other affected flags are set according to the operation's results.

```
r8 = AL AH BL BH CL CH DL DH    r16 = AX BX CX DX BP SP SI DI
sr = CS DS SS ES
m8 = 8-bit memory data          m16 = 16-bit memory data
i8 = 8-bit immediate data       i16 = 16-bit immediate data
d8 = 8-bit signed displacement  d16 = 16-bit signed displacement
```

The Extended ASCII
Code and Symbol Set

Dec	Hex	Binary	Symbol	Dec	Hex	Binary	Symbol
0	00	00000000		19	13	00010011	‼
1	01	00000001	☺	20	14	00010100	¶
2	02	00000010	☻	21	15	00010101	§
3	03	00000011	♥	22	16	00010110	▬
4	04	00000100	♦	23	17	00010111	↕
5	05	00000101	♣	24	18	00011000	↑
6	06	00000110	♠	25	19	00011001	↓
7	07	00000111	·	26	1A	00011010	→
8	08	00001000	◘	27	1B	00011011	←
9	09	00001001	○	28	1C	00011100	∟
10	0A	00001010	◙	29	1D	00011101	↔
11	0B	00001011	♂	30	1E	00011110	▲
12	0C	00001100	♀	31	1F	00011111	▼
13	0D	00001101	♪	32	20	00100000	
14	0E	00001110	♫	33	21	00100001	!
15	0F	00001111	☼	34	22	00100010	"
16	10	00010000	►	35	23	00100011	#
17	11	00010001	◄	36	24	00100100	$
18	12	00010010	↕	37	25	00100101	%

Dec	Hex	Binary	Symbol	Dec	Hex	Binary	Symbol
38	26	00100110	&	74	4A	01001010	J
39	27	00100111	'	75	4B	01001011	K
40	28	00101000	(	76	4C	01001100	L
41	29	00101001	)	77	4D	01001101	M
42	2A	00101010	*	78	4E	01001110	N
43	2B	00101011	+	79	4F	01001111	O
44	2C	00101100	,	80	50	01010000	P
45	2D	00101101	–	81	51	01010001	Q
46	2E	00101110	.	82	52	01010010	R
47	2F	00101111	/	83	53	01010011	S
48	30	00110000	Ø	84	54	01010100	T
49	31	00110001	1	85	55	01010101	U
50	32	00110010	2	86	56	01010110	V
51	33	00110011	3	87	57	01010111	W
52	34	00110100	4	88	58	01011000	X
53	35	00110101	5	89	59	01011001	Y
54	36	00110110	6	90	5A	01011010	Z
55	37	00110111	7	91	5B	01011011	[
56	38	00111000	8	92	5C	01011100	\
57	39	00111001	9	93	5D	01011101	]
58	3A	00111010	:	94	5E	01011110	^
59	3B	00111011	;	95	5F	01011111	_
60	3C	00111100	<	96	60	01100000	`
61	3D	00111101	=	97	61	01100001	a
62	3E	00111110	>	98	62	01100010	b
63	3F	00111111	?	99	63	01100011	c
64	40	01000000	@	100	64	01100100	d
65	41	01000001	A	101	65	01100101	e
66	42	01000010	B	102	66	01100110	f
67	43	01000011	C	103	67	01100111	g
68	44	01000100	D	104	68	01101000	h
69	45	01000101	E	105	69	01101001	i
70	46	01000110	F	106	6A	01101010	j
71	47	01000111	G	107	6B	01101011	k
72	48	01001000	H	108	6C	01101100	l
73	49	01001001	I	109	6D	01101101	m

Dec	Hex	Binary	Symbol	Dec	Hex	Binary	Symbol
110	6E	01101110	n	146	92	10010010	Æ
111	6F	01101111	o	147	93	10010011	ô
112	70	01110000	p	148	94	10010100	ö
113	71	01110001	q	149	95	10010101	ò
114	72	01110010	r	150	96	10010110	û
115	73	01110011	s	151	97	10010111	ù
116	74	01110100	t	152	98	10011000	ÿ
117	75	01110101	u	153	99	10011001	Ö
118	76	01110110	v	154	9A	10011010	Ü
119	77	01110111	w	155	9B	10011011	¢
120	78	01111000	x	156	9C	10011100	£
121	79	01111001	y	157	9D	10011101	¥
122	7A	01111010	z	158	9E	10011110	₧
123	7B	01111011	{	159	9F	10011111	ƒ
124	7C	01111100	¦	160	A0	10100000	á
125	7D	01111101	}	161	A1	10100001	í
126	7E	01111110	~	162	A2	10100010	ó
127	7F	01111111	⌂	163	A3	10100011	ú
128	80	10000000	Ç	164	A4	10100100	ñ
129	81	10000001	ü	165	A5	10100101	Ñ
130	82	10000010	é	166	A6	10100110	ª
131	83	10000011	â	167	A7	10100111	º
132	84	10000100	ä	168	A8	10101000	¿
133	85	10000101	à	169	A9	10101001	⌐
134	86	10000110	å	170	AA	10101010	¬
135	87	10000111	ç	171	AB	10101011	½
136	88	10001000	ê	172	AC	10101100	¼
137	89	10001001	ë	173	AD	10101101	¡
138	8A	10001010	è	174	AE	10101110	«
139	8B	10001011	ï	175	AF	10101111	»
140	8C	10001100	î	176	B0	10110000	░
141	8D	10001101	ì	177	B1	10110001	▒
142	8E	10001110	Ä	178	B2	10110010	▓
143	8F	10001111	Å	179	B3	10110011	│
144	90	10010000	É	180	B4	10110100	┤
145	91	10010001	æ	181	B5	10110101	╡

Dec	Hex	Binary	Symbol	Dec	Hex	Binary	Symbol
182	B6	10110110	╢	219	DB	11011011	■
183	B7	10110111	╖	220	DC	11011100	▬
184	B8	10111000	╕	221	DD	11011101	▌
185	B9	10111001	╣	222	DE	11011110	▐
186	BA	10111010	║	223	DF	11011111	▀
187	BB	10111011	╗	224	E0	11100000	α
188	BC	10111100	╝	225	E1	11100001	β
189	BD	10111101	╜	226	E2	11100010	Γ
190	BE	10111110	╛	227	E3	11100011	π
191	BF	10111111	┐	228	E4	11100100	Σ
192	C0	11000000	└	229	E5	11100101	σ
193	C1	11000001	┴	230	E6	11100110	μ
194	C2	11000010	┬	231	E7	11100111	τ
195	C3	11000011	├	232	E8	11101000	φ
196	C4	11000100	─	233	E9	11101001	Θ
197	C5	11000101	┼	234	EA	11101010	Ω
198	C6	11000110	╞	235	EB	11101011	δ
199	C7	11000111	╟	236	EC	11101100	∞
200	C8	11001000	╚	237	ED	11101101	ø
201	C9	11001001	╔	238	EE	11101110	ε
202	CA	11001010	╩	239	EF	11101111	∩
203	CB	11001011	╦	240	F0	11110000	≡
204	CC	11001100	╠	241	F1	11110001	±
205	CD	11001101	═	242	F2	11110010	≥
206	CE	11001110	╬	243	F3	11110011	≤
207	CF	11001111	╧	244	F4	11110100	⌠
208	D0	11010000	╨	245	F5	11110101	⌡
209	D1	11010001	╤	246	F6	11110110	÷
210	D2	11010010	╥	247	F7	11110111	≈
211	D3	11010011	╙	248	F8	11111000	°
212	D4	11010100	╘	249	F9	11111001	·
213	D5	11010101	╒	250	FA	11111010	·
214	D6	11010110	╓	251	FB	11111011	√
215	D7	11010111	╫	252	FC	11111100	^{n}
216	D8	11011000	╪	253	FD	11111101	^{2}
217	D9	11011001	┘	254	FE	11111110	■
218	DA	11011010	┌	255	FF	11111111	

Segment Register Assumptions

Where allowed, segment assumptions can be overridden with the segment override prefixes. These are DS: SS: CS: ES:. For example:

```
mov ES:[BX],AX
```

The assumptions are these:

1. When the offset is specified in BX, SI, or DI, the assumed segment register is DS.
2. Whe the offset is specified in SP, the assumed segment register is SS. CANNOT BE OVERRIDDEN.
3. When the offset is specified in BP, the assumed segment register is SS.
4. For string instruction LODS, the assumed segment is DS and the assumed offset is SI. CANNOT BE OVERRIDDEN.
5. For string instruction STOS and SCAS, the assumed segment is ES and the assumed offset is DI. CANNOT BE OVERRIDDEN.
6. For string instruction MOVS, the source must be pointed to be DS:SI and the destination must be pointed to by ES:DI. CANNOT BE OVERRIDDEN.

Index

ASSEMBLY LANGUAGE STEP-BY-STEP
Listings Diskette Offer!

Why spend time typing and risk making mistakes? All the listings and tools presented in this book are available inexpensively on diskette, directly from The Coriolis Group.

Just fill out the coupon below, telling us how many diskettes you want. Check the appropriate box for diskette type: 5 1/4" 360K, or 3 1/2" 720K. Add 6% sales tax if the order is to be shipped in Arizona.

Include payment in the form of check or money order in U.S. funds, or else VISA/MasterCard authorization. CODs and open account purchase orders are not accepted.

Mail the coupon to:

The Coriolis Group
Book Diskette Offers
7721 E. Gray Road, #204
Scottsdale AZ 85260

Shipping and handling is $2 for orders shipped to the U.S. and Canada, and $6 for airmail shipping to the rest of the world. Please make all checks and money orders payable to The Coriolis Group.

See other side of coupon for *PC TECHNIQUES* discount subscription offer!

Qty	Listings diskette for:	Each	Total
___	*Assembly Language Step By Step*	$10	_____
	Arizona orders please add 6% sales tax:		_____
	Shipping and handling:		_____
	Total due, in US funds:		_____

Diskette size: 5 1/4" 3 1/2"
☐   ☐

Phone (602) 483-0192
Fax: (602) 483-0193

Name _____

Company _____

Address _____

City/State/Zip _____

Phone _____

VISA/MC # _____   Expires: _____

Signature for charge orders: _____

READ THE MAGAZINE
THAT JEFF DUNTEMANN BUILT!

Published by The Coriolis Group

For years, Jeff Duntemann has been known for his crystal-clear, slightly-be-mused explanations of programming technology. He's one of the few in computer publishing who has never forgotten that English is the one language we all have in common. Now he's teamed up with author Keith Weiskamp and created a magazine that brings you a selection of readable, practical technical articles six times a year, written by himself and a crew of the very best technical writers working today. Michael Abrash, Tom Swan, Keith Weiskamp, David Gerrold, Brett Glass, Michael Covington, Peter Aitken, Marty Franz, Jim Kyle, and many others will perform their magic before your eyes, and then explain how *you* can do it too, in language that you can understand.

If you program under DOS or Windows in C, C++, Pascal, Visual Basic, or assembly language, you'll find code you can use in every issue. You'll also find essential debugging and optimization techniques, programming tricks and tips, detailed product reviews, and practical advice on how to get your programming product finished, polished and ready to roll.

Don't miss another issue—subscribe today!

See other side of coupon for listings diskette offer!

- -

☐ 1 Year $21.95   ☐ 2 Years $37.95

☐ $29.95 Canada; $39.95 Foreign   ☐ $53.95 Canada; $73.95 Foreign

Total for subscription: _____
Arizona orders please add 6% sales tax: _____
Total due, in US funds:_____

Send to:
PC TECHNIQUES
7721 E. Gray Road, #204
Scottsdale AZ 85260

Name _____
Company _____
Address _____
City/State/Zip _____
Phone _____

Phone (602) 483-0192
Fax: (602) 483-0193

VISA/MC # _____ Expires: _____

Signature for charge orders: _____